Introduction to Sociology

Jerry D. Rose

State University College
Fredonia, New York

RAND MᵋNALLY & COMPANY · CHICAGO

Rand McNally Sociology Series
Edgar F. Borgatta, Advisory Editor

Third Printing, 1972

For LoVetra and Christopher

Preface

The aim of this textbook is to provide a bridge of communication between the professor and the student of sociology. The raising of provocative questions and the delineation of areas for discussion is thus the principal orientation.

An introduction to a field of study, like an introduction to a new person, should encourage the newly introduced person to want more information and a closer insight into the nature of his new acquaintance. It should also be candid enough to inform the neophyte about what he might expect to encounter if he continues to think, talk, and write about the field with professionals.

The professor in the classroom is on the firing line of this most difficult task of introduction. If he is faithful to his discipline, he must guide his students in finding a vocabulary and a way of thinking that will enable them to think and talk about *their* experience from the perspective of *his* discipline. To teach a new language is difficult enough; to impart a new way of thinking about familiar problems within the confines of a one- or two-semester course may seem well-nigh impossible. This book aims to make this task seem a little more possible. The book represents the author's own introductory lectures in sociology, not as he delivers them in the classroom but as he *would* deliver them if he had time for this much systematic exposition.

The book may, then, appeal most to that professor who wants his classroom to be a forum of discussion between himself and his students. If the book succeeds in its aims, it will provide the systematic treatment of the field which will give the student the intellectual base for his discussion, with a minimum of exposition and correction of text materials by the instructor. For this purpose, the attempt throughout has been to write in a nontechnical style that will make sociological abstractions meaningful in terms of the everyday experience of the student.

Fundamental to this notion of the book as a base for thought and discussion is the rather strongly classic and theoretical emphasis to be found in these pages. Attempts are made in the discussion of most topics to relate the analysis to the classic formulations of the founders of our discipline and to discuss some of the landmark empirical studies in the discipline. This classic emphasis does not, however, preclude frequent reference to very recent theoretical and empirical studies. This combination of citations of the ancient and the very new in sociological work is aimed, as is most else in this book, at demonstrating the character of sociology as an ongoing research science.

Although this book carries the name of one man as its author, its authorship has many collaborators. To list them all would be to evoke a giant procession of persons who have passed in and out of one man's life. If blame as well as credit must be ascribed to the author, let his critics acquaint themselves with his parents, his wife and child, his friends, enemies, colleagues, teachers and students, and, especially perhaps, with all those sociologists who previously have performed the service or committed the sin of putting their thoughts in print.

To name a few names, however. To my colleagues at Fredonia— Lee Braude, Paul Dommermuth, Edward Ludwig, Alvin Morrison—I am especially grateful for encouragement, advice, and for their forbearance for the lapses in colleagueship that a textbook project has necessitated. The editorial staff at Rand McNally and their sociologist consultants—Lawrence Malley, Martha Urban, Edgar Borgatta, Betty Metz, Clifton Bryant—have acquainted me with the rather startling fact that book publication can be a humane adventure, and therefore worthwhile to its publishers if not to its readers.

Jerry D. Rose

Fredonia, New York
October, 1970

Contents

SOCIOLOGY

PART ONE

Sociology is one of the newer of the academic disciplines, tracing its origins no further back than the middle of the nineteenth century. Today, in the growing pains of its "adolescence," sociology is the focus of much self-consciousness concerning the nature of its identity and its methods of operation. In this section we examine some of the fruits of this self-consciousness.

The Field of Sociology

HUMAN BEHAVIOR AS SUBJECT OF HUMAN INTEREST

The intellectual enterprise called sociology is an attempt to apply the perspectives of science to the understanding of human behavior. The impulse to engage in sociological study is simply one manifestation of the urge of the human mind to make sense out of the apparently chaotic jumble and buzz of things and events in the world.

The urge to understand human behavior is by no means unique to the sociologist. "The way of a man with a maid" excited the curiosity of the biblical writer, and poets and novelists have, through the ages, concerned themselves with untangling the riddle of human nature. It was a poet, Alexander Pope, who urged that "the proper study of mankind is man." News analysts and criminal investigators, diplomats and merchandisers—all have commitments to discover and interpret the meaning of "the facts" in specific episodes of human behavior.

In inquiring into the origin of this urge to understand, we shall suggest one aspect of human nature which will concern us throughout this book: the tendency of humans to reflect upon the behavior of themselves and their fellows. Dogs clearly do not reflect on canine nature if, indeed, they reflect even on their individual life conditions. What is there in human nature that impels us to analyze the nature of our species? If we can indicate some answers to this question, we can anticipate an analysis of some of the motives that actuated the founders of sociology and that today sustain the behavior called sociology.

One answer is that we have some very practical reasons for wanting to understand the behavior of ourselves and others. Visualize a scene on a public highway and try to imagine the chaos that would exist unless each driver had some clear and accurate understanding of the probable behaviors of each other driver. We try to keep idiots and young children from behind the wheels of moving vehicles because they would introduce intolerable elements of unpredictability in driver behavior.

To generalize this point: the search for knowledge of human behavior is motivated by the human urge for *prediction* and *control* of the events that occur in the human environment. "You shall know the truth and the truth shall make you free." The "enslavement" of primitive man is often attributed to his excessive fear of the forces in his natural environment, forces that modern man has been able to harness for his greater ease and comfort. Among the most frightening aspects of the human environment has been the possibility of violence or other hostile action by other humans; warfare, revolution, and crime are among the endemic problems of human existence. To control these and other undesirable manifestations of human behavior has been among the principal motives for understanding that behavior.

The urge to understand human behavior may also be based on a desire for knowledge "for its own sake." It is not so easy to give a coherent account of the psychological origins of this impulse. Perhaps the young child's natural curiosity about all aspects of his environment survives into adulthood despite parental repressions of the more bothersome manifestations of that curiosity. Even if we discount "instinctive" curiosity, we still have to acknowledge that men frequently seek to become known as authorities in some particular subject matter without any great concern for its practical applications. Perhaps the relevant motivation stems from the sheer impressiveness of knowledge and the desire of persons to appear "in the know": you shall know the truth—and the truth shall set you upon a pedestal.

Western man tends to look with some condescension on the pattern of career advancement in Mandarin China which depended on a person's mastery of "classical" learning which had little or no practical application. Even the modern intellectual tends to reject as sterile scholasticism any elaborate philosophical speculations that do not lead anywhere practically. Nevertheless, we seem to be well impressed with the erudition displayed by the participants in spelling bees, quiz shows, and TV "college bowls." The man of learning is an honored figure in today's so-called pragmatic societies, even though we may look slightly askance at the ivory tower preoccupations of our eggheads.

MOTIVES FOR SOCIOLOGICAL STUDY

There is little doubt that the nineteenth century founders of the science of sociology were actuated by motives of the more practical kind. In Europe, this century was a time of troubles, manifested in the frequent international wars and intranational revolutions of the period. First the French Revolution and then the Communist upheaval predicted by Marx preoccupied the minds of European sociologists.[1]

The French sociologist Auguste Comte gave sociology its name and a program for its development. Comte's aim was to establish sociology on the same "positivistic" footing that had been already attained by the natural sciences. Each of the sciences, like human thought in general, is subject to a process of evolution through three stages: thus, Comte's famous "Law of the Three States."[2] These evolutionary stages are the theological, the metaphysical, and the scientific or positivistic. At all stages, the aim of human thought is for more complete control or "prevision" (prediction) of natural phenomena.

The "error" of the primitive or theological stage of thought is the notion that natural phenomena are alterable at the command of human or supernatural will. Like the naive child, the primitive believes that all things are possible at the urging of God, if not of man. In the metaphysical stage, there is still the assumption that natural phenomena are controlled externally: not by human or supernatural will, but by some abstract principles or ideas such as *Reason* and *Freedom*, to use Hegel's terms. At the final or positivistic stage it is recognized that phenomena are regulated by a natural constitution inherent in them. Man's task—the task of science—is, in the words of Francis Bacon, to "find out how nature operates."

Each science, according to Comte, has gone through or will go through each of these stages. Natural science has already abandoned the earlier assumption that natural things could be consti-

---

[1] For a review of nineteenth century sociology in this vein, see Raymond Aron, *Main Currents in Sociological Thought,* 2 vols. (New York: Basic Books, 1965).

[2] *The Positive Philosophy of Auguste Comte,* trans. by Harriet Martineau (London: Bell, 1896).

tuted according to human will (the alchemy stage of chemistry, for example) and has arrived at the assumption that these things have their "nature" which man must understand if he is to control the effects of their operation. Comte found that, in his time, most thinking about human behavior was still infected by theological and metaphysical elements; "wishful thinking" was still the rule of politicians and other men of affairs in planning the arrangement of organized human activities. The new science of sociology that Comte hoped to found would put the study of human behavior on a firmly positivistic base. Men would learn that *society* has a natural constitution, the laws of which must be understood before it can be regulated in any effective way.

The practical applications of Comte's new science of sociology are fairly obvious, and Comte made them quite explicit in his long treatise on "positive polity," which describes the political implications of sociology.[3] One sociologist has called Comte's sociology "a conservative answer to socialism,"[4] providing an ideological justification for repression of the revolutions that swept through Europe in the 1840s. Comte believed that sociology would teach men "the limits of political action" and the adoption of a "wise resignation" in the face of inevitable disappointment.[5]

The British sociologist Herbert Spencer took up the conservative theme of Comte and articulated it into a polemic against interference with the "natural" evolution of human society.[6] While arguing for the ultimate beneficence of the process of natural evolution, Spencer heaped scorn on those naive social reformers who believed that they could impose "obvious" solutions to unfortunate social conditions. He likened their misguided efforts to those of a novice in metalworking:

You see that this wrought-iron plate is not quite flat; it sticks up a little here towards the left—"cockles," as we say. How shall we flatten it?

---

[3] Auguste Comte, *System of Positive Polity,* trans. by John Henry Bridges (London: Longmans, Green, 1875–1877).

[4] Don Martindale, *The Nature and Types of Sociological Theory* (Boston: Houghton Mifflin, 1960), p. 62.

[5] For a summary and critique of the political conservatism of Comte's "positive" sociology, see Herbert Marcuse, *Reason and Revolution* (New York: Oxford University Press, 1941), pp. 340–360.

[6] Herbert Spencer, *Social Statics* (New York: D. Appleton, 1904). First published in 1850.

Obviously, you reply, by hitting down on the part that is prominent. Well, here is a hammer, and I give the plate a blow as you advise. Harder, you say. Still no effect. Another stroke? Well, there is one, and another, and another. The prominence remains, you see: the evil is as great as ever—greater, indeed. But this is not all. Look at the warp which the plate has got near the opposite edge. Where it was flat before it is now curved. A pretty bungle we have made of it. Instead of curing the original defect, we have produced a second. Had we asked an artisan practiced in "planishing," as it is called, he would have told us that no good was to be done, but only mischief, by hitting down on the projecting part. He would have taught us how to give variously-directed and specially-adjusted blows with a hammer elsewhere: so attacking the evil not by direct but by indirect actions. The required process is less simple than you thought. Even a sheet of metal is not to be successfully dealt with after those common-sense methods in which you have so much confidence. What, then, shall we say about a society? "Do you think I am easier to play on than a pipe?" asks Hamlet. Is humanity more readily straightened than an iron plate?[7]

One element of Spencer's analysis of the natural evolution of society that scandalized social reformers was his view that the progress of the human species requires the survival of the fittest and the elimination of the unfit members of society. From the viewpoint of this "social Darwinism," any effort to ameliorate the condition of the weak or incapacitated members of a society is tampering with the beneficent laws of nature.[8]

When sociology as a field of study was introduced in the United States at the turn of the century, this preoccupation with the practical implications of the study was carried over to this country. A vigorous debate soon developed between an ultra–social Darwinist, William Graham Sumner of Yale University, and Lester Frank Ward, a career government official and free-lance sociologist.

Sumner's employment of the concept of social survival of the fittest (his message has been summarized as: "millionaires are the bloom of a competitive society")[9] appealed to the need of the business leaders of the day to justify their positions of economic privilege. But Ward's view touched more directly the humanitarian

---

[7] Herbert Spencer, *The Study of Sociology* (New York: D. Appleton, 1902), pp. 245, 246. First published in 1873.

[8] Richard Hofstadter, *Social Darwinism in American Thought* (Philadelphia: University of Pennsylvania Press, 1944).

[9] Ibid., p. 58.

and optimistic strains in American thought. While conservative thinkers since Comte had urged the necessity of a "wise resignation" before the inevitabilities of a natural order of things, Ward emphasized the uniquely human capacity of *telesis,* or the ability of man to adapt to his environment by changing the character of the environment to suit his needs.[10] "Social engineering," an activity that the conservatives would see as limited at best and as a throwback to theological ways of thinking at worst, became the focus of interest of Ward and the many other American sociologists who were influenced by him or by the same optimistic conditions that shaped his views. American sociology for several decades became very nearly synonymous with the study of solutions to "social problems."

The current situation in American sociology is much more complicated than this. A vigorous reaction against the social engineering style of sociology began shortly before World War II and was greatly accelerated after the war. Sociologists who contributed in different ways to this reaction were George Lundberg, Robert Merton, and Talcott Parsons.

In Lundberg's book *Can Science Save Us?*[11] he answers the question in his title by saying that, yes, (social) science can save us (i.e., solve problems for us), but *only* if we are willing to wait until much basic research has been done and if we are willing to support social scientific activity to a much greater extent. Like Spencer, Lundberg would emphasize the complexity of human society and the fact that we do not yet have the knowledge to apply directly to the solution of our outstanding social problems. This stance has led Lundberg and his followers to what one critic[12] has called a kind of "abstracted empiricism" in which problems for sociological study are selected because they are amenable to objective measurement rather than because they have any relevance to human concern. From one viewpoint, such research is "basic" in that it will provide a base for more general understandings of human behavior when the fund of detailed knowledge is sufficiently built up. From the other, critical viewpoint, the research is hopelessly trivial and will *never* add up to anything significant.

---

[10] Lester Frank Ward, *Dynamic Sociology*, 2 vols. (New York: D. Appleton, 1883).

[11] George A. Lundberg, *Can Science Save Us?* (New York: Longmans, Green, 1947).

[12] C. Wright Mills, *The Sociological Imagination* (New York: Oxford University Press, 1959), Ch. 3.

Robert Merton's work, like that of Lundberg, has emphasized the complexity of human social organization. Merton was strongly impressed with the frequency with which there are "unanticipated consequences" of men's attempts to control human affairs; things never turn out quite as they are planned.[13] Later, he developed the notion of *latent function* to describe those situations in which social practices have consequences that were neither recognized nor intended by the people involved.[14] The historical pattern of domination of city politics in the United States by political bosses is an example of a latent function of a social practice. Although it was not planned that way, and although many "good government" reformers refused to admit it, it appears to be a fact that this pattern provided many essential services to residents of American cities. Students of Merton have emphasized the essentially conservative character of human social organization, the "recalcitrance," as Selznick puts it, of human beings as "tools of action."[15] Would-be social reformers who read in contemporary sociology are thus frequently prompted to beware of the unanticipated consequences of their own reform efforts, the latent functions of the social "evils" that they may wish to attack.

Talcott Parsons is the key figure in contemporary sociology. His work is sometimes criticized for creating a new conservatism through its emphasis on the social system, which is conceived as a set of forces that maintain the status quo or equilibrium of a given state of social relations.[16] Another feature of Parsons' work is his argument for a more highly theoretical or abstract level of sociological analysis. Parsons calls for a "general theory" of social systems.[17] One critic has argued that the resulting theory is so abstract that, in the attempt to explain social systems in general, it offers no help at all in dealing with the specific issues that arise at specific points in the history of a society.[18] Whether or not this criticism is

---

[13] Robert K. Merton, "The Unanticipated Consequences of Purposive Social Action," *American Sociological Review*, 1(1936):894–904.

[14] Robert K. Merton, *Social Theory and Social Structure*, rev. ed. (Glencoe, Ill.: Free Press, 1957), p. 51.

[15] Philip Selznick, "Foundations of the Theory of Organization," *American Sociological Review*, 13(1948):25–35.

[16] Ralf Dahrendorf, "Out of Utopia: Toward a Reorientation of Sociological Analysis," *American Journal of Sociology*, 64(1958):115–127.

[17] "The Present Position and Prospects of Systematic Theory in Sociology," in Talcott Parsons, *Essays in Sociological Theory* (Glencoe, Ill.: Free Press, 1949).

[18] Mills, *The Sociological Imagination*, Ch. 2.

valid, it does appear that the "theoretical" emphasis of contemporary sociology represents a significant retreat from the social-engineering emphasis of earlier American sociology.

Many contemporary sociologists have withdrawn so far from the melioristic tendency of their intellectual forebears that they participate in what Peter Berger calls the "debunking motif" in modern society.[19] The contemporary skeptic "knows" that behind the facade of official reality, beyond the "conventional wisdom" that is articulated by political leaders, there is an unofficial level of reality, and no sophisticated man is taken in by these official versions. The sociologist simply systematizes this skeptical tendency in, for example, his concern with the informal dimension of political power in a community, a focus not on who holds what offices but on "who runs things around here."[20] Sociology becomes politically neither conservative nor liberal. If anything, it is *apolitical,* since the sociologist is taken in neither by the moralizing of defenders of the status quo nor by the utopian plans of the revolutionary. The motives that drive this sort of sociologist are not the motives of the "people-helper" or the "social reformer";[21] they are the motives of unrationalized curiosity—a desire to know simply, What is man really like?

Such declining concern for social problems is a cause for lament among some contemporary sociologists. C. Wright Mills criticizes the tendencies toward retreat into either "abstracted empiricism" or "grand theory" and advocates a return to what he calls the "classic tradition" of sociology, a tradition founded by men like Weber, Durkheim, Simmel, Cooley, and Veblen, all of whom were notably alive to the social problems of their day and deeply concerned about these problems in their sociological writings.[22] The sociologist cannot, Mills believes, isolate himself from the problems of his particular time and country; indeed, it is the promise of sociology that it will enable men to find solutions to their private *troubles* (e.g., marital difficulties) by helping them to trace these troubles to institutional factors (e.g., change in structure of the

---

[19] Peter Berger, *An Invitation to Sociology* (Garden City, N.Y.: Doubleday, 1963).

[20] Floyd Hunter, *Community Power Structure: a Study of Decision Makers* (Chapel Hill: University of North Carolina Press, 1953).

[21] Berger, *An Invitation to Sociology,* pp. 1–8.

[22] Mills, *The Sociological Imagination.*

family) that can be translated into public *issues* amenable to solution at the societal level.

The degree to which sociology must be relevant to immediate social concerns is a continuously debated point. Sometimes the debate proceeds from the question of whether a value-free sociology, as advocated by Weber,[23] is possible, of whether the sociologist can or should divorce his sociological work from his commitment to political or other beliefs. An increasingly prominent school of radical sociology asserts the impossibility of this divorce.

Sometimes this debate surfaces at sociological meetings when politically activist groups present resolutions which would have a sociological association take a stand on a topical issue like the war in Vietnam. The resolutions are usually defeated by the more academically oriented majorities. However, even the academicians must take account of one very significant fact of life. In a pragmatically oriented society like the United States, where the question, Knowledge for what? is frequently raised, sociologists must at least justify their activity by citing its relevance for some practical concerns. An urban college administration may support an expanded sociology department only if it believes that the department has much to offer to the solution of urban social problems. A government funding agency like the National Institute of Mental Health may support sociological research only if it believes this research will contribute to the reduction of mental illness or to its more effective treatment. Sociology is, in short, *expected* by much of the public to be relevant to immediate social problems, and this public expectation may influence the behavior of the sociologist as much as do the professional expectations that sociologists hold for one another.

SOCIOLOGY AMONG THE SOCIAL SCIENCES

Sociology is one of the several social sciences. Each of the social

---

[23] Max Weber, *The Methodology of the Social Sciences,* trans. by Edward A. Shils and Henry A. Finch (Glencoe, Ill.: Free Press, 1949).

[24] For a statement of the viewpoint that sociology is committed by its nature to take the side of the underdog in social issues, see Howard S. Becker, "Whose Side Are We On?" *Social Problems,* 14(1967):239–247. For a critique of this article by a sociologist who is generally sympathetic, see Alvin W. Gouldner, "The Sociologist as Partisan: Sociology and the Welfare State," *American Sociologist,* 3(1968):103–116.

sciences represents a particular way of looking at a common subject matter—human behavior. There are no hard-and-fast boundary lines between the social sciences since each of these perspectives has implications for each of the others. Still, it is useful at the outset of a survey of sociology to distinguish its particular perspective from those of the other social sciences.[25]

Sociology: a Generalizing Science

History is a study of human behavior from a *particularizing* perspective. The historian is interested in describing unique events and explaining these in terms of their relation to other unique events. (The identification of history as a study of the past is probably a naive one, since it is possible to apply the historical perspective to the understanding of contemporary events.) Sociology is *generalizing* in its perspective. The interest is not in the unique but in the recurring pattern of events. Generalizing social sciences look for the "principles" or the "laws" that describe regularities in human behavior. These laws presumably apply in *any* historical situation.[26]

The interdependence of history and sociology should be quite clear. To explain unique events the historian needs sociological principles which define the kinds of unique events that are *usually* associated with other kinds of unique events. The historian of the Civil War can use a sociology of war to guide him in the search for causes of that war. On the other hand, the sociologist must use historically unique events (unique societies or communities or political parties) to test and verify his generalizations about human behavior. History is an important tool in the verification of sociological hypotheses.

Sociology: a Generalized Science

Having identified sociology as one of a number of social sciences that are generalizing in their perspectives, we can now note how sociology differs from some of these other generalizing social sci-

[25] For outlines of the relationship of sociology to other social sciences that differ somewhat from ours, see Pitirim A. Sorokin, *Society, Culture and Personality* (New York: Harper, 1947), pp. 6–17; and Neil J. Smelser, "Sociology and the Other Social Sciences," in Paul F. Lazarsfeld, William H. Sewell, and Harold L. Wilensky (eds.), *The Uses of Sociology* (New York: Basic Books, 1967), pp. 3–44.

[26] Robert Bierstedt, "Toynbee and Sociology," *British Journal of Sociology,* 10(June, 1959):95–104; Alan P. Bates, *The Sociological Enterprise* (Boston: Houghton Mifflin, 1966), p. 4.

ences. Within the social sciences, we find certain areas of study that are specialized or limited in the scope of their interest in human behavior. Only certain kinds of behavior engage their attention. The *economist,* for example, is interested in generalizing about only one kind of behavior, economic behavior. The *political scientist* likewise is concerned only with political behavior.

In contrast with these specialized sciences, the generalized sciences of sociology, psychology, and anthropology recognize no such limitations of scope of interest. While one may readily speak of noneconomic or nonpolitical behavior, it simply makes no sense to speak of nonpsychological or nonsociological or nonanthropological behavior. *All* behavior has psychological, sociological, and anthropological dimensions, and the scientist in any one of these fields must necessarily take all kinds of behavior into account.

Much of the dialogue between practitioners of the specialized and of the generalized social sciences seems to revolve around the question of whether behavior can profitably be studied from a narrowed perspective. The economist or political scientist may feel that this limitation is justified because man is, in some respects, *homo economicus* or *homo politicus.* From the perspective of the generalized sciences, however, one often finds the specialized studies criticized for not taking into account the fact that economic or political behavior always occurs in a wider social context.[27] In his voting or buying habits a person may be reflecting sentiments that cannot be explained by any primary human urge for monetary profit or political power.

Such critical positions sometimes arise *within* a specialized social science. Economists like Thorstein Veblen, John R. Commons, and Alfred Marshall, sometimes operating under the label of "institutional economics," have emphasized this broader context of economic behavior.[28] Political scientists like Robert Lane, Gabriel Almond, and Heinz Eulau represent a behavioral persuasion in political science that approaches more nearly the generalized perspective of political sociology.[29]

---

[27] For a criticism of the narrow scope of traditional economics, see Talcott Parsons and Neil J. Smelser, *Economy and Society* (Glencoe, Ill.: Free Press, 1956).

[28] For a general discussion, see "Economics and Sociology," in Mirra Komarovsky (ed.), *Common Frontiers of the Social Sciences* (Glencoe, Ill.: Free Press, 1957), Part II.

[29] See Robert E. Lane, *Political Life* (Glencoe, Ill.: Free Press, 1959); and the

Sociology: a Special Kind of Abstraction

Psychology, anthropology, and sociology have in common their interest in all aspects of human behavior. The difference between them seems to lie in their different ways of thinking about human behavior in general. These differences may be understood by noting that human behavior is a *variable* and that these three social sciences represent different systems of explanation of this variability. To illustrate this, we can cite three different kinds of explanation of a single fact of human behavior, namely, the variability in the amount of discrimination practiced by people against other racial groups.

The psychologist tends to explain variability in behavior in terms of the *personalities* of the behaving persons. Each kind of behavior is a specific manifestion of a kind of organization of psychological elements. Thus, persons vary in the degree to which they possess what has been called an "authoritarian personality." The discriminatory actions of persons against members of an "inferior" group is thought to be a reflection of such authoritarian personality traits as insecurity and the need to see the world in black-and-white terms.[30] Psychological generalizing tends to revolve around the concept of personality.

For the anthropologist, variations in human behavior tend to be explained by variations in *culture*. Different groups of people have different ideas and moral conceptions, and persons living in groups with different cultures may be expected to display different patterns of behavior. The Eskimo behaves in one way, the Zulu in another, reflecting a quite different culture. Racial discrimination is part of the way of life of certain groups; that is, the behavior is as "normal" for members of those groups as it is "abnormal" for persons in groups with cultures that prescribe egalitarian interracial relations.

Anthropology is often distinguished from sociology by its emphasis on the study of *primitive* groups of people. Although this difference in emphasis is a fact of social scientific life—anthropologists did and still do study primitives most often—it may not be a very basic or essential fact. Some anthropologists believe that analysis of cultures can extend to the study of modern societies or com-

---

work of political scientists represented in Heinz Eulau, Samuel J. H. Eldersveld, and Morris Janowitz (eds.), *Political Behavior* (Glencoe, Ill.: Free Press, 1956).

[30] T. W. Adorno, E. Frenkel-Brunswik, D. J. Levinson, and R. N. Sanford, *The Authoritarian Personality* (New York: Harper, 1950).

munities.[31] New York University has recently instituted a department of urban anthropology to study the adjustment of persons to the culture of modern cities.

Sociology tends to explain variability in human behavior in terms of variation in *society* or *social structure.* Different persons are seen as occupying different positions or statuses in that structure, and these positions condition the behavior of their occupants in a number of ways. Men and women, employers and employees, leaders and followers—these are categories of social structure which are thought to be related to variations in behavior. Interracial discrimination, for example, seems to be practiced more by persons in lower-class social positions than by those in upper-class social positions.

These differences among psychology, anthropology, and sociology are differences of emphasis rather than absolute differences. Sociology does, as we shall see, make use of the concepts of *culture* and *personality;* it simply does not make either concept central to its system of explanation. The close relationship of these three social scientific disciplines is shown in the fact that, in many American colleges and universities, the departments of sociology and anthropology are administratively combined.[32] In a few (Harvard, for example), the three departments are merged into a Department of Social Relations.

SUMMARY

Sociology has been described as a kind of human behavior, marked by the disposition to subject human behavior itself to inquiry and analysis. The motives for sociological study tend to vary in the same way that human beings generally vary in the reasons for their

---

[31] An example of such anthropological study of modern communities is found in the "Yankee City" and other community studies directed by Warner at the University of Chicago. See W. Lloyd Warner and Paul S. Lunt, *The Social Life of a Modern Community* (New Haven: Yale University Press, 1941).

[32] It is one indication of the greater organizational development of sociology in the United States that, in many colleges and universities, combined departments of sociology and anthropology are dominated by sociologists, with the lone anthropologist in a department often finding himself and his courses tacked on to the sociology curriculum. In much of Europe the reverse is true. There are no departments of sociology in many major universities, and the sociologists may have to tack on to a department of anthropology, most often by specializing in social anthropology (as compared to cultural or physical anthropology).

interest in self-analysis. Sometimes this self-consciousness is seen as a practical necessity to deal with persistent problems of adjustment.

Depending on whether sociological analysis encourages change or stability of existing social patterns, sociology may have conservative or radical political implications. Such founders of the discipline as Comte and Spencer tended to see the study of sociology as conducive to greater appreciation by people of the complexity and the limited alterability of society in its existing forms. In the early part of the twentieth century, largely under the impact of its Americanization, sociology came to be more closely associated with a reformist or liberal critique of existing society and to be seen as a tool for social engineering. The current wave of radical sociology is a continuation and a deepening of this tendency.

An alternative set of motives is threaded through the history of sociology, namely, the view that the discipline is justified not by its association with any practical or political viewpoint, but by its position as a dispassionate or "value-neutral" analysis of a natural phenomenon. From this perspective, sociological study is seen as a liberal discipline or an end in itself. The main focus of controversy among sociologists today is a struggle for the "soul" of sociology between those advocates of a relevant and politically involved discipline and those who continue to maintain the view of sociology as an ethically neutral discipline.

Regardless of the motives for its study, there is fairly high agreement among sociologists concerning the subject matter of the discipline compared with the other social sciences. Sociology can be characterized by its interest in the general principles or recurring patterns in human behavior, its concern with all facets of human behavior, and its special orientation toward the social organizational or structural dimension of human behavior.

Methods
in Sociological Study

SOCIOLOGY AND THE SCIENTIFIC METHOD

As we noted at the start, the sociologist holds no monopoly in his interest in understanding human behavior. Human behavior is grist not only for the social scientist but for the novelist, the essayist, the playwright, the poet. In the mill of his mind the creative writer turns over the behavior of his fellows and, depending upon his motivation, produces a view of humanity—or of a very small piece of it—that will arouse, or placate, educate, or simply entertain and inform his readers. His range of motives, in fact, is probably very similar to the variations in motives for sociological study that we discussed in chapter 1.

If the sociologist is not distinguished from the artist by his *aims,* however, he clearly is distinguished from him in his *methods.* Sociology attempts to apply the methods of science to the understanding of human behavior. Men of letters are not scientists; the sociologist is, or he at least aspires to apply scientific methodology to his study of human behavior. The essence of this method is a suspension of judgment about the apparent facts in a given area until any hypothesis that has been formulated is supported overwhelmingly by empirical evidence. Two features of this definition of the scientific method will now be discussed.

Doubt

The scientist is sensitive—some critics would say overly sensitive[1]

---

[1] William James, "The Will to Believe" in *The Will to Believe, and Other Essays in Popular Philosophy,* new ed. (New York: Longmans, Green, 1937).

—to the "error" of accepting as fact some proposition that is in fact false. The prototype of the scientific attitude is Descartes' seventeenth century exercise in "methodological scepticism,"[2] in which he proposes to doubt literally everything until it can be established on the level of absolute certainty, that is, to "make it a rule to trust only what is completely known and incapable of being doubted."[3] This rule can be carried to a ridiculous extreme, of course, as in the story of a scientist riding on a train whose companion points out the window and says, "Look, those sheep have been shorn," to which the scientist replies, "To be sure, they have been shorn on one side."

Contrary to Descartes, the modern scientific attitude takes account of the likelihood that most or all of our knowledge is inferential or probabilistic in nature. If we waited for knowledge which is "incapable of being doubted," we apparently should wait forever to find any propositions that we can "trust." Still, the scientist is likely to be less trusting of his impulses and intuitions than is the artist. Scientific attitudes demand and scientific procedures provide for systematic generation of empirical *evidence* for or against any proposed facts.

Evidence

How does one gather scientific evidence for or against a proposition that will allow him to suspend his suspended judgment and reach a conclusion about some matter of fact? What counts as evidence for or against the proposition?

The basic scientific method for accumulating evidence is the method of empirical *observation;* one uses his sensory faculties— sight, hearing, taste, touch, and smell—to apprehend the facts of the world. The chemist sees the changes of color and texture that accompany the mixing of chemical reagents; the sociologist hears men saying certain things to their fellow men, or to himself. These observations are recorded in painstaking detail, and one's conclusions must be strictly consistent with the facts that one has observed in the empirical world.

This fact-gathering may or may not be preceded by some tenta-

---

[2] John H. Randall, Jr., and Justus Buchler, *Philosophy: An Introduction* (New York: Barnes & Noble, 1942), p. 93.

[3] Ibid., p. 79.

tive idea of what the final conclusion might be. One model of scientific operation is the idea of the *inductive* method: the investigator begins with a set of observed facts on which he can base some overall conclusion or some abstract *theory* about the facts in a particular area of study. The frequently cited model of the inductive method is Darwin's description of the laborious biological observations by which he finally arrived at the theory of natural selection.[4] However, much scientific investigation is in the nature of hypothesis-testing. Hypotheses are tentative statements about the facts in a particular area of study. One frequent justification of scientific *theory* (e.g., Darwin's theory of natural selection or Freud's libido theory of human psychology) is that it allows the investigator to hypothesize facts before he has gathered them; he then proceeds *deductively* from an existing theory to a specific hypothesis about some phenomenon.

Whether he proceeds from a basis of induction or deduction, the scientist must devise observational "tests" of the facts that he is investigating. Frequently scientists think in terms of entities that are unobservable by the senses: light waves, for example, or the superego. To make any observations at all about such phenomena, he must develop operations that provide the rules for determining what sensory observations will be treated as evidence for or against a proposition.[5] Much of the uncertainty and controversy in science arises from disagreements about the appropriateness of using a particular operation as a measure of some unobservable phenomenon. (A familiar example: Do intelligence tests *really* measure intelligence?)

Assuming his ability to develop adequate measures of some phenomenon, the scientist is frequently faced with a problem of *interpreting* the data that his observations have generated. What does it all mean? is a question that will arise in any science as the scientist confronts the hard facts of his area of study. Even if all scientific effort were concerned with testing specific hypotheses (it is not), the process of hypothesis-testing would generate many puzzling facts that have yet to be explained scientifically.

Some students have found encouragement in the frequency in

4 Sir Gavin De Beer, *Charles Darwin* (Garden City, N.Y.: Doubleday, 1965).

5 Carl G. Hempel, "A Logical Appraisal of Operationism," in Philipp Frank (ed.), *The Validation of Scientific Theories* (Boston: Beacon, 1956), pp. 52–58.

scientific research of *serendipity:* the discovery of new facts for which one was not looking at the time of their discovery.[6] An antibiotic drug, penicillin, was supposedly discovered serendipitously, and the story of the apple falling on Newton's head before he "discovered" the law of gravity is a popularized version of the fact that, frequently, the scientist must be "hit on the head" by facts before he recognizes their scientific value. Whatever the degree of importance one assigns to serendipitous findings, it is clear that much scientific thought is post-factum and involves the problem of interpreting the meaning of preexisting facts. This situation leads to one of the persisting criticisms of scientific interpretations; that is, being after the fact, the interpretation represents a plausible explanation of the facts but does not preclude the possibility that someone else may dream up an alternate interpretation that is equally plausible.[7]

In the balance of this chapter we shall consider some of the problems and proposed solutions to the problems of applying scientific methods to sociological subject matters. In the light of the foregoing discussion, the reader may need to remind himself from time to time that these methodological problems are not unique to sociology. If sociological research is sometimes (or always) characterized by slipshod methodology, we may at least take some comfort in the realization that the development of knowledge which is "completely known and incapable of being doubted" is an extremely difficult feat in *any* line of scientific inquiry.

PROBLEMS IN OBJECTIVITY

The sociologist, like any scientist, is expected to take a quite different stance toward the material of his study than does the artist or literary person. Self-expression is the ideal stance of the artist, as indicated in Cooley's approving characterization of Goethe's writing which allows the reader to "get the feeling of something calm, free, and onward which is Goethe himself, and not to be had elsewhere."[8] The scientist, by contrast, is expected to disengage his own personality from his scientific findings, producing results

---

[6] Robert K. Merton, *Social Theory and Social Structure* (Glencoe, Ill.: Free Press, 1956), pp. 103–108.

[7] Ibid., pp. 93–95.

[8] Charles H. Cooley, *Human Nature and the Social Order* (New York: Scribner's, 1902), p. 110.

that can be verified by any other scientist who uses the same methods of study. In the realm of human behavior, that novelist who writes about social life as *he* has experienced it is considered "authentic." The social scientist is discouraged from allowing his own biased sample of social experience to substitute for the whole of human behavior. In every respect, the rule is one of subjectivity for the artist, objectivity for the scientist.

The social scientist does not, however, derogate the importance for scientific discovery of the element of subjectivity, either his own or that of persons in the subjectively oriented professions. The beginning of sociological investigation is frequently the provocative hypothesis or hunch, and literary sources may be rich mines of material for the sociologist's hypotheses.[9] The insights on human behavior of a Dostoevsky, a Goethe, or a Shakespeare may be more illuminating than the most sophisticated sociological theories. But, valuable as these insights may be as starting points for sociological study, they do not enter the body of sociology proper until they have been tested with research instruments that are independent of the brilliant intuitions of individual thinkers.

The positivistic program advocated by Comte aimed at removing sociology from the realm of speculation and establishing it as an objective or research science.[10] Comte's fellow countryman, Emile Durkheim, shared this vision of an objective sociology and, in his *Rules of Sociological Method,* urged that the sociologist must "eradicate all preconceptions" and deal with facts rather than with his ideas about social facts.[11] The eminent German sociologist Max Weber devoted major essays to the problem of objectivity or "value-neutrality" in sociology, arguing that the sociologist may well be involved in partisan political activity to stimulate his intellectual curiosity but that, as a social scientist (e.g., a teacher of sociology), he must leave out his personal biases, remembering always that a "podium is not a pulpit."[12]

Objectivity is easily articulated as an ideal but not so easily

---

[9] Lewis Coser, *Sociology Through Literature* (Englewood Cliffs, N.J.: Prentice-Hall, 1963).

[10] *The Positive Philosophy of Auguste Comte,* trans. by Harriet Martineau (London: Bell, 1896).

[11] Emile Durkheim, *The Rules of Sociological Method,* trans. by Sarah A. Solovay and John H. Mueller (Chicago: University of Chicago Press, 1938).

[12] Max Weber, *The Methodology of the Social Sciences,* trans. by Edward A. Shils and Henry A. Finch (Glencoe, Ill.: Free Press, 1949).

practiced, perhaps especially so in the social sciences. It is quite common in treatises on social science to note that the control of personal bias is an especially difficult feat when the subject matter is human behavior.[13] Whether concerned with the study of prejudice, or voting, or lovemaking, the social scientist is trying to understand behavior in which he himself is engaged. This is in contrast with, say, the geologist, who studies phenomena with which he does not personally identify.

This contrast in the ease of maintaining objectivity in the social and physical sciences can easily be overdrawn. The working habits of the professional scientist in any field are such that he tends to develop preferences for finding one set of facts rather than another. Scientists develop hypotheses or theories which they publish, thereby committing themselves professionally. The reluctance with which a geologist gives up his hypothesis about the surface of the moon, despite the introduction of new facts, suggests that, even in the physical sciences, human preference is an ever-present factor.

Most scientific fields recognize individual bias and control it by institutionalizing a system of internal checks by which one scientist's biased thinking is reviewed by other scientists, who presumably operate with other kinds of bias. However, there are many flaws in this system. A scientist may be too specialized for many others to be able to check his work. The weight of an investigator's reputation or mere politeness toward a colleague may produce in the reviewers a reticence to criticize.[14] The training of scientists still involves indoctrination in the necessity of individual intellectual integrity. Exercising this integrity may be more difficult for the social scientist, who is influenced by his identification with his subject matter as well as by his professional commitments.

PROBLEMS IN MEASUREMENT
When the poet writes that "these are the times that try men's souls," he is making a statement about social conditions that no one is

---

[13] One of the earliest examples was Herbert Spencer, *The Study of Sociology* (New York: Appleton, 1902).

[14] One of the problems of becoming an expert or a "big name" in a scientific field is that other scholars are often more inclined to cite the expert's work with approval as a way of gaining prestige for themselves than they are to criticize the work of a "great man." See Norman Storer, *The Social System of Science* (New York: Holt, Rinehart & Winston, 1966).

inclined to reject because the poet does not specify *how much* men's souls are currently being tried. The scientific interest is quite different. When the physical scientist describes a chemical element, it is not sufficient to call it a light or a heavy element; the chemist, at the least, will be expected to identify the different elements by different degrees (more or less) of weight (a measuring device which will allow such relative measurements is called an *ordinal scale*). Better, the weights of different elements might be described as falling at a point along a continuous scale (e.g., so many pounds and ounces) that will tell one by *how much* the weight of a given element exceeds that of any other element (*interval scales* permit such measurements).

Likewise, the sociologist will seldom be content to assert that "times are trying" or that "there is a lot of unrest on college campuses today." There are any number of sociological questions that assume the capacity to make accurate measures of, say, the amount of unrest now compared with five years ago, or in Europe compared with the United States, or in one situation compared with another.

The two criteria of accurate sociological measures are *reliability* and *validity*.[15] A reliable measure is one which yields the same results upon repetition of the measuring procedure or upon application by other investigators. Reliability is one indication of the objectivity of sociological knowledge: a judgment, for example, about the degree of unrest is not subject to the vagaries of viewpoints of persons making the judgment if this trait is measured by reliable instruments. A valid measure is one which in fact measures whatever it is purported to measure. The validity of a measure of unrest might be challenged by arguing that sociologists are not really measuring unrest but only the degree of willingness or reticence of people to express discontent in interviews.

Of the two kinds of measurement problems—reliability and validity—the degree of reliability of a sociological measure can be much more easily determined. The degree to which measuring scales yield comparable results upon repeated measurement can be stated in precise mathematical terms.[16] Validity, however, can

---

[15] Claire Selltiz et al., *Research Methods in Social Relations,* rev. ed. (New York: Holt, Rinehart & Winston, 1961), pp. 154–186.

[16] J. P. Guilford, *Psychometric Methods,* 2nd ed. (New York: McGraw-Hill, 1954), pp. 373–398.

only be inferred, never proven. If we want to know, for example, whether we are really measuring social unrest, we have no perfect device for reassuring ourselves. We might consider whether our measure has "face validity"; that is, whether, in the judgment of ourselves or some panel of experts, it appears obvious that the questions we ask people are well designed to measure their degree of discontent. But what is obviously valid to one investigator may be just as obviously invalid to another investigator with another set of intuitions. Even if all investigators were to agree on the face validity of a measure, they could not be sure of its validity. Sociology itself will teach us that forty million Frenchmen *can* be wrong (at least to the extent that what is judged as right in one place may be judged as wrong elsewhere, or that what seems right today may be proven wrong tomorrow) and that a panel of seven experts can indeed all operate under the same illusions.

We might also infer validity by comparing results yielded by a measure with unknown validity with results yielded by a measure with known validity, much as psychologists validate a new test of intelligence by determining whether people make scores on it comparable to scores they make on some established or standard test. The rub here, of course, is that we have made an inference about the validity of the established measure. All we actually measure by these techniques is the reliability of different measures of the same characteristics. It is still possible that we err (albeit "reliably") in *all* our measures.

Finally, we might resort to some form of *scaling* technique.[17] A *scale* involves a number of measures of the same characteristic and is constructed on the theory that the sum total or pattern of responses on a number of measurement items will be more valid than a single measurement. Any professor who bases exam grades on the total number of correctly answered questions is using a kind of scaling technique. If the students' grades were based on a single question, a student might well claim that his grade was an invalid measure of his overall knowledge of the course materials ("You just happened to hit me with the one thing I didn't know" or "My pencil slipped"). But if the student missed thirty-five out of forty questions, he would appear foolish if he made such arguments. Similarly, in measuring unrest, if a subject answers one question

---

17 Selltiz et al., *Research Methods in Social Relations*, Ch. 10.

about the degree of his contentment in negative terms, it may be that the investigator accidentally hit upon the one area of dissatisfaction in an otherwise contented existence. However, we are unlikely to attribute to accident those similar events that occur repeatedly. A pattern of discontented responses allows a more valid inference that a subject is, in fact, discontented.

Although scaling is a common and reputable way of dealing with the problem of validity, it is not a panacea. Anyone who has objected to a course examination on the grounds that the professor's questions are too vague or that the expected pattern of responses is too idiosyncratic to the professor's way of thinking will recognize the problem. High and low total scoring on a number of items, instead of measuring the course knowledge as intended, may measure the student's ability to parrot the professor or the text or may reflect the student's familiarity with testing rules-of-thumb such as, on a true-false question, the statement is false if the words *always* or *never* are used or, on a multiple choice question, the alternative with the most words is the correct one. Similarly, a generalization like "men display more social unrest than women" may be challenged (even though research shows this to be the case) if, for any reason, men are simply more willing to admit their discontent when certain kinds of questions are used.

To deepen a bit the perplexity introduced by the problem of validity of sociological measures, consider the problem of what may be called "observer effect." The problem, briefly, is whether or not a person's awareness that his behavior is being observed will alter his behavior. Most of us have experienced the sensation of stage fright or seen the effects of an audience on the behavior of the inveterate ham. With the physical scientist, observer effect is much less a problem. When the physicist measures the temperature of a liquid, he is not likely to be much concerned with the question of whether the insertion of the thermometer into the thermal system being measured will itself change that temperature. The sociologist, in assessing the validity of his measuring techniques, must consider a variety of problems involving the reactions of people to the act of observation: the hostility of subjects to a questionnaire, the constraints imposed by an interviewer taking notes, the fear of self-incrimination, and so forth.

In dealing with observer effect, the investigator can resort to various tricks of the researcher's trade.[18] An assurance of anonymity may neutralize a subject's fear of negative consequences if certain answers are given. Note-taking may be eliminated in favor of an unobtrusive tape recorder. *Projective* techniques—questioning people more indirectly about sensitive matters—may be used. The rapport of the investigator with his subjects is a concern of virtually every sociological study.[19] But even when all the tricks are used by a trained and skillful investigator, he can never be sure that the behavior he observes or is told about corresponds to the behavior that occurs in the absence of his investigations.[20]

There seems to be no ultimate solution to the problem of the validity of sociological measures. Sociologists employ a wide variety of validating techniques, but the usual understanding is that we strive for the most valid possible measure, knowing that we shall never entirely succeed.

PROBLEMS IN SAMPLING

Even assuming that our measures of behavior are valid, the problem remains that, given the limited amount of time, energy, and money that can be devoted to sociological investigations, it is unlikely that we shall be able to apply our valid measuring instruments to all possible instances of the kind of behavior we are studying. A study of unrest on American college campuses, for example, would be able to measure the degree of discontent avowed or displayed by only a limited number of students or faculty. To deal with this situation, the sociologist typically *samples* human behavior and, on the basis of a limited number of observations made on that sample, he hopes to generalize about the behavior of persons in a larger *universe* or *population*. This generalization has to be based

---

[18] Aaron V. Cicourel, *Method and Measurement in Sociology* (New York: Free Press of Glencoe, 1964), Chs. 2 and 3; Eugene J. Webb et al., *Unobtrusive Measures* (Chicago: Rand McNally, 1966).

[19] For discussion of the problem of establishing rapport in participant-observer situations, see William F. Whyte, *Street Corner Society* (Chicago: University of Chicago Press, 1943), Appendix; John Dollard, *Caste and Class in a Southern Town* (Garden City, N.Y.: Doubleday, 1957); Leon Festinger et al., *When Prophecy Fails* (Minneapolis: University of Minnesota Press, 1956), Methodological Appendix.

[20] In addition to observer effect, the reverse situation, namely, the effect of his subjects on the observational powers of the observer, has also been discussed. See John F. Glass and Harry H. Frankiel, "The Influence of Subjects on the Researcher: a Problem in Observing Social Interaction," *Pacific Sociological Review*, 11(1968):75–80.

on an *inference,* since the sociologist cannot prove that people whose behavior he has not observed are behaving in the same way as those he has observed. A major problem in sociological methodology is the construction of samples for study that will insure that the inference is a valid one.[21]

A *representative* sample is the aim of the sociologist because it is this kind of sample that permits a valid inference about a larger population. A sample is representative when the various elements of a population are represented in the sample in the same proportion that they constitute in the population from which the sample was drawn. A sample of college students is representative with reference to sex if, in a college with 75 percent females, there are 75 percent females in the sample. A *biased* sample is one in which some population elements are underrepresented and others are overrepresented. A class in introductory sociology (a frequent "sample" in sociological studies) would, in most colleges, have an overrepresentation of freshmen and sophomores and an underrepresentation of upperclassmen (as well as, probably, some other kinds of bias in the kinds of people who are found in such a course).

A representative sample, like a valid measure, is easier said than done. Some techniques can be mentioned, along with some of their difficulties and limitations. The most familiar technique is the *random sample.* Contrary to the popular conception that a random sample is an arbitrary selection of cases for study ("I just went around randomly and talked to any student I happened to run across"), a random sample employs a technique that eliminates entirely the arbitrary or willful element in sample selection. A random sample begins with an enumeration (listing) of all members of a population (a roster of members of a labor union, for example) and selects cases from that list by a mechanical procedure similar to drawing names from a hat, or selecting the cases whose numbers correspond to a group of numbers drawn from a table of random numbers. The investigator thus may exercise *no* discretion in the selection of his sample for study.

The value of random samples can well be emphasized. A random-

---

[21] For a general discussion of problems in sampling, in this case revolving around the failure of the public opinion polls to predict the outcome of the 1948 presidential election, see Rensis Likert, "Public Opinion Polls," *Scientific American,* 179 (Dec.,1948):7–11. For a more recent discussion, see Gideon Sjoberg and Roger Nett, *A Methodology for Social Research* (New York: Harper & Row, 1968), pp. 144–159.

sampling technique is likely, with a degree of probability that can be stated statistically, to generate a representative sample, since the likelihood of persons from various elements of the population being included in the sample is directly proportional to the numbers of each kind of persons in the population. (Thus, a random sample is sometimes called a *probability sample*.) Obviously, the size of the sample is important in determining this probability. In a population with half females, the probability of randomly selecting an all-male sample of two or three persons is quite high (like the chance of flipping a coin and getting "heads" three times in a row). However, the probability of such a chance selection of a fifty-person all male sample from such a population is extremely slight.

Random samples, though valuable, have their limitations. In the first place, they assume an enumeration of the population, and for many populations that the sociologist would study there is no such listing. (Where would you find a complete enumeration of unwed mothers or Italian-American residents of a city?) They assume, also, that the investigator will be able to study all the cases selected for his sample. In a random sample of the residents of a city, some of the sample persons may be extremely difficult to locate and many may refuse to cooperate with the study (e.g., refuse to grant an interview or return a questionnaire). This would introduce a possible bias if those who cooperate are different in any way relevant to the research from those who refuse to cooperate. (It is sometimes thought, for example, that only those persons cooperate with researches on sex behavior who have "nothing to hide" or "much to brag about" sexually.)

Some of these problems may be skirted by the adoption of other sampling techniques. Even without a names-and-addresses listing of the persons in a population, we may know enough about the general composition of the population to give us leads in constructing a sample. We may know, for example, that 40 percent of unwed mothers are under seventeen years of age, and that 55 percent of Italian-Americans are men. We may construct a *quota sample* in which we select enough persons of each type to correspond to their proportions in the population. We can thus construct by design a sample that is representative with reference to the criteria of representativeness (e.g., age, sex, marital status, social class) that we may think are relevant to the results of our research.

The limitation of the quota-sampling method should be clear. We have allowed an arbitrary element to remain. Assume that the sample must contain twelve women to be representative with reference to sex, but the question of *which twelve* are to be chosen from the population is left to the investigator's discretion. The bias may come if there is some criterion of representativeness that we have not considered but that affects the outcome of our research. The investigator might use his discretion to select *twelve pretty women;* if physical attractiveness affects the behavior being studied (attitudes toward the opposite sex, for example), we could not infer that the behavior measured in our sample would be found with equal frequency in a population with a different proportion of attractive and unattractive women. Most of the public opinion polls in the United States use a quota-sampling technique, and some of the error in their results comes from the inability of the pollsters to know precisely which population variations (e.g., age, sex, region of country, or religious affiliation) will be relevant to variations in public opinion on a given issue; they are never quite sure, therefore, which criteria to use in constructing a quota sample.

Finally, the least respected but probably most used sampling technique involves the use of what can be called a *convenience sample,* that is, a sample of those persons who happen to be available to be studied. Two familiar recruitment techniques are (1) advertising for volunteers or for paid participants in a study, and (2) the use of a captive audience such as the members of a school classroom or employees of a company that will give them time off to participate in a study. The biasing possibilities in such samples are obvious. College freshmen are not "the world," and what is true of their behavior may not be true of "real-life" people. However, such samples do have the advantage of their label—convenience—and it may be possible to dismiss the significance of a given form of bias by showing that, in relevant respects, the sample of available subjects is reasonably typical of some wider population. For example, introductory sociology students may not be a bad representation of college underclassmen if most or all students at a given college take such a course. If the sample *is* biased in some significant way, it is at least possible to take the bias into account and exercise the proper caution in any suggestion of a generalization of one's findings.

PROBLEMS IN CAUSAL INFERENCE
The measurement and sampling problems we have just discussed refer to the sociologist's problem of providing accurate *descriptions*

of some of the facts about human behavior. Another side of socio-logical interest in human behavior is its concern with the *explana-tion* of human behavior: *Why* is there more campus unrest today than yesterday? *Why* is there more unrest on the large campuses? etc. Human behavior is a *variable,* and sociology is concerned with explaining this variability. The explanation of a given kind of be-havior presupposes the existence of measuring and sampling operations that indicate the frequency of that behavior, but the problems of explanation have only begun when these other prob-lems are solved.

Correlation

Sociological explanation, like scientific explanation in general, begins with the attempt to discover *correlations* in the phenomenal world. Correlation means covariance, the tendency for variation in one variable to accompany variations in other variables. The Boyles Law and Charles Law of physics state the covariance of the vari-ables of temperature, pressure, and volume. A sociological study of, for example, campus unrest would tend to try to discover varia-tions in other social conditions that are correlated with variations in campus unrest. Questions might be raised, for example, about whether unrest varies with (1) the time of the school year (more of it around examination time, for example), (2) the social-class com-position of the student body, and (3) the degree of "social distance" between faculty and students. These are all *variables,* and the soci-ologist may hypothesize a correlation between one or more of such variables and the variable of campus unrest.

The introductory student should acquaint himself with a few of the technicalities involved in the reporting of sociological corre-lations. Two major devices for the demonstration of correlation will be discussed.

The first device may be called the technique of *contingency anal-ysis,* used especially when one or more of the correlated variables is a discrete (either-or) kind of variable. Suppose a sociologist of campus unrest observed that, during the disturbances on American campuses that occurred in the spring of 1970, some colleges closed early in accommodation to student demands while other colleges remained in operation to the end of the semester. The sociologist might believe that there is a correlation between closing or not closing and, say, the kind of financial support—private or public—on which the school is primarily dependent. Each college in a sample of 100 colleges is classified on these two variables. There are four combinations of closing policy and type of financial support; any correlation would show up in an uneven distribution of closing policies in the schools with the two types of financial support. We might tabulate our 100 cases as follows:

CLOSING POLICY

		Closed Early	Stayed Open	
TYPE OF FINANCIAL SUPPORT	Private	40	10	50
	Public	20	30	50
		60	40	100

According to the table, there *appears* to be a relationship between the two variables, i.e., a private school was more likely than a public one to close early.

If we want a more precise statement of the probability of a relationship between these two variables we may use a *test of statistical significance.* Very frequently, the *chi*-square test is used in such cases.[22] To understand something of the logic of the *chi*-square test, let us construct a table that would show the distribution of measurements on these two variables if there were *no* relationship between the two variables. Such a no-relationship or theoretical frequency table would be as follows:

CLOSING POLICY

		Closed Early	Stayed Open	
TYPE OF FINANCIAL SUPPORT	Private	30	20	50
	Public	30	20	50
		60	40	100

Since half of the sample's schools are private and half are public, half of the schools that closed early should be private and half should be public, etc. The *chi*-square statistic is arrived at by computing the degree of discrepancy between this theoretical fre-

---

[22] Sidney Siegel, *Nonparametric Statistics for the Behavioral Sciences* (New York: McGraw-Hill, 1956).

quency of cases in each cell and the actual or measured distribution (the first model); the greater the discrepancy, the greater the *chi*-square value. The statistical significance of this value is determined by consulting a statistical table which indicates the probability that any apparent correlation of the variables is actually the result of "chance" factors (such as the kind of sample we happen to have drawn). The *smaller* the size of this number, the greater the investigator's confidence that there is actually a relation between the variables. A limitation of this technique is that it does not indicate the degree of correlation or "strength of association" of the variables. A probability of .001 does *not* indicate ten times as much correlation as does a probability of .01; it simply reflects that much greater confidence that there is *some* relationship.

Dissatisfaction with this limitation of contingency analysis has led many sociologists to prefer another technique that does not have this limitation, namely, some form of a *coefficient of correlation*.[23] This technique is useful when variables are measured on a *continuous* scale, i.e., where measurements yield scores on both variables. To consider again our campus unrest example, our interest in the relationship between the type of financial support and the closing policy may have been based on the view that the governing boards of private colleges are composed of wealthier people who are more sympathetic to the aims and tactics of student protest. We might, now, measure our 100-case sample of colleges on two variables: (1) the average income of the members of the governing board of each college and (2) the number of public statements by board members of each college that indicate sympathy for student protest. Each college would receive a numerical "score" for each of these two variables and a coefficient of correlation would show the degree of covariance of these scores.

The mathematics involved in computing a coefficient of correlation need not concern us here; suffice it to understand the meaning of a given correlation. Coefficients of correlation range from a perfectly negative correlation of -1.0 to a perfectly positive correlation of $+1.0$, with *no* correlation at the midpoint of 0. Negative correlations mean that an individual or institution with a high value on one variable is likely to have a low value on another (colleges with wealthy board members have few sympathetic public statements

---

[23] Bernard S. Phillips, *Social Research Strategy and Tactics* (New York: Macmillan, 1966), pp. 45, 46.

by board members). Positive correlations show similarity of value on the two variables (colleges with wealthy board members have many sympathetic public statements by board members).

The magnitude of a correlation (.40, for example) indicates the degree to which variability in one variable can be accounted for by variation in another variable. The degree of this predictability is not, however, the decimal of the given coefficient, but the mathematical square of this value. A .40 correlation indicates 16 percent variability accounted for, .30 means 9 percent, etc. This information is useful to the student in assessing the scientific value of a given coefficient of correlation. The statistical probability that a correlation of a given magnitude indicates *some* relationship between variables can be computed, as in the case of a *chi*-square of a given value. Correlations on the order of .20 to .30 are often reported as being statistically significant. When the reader is reminded that correlations of this magnitude account for only 4 to 9 percent of variability, he may want to question whether the correlation is very significant in terms of its power to explain the phenomenon in question.

Causality

So far we have, by design, said nothing about any *causal* relation between variables. We have not spoken, for example, of the causes of campus unrest. However, when the sociologist (or the man in the street) asks for explanations of phenomena, he does want to know what forces or factors have produced the phenomenon in question, whether it be a crime wave, an economic depression, or a championship football team. Philosophers like David Hume might argue that we experience "concomitant variation" (correlation) and imagine cause-and-effect relations only as a matter of "habit"; but it is a strongly ingrained habit in human thought, and the sociologist takes it over.

The terms *independent variable* and *dependent variable* are used to denote cause and effect, respectively. The demonstration of correlation is necessary but not sufficient to support an inference that variation in one variable "causes" variation in another. For one thing, even if the variables are causally connected, it is not always possible to determine which is cause and which is effect. If there is a high correlation between poverty and mental illness, it may be that being poor is a causal factor in becoming mentally ill, but it may also be that the expense incurred by mental illness is a causal factor in precipitating poverty. (There may also, of course, be an interaction or mutual dependence of variables—the proverbial vicious circle.) Our judgments in these matters are likely to be rather intuitive. If there is a correlation between wealth and liberalism in social attitudes, we may doubt that liberalism contributes very much to a person's becoming wealthy, whereas wealth does make it possible for one to indulge in the "luxury" of liberalism in the *noblesse oblige* style. Such judgments, being intuitive, are subject to controversy because of variations in individual intuition.

Another and probably more serious problem in inferring causality from correlation appears when we reflect that two classes of events may be correlated without there being *any* causal connection between them. The blooming of the dogtooth violet and the northward migration of the bobolink coincide closely in time, but no one would seriously suggest that flower-blooming is the cause of bird migration or that bird migration is the cause of flower-blooming. Clearly they are both dependent variables (effects) of a third variable, the change of the seasons.

A closely analogous situation often exists in sociological explanation and creates a major problem in causal inference. Consider again the hypothetical correlation of financial support of colleges and their responses to student demonstrations. The fact that the private colleges are more likely to close early could mean that financial support is a determinant of school policy in such cases, but it is also quite possible that both financial support and school policy are dependent effects of a third variable, say, the social-class composition of the student body. If colleges with "upper class" student bodies are privately supported colleges and are also colleges where the pressure of student demands to close early is greater (as a reflection of upper-class life styles), then the pattern of coincidence of private financial support and early school-closing may have no more causal significance than does the correlation of flower-blooming and bird migration. The influence of third or *intervening* variables is an ever-present problem in the making of causal inferences.

There are, of course, long-established scientific techniques for dealing with the effects of intervening variables. The physical scientist's laboratory experiment is an attempt to study the effects of one variable on another by holding constant all other variables. The typical small-groups experiment uses control and experimental groups in which the situation of each group is identical except for the introduction of one variable (say, the raising or lowering of group morale) whose effects the investigator wants to study.[24]

Many kinds of sociological explanation are not amenable to such treatment, however. Were the sociologist interested in the effects of capital punishment in encouraging or discouraging capital crimes, he might suspect that any correlations are the result of intervening variables; for example, the lower rates of capital crimes in those states that have abolished capital punishment may mean simply that general social enlightenment has produced both a reduction in crime and a reduction in the severity of punishment. He might be tempted to wish himself in a position to impose on one state an elimination of capital punishment (his experimental group) and impose on an otherwise similar state a maintenance of capital punishment (his control group). Any differences in the subsequent capital crime rates of the two states could properly be ascribed to the effects of the treatment. But, of course, the sociologist is restrained from making some of the experiments that could answer difficult questions of explanation either by his lack of political power or by his ethical notions about appropriate ways of treating human subjects.[25]

Fortunately, there are alternatives to experimental manipulation in dealing with the effects of intervening variables. One possibility is that, while sociologists are seldom in power positions that would allow them to make random assignments of subjects for different experimental treatments, other people *do* sometimes make such assignments and, in a sense, set up experiments for us. Students may be assigned to one section or another of a class, to one dormitory roommate or another on an essentially random basis. The alert sociologist can use such situations as "natural experiments" in the factors that influence human behavior.

Another possibility is that one may, by statistical manipulation of data, control for the effects of a third variable. This is done by computing some kind of *partial correlation,* the correlation that remains between two variables when the effects of a third variable

---

[24] See, for one example, Muzafer and Carolyn Sherif, *Reference Groups* (New York: Harper & Row, 1964).

[25] For one discussion of the ethical problems involved in social research, see Edward A. Shils, "Social Inquiry and the Autonomy of the Individual," in Daniel Lerner (ed.), *The Human Meaning of the Social Sciences* (Cleveland: World, 1959), pp. 114–157.

have been held constant. The assertion, for example, that the correlation of mode of financial support and college response to student demonstration is accounted for by the higher social-class composition of the private schools would have to be rejected if it could be shown that, *within* a group of colleges with student bodies of equivalent class standing, the private ones are more likely to respond favorably to the student demonstrations. Here we have the statistical equivalent of the "holding constant" of intervening variables by laboratory controls. Although we obviously cannot *impose* any lack of variation in social-class composition of student bodies at different colleges, we can see whether correlations of our independent and dependent variables hold up within a subgroup of our sample for which there is no variation of class position.[26]

A critic of sociological explanations (and sociologists tend to be their own severest critics) may point out that causal inferences based on such statistical manipulations are always risky because it is always possible that the investigator has overlooked some hidden variable that is influencing his results. If you believe that human behavior is the resultant of a complex of causal factors that are hopelessly intertwined, you may doubt that the human mind will ever be able to apprehend all the obscure interconnections of things. The sociologist is continuously made aware of these problems by the criticism of his research by his colleagues, if not by himself.

For the nth and final time in this chapter it must be said that there are no ultimate answers to the problem of applying scientific methodology to the study of human behavior. When sociology was characterized, at the outset, as an "intellectual enterprise," it was in the author's mind that sociology is, for those who choose to indulge in it, a tantalizing, often frustrating, sometimes rewarding effort to apply a discipline of method to the recalcitrance of human behavior. When asked why he studied sociology, Max Weber was said to have replied, "To see how much I can stand." In so answering, he may well have had in mind the incredible complexity of human behavior and the necessity for the student of that behavior to exercise continuous and critical self-consciousness about his methods of study.

---

[26] An example of a study which deals in this way with intervening variables is Samuel A. Stouffer, *Communism, Conformity and Civil Liberties* (Garden City, N.Y.: Doubleday, 1955).

SUMMARY

A contemporary sociologist, C. Wright Mills, has criticized some of his colleagues for a "methodological inhibition," an overconcern for "how to do it" in research that leads to a poverty of imagination in insightful understanding of human behavior.[27] The reader may suspect by now that this criticism is justified, that with all the things that can go wrong in sociological research, the sociologist must be discouraged from attempting anything really bold or creative.

It has not been the purpose of this chapter to scare the reader into extreme caution in his own research or extreme skepticism about the validity of the research done by others. Rather, the aim has been to introduce the reader as frankly as possible to the problems faced daily by practicing sociologists. Sociological investigation is carried on in a pervasive atmosphere of criticism that is likely to be painful to the recipient but is a necessary part of the system of checks and balances by which sociological findings are kept honest.

We have discussed three troublesome areas of methodological concern in sociology: (1) the problem of developing reliable and valid measures of human behavior; (2) the problem of constructing representative samples that allow an inference from a limited number of measurements to a wider universe of human behavior; and (3) the problem of apprehending the relationships, especially cause and effect, between different aspects of human behavior. In none of these areas is there any easy solution to the problem; but in none is the sociologist completely bereft of techniques for dealing with the problem. Research *style* is as important a consideration in sociology as it is elsewhere. Just as there may be graceful or clumsy styles of public address or lovemaking, there are sociologists who command the respect of their colleagues for the elegance of their methodological style, and others whose styles are best overlooked in the interest of charity.

---

[27] C. Wright Mills, *The Sociological Imagination* (New York: Oxford University Press, 1959).

CULTURE

PART TWO

In a popular treatise on the accomplishments of social science, Stuart Chase characterizes the concept of culture as "the foundation stone of the social sciences."[1] Whether or not the sociologist fully shares this exalted view of the importance of the concept of culture, he, along with the anthropologist, is ready to see the highly conventional character of much of human behavior. Even the so-called nonconformist is likely to accept rather unconsciously most of the life styles that prevail in the groups to which he belongs. The pervasiveness of this tendency of people to go along with the ways of life that they find around them is a major reason for the sociological interest in culture.

---

[1] Stuart Chase, *The Proper Study of Mankind* (New York: Harper, 1948), p. 59.

Culture
and Human Behavior

3

DEFINITION OF CULTURE

The classic definition of culture is Tylor's "Culture is that complex whole which includes knowledge, belief, art, morals, law, custom, and any other capabilities acquired by man as a member of society."[1] If this sounds more like a catalog than a definition, we can look to the other extreme of specification of detail. Kluckhohn has defined culture very simply as "the total life way of a people."[2] This definition has the merit of pointing out the way in which the technical sociological definition differs from the everyday usage of the term. Popular usage tends to equate culture with the "finer things of life"—art, music, and philosophy, for example—and to define the "cultured" man as one who participates in this elevated way of life. The sociological definition is quite different. Culture is not limited to the more refined ways of behavior but includes the total way of life of a group of people. The life styles of mechanics and kings are equally cultural by this definition.

In addition to the identification of culture with *total* life ways, there are a few other distinguishing characteristics of the concept of culture as employed in social science. Most of these features are implicit in Tylor's definition.

First, culture is a way of life which is *shared* among the people in some social grouping—a nation, a region, an occupation, for example. Not all the life ways of people are cultural, since some

---

[1] Edward B. Tylor, *The Origins of Culture* (New York: Harper, 1958), p. 1. First published in 1871 as *Primitive Culture*.

[2] Clyde Kluckhohn, *Mirror for Man* (New York: McGraw-Hill, 1949), p. 17.

41

are highly idiosyncratic to a single person or to a tiny cult of eccentrically acting persons.

The distinction between shared and idiosyncratic life ways cannot always be easily drawn. We frequently find that, in a group within which most members share a way of life, there are significantly large subgroups of people who do not fully share this dominant culture, but who have life ways that are limited to these smaller groups. Adolescents may, for example, share a "youth culture" which emphasizes certain themes (such as teen-age enthusiasm for rock music) that are not so highly emphasized in the larger societies of which these adolescents are members. The sociologist calls such minority life ways *subcultures* and, as we shall see, makes frequent use of the concept in his explanations of variations in social behavior.

Second, culture is a life way that is more or less permanent or stable, providing a tradition that is passed on from one generation to the next. It is on this basis that culture is distinguishable from fashion. Fashionable ways of life are those that become prominent for a brief period but do not become the basis for a tradition that is taught to the next generation. Members of one generation frequently cannot understand why their elders were so wild about a particular form of dance or a particular theatrical personality.

The line between culture and fashion, like other definitional lines in sociology, is not always simply drawn. Some fashionable forms of dancing do become traditional and are taught to the next generation of children, and some theatrical idols of one era do enter a "hall of fame" and are honored by succeeding generations. Also, as we shall see in chapter 4, traditional ways of life do fall into disuse at times. The westernization of Oriental life or the Americanization of European life are examples of the instability of traditional cultural ways.

Third, in many definitions of culture, the concept does not refer to the actual ways of behavior of people in a group but is limited to the socially approved or expected behavior. Culture has been called a "design for living"[3] with perhaps the idea that human behavior bears the same relation to culture that a building bears to the set of designs or blueprints used by its builder. Every build-

---

[3] Clyde Kluckhohn and W. H. Kelly, "The Concept of Culture," in Ralph Linton (ed.), *The Science of Man in the World Crisis* (New York: Columbia University Press, 1945), pp. 78–107.

ing has its flaws and deviations from the blueprint; in the same way human behavior is never perfect since it never follows exactly the socially approved designs. Another way of making this point is to insist that culture is *ideational*,[4] that it exists in the minds of members of a society. If one follows this approach, perhaps the phrase "way of thought" is a more accurate definition of culture than is the phrase "way of life."

ELEMENTS OF CULTURE

The "total life way of a people" includes at least three elements: (1) the people's prevailing notions about reality, (2) their moral judgments of good and bad or right and wrong, and (3) their definitions of those things in life which are attractive or unattractive as objects of desire. We shall refer to these three elements, respectively, as *cultural beliefs, ideals,* and *preferences*.[5]

Beliefs

Everywhere men entertain certain notions about the nature of the world in which they live. These notions range from the most objectively verified theories of science about natural phenomena to the most fanciful or metaphysical beliefs about the nature of supernatural or transcendent beings.

A defining characteristic of beliefs is that they are susceptible to arguments about their truth or falsity. A belief is an existential element in thought, a notion about what is in the universe, and is always subject to verification or refutation on the basis of evidence. Some beliefs are easier to refute than others. Scientific beliefs are held only tentatively and are always subject to revision with subsequent experiments (with some qualifications of the kind we discussed in chapter 2). Religious beliefs, on the other hand, are likely to die hard since they make claims about reality that are not easily refuted.

One of the features of culture in general that is of special sociological interest is the *shared* quality of a belief system. People who share a given culture tend to take a rather unified position on just

---

[4] George P. Murdock, "The Cross Cultural Survey," *American Sociological Review,* 5(1940):361–369.

[5] Compare the following analysis with the cognitive, cathectic, and normative types of "definition of the situation" as outlined in Harry C. Bredemeier and Richard M. Stephenson, *The Analysis of Social Systems* (New York: Holt, Rinehart & Winston, 1962), pp. 11–14.

what are the so-called facts of the universe and to take a hostile attitude toward those within their midst who cannot or will not accept conventional definitions of fact. If, on religious or scientific grounds, "everybody" believes that the earth is the center of the universe, a "deviant" astronomer like Galileo is likely to experience rejection and pressure to bring his beliefs in line with the prevailing ones. We typically reserve adjectives like "insane" or "kooky" for individuals who apprehend the facts of the world in highly individualized styles. Given the various popular delusions that have existed throughout history, it is quite possible, of course, that a deviant thinker is more in line with reality than is the society of people who reject him as a madman.[6]

One important kind of belief or existential idea system is represented in the *technology* of a culture. A technology is a belief about how reality can be manipulated effectively by human beings for human purposes. Technology is not, as sometimes thought, limited to prevailing ideas about how to manipulate material aspects of reality. A culture does have systems of engineering by which material goods are made to yield to the desire for artificial production; it also contains technologies for the manipulation of such nonmaterial realities as popularity ("how to win friends"), happiness, and mental health. As with all culture, technologies tend to be highly conventional and traditional. Although there may be many effective alternative strategies for raising crops or children, the tendency is to do these things "like everybody else is doing" or "like grandfather and grandmother did it."[7]

Ideals

In addition to a belief system which defines notions of *what is,* culture includes a system of ideas about *what ought to be.*[8] It seems to

---

[6] In the realm of economic behavior there may be a kind of "conventional wisdom" shared by almost everybody concerning the nature of economic processes which is, in fact, a delusionary view of these processes. John Kenneth Galbraith, *The Affluent Society* (Boston: Houghton Mifflin, 1958).

[7] One study dealing with resistances to technical change is Margaret Mead, *Cultural Patterns and Technical Change* (New York: New American Library, 1955). On resistance to changes in medical practices, see Catherine M. Una MacLean, "Traditional Healers and Their Female Clients; an Aspect of Nigerian Sickness Behavior," *Journal of Health and Social Behavior,* 10(1969):172–186.

[8] There is clearly a large difference between a *belief* of the type, "there has been an increase in the amount of crime in the last year," and a judgmental reaction like "crime is probably our worst social problem."

be a universal characteristic of people to make judgments about reality in terms of some standard by which reality is approved or condemned. Every culture involves a moral order in which certain forms of conduct are considered as acceptable while other forms of conduct are rejected as wrong or evil. *Indignation* can be aroused among any group of people who possess a set of standards for judging behavior, and the indignation is always righteous and directed against the wrongdoer.

An important distinction can be made between norms and values, as two types of ideals or standards. *Norms* are the standards by which specific human acts are approved or condemned.[9] They are either *prescriptive,* demanding certain kinds of behavior ("thou shalt . . .") or *proscriptive,* requiring the abstinence from tabooed sorts of behavior ("thou shalt not . . ."). *Values* are more abstract kinds of ideals, expressing the general aspirations of a people without specifying standards for the details of behavior. American culture, for example, is sometimes characterized as emphasizing such values as democracy and progress.[10] Each of these general ideals implies a great many norms which specify the behaviors that are appropriate to the realization of this value. If one of the values of a culture is democracy, we can expect to find many norms which will encourage participation in decision-making processes (get out and vote!) and condemn any actions that tend to restrict this participation (outlaw literacy tests!).

Preferences

A third element of culture is one which is frequently not carefully defined by essayists on culture. A striking difference in the cultures of different peoples may be their different notions about what is desirable in human existence. We may occasionally forget that our judgments of the ideal or "proper" do not always correspond to our judgments of the pleasant or enjoyable. These discrepancies are revealed in notions like "onerous duties" (not desirable but proper) and "temptations" (not proper but desirable)—"All the

---

[9] Students may need to remind themselves occasionally that in sociology the term *norm* does not (as it often does elsewhere) denote the average or typical behavior of people. Although a norm or ideal for behavior may be held by everyone in a group, it is entirely possible that *no one* actually behaves in a way that fully lives up to the norm.

[10] A major study of American values is found in Robin M. Williams, Jr., *American Society* (New York: Knopf, 1960).

things I really like to do are immoral, illegal or fattening," declared Alexander Woollcott. In the area of preferences, cultural standards may define the "good life" in terms that range from the very general to the very specific.

The general goals of human existence (what is life all about?) are differently defined in different cultures, and the misery or happiness of people depends on the standard being applied. Among some peoples, spiritual salvation or immortality is a principal goal of existence, and the miserable man is the "sinner." Among others, accumulation of wealth represents the goal of existence and the happy man is one who has done well by these more earthly standards. In every society there are people who are successes and those who are failures; it is the culture that provides the criteria by which these judgments about success or failure are made.

A culture tends to provide the canons of taste in specific lines of human activity. Taste, in the most literal sense, varies greatly with the food-consumption preferences of different cultures. But there is also taste in clothing, housing, sexual practices, and in an endless variety of possessions and activities. What is tasteful in one culture may be highly distasteful in another. The rule of *De gustibus non est disputandum* ("there is no disputing about tastes") is rather frequently violated, as when a person from one cultural background attempts to "educate" an acquaintance who is too gauche because his tastes (in music or novels, for example) were formed in another cultural environment.

CULTURAL INTEGRATION

A major trend in recent anthropological study of culture is the insistence that the culture of a people is not a conglomeration of individual traits (specific beliefs, ideals, and preferences) but an integration of these traits into some meaningful whole. The meaning of an individual trait can be discerned only if we understand the basic theme or pattern of cultural traits in the culture in which the trait prevails.

A forerunner of this trend toward a "holistic" approach to cultures was Benedict's description of cultures as embodying a Dionysian or an Apollonian theme.[11] A Dionysian culture emphasizes the importance of emotional expression and extraordinary religious ecstasy, while an Apollonian culture emphasizes the ne-

---

[11] Ruth Benedict, *Patterns of Culture* (New York: Mentor, 1959).

cessity of living a harmonious life based on the calm repetition of traditional rituals. The Zuñi Indians of the southwestern United States are described as having an Apollonian culture; the Kwakiutl Indians of the northwest coast of North America are seen as Dionysian.

Such characterizations of the total culture of a people are hazardous, and the social scientist engages in such generalizations at his own risk. The assumption that cultural traits always form an integrated pattern can be challenged.[12] When one observes the conglomeration of architectural styles represented in the buildings of any large American city or the eclecticism of home-furnishing styles in the typical American living room, one may wonder whether there is any integration here except the "mechanical integration" of various things coexisting in the same place.[13]

Even the characterization of the way of life of a people as being "basically" Apollonian or Dionysian may be dubious. How would one characterize American culture, for example? Apollonian, if one has in mind the ritualism of the nine-to-five, five-days-a-week working habits of the typical American wage earner or the daily drudge of the housewife-mother. But weekends in general, and Saturday nights and holidays in particular, are likely to be defined as occasions to "live it up" in a search for Dionysian excitement. Does this mean that the culture is imperfectly integrated? Or does it mean, perhaps, that any functionally viable society must make provision for *both* the disciplined behavior of the Apollonian type and the self-expressive behavior of the Dionysian type?[14]

Some further complexities about cultural integration arise if we consider again the phenomenon of *subculture*—the existence of subgroups whose values depart from those of the larger group. The new breed of American college student seems, especially to his critical elders, to hold values that are rather strongly Dionysian in character. The search for self-expression among the young, the

---

[12] Benedict herself recognized that not all cultures are completely integrated, but her analysis emphasized the tendency toward such integration. *Patterns of Culture*, pp. 200–202.

[13] Pitirim A. Sorokin, *Social and Cultural Dynamics*, Vol. I, *Fluctuation of Forms of Art* (New York: Bedminster, 1937), pp. 10–13.

[14] See the interpretation of the Zulu "rituals of rebellion" as a device for allowing women a kind of Dionysian compensation for the usual tight rein that is kept on their behavior. Max Gluckman, *Custom and Conflict in Africa* (Glencoe, Ill.: Free Press, 1956).

desire to do their own thing, is partly a reaction against what they see as the ritualism and apathy of the older generation. Again, however, we can pose alternative consequences of such facts for cultural integration. Do subcultural variations in values indicate the imperfect integration of the culture? Or does an integrated society require that some groups specialize in Apollonian ways while others specialize in Dionysian behavior? In support of the latter alternative, it can be noted that sometimes older people take a measure of pride in the freedom and nonconformity of youth; and young people, in their more candid moments, may admit the value of the maturity of their elders. Many social organizations try to balance their memberships by age in order to take advantage of both the freshness of youth and the experience of maturity.

One final problem: It is often observed that the values that people verbalize are in conflict with the values that are operative when they are choosing how to act. They profess the value of sobriety but are consumers of alcohol; they say they value peace but support acts of war by their government.

This behavior, popularly called "hypocrisy" or "paying lip service" to cultural values, may, again, have alternative implications for cultural integration. One view is that this hypocritical behavior is an indication of lack of cultural integration and that it introduces a "strain toward consistency" between professed beliefs and actions. This was approximately Myrdal's view of American race relations in his characterization of these relations as involving a "dilemma."[15] The dilemma arises from the fact that, although the American believes strongly in the American creed which holds that all men are created equal, the white man in fact discriminates against the black and denies him equality of treatment in many overt and subtle ways. Myrdal believes that the white American feels strongly this lack of integration of his beliefs and actions and is motivated to an elimination of the discrepancy.

An alternative view about cultural hypocrisy is that a community requires an "official morality" to which everyone verbally adheres even if this morality is often violated in practice.[16] Similarly, a society may require a kind of division of moral labor in which some persons—such guardians of morality as clergymen and school-

---

[15] Gunnar Myrdal, *An American Dilemma* (New York: Harper, 1944).

[16] Charles K. Warriner, "The Nature and Functions of Official Morality," *American Journal of Sociology*, 64(1959):165–168.

teachers—are able to adhere to the official morality because they are protected from knowledge of the compromises and the dirty work that exists at the level of practical behavior. Men of affairs— politicians and lawyers, for example—are expected to perform that very dirty work that is necessary to get things done in the real world. One study of attitudes toward corruption in a community found that most citizens professed to be unaware of any great amount of corruption by public officials and to be concerned about the problem only if forced into the open by some adverse publicity.[17] Findings like these suggest that a society may very well sustain and even require a certain degree of conflict or lack of integration of the values by which its various members act.

FUNCTIONS OF CULTURE

Among all groups of people we find widely shared beliefs, norms, values, and preferences. Since culture seems to be a universal human phenomenon, it occurs naturally to wonder whether culture corresponds to any universal human needs. This curiosity raises the question of the functions of culture. Social scientists have tended to emphasize one or both of two kinds of functions that culture performs for man: (1) it liberates his capacities; and (2) it channels or limits his activities.

Culture as Liberating

Culture enables man to do things that are impossible for any other animal. Other animals are sharply limited in their ability to apply social experience to the solution of their problems. The higher animals can learn through experience and may even succeed in some rudimentary teaching of personal experiences to others of their kind. For the most part, however, animal behavior is determined by instinct rather than by learning. The process of organic evolution has produced an instinctive ability of fish to swim and breathe in water and of birds to migrate seasonally to appropriate habitats.

The human species is not well adapted biologically to adjust behavior automatically to the requirements of existence. The human infant is among the more helpless of animal young. He is completely dependent for his survival on the care he receives from

---

[17] John A. Gardiner, "Public Attitudes Toward Gambling and Corruption," *Annals of the American Academy of Political and Social Science,* 374(1967):123–134.

adults. However, this lack of instinctive survival equipment is compensated by another biological characteristic, namely, his great capacity for learning or incorporating the ideas of others about techniques of survival. Cooley contrasts the plasticity of human heredity with the fixity of animal heredity:

> Roughly speaking, then, the heredity of the other animals is a mechanism like that of a hand-organ: it is made to play a few tunes; you can play these tunes at once, with little or no training; and you can never play any others. The heredity of man, on the other hand, is a mechanism more like that of a piano: it is not made to play particular tunes; you can do nothing at all on it without training; but a trained player can draw from it an infinite variety of music.[18]

The "infinite variety" of the forms of human behavior is a product of the influence of different cultures on the "tunes" that different people play. Without his ability to learn from his immediate associates and from previous generations who have developed traditions for him to follow, without the aid of this "superorganic" level of adjustment to his environment,[19] man would probably play a very poor tune, indeed. Thus, many writers refer to culture as a social heritage, a stock of knowledge from which the individual learns what he must know as he goes about the process of living.

Culture as Limiting

If men use culture to advance their purposes, it seems clear also that a culture imposes limits on human purposes and activities. The need for order calls forth another function of culture, that of so directing behavior that disorderly behavior is restricted and orderly behavior is promoted. A society without rules or norms to define right and wrong behavior would be very much like a heavily travelled street without traffic signs or any understood rules for meeting and passing vehicles. Chaos would be the result in either case.

Social order cannot rest on the assumption that men will spontaneously behave in ways conducive to social harmony. The "social contract" theory of the state assumed that men agreed to give up some of their liberties in favor of social regulation because they

---

[18] Charles H. Cooley, *Human Nature and the Social Order* (New York: Scribner's, 1902), p. 19.

[19] Alfred L. Kroeber, *The Nature of Culture* (Chicago: University of Chicago Press, 1952).

experienced the terror of the primeval war of each against all. Actually, the view of "primitive" society that is embodied in the social contract theory has been challenged by sociologists and anthropologists who are skeptical of a "state of nature" in the early history of man that was chaotic and without rule.[20] From this viewpoint, the normative regulation of human behavior is a functional requirement for *any* society, primitive or modern. The form of this regulation may change and may vary from society to society, but anarchy seems to be contradicted by the very nature of human society.

SUMMARY

Human behavior is marked by the pervasive influence of the *ideas* that people have about that behavior. Culture might be thought of as the analogy, on the level of the group, of that self-consciousness that is a prominent feature of individual human psychology. Men not only act, they think about their acts and, when this thinking takes forms that are widely shared among a group of people and that are transmitted across generations, we see the influence of culture on human acting.

Whether these modes of thought involve ways of apprehending the "facts" of the universe or ways of responding morally or emotionally to these facts, there tends to be a pervasive group definition of correct and proper ways of thinking, and the individual who does not think "rightly" is rejected as a deviant. These elements of culture tend to take an integrated or self-consistent form as the various traits of a culture are arranged into some consistent theme or configuration. However, certain cultural inconsistencies may be tolerable or even necessary if a group of people are to remain in association with one another. Although inconsistency of culture is tolerable, the absence of culture would apparently violate the necessary conditions of human existence. Men require culture to provide them with the knowledge they need to insure their survival; it also provides a set of rules for behavior that makes orderly social life possible.

---

[20] Emile Durkheim, *On the Division of Labor in Society,* trans. by George Simpson (New York: Macmillan, 1933).

Cultural Variability
and Change

CULTURAL VARIABILITY

The discussion in the last chapter of the functions of culture emphasizes the universal aspect of the phenomenon, but the fact of cultural variability is impressive and introduces some of the most basic problems for sociological analysis of human behavior. If all men in all societies possess culture, the form of that culture varies greatly from one society to another. We shall consider now some of the forms of this variability and some speculations on the causes and consequences of cultural variability.

Cultural Specificity of Human Behavior

The range of human behaviors that is determined by variations in culture is sometimes surprising to the student. We are ready enough to grant the fact that there are different religious or political values incorporated in different cultures because it is generally understood that religion and politics are "social" phenomena. We are less likely to see that some of the behaviors attributed to the universal, biologically determined "human nature" of man are also highly subject to variation under the influence of different cultures.

At one time it was fashionable to attribute war to a "pugnacity instinct" in man, and to attribute human sociability to a "gregarious instinct." The notion that warfare is instinctively determined flounders on the evidence that contradicts the universality of this so-called instinct. Eskimo people are reported as being unable to understand the killing of a man as an act of war. Benedict found that some Indian people whom she studied were unable to understand the cultural pattern of war:

. . . and their attempts to reason it out reduced the great wars to which we are able to dedicate ourselves with moral fervour to the level of alley brawls. They did not happen to have a cultural pattern that distinguished between them.[1]

The relation between human biology, human culture, and human behavior is frequently formulated as a relation in which biology furnishes the *necessary* but not the *sufficient* conditions for the determination of human behavior. Man's biological nature fixes the behavioral problems (for example, eating, sleeping, sexual activity) which must be dealt with, but culture determines the specific direction of the solution to these problems.

Consequences of Cultural Variability

The *fact* of cultural variability in human behavior has been impressively documented by contemporary anthropologists. So long as people remain unaware of other people with life ways that differ from their own, the strictly sociological consequences of this fact are rather limited. Interesting problems do arise when people become aware of these cultural differences. Some possible effects of such awareness on social interaction or social organization will now be discussed.

Ethnocentrism. A possible and frequent reaction to the awareness of cultural differences is rejection of the "foreign" ways. Alien *beliefs* may be seen as incomprehensible (How can anyone adhere to such a silly superstition or inefficient technology?). Alien *norms* and *values* may be rejected as immoral (How can the Eskimo possibly think it right to offer sexual relations with his wife to a guest in his home?). Alien *tastes* may be seen as repulsive (How can the Japanese eat that nasty tasting marinated seaweed?). This rejection of alien ways because they fail to conform to standards derived from one's own culture, which is usually considered superior, is called *ethnocentrism.*

The human tendency toward ethnocentric thought has often been commented upon. Sumner noted the tendency everywhere to divide the world into "we" and "they," and to reject the culture of "they" because it involves ways of which "we" disapprove:

Each group nourishes its own pride and vanity, boasts itself superior,

---

[1] Ruth Benedict, *Patterns of Culture* (New York: Mentor, 1959), p. 41.

exalts its own divinities, and looks with contempt on outsiders. Each group thinks its own folkways the only right ones, and if it observes that other groups have other folkways, these excite its scorn. Opprobrious epithets are derived from these differences. "Pig-eater," "cow-eater," "uncircumcised," "jabberers," are epithets of contempt and abomination. The Tupis called the Portuguese by a derisive epithet descriptive of birds which have feathers around their feet, on account of trousers.[2]

Many anthropologists have seen as part of their civilizing mission to mankind the obligation to render ethnocentrism in an unacceptable light. In her famous book *Patterns of Culture,* Ruth Benedict notes that men in Western society are especially ethnocentric because, given the power and extent of Western culture, there has been little practical necessity for Western man to expose himself to non-Western ways.[3] She hoped that her book about alien cultures would serve as an antidote to this ethnocentric tendency. The viewpoint of "cultural relativity" (there is no absolute right and wrong, but moral judgments are relative to the standards of a given culture) that Benedict attempts to promote appears to be a most difficult attitude for humans to maintain. There is a well-established tendency in everyday life for people to behave on the basis of ethnocentric viewpoints. Two kinds of sociological consequences of this tendency might be mentioned.

First, the fact that a person comes from a cultural background in which the way of life is judged to be inferior or unworthy may have many consequences for that person's social life. In the United States, for example, there is a great deal of rural and urban ethnocentrism. Rural dwellers glorify the neighborliness of their way of life;[4] city dwellers emphasize the superior cosmopolitanism and the cultural advantages of their way of life. A person with an urban upbringing who happens to live in a rural area may find himself rejected as a "city slicker" by his rural neighbors. Similarly, the rural migrant to the city may be handicapped socially by the tendency of city natives to reject him as a "hick." Also in the United States, immigrants from eastern and southern Europe have been less easily accepted as full-fledged Americans than have those from northern and western Europe because the cultural dissimi-

---

[2] William Graham Sumner, *Folkways* (Boston: Ginn, 1906), p. 13.

[3] Benedict, *Patterns of Culture,* p. 20.

[4] For a description of rural ethnocentrism, see Arthur J. Vidich and Joseph Bensman, *Small Town in Mass Society* (Princeton: Princeton University Press, 1958).

larity to "native" populations has been greater among southern and eastern Europeans. The immigration legislation of the 1920s set quotas for allowable immigration from each country that reflected most dramatically the desire to restrict any influx of people from those countries with more alien or "un-American" ways.

Second, the sense of inferiority of alien ways may lead to the attempt to isolate one's own culture from influence by these alien ways. Contemporary parents who reject the subculture of the hippie try to discourage any tendency of their children to associate with "bad companions" from among the hippie group. Some churches similarly try to insulate their younger members from some of the more bohemian aspects of the youth culture by maintaining a full round of youth activities that will engross their members' time and exhaust their sociable contacts.

An almost invariable feature of social organization of a "radical" cult or subculture of any kind is the attempt to insulate members from contact with a wider culture. "Be not conformed to this world" is the watchword of many radical religious communities, and their ways of life are typically well designed to prevent intimate contact with persons from "this world."[5] These practices are understandable when seen as consequences of ethnocentrism, as an attempt to protect one's group from the influence of another culture that is seen as less worthy.

From one value position, that of cultural relativity, ethnocentrism is a negatively valued form of human thought, and the question is frequently posed, How can people be brought to be less ethnocentric? Probably the most frequently proposed remedy, seen already in Benedict's motives for writing *Patterns of Culture,* is the exposure of people to alien ways through the study of anthropology, foreign travel, cultural-exchange programs, international games and festivals, etc.

Experimental studies of the effectiveness of cultural contact in reducing ethnocentrism have generally been encouraging.[6] How-

---

[5] John A. Hostetler, *Amish Society,* rev. ed. (Baltimore: Johns Hopkins Press, 1968).

[6] There are reviews of some of these studies contained in the following: Daniel M. Wilner, Rosabelle P. Walkley, and Stuart W. Cook, *Human Relations in Interracial Housing: a Study of the Contact Hypothesis* (Minneapolis: University of Minnesota Press, 1955); Edward A. Suchman, John P. Dean, and Robin M. Williams, Jr., *Desegregation: Some Propositions and Research Suggestions* (New York: Anti-Defamation League of B'nai Brith, 1958); and Gordon W. Allport, *The Nature of Prejudice* (Garden City, N.Y.: Doubleday, 1958), Ch. 30. On international student

ever, some caution should be exerted in treating such programs as panaceas. For one thing, people who participate in such activities are likely to be already well-disposed toward a cultural relativist viewpoint. Those who are not so disposed are unlikely to expose themselves; if they are involuntarily exposed (every student may be required to take an anthropology course, a soldier may be ordered to a military post in Germany), they may have their prejudices confirmed by the fact that they will selectively attend to those aspects of alien ways of life that they had rejected. Cultural relativity is not, apparently, a natural or easy tendency of the human mind, and no well-meaning but naively conceived program to promote appreciation of foreign cultures is likely to have much success.

Communication difficulties. Communication between people assumes that they mutually understand the meaning of the symbols—words, gesture, etc.—employed in communication. A language is a set of such communication symbols. The lack of a universal human language, the specificity of each language to a particular culture, creates major problems of communication between people of different cultures. A given linguistic symbol, like all symbols, is completely arbitrary; there is no reason other than variation in traditional usage that the nominative form of the first person singular is designated by the symbol *I* in English, *ich* in German, *jeg* in Norwegian, etc.

Learning the language of an alien culture is a difficult process, partly because it is never simply a matter of learning which symbol in one language means the same thing as which other symbol in another language. Given the subtle connotations that grow up around words, it may be impossible to "say the same thing" in one language that was said in another.[7] The same problems may apply where there has evolved a special or esoteric jargon for a particular field of human knowledge and where the specialist is faced with the problem of communicating with a layman. Can the doctor translate

---

exchange, see Steven E. Deutsch, "The Impact of Cross-Cultural Relations on the Campus," *Sociology and Social Research,* 53(1969):137–146. On foreign travel, see Willis A. Sutton, Jr., "Travel and Understanding: Notes on the Social Structure of Touring," *International Journal of Comparative Sociology,* 8(1967):213–223.

[7] Some of Max Weber's English translators have complained, for example, of the difficulty of retaining the nuances of his ideas when they are translated from the German. See H. H. Gerth and C. Wright Mills (eds.), *From Max Weber: Essays in Sociology* (New York: Oxford University Press, 1958), pp. v–vi.

a patient's medical condition into terms the patient can understand? Can the mystic verbalize his religious experience? Can the teacher of sociology find words to explain the anomic theory of deviance?

Countering such culturally relativistic views of human thought and language are ideas about some form of universal human language. Music, art, and love are sometimes advanced as candidates for such universal languages on the theory that they are generally human experiences that can be communicated without specific languages. There is some truth in this. A German and an Englishman can perhaps equally appreciate a Beethoven symphony, and people from radically different cultures do fall in love in spite of the possibility of "Madame Butterfly" complications in such affairs. But the assertion that music is a universal language may presume too much about the universality with which, for example, Western, Oriental, and African music is experienced by people outside these cultures. Love, if a universal experience, certainly is quite differently experienced in different times and places.[8]

Some less obvious kinds of cultural differences are analyzed in a study of communication difficulties between people from different cultures.[9] For example, there is a striking cultural difference in definition of the appropriate distance apart for two people to stand while carrying on a conversation: the Latin American culture defines as appropriate a closer proximity than does the "North American" culture. The consequences of such differences in the direction of uneasy conversational situations was described by Hall:

A conversation I once observed between a Latin and a North American began at one end of a 40-foot hall. I watched the two conversationalists until they finally reached the other end of the hall. This maneuver had been effected by a continual series of small backward steps on the part of the North American as he unconsciously retreated, searching for a comfortable talking distance. Each time, there was an accompanying closing of the gap

---

[8] Related to this is the notion that each language captures a unique spirit of a people that is not expressible in any other language. "A Minneapolis clergyman is supposed to have said that he and his wife know all three languages—Swedish, Norwegian and Danish—but that if he wanted to talk over everyday things with his wife he would talk Swedish, if he wanted to talk over serious matters he would talk Norwegian, and if he were to talk lovingly it would be in Danish." Gerhard Neubeck, "Patterns of Affection," International Journal of Comparative Sociology, 8(1967):21.

[9] Edward T. Hall, The Silent Language (Garden City, N.Y.: Doubleday, 1959).

as his Latin friend attempted to reestablish his own accustomed conversation distance.[10]

Causes of Cultural Variability

One of the most natural questions to ask the student of culture is, Why is there this great variability in the forms of human culture? Unfortunately, this is also one of the questions to which the least satisfying answers have been developed. To answer a "why?" with "just because" is not likely to be satisfying to a child or anyone else; but the social scientific answer to the explanation of cultural variability comes close to being "just because." Only a step beyond this answer is the explanation that human behavior is not determined by any set of instincts that is universal to the species; there is no universal "human nature" as there is a universal "dog nature" because man, unlike the dog, does not have his way of life predetermined by his biological nature.

This last observation indicates the *possibility* for cultural variability. It says nothing about the correlates or the causes of variability; nothing, for example, about what conditions have produced an "Apollonian" culture among the Zuñi, a "Dionysian" culture among the Kwakiutl. On this point, social scientific explanation comes close to a void. Most of its effort has been expended in exploding popular and scientific theories about the causes of cultural variability. Although negative, this effort has at least eliminated, to the satisfaction of most social scientists, two popular contenders as major explanations—the biological and the geographic.

Biological explanations. The biological interpretation of human behavior is by no means disposed of when it is shown that there is no behavior that is universal to all members of the human species. The *races* of man constitute biological varieties within the species, and it is entirely possible and has been frequently asserted that cultural differences are the result of racial differences. If one looks at the phenomena of race and culture in the world historically, it may be true that there has been at least a rough correlation between the distribution of racial types and of cultural forms: an African

---

[10] Edward T. Hall, "Our Silent Language," *Américas,* 14(Feb.,1962):6. Reprinted from *Américas,* monthly magazine published by the Pan American Union in English, Spanish and Portuguese.

culture among blacks, an Oriental culture among yellows, an Occidental culture among whites.

Many racial theories of cultural variation have been tied to ethnocentric assumptions; that is, cultural inferiority or superiority has been related to an assumed quality of a racial "stock." Programs of genocide (extermination of "inferior" races), restriction of immigration by race, and racial segregation in schools have been justified by the notion that racial mixture will produce a corruption of cultural standards.

In the negative spirit mentioned above, social scientists have raised a number of objections to the adequacy of racial explanations of cultural variability.

First, the correlation between racial and cultural distribution, while it may exist roughly, is by no means perfect. The people of India, considered Caucasian by some systems of racial classification, have a traditional culture that is far more Oriental than Occidental. American Negroes are "Afro-Americans" culturally only if they make vigorous efforts to recapture an African cultural tradition that was allowed to lapse for many generations. (Even so, they tend to be more "American" than "Afro" culturally.) Such correlation as does exist between race and culture may be explained by an intervening variable (as we discussed that term in chapter 2). Perhaps the real causal factor in determining both racial and cultural type is the historic isolation of people in different geographic regions of the world. A geographically isolated people tend to develop a special racial type through the accentuation of traits by inbreeding and by the adaptation of biological traits to the geographic conditions of the region. Isolation has also made possible the elaboration of cultural forms in different directions because of the same tendencies toward accentuation and adaptation in the realm of culture. Such an explanation would suggest that, as geographic isolation of groups is increasingly broken down, there will be a diminishing correlation between racial and cultural type.

Second, the processes of assimilation and acculturation raise serious questions about the adequacy of a racial theory of cultural variation. *Assimilation* occurs when the culture of one people undergoes a change in the direction of greater similarity to the culture of another people.[11] Rome was Hellenized, Japan was West-

---

[11] In most anthropological and in some sociological writings, the meanings of the terms *acculturation* and *assimilation* are the reverse of those given here.

ernized, much of Africa was Europeanized, yet none of these assimilation processes seems to have been retarded by the fact that
the assimilating peoples were of a racial type different from that
prevailing in the culture to which they were assimilating. *Acculturation* refers to cultural change at the level of individuals, as when
an immigrant to a country gives up his "old country" ways and
adapts his behavior to the ways prevailing in the host country. The
radical de-Africanization of Negro slaves in the United States is a
good example of the possibility for persons of different racial types
to adapt themselves to a common culture.

Finally, when one considers the rapidity of cultural change and
the slowness of evolutionary biological changes, the racial explanation of cultural variability makes very little sense. Biologically, four
generations (four completions of the reproductive cycle) can have
only an infinitesimal effect on the nature of hereditary traits. For
all practical purposes, man has the same biological equipment
today that he had four generations (about 100 years) ago. Culturally,
the changes that have occurred in most parts of the world in the
last 100 years have been profound. If these cultural changes had to
wait on a change of racial type, they could not have developed so
rapidly.

Altogether, it seems to take a considerable act of will to hold to
a biological explanation of cultural variability in the face of considerations like these. One kind of rearguard action in the modern
retreat from biological determinism can be discussed, however.
This is the idea and program of *eugenics,* a science based on the
belief that the quality of human life could be greatly improved
through selective breeding, a program to insure the "survival of the
fittest."[12]

The impetus for eugenic programs comes from such observations
as these: (1) reproduction tends to be highest among the poorer
and less educated classes of a society; (2) modern medicine has
spared mankind the rigorous application of the rule of survival of
the fittest, because persons with hereditary defects (poor eyesight,
for example) are kept alive and allowed to reproduce and pass
along their deficiency; and (3) modern warfare is especially geared
to kill off the "fittest" since only the healthiest are selected by
"selective service" to risk the hazards of combat. Such tendencies,

---

[12] Frederick H. Osborne, *Preface to Eugenics,* rev. ed. (New York: Harper, 1951).

eugenicists argue, will affect human society adversely by lowering the level of biological capacity for the development of cultural products. Eugenic programs aim at the encouragement of reproduction by the "fit" and at control of reproduction among the "unfit." Eugenic programs may or may not involve racist overtones, depending on whether they classify different races as fit or unfit. Where judgments of racial fitness are made, they tend to be highly ethnocentric.

Eugenics is based probably on an overestimation of the role of genetic factors in the determination of human behavior. Given the accentuated technological developments in the world, it is possible to argue that cultural "progress" is not at all inconsistent with a somewhat diminished level of biological capacity. Even where sheer physical accomplishments are concerned, it may be that technological improvements can override genetic deteriorations. Contemporary athletes can certainly outperform their predecessors (the "four-minute mile" was once considered impossible for runners; now it is almost commonplace), this greater physical performance being based on such technological gains as a better knowledge of nutrition and of ways to train the body for athletic efforts. So long as facts like these can be readily cited, it seems that eugenics will remain a minor factor in the determination of human culture.

Geographic explanations. Another tempting explanation of cultural variability is that of geographic determinism. Ways of life certainly vary between people in different parts of the world, and the possibility that variations in culture are causally related to variations in geographic conditions must seriously be considered. Geographic determinism comes in two flavors, mild and sharp.

The milder form of geographic determinism makes note of the fact that the physical environmental conditions of a given region furnish both the materials and the motives for the elaboration of cultural forms in given directions. The fact that the physical environment is dominated by mountains, a sea coast, a desert, or a tundra will determine much about the technology and, perhaps, the moral outlook of a people. The appellation "hillbilly" denotes a cultural orientation, suggesting the importance to this way of life of the physical isolation between families and communities that a mountainous topography tends to produce.

One measure of the influence of geography on culture is the observation that the language of a people tends to include an elaborate vocabulary to differentiate the various aspects of a dominant geographic consideration. Thus, Arabs are reported to have some six thousand words to denote variations in kind and condition of the camel, the principal animal in this desert culture.[13] Seacoast people similarly have rich vocabularies of terms referring to life at sea; and great rivers produce along their banks a way of life and a vocabulary which are preoccupied with the vagaries of "old man river."

Impressive as these correlations of geography and culture may be, it can be noted that the degree of this relationship may be declining under the influence of technological developments. A technology for flood control, when applied, can remove a part of the river's impact on the culture of the people living along its banks. The introduction of air conditioning into tropical and subtropical regions allows for ways of life that are not so heavily influenced by the local physical environment. The technological development that makes possible rapid transportation exposes people to a variety of geographic environments. For some favored persons, at least, the geographic setting may be altered to suit the mood: the Swiss Alps in the summer, the Riviera in the winter. The geographic environment of Miami, Florida, or Boulder, Colorado, does, indeed, determine largely the ways of life found there; but, given the mobility of people into and out of such places, they are not the best examples of geographic determinism, which assumes that persons inhabit a given region permanently and that their culture is dictated by geographic conditions of that region. The fact that persons may choose their geographic locales under modern conditions weakens the explanatory power of the theory.

A more extreme form of geographic determinism would hold that the overall mentality, temperament, or "civilizing" energy of a people is influenced by geographic conditions. Popular notions of this kind abound; passions are more easily aroused in tropical climates, sexual frigidity is common in polar regions, intellectual vitality is low in the tropics, etc. A major scientific theory of this type was Huntington's attempt to show that the more highly complex ways of life have developed in the temperate regions of the

---

[13] Otto Kleinberg, *Social Psychology* (New York: Holt, Rinehart & Winston, 1954), p. 50.

earth; neither extreme heat nor extreme cold is conducive to the development of "civilization."[14]

The historian Arnold Toynbee has similarly attempted to relate "civilization" to geographic conditions, although his theory is somewhat different.[15] Toynbee sees civilization developing through a series of "challenges" to a society's existence which are met by adequate societal "response." A somewhat harsh or difficult geographic environment is seen by Toynbee to be most conducive to civilization because such environments present challenges severe enough to begin the challenge-response cycle. The influence of the lowland topography of Holland, with the ever-present danger of flooding from the sea, is a familiar example of such a challenging environmental condition. In contrast to Huntington, Toynbee suggests that some environments may be *too* temperate to stimulate the work of civilization.

Theories of this type tend to falter on their inadequate consideration of the range of human cultures in different times and places. With reference to Huntington's theory, it is true that the contemporary major world powers are concentrated in the temperate geographic zones and, from an ethnocentric viewpoint, these might be considered the more "civilized" peoples. But historical analysis would indicate many exceptions to this theory at earlier periods. By present Western standards, the Maya and Aztec civilizations of subtropical Mexico were more culturally "advanced" than the nomadic tribes of American Indians who, during the same period, inhabited the more temperate regions of North America. The Middle Eastern "cradle of civilization" was in an essentially desert region, hardly a temperate climate.

Toynbee's theory also has its difficulties. Granting his view that "challenge" is necessary to the development of a complex culture, it may be doubted that geographic conditions have been the only or even the major challenges to a society's existence. Famine, disease, and war—to cite one trilogy of historical miseries—have perhaps been of greater historical importance as cultural challengers. A critical point has also been made that the people who inhabit "difficult" geographic regions like Holland may have migrated to the territory and brought with them technological know-

---

[14] Ellsworth Huntington, *Mainsprings of Civilization* (New York: Wiley, 1945).

[15] Arnold J. Toynbee, *A Study of History*, Vol. 2, *The Genesis of Civilizations* (London: Oxford University Press, 1934), pp. 31–73.

how developed in other areas in which geographic challenges were less severe.[16]

CULTURAL CHANGE

We defined culture in the previous chapter as a *traditional* way of life, one which tends to be "here today and here tomorrow." The fact of ethnocentrism alone would tend to perpetuate a way of life; people tend to value the ways to which they are accustomed and to "uphold and defend" that way. Nevertheless, changes in culture do occur. Sociological analysis is concerned with how and why these changes in a group's way of life occur.

Evolutionary Theories

The notion of an evolutionary process of cultural change has been borrowed from biology, where the evolutionary theory is a highly respectable version of the process involved in the "origin of species." As an explanatory approach in social science, evolutionism has involved, in various proportions of emphasis, the notions of: (1) the extremely slow rate of cultural change, and (2) a series of "stages"—from primitive to modern—that all cultures tend to go through.

Slow rate of change. The view that human culture changes only very slowly was well expressed in Sumner's book, *Folkways*:

We see that we must conceive of the mores as a vast system of usages, covering the whole of life, and serving all its interests; also containing in themselves their own justification by tradition and use and wont, and approved by mystic sanctions until, by rational reflection, they develop their own philosophical and ethical generalizations, which are elevated into "principles" of truth and right. They coerce and restrict the newborn generation. They do not stimulate to thought, but the contrary. The thinking is already done and is embodied in the mores. They never contain any provision for their own amendment. They are not questions, but answers, to the problem of life.[17]

Any wholesale "reorganization" of culture is thus impossible, ac-

---

[16] Patrick Gardiner (ed.), *Theories of History* (Glencoe, Ill.: Free Press, 1959), pp. 309, 310.

[17] Sumner, *Folkways*, p. 79.

cording to Sumner. "We might as well plan to reorganize our globe by redistributing the elements in it."[18]

An important modification of the view of the conservative character of culture is the theory of *culture lag.*[19] Ogburn distinguishes between "material culture" and "nonmaterial culture" and points out that many parts of the nonmaterial culture are *adaptive* to material conditions in that they involve the regulation of human behavior in relation to material objects. Government, for example, is an adaptive part of the nonmaterial culture, enacting and enforcing laws that deal with permissible uses of land or of an automobile. A problem arises for a society when material conditions change more rapidly than the society can evolve new forms of nonmaterial culture to regulate them. An example cited by Ogburn is a "lag" in the development of U.S. conservation laws to match the very rapid changes in the material culture which threaten the destruction of virgin forests. Another frequently cited example is the lag in development of required safety features in the manufacture of automobiles that will compensate for the escalation in power of automobile motors.

The culture-lag theory seems to suggest that what is needed is a speeding up of changes in nonmaterial culture to catch up with faster changes in material culture. This implication may contain a value judgment with which not everyone would agree. Why not just as well make the judgment that change in material culture is proceeding too rapidly and should be slowed down? (A "moratorium on inventions" has occasionally been seriously proposed.) Despite such controversies in practical policy as to what should be done about culture lag, the generalization about the differential rates of growth of the two aspects of culture seems to be valid.

Evolutionary stages. Early anthropology was preoccupied with the notion of inherently "primitive" and "modern" forms of culture. The first sociologist, Auguste Comte, likewise articulated an evolutionary theory of human culture, the Law of the Three States (see the discussion in chapter 1). Sir Henry Maine, a British anthropologist, postulated a primitive form of culture based on *status* and a modern

---

[18] Ibid., p. 95.

[19] William F. Ogburn, *Social Change* (New York: Huebsch, 1923).

form based on *contract*.[20] A comparison of primitive and modern forms of marriage would suffice to indicate the difference. In primitive marriage, wives were the property of their husbands; in modern marriage, the wife is free to contract or dissolve the union, and the marriage is based on mutual obligations.

Spencer argued that primitive society was inherently egoistic and militaristic. One aspect of his grand "law of evolution" is the increasing heterogeneity of social life and, along with this, the growth of an altruistic morality and an industrial social organization.[21] Durkheim agreed with Spencer about the evolutionary tendency toward increasing heterogeneity but challenged vigorously the notion of "primitive egoism," arguing instead that primitive man is characterized by an excess of altruism or, in Durkheim's terms, by a strong *collective conscience* that dominates the individual consciousness. Far from having evolved a greater altruism, modern society has, in Durkheim's view, elevated individuality to something of a religious principle, creating the "cult of the individual."[22]

Evolutionary theory of this type has lost favor among contemporary social scientists. One critic, having asked what happened to the popularity of Spencer among intellectuals, concluded that "Spencer is dead." "He was the intimate confidant of a strange and rather unsatisfactory God, whom he called the principle of Evolution. His God has betrayed him. We have evolved beyond Spencer."[23]

Better acquaintance with the variety of forms of primitive culture has led to a skepticism about the possibility of establishing any one form of culture as more "primitive" than any other. It has been discovered, for example, that so-called primitive people have ways of life that are, in some respects, more complicated than those of so-called modern people. For instance, some primitive people have systems of reckoning kinship that make many subtle distinctions of family relationship that are completely ignored in the family systems of some of the more "advanced" societies.

---

[20] Henry Sumner Maine, *Ancient Law* (New York: Henry Holt, 1906). First published in 1861.

[21] Emile Durkheim, *On the Division of Labor in Society,* trans. by George Simpson (New York: Macmillan, 1933).

[22] Emile Durkheim, *The Elementary Forms of the Religious Life,* trans. by Joseph W. Swain (New York: Collier Books, 1961), p. 472.

[23] Crane Brinton, *English Political Thought in the Nineteenth Century* (London: Ernest Benn, 1933), pp. 226, 227.

Another observation damaging to the evolutionary approach is the discovery that the cultural ways of modern people are not so different from those of the primitives as we would perhaps like to believe. Horace Miner made this point rather humorously in his satirical essay on the body rites of the "barbarous" Nacirema (whose resemblance to the American who "brushes his teeth twice a day and sees his dentist twice a year" is purely intentional). According to Miner, the "mouth-rite" of the Nacirema involves "inserting a small bundle of hog hairs into the mouth, along with certain magical powders, and then moving the bundle in a highly formalized series of gestures." The mouth-rite is followed up by periodic visits to the "holy mouth-man," who has a "variety of augers, awls, probes and prods" with which to "enlarge any holes which decay may have created in the teeth."[24] Perhaps it takes more than a touch of ethnocentrism to look at primitive culture in the condescending way of Malinowski:

Looking far and above, from our high places of safety in the developed civilization, it is easy to see all the crudity and irrelevance of magic. But without its power and guidance early man could not have mastered his practical difficulties as he has done, nor could man have advanced to the higher stages of civilization.[25]

Although unilinear evolutionary theory (from *this* stage to *that* stage) is today dead or dying, there are some attempts to maintain a multilinear evolutionary approach to cultural change. Steward, a contemporary anthropologist, argues that there may, indeed, be inherent stages in the development of culture but that we must first identify some of the major types of cultures and then describe how different types evolve along different lines.[26] For example, farming societies which are widely separated have followed similar evolutionary lines of early settlement in small permanent villages along moist river banks, followed by irrigation and canal-building activities that have produced major changes in general culture and social organization. Other kinds of societies—those based on hunting

---

[24] Horace Miner, "Body Ritual Among the Nacirema," *American Anthropologist,* 58(1956):503–507.

[25] Bronislaw Malinowski, *Magic, Science and Religion and Other Essays* (Boston: Beacon Press, 1948), p. 70.

[26] Julian Steward, *Theory of Culture Change* (Urbana: University of Illinois Press, 1955).

or food-gathering modes of subsistence, for example—have followed quite different evolutionary lines.

Contingent Theories

The major alternative to evolutionism as an approach to explaining cultural change is the view that culture may or may not change in a given direction, depending on the presence or absence of certain factors which are seen as causing change. From this contingent view of cultural change, the problem is not one of discovering any general direction of cultural evolution but of assessing the weight of various factors in producing change. In dealing with such questions, all the problems of causal inference as discussed in chapter 2 are involved. It may be, for example, that certain variables (such as population growth) are related to certain cultural changes (such as the growth of secularism) without there being any causal connection between them. This is possible if population growth and secularism are both the result of some other causal factor, say, the industrial revolution.

One variety of contingent explanation of cultural change is the one-factor or deterministic theory of change. *Economic determinism,* for example, would argue that changes in patterns of organization of productive activity have the major influence on changes in all aspects of culture. Marx contends that the "real facts" of any society are the relations that men enter into with other men in the process of producing their subsistence.[27] If culture is ideational, Marx would say that culture is economically determined since prevailing ideas are simply rationalizations for the position of the dominant economic class; "the ruling ideas" are the ideas of the "ruling class."[28] *Technological determinism* places primary emphasis on the techniques that prevail in a society. The anthropological classification of cultures as plow culture or basket-making culture is an implicit assertion of the influence of technology on all aspects of culture.

Deterministic or one-factor theories of all kinds tend to run into some of the same kinds of problems as those encountered with the biological and geographic determinisms that we discussed previously. Correlations between any one form of culture and any one

---

[27] T. B. Bottomore (ed.), *Karl Marx: Selected Writings in Sociology and Social Philosophy* (New York: McGraw-Hill, 1964), pp. 51–66.
[28] Ibid., p. 78.

form of technology, economy, or any other "factor" tend not to be perfect. A *multifactor* theory of change would emphasize the complexity of causation of cultural change and insist that (1) the impetus to cultural change may come from a variety of sources, not simply from changes in one factor; and (2) whether change develops or is arrested at an early stage depends on a variety of contingent factors.

Concerning sources of change, a distinction can conveniently be made between internal *innovation* and external *culture contact.* Some changes are initiated within a society as discoveries and inventions are made, as persons learn to deal with old problems in new ways. Exactly why some societies are inventive in this way and others seem to produce few new ideas is not at all clear. Perhaps the sociologist's contribution to understanding the matter is his suggestion that invention occurs in those societies that institutionalize it, where there are definite social mechanisms (such as funded research) to support and reward innovative activity. A society which gives vigorous support to research activities in science and engineering will tend to produce many inventions.[29]

If the isolation of peoples produces separate cultures, the mingling of people from different cultures should lead to assimilation or the disappearance of cultural differences. The process of *cultural diffusion* refers to the passage of traits native to one culture into a culture in which these traits have heretofore been alien. The recent diffusion of American culture throughout the world has been a source of dismay to many travelers who go in search of exotic cultures only to find the natives drinking Coca-Cola and dancing the latest American dances.

Whether cultural change originates in internal innovation or external contact, the process by which a new idea spreads is likely to be a complex one, with many new ideas never catching on. In most societies, most inventions are at least temporarily ignored or resisted, and ethnocentrism tends to guarantee that cultural contact will not lead immediately to the adoption of "alien" ways.

One factor influencing the acceptance of an invention or an alien way is the degree of material content of the cultural element. Change tends to be accepted more readily when it involves ideas about the use of material things. Such nonmaterial aspects as religious ideas or ideas about appropriate systems for the punish-

---

[29] S. C. Gilfillan, *Sociology of Inventions* (Chicago: Follett, 1935).

ment of crime tend to change less rapidly. There may be two major reasons for this difference. First, the superiority of a new idea about material things can be more easily demonstrated. A people confronted with a new system of crop-raising can readily test that system in comparison with the old system (especially if they have an institutionalized testing system like the agricultural experiment station). The tests of superiority or inferiority in something like a religious system are far less obvious. Second, the nonmaterial aspects of culture are likely to be more fundamental to the people who adhere to that culture. The basic values of a culture are the core around which other cultural elements are arranged. People can accept a new mode of transportation without disturbing this central core,[30] but a competing system of values is much more threatening to the total integration.

Even with purely material technologies, however, people tend to resist the adoption of new ways, and sociologists have been interested in some of the factors that influence the rate of "diffusion of innovation" in a population. Farming and medical practice are two areas that have been much studied in this regard.[31] Farmers do not always immediately adopt a superior farming technique, sometimes preferring an older way of doing things that is less efficient, perhaps, but also more "satisfying"; for example, the preference for handpicking crops over harvesting them by machine. Nor do doctors always prescribe a "new and better" drug to their patients as soon as it comes on the market.

Studies in the diffusion of innovation have been concerned with assessing the relative effects of formal and informal channels of communication. Do farmers, for example, find out about a new technique and become persuaded to use it primarily through reading experimental station bulletins or upon the recommendation of the agricultural extension agent, or are they more influenced by the attitudes of their friends and neighbors toward innovations? A study

---

[30] This is not to deny that a strictly material invention may have many unanticipated consequences for various aspects of social life. For a treatment of the ramifying social effects of the radio on American life, see President's Research Committee on Recent Social Trends, *Recent Social Trends* (New York: McGraw-Hill, 1933), pp. 153–156.

[31] On farming, see Everett M. Rogers, *Diffusion of Innovations* (New York: Free Press of Glencoe, 1962), and the many studies reported in recent issues of the journal, *Rural Sociology*. On medical practice, see James Coleman, Elihu Katz, and Herbert Menzel, "The Diffusion of an Innovation Among Physicians," *Sociometry*, 20(1957):253–270.

of innovation in medical practice[32] suggests that there is a kind of "two-step flow" of information and persuasion to doctors. A few "opinion leaders" in the medical community are influenced by advertising and other "outside" agents (such as drug company representatives) to adopt an innovation; the colleagues of these opinion leaders tend to follow their lead. Persons interested in bringing about a cultural change in an area are likely to be sensitive to the necessity of "converting" opinion leaders. When a President of the United States used the slogan of the civil rights movement— "we shall overcome"—in a public statement, there was much rejoicing that an influential leader had thus identified himself with the change that this movement was trying to bring about.

SUMMARY

In popular anthropology it is fashionable to refer to the bewildering variety of human cultures. The social scientist shares to some extent the popular sense of wonder at the variety and instability of culture, but his professional concern is with the analysis of variability and change, both the causes and the consequences of these phenomena. The sociologist is especially interested in those effects of cultural variability that introduce problems in the interaction between people from different cultures. The ethnocentric rejection of people with "alien" ways and the communicative "misunderstandings" of people who speak different languages are typical sociological concerns.

The causal explanation of cultural variability and change involves many complex problems of causal inference. Sociologists have tended to reject as oversimplified such theories as the biological or geographic determinism of variability or, indeed, any one-factor explanation of the origins of variability and change in human culture. The evolutionary theory of social change, postulating a set of steps or stages through which every culture inevitably passes, is likewise often rejected as too easy an explanation of a complex phenomenon.

Given these skepticisms about simplified or monistic explanations, sociological explanation tends to move to a less rigid structure of explanation, committing itself only to a search for "factors" or "contingent" events which, if they occur, will produce certain kinds of cultural change. In this more open explanatory structure,

---

[32] Coleman, Katz, and Menzel, "Diffusion of an Innovation."

the sociologist is freer to exploit some of his more general notions about the determinants of human behavior. He can apply, for example, the general notion of the importance of "informal" levels of social influence to an understanding of the process by which a technological change is introduced into a culture.

SOCIAL ORGANIZATION

PART THREE

The assertion was made in chapter 1 that the concepts of "social organization" and "social structure" represent ideas that are fundamental to what is most uniquely sociological in the study of human behavior. In this section we attempt to elaborate on these basic concepts.

Perhaps the most basic feature of social organization is its *interindividual* feature, the fact that the organization of human behavior can be understood only if that behavior is thought of as something occurring *between* two or more persons. It takes two to tango and nine to make a baseball team, and the quality of relationship between this two or among these nine is a problem of preeminent sociological interest.

In the three chapters in this section we examine social organizational matters from three different perspectives, ranging from *society* at the largest or most macroscopic level to *social interaction* at the microscopic level, with the discussion of *groups* representing problems of social organization at an intermediate level of inclusiveness. Although not all problems of social organization will locate themselves neatly and obligingly in one of these three categories of inclusiveness, we can at least illustrate something of the range of emphases in different kinds of sociological studies of social organization.

Society

DEFINITION OF SOCIETY

The sociological usage of the term *society* differs from some of the popular usages of that term. Most notably, in sociology *society* does *not* denote a group of persons of superior social status whose activities would be reported in the "society" pages of a newspaper. Like the term *culture,* society has a wider meaning than the popular restriction of the term to refer to an elite group of people.

Society as External Constraint

A closer approximation in popular usage to the sociological meaning is expressed in references to the effects of prison in rehabilitating an inmate to prepare him to go back *into* society as a law-abiding citizen. In sociological usage, a society is also the sort of entity that a person may be *in;* he may also be out of or *alienated* from society, the latter view being expressed by Simmel, who insists that "the fact that in certain respects the individual is not an element of society constitutes the positive condition for the possibility that in other respects he is."[1]

Following the lead from popular thought that an individual exists *in* or surrounded by society, let us consider what it may mean from the individual's viewpoint to live in a society. Whatever a person does or even thinks, he may find that there are prevailing "arrangements" for that doing or thinking among the people with whom he associates. If, for example, he considers marriage, he finds that

---

[1] Kurt Wolff (ed.), *Georg Simmel, 1858–1918* (Columbus: Ohio State University Press, 1959), p. 345.

the necessary arrangements for this event are already largely anticipated in the customary ways of his society. He may even feel that, once he has committed himself to this fatal step, the implementation of his decision will be taken over by others and executed according to *their* plan; he may feel himself almost a passive spectator of these socially enforced events.

This conception of society is summarized quite well in Durkheim's view of society as having the twin characteristics of *exteriority* and *constraint*.[2] Society is exterior to the individual in that it exists independently of and often in spite of his own will; it is in the nature of "social facts" that, as with the other hard facts of life, he must accept society and find a way to live with it. Society is constraining in that, as we shall discuss in chapter 13, there are numerous devices by which the society can enforce its expectations on the individual.

Sociologists have, at least since Durkheim, insisted on the existence of a level of "reality" beyond that of the individual psychologies of human beings. Much of the rationale for the existence of sociology as a discipline distinct from psychology is based on this assertion that the societal order of reality cannot be "reduced" to the level of individual psychology.

Society as a Social System
We began with the popular conception of society as a kind of Leviathan or superpersonal entity existing over and above the individual person. The wisdom of popular usage can carry us a step further, toward the notion of society as a social system. Popular complaints about the constraints of "the system"—I hate to buck for promotion in that way, but that's "the system" around here—indicate popular awareness of the term. The sociologist likewise tends to think of a society as a "system," but he adds to the popular notions certain more technical characteristics which we can call the system properties of *integration* and *equilibrium.*

Integration. Any system—physical, biological, or social—can be analyzed as having *parts:* organs of a body, molecules of a compound, etc. The idea of integration is that there is some relationship among those parts and between the parts and the whole system.

---

[2] Emile Durkheim, *The Rules of Sociological Method,* trans. by Sarah A. Solovay and John H. Mueller (Chicago: University of Chicago Press, 1938).

Sorokin defines two fundamentally different kinds of integration: causal-functional and logico-meaningful.[3] *Causal-functional* integration refers to the notion that the parts of a system are causally related to one another and perhaps to the whole system of which they are parts. Variability in one part is a "function" of variability in other parts. Also, the maintenance of the whole system is a function of the operation of the parts; a living organism as a system cannot continue to exist unless its various "vital functions" are being performed by its various parts. These ideas about system integration lead directly into the controversial area of sociological *functionalism,* which we shall discuss a little later.

Logico-meaningful integration refers to a quite different relationship between system parts and wholes. A system is logical when it "makes sense" to the human mind and meaningful when its characteristic features can be described in a communicative process. The various parts (notes) of a symphony are not related to one another in any causal way, but they are related in that, when played together, they create an overall sound that is called music. We have encountered an idea similar to that of logico-meaningful integration in the discussion of cultural integration: the insistence that the meaning of cultural parts or traits can only be established when one sees the theme or pattern that integrates these various traits. In the same way, there may be societal themes or patterns that distinguish between different kinds of social systems.

Equilibrium. The equilibrium conception of a system is the notion that a system tends to be self-maintaining, resisting change in existing patterns of integration. A physical system like a rock and a biological system like an animal are systems in the sense that they resist environmental forces that might disintegrate them. Rocks resist being broken up by blows, animals have food-gathering instincts to ensure their nourishment, etc. Typically, the scientist is interested in the "mechanisms" by which a system insures its survival; for example, the metabolic mechanism of a "warm-blooded" animal functions to maintain a constant internal body temperature in the face of fluctuations in external temperature. The application of the idea of equilibrium to society as a self-maintaining entity is a highly controversial one, as we shall see.

---

[3] Pitirim A. Sorokin, *Social and Cultural Dynamics,* Vol. 1, *Fluctuation of Forms of Art* (New York: Bedminster, 1937), pp. 14–21.

The application of system concepts to society has a long history in sociology. Herbert Spencer, in his *Principles of Sociology*,[4] has an early chapter entitled "Society Is an Organism" in which he argues that, like a biological organism, a society is sustained by the operation of its major vital systems. The long treatise which followed was largely an elaboration on this theme, analyzing in detail the various systems or "institutions" of a society. More recently, works like *Human Society* by Kingsley Davis[5] and *The Social System* by Talcott Parsons[6] have carried forward this tradition of examining society from a social-systems perspective.

To complete our preliminary definition of society, we should note that not every social system is a society in the usual definition of the term. Although the concept *social system* can apply to units of analysis as simple as the association of two persons, if this association is characterized by integration and equilibrium maintenance, these simpler units are not ordinarily called societies. *Society* refers to a system with a structure which is complex enough that it approaches the level of self-sufficiency.[7] People may live and die within the confines of a society; although a boardinghouse or a college classroom may be "social systems" in some respects, they clearly are not societies by virtue of their lack of self-sufficiency. In this sense, a society is simply a very complex social system.

FUNCTIONAL ANALYSIS OF SOCIETY

The school of sociological analysis that most consistently employs social-systems analysis of society is the approach called *functionalism,* the focus of a major controversy in contemporary sociology. Some varieties of functional analysis emphasize equilibrium properties, others focus on integrative properties of systems. The views of Robert Merton and of Talcott Parsons will illustrate these two approaches.

Merton's Views

Robert Merton defines the "central orientation" of functionalism as "the practice of interpreting data by establishing their conse-

---

[4] Herbert Spencer, *Principles of Sociology,* 3 vols. (New York: Appleton, 1900–1901).

[5] Kingsley Davis, *Human Society* (New York: Macmillan, 1949).

[6] Talcott Parsons, *The Social System* (Glencoe, Ill.: Free Press, 1951).

[7] Ibid., p. 19.

quences for larger structures in which they are implicated."[8] Thus Merton identifies functionalism with an interest in one kind of causal-functional integration: the functional relation between parts of social systems and the whole system. The part-to-part relationships seem to be outside the scope of functional analysis as Merton describes it.

In ascribing societal consequences or functions to social practices there are, Merton believes, important cautions that the sociologist should observe, and he criticizes many of his colleagues for failing to observe them.[9] One frequent error is in adopting a "postulate of functional unity," which assumes that each part of a social system is so thoroughly integrated with the whole that a given practice has the same consequences for each other part; what's "good" for one part is equally "good" for others. In fact, Merton suggests, there are numerous conflicts of interest between, say, the workers and managers in a factory social system. The fact of such conflict introduces the necessity of indicating *what* consequences there are for *which* persons in a society whenever functions are being ascribed.

Merton's viewpoint can be criticized by showing that you can carry this caution to the extreme by denying that there is *any* functional unity between *any* persons, by denying really the whole idea of integration.[10] Functionalists who are a little more tough-minded than Merton have tried to show that social systems have developed mechanisms to overcome just such conflicts of interest. American society, with its multiplicity of potentially warring religious denominations, has apparently evolved a kind of nonsectarian religion of "Americanism" as a new sort of functional unity in the area of religion.[11]

A second criticism by Merton is the tendency of functionalists to adopt a "postulate of universal functionalism" which insists that *all* existing practices contribute in a vital way to the maintenance of some social system. Some practices are, in fact, *dysfunctional*, tending to the destruction or change of society, and some are

---

[8] Robert K. Merton, *Social Theory and Social Structure* (Glencoe, Ill.: Free Press, 1956), pp. 46–47.

[9] Ibid., pp. 25–37.

[10] Jerry D. Rose, "The Moderate Approach to Sociological Functionalism," *Acta Sociologica*, 13(1970):127–131.

[11] Will Herberg, *Protestant-Catholic-Jew* (Garden City, N.Y.: Doubleday, 1955).

simply nonfunctional, perhaps because they are survivals from an earlier time in which they had some function. Merton may be suggesting a valuable liberalization of viewpoint in ascribing functions, although the idea of dysfunction introduces some very serious problems in sociological explanation. It would seem that you cannot explain some practice (the requiring of a college degree for a particular line of work, for example) by ascribing to it a positive function in a social system if the system tolerates dysfunctional parts as well as it tolerates functional ones. (How can one argue that attaining a college degree is dysfunctional for a woman who is destined to be "only" a housewife if most college-educated women turn out to be tolerable wives?) Many sociologists prefer to remain with the "postulate of universal functionalism," trying to discover hitherto unknown positive functions of "undesirable" social conditions. This strategy may have motivated Durkheim to the "discovery" of a positive function of crime: the fact that crime creates the occasion for collective punishment which reinforces the sense of righteousness on the part of the people who participate in a ritual of punishment.[12]

Merton also criticized the adoption of a "postulate of indispensability," i.e., because a practice is vital to a social system, it is also necessary to it. The mistake here is illustrated in the argument that, because religion produces "social solidarity" (a Durkheim thesis) and because this solidarity is necessary to a society, religion is therefore indispensable to a society. This inference would *not* be valid if there are "functional alternatives" or, in cruder language, if there is "more than one way to skin a cat." A very secular belief system, like communism or humanism, might be an adequate functional alternative to religion in producing social solidarity.

In fact, it seems that most functional analyses do operate with a kind of "indispensability" notion, but only after some examination of the specific historical context which makes a given social practice indispensable in *this* situation. Some exotic customs (such as the "rituals of rebellion" in Zulu society[13] in which, on occasion, women are allowed to attack men physically and verbally) may be explained by showing: (1) it is a functional necessity that dominated

---

[12] Durkheim, *Rules of Sociological Method*, pp. 64–75.

[13] Max Gluckman, *Custom and Conflict in Africa* (New York: Barnes & Noble, 1964), pp. 110–116.

groups (as Zulu women are) have some outlet for their aggressive-ness; (2) the society prohibits the dominated group from expressing aggression in everyday life (Zulu women cannot nag their husbands on a day-to-day basis). Since the "functional alternatives" (e.g., nagging) are closed, the periodic rebellion rituals become indis-pensable, but only in *this* society with these restraints on the adop-tion of functional alternatives.

Finally, Merton criticizes the tendency to confuse function with purpose or aim. Some writers refer to the function of a social prac-tice when they ascribe motives to the people who practice it: the "function" of religious worship is to secure supernatural aid for men's endeavors, etc. In fact, some of the consequences of social practices are *latent functions,* outcomes of social acts that were neither intended nor recognized by the people who engage in them (as opposed to *manifest functions,* whose consequences were intended by the participants). A function of marriage, for example, may be that it reduces conflict between members of the same sex by taking people of the opposite sex out of circulation, that is, re-moving them as a source of sexual rivalry. If this is a social conse-quence of marriage (as we shall argue in chapter 8), it is cer-tainly a latent one, since probably no one ever marries for the purpose of reducing conflict with others of his own sex. As we noted in chapter 1, the idea of latent functions contributes to a sense of the great complexity of the connections between things in the social world. Sociological facts tend to be less obvious than they seem.

Merton thus raises an important problem concerning the relation between the consequences of human action and human awareness of these consequences. Being the *calculating* sort of animal that he is, man tends to act with the intention of producing certain conse-quences and of avoiding others. The idea of latent functions sug-gests that he often fails in his intentions. But suppose a man has studied sociology or simply has unusual insight of human behavior and becomes aware of functions of his actions that previously were beneath the level of his consciousness. How will this new con-sciousness affect the consequences of his future acts?

For those who believe that "awareness" is a panacea for human problems, the effects must clearly be to the person's advantage; recall the Scripture, "Ye shall know the truth, and the truth shall make you free." But consider another possibility. Some things we desire as outcomes of our actions may be attainable only if they come as unconscious or unintended by-products of actions. "Fun" may be most elusive when we are most determined to have it and most accessible when our attention is focused elsewhere, just as we may have to stop trying to go to sleep before we can sleep. The frantic determination of some of our acquaintances to "have fun" or "be happy" because it's New Year's Eve and everybody else is doing it will illustrate the self-defeating character of some of our actions when we pursue our aspirations too directly.[14]

A few examples from sociological research will further illustrate this possibility. According to several observers, including David Riesman, Americans are growing increasingly self-conscious about the necessity of leading sexual lives that will allow them to enjoy a maximum possible amount of sexual "experience," and they worry about this a great deal and may consult friends, psychiatrists, or lonely hearts columnists with their "problems" in this area.[15] Consequently, a great deal of social reinforcement of people's sexual anxieties has developed around sex. In this vein, one sociologist has written of the contradictions and limitations of "sex as a more or less autonomous institution."[16]

In a study of junior colleges, Clark found that one of the functions of this type of college is "cooling out" people who are academic failures, making it possible for them to preserve a modicum of self-respect in a situation in which they could not make the grade elsewhere.[17] Of course, this function is effective only if it remains latent, since people would probably not enroll in such a college if they knew that it had this kind of consequence for the careers they hoped to pursue.

A sociological study of some forms of popular religion has made a similar point.[18] The creation of self-confidence and the promotion of greater earthly success have been among the traditional latent

---

[14] Alan R. Anderson and Omar K. Moore, "Autotelic Folk Models," *Sociological Quarterly,* 1(1960):203–216.

[15] David Riesman, *The Lonely Crowd* (New Haven: Yale University Press, 1950), p. 154.

[16] Jetse Sprey, "On the Institutionalization of Sexuality," *Journal of Marriage and the Family,* 31(1969):432–440.

[17] Burton R. Clark, "The Cooling-out Function in Higher Education," *American Journal of Sociology,* 65(1960):569–576.

[18] Louis Schneider and Sanford M. Dornbusch, "Inspirational Religious Literature: From Latent to Manifest Functions of Religion," *American Journal of Sociology,* 62(1957):476–481.

functions of religious activity. But when popular literature preaches the "power of positive thinking" and other ideas about the earthly value of religious piety, it begins to pursue secular outcomes directly. However, positive thinking may be as difficult to attain as having fun or being sexually satisfied: the very consciousness of the effort detracts from the possibility of success. It may be, in short, that some functions must *remain* latent if they are to be functions at all.

Parson's Views

More directly in the tradition of Spencer's treatment of societies as social systems is the recent work of Talcott Parsons. This work follows earlier attempts to define the "necessary conditions" or the "functional prerequisites" of a society as a social system.[19] Functionalists of this type have tended to follow Radcliffe-Brown's view of functionalism as developing a kind of physiology of social systems, a description of the way the system operates to provide for its vital needs.[20] Parsons developed a theory to the effect that every social system is characterized by four kinds of system problems.[21] Parsons calls these system problems *functional imperatives* and labels them "adaptation," "goal attainment," "integration," and "pattern maintenance and tension management."

To understand these functional imperatives, it is helpful to know that Parsons is interested in two major contrasts in types of human social actions. On the one hand, there is a distinction between *instrumental* and *consummatory* social action. Instrumental action is that by which a system "lays up stores" for the future. Social systems as well as individuals apparently display behavior of this kind. One anticipates a "hard winter" or a "critical audience" and prepares for these contingencies by accumulating fuel or polishing the lecture. Consummatory action, in contrast, is aimed at immediate gratification of desires or fulfillment of needs; the individual or social system "cashes a check" and expends its resources to provide for current needs.

---

[19] David Aberle et al., "The Functional Prerequisites of a Society," *Ethics*, 60(1950): 100–111.

[20] A. R. Radcliffe-Brown, *Structure and Function in Primitive Society* (Glencoe, Ill.: Free Press, 1952).

[21] Talcott Parsons and Neil J. Smelser, *Economy and Society* (Glencoe, Ill.: Free Press, 1956).

On the other hand, certain behavior is focused on some relation of the system to an *external* environment, especially to the accomplishment of some *task* of the system. Other behavior has a more *internal* focus in that persons in a social system are primarily concerned about their interpersonal or intrapersonal relations, for example, an individual with the internal psychological problem of squaring his behavior with his own self-conceptions.[22] Parsons was familiar with and influenced by the findings of Bales, who experimented with small-groups situations and found a sort of "phase movement" in the kinds of action which prevailed in groups at different times.[23] At some times groups with assigned tasks concentrate hard on those tasks, suppressing members who "horse around," and exchanging sharp words in the heat of discussion concerning the best ways to approach a task. At other times, groups seem preoccupied with repairing the social and emotional "damage" sustained in the course of concentrating on a task. Apologies are given, jokes are told to break the tension, and group members generally relax into a more sociable kind of interaction. Bales found, interestingly enough, that different group members specialize in either task or social-emotional leadership. Groups typically have a "most popular" and a "best worker" distinction, and seldom would one member receive both accolades.

The application of the two distinctions in social behavior—type of social action and kind of focus—to one another would yield the four functional imperatives as indicated in the following diagram:[24]

	Instrumental	Consummatory
External	Adaptive function	Goal attainment function
Internal	Pattern-maintenance and tension-management function	Integrative function

Each of these imperatives will now be discussed.

---

[22] Leon Festinger, *A Theory of Cognitive Dissonance* (Evanston, Ill.: Row, Peterson, 1957).

[23] Robert F. Bales, *Interaction Process Analysis* (Cambridge, Mass.: Addison-Wesley, 1950).

[24] Based on the discussion by Talcott Parsons in Robert K. Merton, Leonard Broom, and Leonard S. Cottrell (eds.), *Sociology Today* (New York: Basic Books, 1959), p. 114.

Adaptation. A social system requires that ways be found to produce the general facilities required for the accomplishment of the system's goals. For a society as a social system, this imperative refers mostly to economic activities, the production of the goods and services that people require. With other social systems, there may be other kinds of adaptation imperatives. A school as a social system requires that a certain number of professionally qualified teachers be recruited to provide one of the "facilities" without which educational goals could not be achieved.

Goal attainment. It is never enough for a social system to have a supply of facilities adequate to meet its needs. There is still the problem of the application of these resources in specific programs of collective action. Often the application involves the necessity of deciding whether to apply facilities to one purpose or another. A school system must decide on its curriculum, a family on whether to expend its income to repair the roof or to make a down payment on an automobile. At the societal level, Parsons uses the term *polity* to refer to the goal-attainment mechanisms of a society; the legislative and administrative processes of government are approximately what he has in mind.

Pattern maintenance and tension management. This cumbersome terminology is used by Parsons to denote the imperative of a social system that it maintain, as a condition of its collective existence, properly *motivated* individuals. Apathy, hostility, and a condition of being too "up tight" are personal traits that are dysfunctional for social systems. Pattern-maintenance mechanisms are those which produce individuals imbued with the basic values that the prevailing culture emphasizes. All the indoctrinating or moralizing practices in a society—its educational and religious institutions, for example—have primarily this kind of functional relevance. Tension-management mechanisms are devices which encourage people to let off steam in ways that are not subversive of the system's order. We mentioned earlier the Zulu "rituals of rebellion" as presumably having this kind of function; and it was at least suggested in chapter 3 that our Dionysian weekends and holidays are tension-management devices that allow us to go back to our Monday mornings for another week of Apollonian ritualism.

Integration. Properly motivated individuals are no ultimate guarantee of social order. Though everyone may be properly indoctrinated with a belief in the "sanctity" of a contract, it still may happen that disputes about the conditions imposed by a contract will arise between the contracting parties. Most social systems require "referees" of one sort or another to keep such disputes within the realm of peaceful competition and to avoid violent conflict. At the societal level, Parsons refers to the *legal* system as society's mechanism for mediating disputes between persons. He thus splits the institution of government into a *polity* aspect dealing with the making and enforcement of decisions and a *legal* aspect dealing with judicial procedures for settling disputes and maintaining "law and order."

CHANGES IN SOCIETY

One of the most frequent criticisms of functional analysis is that it emphasizes the sources of continuity or stability in social systems and ignores or slights the element of change in them.[25] Some functionalists have denied the validity of this criticism, claiming that the initial focus on the mechanisms that maintain social systems is not a denial of the fact of change but simply a strategy of adopting the assumption of equilibrium as a starting point.[26] With this controversy in mind, we shall look at several theoretical viewpoints concerning the most effective ways of explaining change in social systems.

Dialectic Theories of Change

There is one perspective on change that tends to reject at once the perspectives of both the functionalists and most of the critics of functionalism. Recall Sorokin's view that the integration of social systems may be of a logico-meaningful rather than a causal-functional nature. If a society has *no* causal connections between its parts, then any attempt to account for change by studying the overall effects of changes in key variables is doomed to failure. To Sorokin, the most important level of integration of social systems

---

[25] David Lockwood, "Some Remarks on 'The Social System,' " *British Journal of Sociology,* 7(1956):134–146. Ralf Dahrendorf, "Out of Utopia: Toward a Reorientation of Sociological Analysis," *American Journal of Sociology,* 64(1958):115–127.

[26] Talcott Parsons, "The Present Position and Prospects of Systematic Theory in Sociology," in Talcott Parsons, *Essays in Sociological Theory* (Glencoe, Ill.: Free Press, 1954), pp. 212–237.

is the logico-meaningful. At any given time, a society tends to be organized around a "first principle." For change to occur, this principle must change, but it can only change because of the inherently unstable or dynamic character of all phenomena.[27] Sorokin's view is one variety of a *dialectic* theory of change, as we shall discuss below.

First, however, since Sorokin's view is somewhat influential and is both continuous with and a departure from earlier views about differences in kinds of societies, it would be worthwhile to look at his idea of the fundamentally different types of first principles existing in social systems. Sorokin sees all of history as a dialectic fluctuation between *sensate* and *ideational* forms of sociocultural organization (with a third mixed type, the *idealistic*, which we shall ignore here).

A sensate society has a logico-meaningful integration around the first principle that the measure of all value is the gratification of individual appetites; that society is seen as "best" which allows maximum individual happiness—the "greatest good of the greatest number" (the classic statement of a utilitarian philosophy, which Sorokin sees as a major element in sensate thought). Ideational societies, in contrast, incorporate the first principle that the measure of value is absolute faith in a supernatural being and that individual wills must be subordinate to that of the supernatural—"not my will be done, O Lord, but thine."

Although existing societies show mixtures of these elements, they tend more and more to approximate one or the other of these polar types. In a basically sensate society, there is little tolerance for the "impracticality" of the man of faith who refuses to "face facts" and, in a basically ideational society, there is little tolerance for the "sin of pride" and a fear of the damage to religion of too much concern for things of "the flesh." The social organizational correlate of this essentially cultural or value conflict is found in Sorokin's distinction between the *contractual* form of social relations that tend to prevail in sensate societies and the *familial* relations that dominate in ideational societies. These essentially self-explanatory terms correspond closely with the distinction made by Tonnies between *gesellschaft* and *gemeinschaft* social forms or by Durkheim

---

[27] Sorokin, *Social and Cultural Dynamics*, Vol. 4, *Basic Problems, Principles and Methods*, pp. 587–620.

between *organic* and *mechanical* forms of social solidarity, terms which we shall define in the following chapter.

The fluctuation between sensate and ideational forms is explained as the result of the operation of a *dialectic* process. As each form comes to be realized in its "pure" state, there begin to appear contradictions that tend to disintegrate the system. Sorokin sees the "crisis of our age"[28] as a disintegration of a sensate system. Here we can see how the dialectic operates.

A purely *contractual* society has great contradictions. The logical conclusion of the individuality that a sensate system encourages is the situation in which the individual is completely amoral, subordinating himself to no principles of right conduct, justifying any action if it is conducive to his personal sensual gratification. When this point is reached, the "law of the jungle" is reestablished; men do anything they can get away with. Warfare, revolution, and crime are typical ways people promote their individual ambitions. At this stage, contractual relations have in fact degenerated into *compulsory* ones.

Sorokin saw the rising authoritarianism of the 1930s and 1940s as a logical outgrowth of an "over-ripe" sensate system. Only when men experience sufficiently the miseries engendered by their personal ambitions will they begin the movement toward a more ideational system. Like Peter Rabbit, man will not be satisfied to "cultivate his own garden" until he has suffered the consequences of overindulging his sensate nature in MacGregor's garden. The "wise resignation" that Comte thought would result from the complete application of science will come, according to Sorokin's view, only when science and other sensate ways of thought are abandoned in favor of more religious faith and a more "godly" form of relationships, namely, the familial form.[29]

Functional Theory of Change

Despite the persistent criticism of functionalism that it is incompetent to deal with the problem of change in social systems, Parsons and other functionalists have attempted to explain change

---

[28] Pitirim A. Sorokin, *The Crisis of Our Age* (New York: Dutton, 1941).

[29] For critiques of Sorokin's views, together with a "reply to my critics" by Sorokin, see Philip J. Allen (ed.), *Pitirim A. Sorokin in Review* (Durham, N.C.: Duke University Press, 1963).

from a functionalist perspective.[30] Parsons identifies two major types of change which he calls *equilibrating process* and *structural change.*

Equilibrating process refers to the changes that are required by a social system as a condition of its maintenance. A society in which social mobility is a strongly emphasized value may require many changes in intimate relationships as families and friendships break up under the pressure of individuals moving physically or in social status. The process of growing up or of change from one age status to another is another instance of equilibrating process. Contrary to the criticism that functionalist views foster an image of societies as utopias in which "nothing ever happens,"[31] there may be much ferment and many traumatic and ecstatic experiences; however, equilibrating-process changes are confined to the smaller units of social interaction.

Structural change is a more radical level of change, referring especially to changes in the basic patterns of values in a society— a change, for example, from a sensate to an ideational set of values. Social systems tend to resist any changes in these values, treating exponents of change as deviants and punishing or otherwise attempting to contain the spread of innovative ways of life. A major question is, How does deviance arise in a social system if it contains so many mechanisms to repress deviance? Parsons distinguishes between *exogenous* and *endogenous* sources of such deviance.

Endogenous sources refer to the stresses and strains that arise from the operation of normal social processes. Perhaps those very people who suffer from the operation of "the system"—those who are widowed by warfare conducted on behalf of the society, those who are losers in a system of survival of the fittest—will tend to become alienated from the system that has inflicted their misfortune.[32] Societies try to deal with such alienation by finding ways,

---

[30] Talcott Parsons et al. (eds.), *Theories of Society,* Vol. 1 (New York: Free Press of Glencoe, 1961), pp. 60–79. For a more recent discussion in this vein, see Barry Sugarman, "Tension Management, Deviance and Social Change," *Sociological Quarterly,* 10(1969):62–71.

[31] Dahrendorf, "Out of Utopia."

[32] Compare this with Merton's view of the "innovator" as the person deprived of legitimate opportunities for success in a society. Merton, *Social Theory and Social Structure,* pp. 141–149.

in the words of one sociologist, to "cool out" such persons, to help them adapt themselves gracefully and peaceably to the fact of their failures.[33] Such practices seem to be illustrations of what Parsons means by the "reequilibrating mechanisms" of a social system for dealing with deviance.

Exogenous sources of change arise from the fact that societies exist in an environment that includes other societies. Culture contact, as we pointed out in chapter 4, leads to the exposure of people from one society to the alien values of people in another society. Deviance may result if people come to prefer those alien ways, if young people in an Oriental society, for example, are attracted by the values of a Western way of life and begin to act in ways that their elders define as subversive of traditional ways. One might hypothesize an interaction between endogenous and exogenous sources of deviance. It may be, for example, that the alienated people within a society—the young or the members of a racial minority, for example—are less influenced by the ethnocentrism of their own people and more likely to take favorable attitudes toward alien ways. It may also be that the fact (or even the suspicion) of alien influences on a person may lead to his failure within a society and a resulting alienation. A scientist may, for example, lose his government job on the suspicion of his Communist connections.

Regardless of the source of deviance, societies tend to resist change through the reequilibrating mechanisms by which sanctions are brought to bear against deviance. But these mechanisms do not always succeed; the behavior of young people may get out of hand. Structural change does not occur, however, until behavior that is widespread but nevertheless deviant is finally accepted as right and proper. In the early history of capitalism, as Weber describes it, the capitalist entrepreneur was generally considered an immoral deviant from traditional attitudes toward right and proper business behavior.[34] (For example, there was a traditional conception of a "fair price" at which goods were to be sold, and the supply-demand pricing based on what the traffic will bear was seen as exploitative.) Only when capitalism became the accepted and ideologically glorified way of life could we speak of a structural change,

---

[33] Erving Goffman, "On Cooling the Mark Out," *Psychiatry*, 15(1952):451–463.

[34] Max Weber, *The Protestant Ethic and the Spirit of Capitalism*, trans. by Talcott Parsons (New York: Scribner's, 1958).

in Parsons' terms. Changes in values tend to develop more slowly than changes in actual behavior; hence the often-noted "hypocrisy" of people in social systems who do not accept the rightness of others' engaging in a behavior in which they themselves quietly indulge.[35]

Conflict Theory of Change

Dahrendorf criticizes the functionalist explanation of change, noting that although it treats deviance as the source of change, it gives no coherent account of how deviance is generated; the tendency is to analyze the effects of deviance from "whatever source."[36] Dahrendorf proposes instead a view of social systems which will show how deviance or the tendency to change is "structurally generated." From this viewpoint, one begins with the observation that, in every social system, some persons are dominant and others are subordinated, and the subordinate persons have an inherent tendency to rebel against the system that works to their disadvantage and to try to change it. Although there is this tendency toward revolutionary change, change may in fact be retarded by the element of "constraint" of revolutionary activity. There are several kinds of "conditions" (independent variables) that have to be favorable if the revolutionary potential is to be realized.

Conditions of organization. Many subordinate groups either are never aware of their common interest in revolution or, if they are aware, they are unable to get together and form effective fighting organizations. Someone may have to plead with them ("workers of the world, unite!") and even then a combination of subordinate-group apathy and dominant-group suppression may keep them from organizing.

Conditions of conflict. Even if they are effectively organized, subordinate-group members may work out compromises or accommodations by which they are able to tolerate their disadvantaged positions. Minor improvements in their social positions under the existing system may deter people from revolution.

---

[35] Charles K. Warriner, "The Nature and Functions of Official Morality," *American Journal of Sociology*, 64(1958):165–168.

[36] Ralf Dahrendorf, "Toward a Theory of Social Conflict," *Journal of Conflict Resolution*, 2(1958):170–183.

Conditions of change. Even if they define their situation as intolerable and use desperate revolutionary tactics, subordinate groups are likely to find that the rulers maintain a near-monopoly on the use of force and will employ it in police-state fashion to suppress any potential revolution. A successful revolution may depend on some failure of will on the part of rulers, some hesitance in the use of the force they possess.[37]

Comparison of Functionalist and Conflict Theories

Dahrendorf's theory of social conflict does not seem to eliminate the difficulty that he raised with functional theory, namely, that it leaves an untidy situation of granting that change may come from "whatever source." If Parsons does not explain the origins of *deviance* systematically, Dahrendorf likewise does not explain the origins of *constraint* systematically. The tendency toward change is "structurally generated" in Dahrendorf's theory, but the constraints that retard change are not so generated. Rather, these constraints are the "independent variables" in Dahrendorf's theory, and independent variables are *never* explained in the explanatory system in which they are the explaining factors. Parsons prefers to treat deviance and the attempt to control deviance as the independent variables in explaining change.[38]

This controversy can say something useful to us about the use of "models" such as the notion of a social system in sociological explanations. Is a society *really* an equilibrium-maintaining entity, as in the models of Spencer and Parsons, or is it *really* an arena of conflict of the powerful and the weak, as in the model that Dahrendorf inherited from Marx? Perhaps it is *really* neither, or at least there is no way to show which is the "true" conception of society. The value of any scientific model is perhaps in its power to stimulate fruitful kinds of questions about some phenomenon.[39] For instance, does one get more explanatory mileage by assuming

---

[37] According to Brinton, this will is based largely on ideological support by intellectuals, and a key to a successful revolution is a "desertion of the intellectuals" to the side of the revolution. Crane Brinton, *The Anatomy of Revolution* (New York: Vintage, 1965).

[38] For another critique of the Dahrendorf approach, see Peter Weingart, "Beyond Parsons? A Critique of Ralf Dahrendorf's Conflict Theory," *Social Forces*, 48(1969): 151–165.

[39] This is the "pragmatic" view of theories, as discussed in Ernest Nagel, *The Structure of Science* (New York: Wiley, 1961).

inherent stability and treating change as problematic (Parsons) or by assuming inherent change and treating stability as problematic (Dahrendorf)? Each sociologist has his opinion and the student will form his own as he learns more about the field of sociology and comes to know more about what is his "own thing" in the study of sociology.

SUMMARY

Society is that inclusive level of social organization that provides a social environment within which all the major activities of a person are promoted and regulated. Societies are often analyzed from the viewpoint of their being social systems, complex entities with self-maintaining properties and/or a functional interdependence of their parts.

Three major differences about the most appropriate way to study society have been suggested in this chapter. The first involves the relative importance of the *integration* and the *equilibrium* characteristics of society. Are social systems to be studied by analyzing the functional and dysfunctional consequences of social practices for a society (Merton) or by analyzing the "mechanisms" that enable a society to survive as a "living" entity (Parsons)? Second, should a society be conceived primarily as a social system with integrative and equilibrium properties (the functionalists) or as a "meaningful" integration of elements which can only change by the operation of dialectic contradictions in the various forms of integration (Sorokin)? Third, should one assume, for purposes of dealing with social change, an inherent tendency toward stability and attempt to explain change (Parsons) or an inherent tendency toward instability and an attempt to explain restrictions of change (Dahrendorf)?

Since all of these controversies represent quite fundamental variations in ways of studying societies sociologically, the reader may find it worthwhile to spend the time necessary to acquaint himself with some of the technicalities of theoretical viewpoints of the type presented here.

Groups

In this chapter we shall undertake to analyze the kind of social organizational "arrangements" that take place at a level of inclusiveness one notch below that of "society." If a person lives *in* a society, he typically is also a member *of* a number of groups which may themselves be considered as existing *in* a society. A group is a number of people involved in a pattern of association with one another; typical groups are a clique of friends, a political party, a flying saucer club. The key to the nature of human grouping is the notion of *association,* and we shall open with a consideration of some of the meanings and implications of human association. Later, we shall consider special associational problems involved with different types of human groups.

NATURE OF HUMAN ASSOCIATION

Man is a social animal in the sense that he lives with others of his own kind. This living together of men is called *association* by the sociologist, who insists that the patterns of association between men as they form groups constitute a level of reality that cannot be reduced to the psychologies of the individual actors.[1]

What does it mean to individuals to be members of groups? The fact of association has a number of implications for the behavior of persons involved in these patterns of association. A few of these implications will now be discussed.

---

[1] Charles K. Warriner, "Groups Are Real: a Reaffirmation," *American Sociological Review,* 21(1956):549–554.

Sharing of Fate

The phrase "guilt by association" is a recognition of the fact that persons tend to be judged by the company they keep. This is one illustration of the fact that what happens to one member of a group tends to happen in a similar way to those who are associated with him. John Donne gives poetic expression to this sociological fact in asserting the shared fate of *all* men:

No man is an island, entire of itself; every man is a piece of the continent, a part of the main. If a clod be washed away by the sea, Europe is the less, as well as if a promontory were, as well as if a manor of thy friend's or of thine own were; any man's death diminishes me, because I am involved in mankind, and therefore never send to know for whom the bell tolls, it tolls for thee.[2]

Without quarreling with Donne's important insight on the interdependence of human fates, we could note that this sharing of fate among group members is clearly a variable in different conditions of association. The "black sheep" of a family in a small rural community will probably have a greater effect on the social reputation of his entire family than would be the case in an urban community, where the anonymity of life insures the possibility of concealing such family problems. The interdependence of fates of the world's nations—expressed positively in movements such as the formation of common markets and negatively in the real possibility of local arguments between small countries expanding into world wars—is a product of recent changes in the patterns of international association. The social conditions which promote involvement and disinvolvement of persons and groups with one another are prime problems of sociological explanation.

One feature of human behavior with reference to shared fate is the tendency of persons to try to avoid being blamed for the failures of the organized groups to which they belong. A family breaks up, a political party loses an election, a baseball team misses the pennant. The tendency is to treat the failure as a kind of crime and ask, Who did it? (Only sometimes are the involved persons satisfied with the explanation, "It's just one of those things.") People are notorious for their tendency to point fingers away from themselves, but

---

[2] John Donne, *Devotions Upon Emergent Occasions* (Ann Arbor: University of Michigan Press, 1959), pp. 108, 109.

certain people are highly suspect in cases of organizational failure —the eldest son of a family, the chairman of a political party, the manager of a baseball team, for instance.

The more *specialized* the individual's contribution to the success of the groups of which he is a member, the more he is judged by his personal "record" and the less he is blamed for organizational failures. Thus, a pitcher on a baseball team and an "extra-point kicker" on a football team have very specialized roles in organized groups, and pitchers are less likely than other players to end their playing careers with failing teams.[3] It can be argued that managerial and other "generalist" responsibilities involve a greater sharing of individual fate with that of the group. Being "dangerous" in this way, such positions may be filled only because people in these positions are more highly rewarded in money and prestige.

Organization

When people are moved to get together, it is often in the interest of accomplishing some task in an orderly and organized fashion. The motive for this getting together is often a recognition of the shared fate of persons; we had better "hang together" else we shall surely "hang separately." The organization of a group of persons gives each individual his part to play in the accomplishment of a collective task and insists on the loyalty of each person to those other group members who rely on him.

Groups of associated persons display wide variation in their degree of organizational effectiveness. The well-drilled football team and the well-oiled political machine are examples of highly organized associational endeavors. On the other hand, there are notoriously underorganized systems; Will Rogers pointed up a classic political example when he remarked, "I don't belong to any organized political party; I'm a Democrat." We shall look now at two major variables in determining the organizational effectiveness of a group: the problem of *competence* and that of *experience*.

Competence. Effective organization assumes the competence of individuals to play their individual roles. The importance of competence is seen in the effort during recruitment to secure the "best qualified" persons to join the group. This is perhaps especially so

---

[3] Jerry D. Rose, "The Attribution of Responsibility for Organizational Failure," *Sociology and Social Research*, 53(1969):323–332.

in the selection of *leaders;* sometimes a special committee is established to conduct a nationwide search for a highly qualified man to serve as president of a college or as a member of the cabinet of the President of the United States. On the other hand, a recent work, written with facetious intent but with a degree of sociological insight, has suggested that selective processes tend to choose incompetent people for leaders.[4] More precisely, the "Peter Principle" states that people tend to be promoted in rank and responsibility until they reach the "level of their incompetence," a job that is just beyond their capacity to fulfill. The competent worker is made foreman, a job that is just a little "beyond him," a competent professor becomes an incompetent dean, etc.

There is certainly a degree of plausibility in the "Peter Principle" although it assumes a cultural condition which values "getting ahead" professionally or "bettering oneself" socially. Assuming the prevalence of such values, one could criticize the practicability of Peter's prescriptions for avoiding the operation of the "principle" that he articulated. "Peter's prophylactics" consist mostly in urging men to resist the temptation to seek or accept promotion from a position that they can fill competently to one in which they must fail. Such suggestions seem to run against the spirit of a "get ahead" society.

Perhaps the most important truth in the "Peter Principle" is that men *do* perform more competently before they reach their highest levels of responsibility, but part of this competence may be stimulated by the persistent failure of organizations to promote people as rapidly as people believe they deserve to be promoted. In many organizations there are "bright young men" waiting in the wings to assume leadership when the incompetent but tenured leader finally dies, retires, or transfers. There thus tends to be a persistent sense of frustration or alienation from "the system" that holds people back. The securing of competent performance by these "underemployed" persons may depend on a creative use of their frustration; perhaps a person tends toward high-level performance "to show the bastards" how wrong they are in retarding his promotion.

Experience. In addition to competent performers, an effectively organized group usually assumes some experience on the part of

---

[4] Laurence Peter and Raymond Hull, *The Peter Principle* (New York: Morrow, 1969).

the members in dealing collectively with a given kind of problem. A seasoned combat outfit is likely to be more effective than a green or inexperienced one. It is also true, however, that veteran troops may suffer from battle fatigue and may therefore be less effective than a fresh batch of troops. Likewise, a person who has been "burned" in a first marriage may be less able to surrender himself fully to the spirit of a second.

This reservation aside, effective organization requires that associated persons somehow acquire experience. Ideally, people like to develop experience through "rehearsal" situations before they are expected to perform "live." Armies hold maneuvers, sports clubs schedule practice sessions, publishers critique manuscripts before they publish them. Even the period of premarital engagement can be seen, in many respects, as a rehearsal or trying-out of a couple's relations to one another and to friends, relatives, and the general public.[5]

A limitation of rehearsals for gaining experience is that, no matter how realistic the training conditions, they can never quite duplicate the real-life situation. However rigorous their rehearsals, the cast of a play cannot know how they will perform until they actually are on stage opening night, and many a carefully trained combat team has panicked when the first real bullets began to fly. Some interesting compromises between rehearsal and performance are sometimes developed. Broadway plays usually open in New Haven or Boston for a preseason testing, and ball clubs hold exhibition and spring-training games which do not count in the season's standings. On a more individual level, sometimes a would-be college student, unsure of his capacity for academic work, decides to try himself by enrolling in a two-year college with the idea of transferring later if he finds he can make it here.

In no case does it appear that completely satisfactory experience can be gained in any of these anticipatory ways. The school of "hard knocks" may ultimately be the training ground for the acquisition of experience. The veteran members of a group tend to hold this view, looking with disdain on the "ninety-day wonders" fresh out of a training institution and still infected with the impractical theories that are taught in the schools.

---

[5] Willard Waller and Reuben Hill, *The Family: a Dynamic Interpretation*, rev. ed. (New York: Dryden, 1951), Ch. 12.

Sociability

People do not always have specific purposes in mind when they associate with others. "Let's get together" may mean "let's get on the ball and get this job done," but it may also mean "let's have lunch together" or "let's make love." Sometimes such associations are rather formally structured social occasions or get togethers, but often the association is informal or spontaneous: a chat with an acquaintance, the exchange of greetings on a street, a petting episode in an automobile on a Saturday night. Whether formal or informal, such nonpurposive kinds of association will be called *sociability* by the sociologist.

The human tendency to engage in sociable forms of interaction has excited the curiosity of some sociologists. Simmel believed that each of the serious or purposive kinds of human association has its counterpart in a "play-form"; conversation is the play-form of discussion (serious talk), contest games are the play-form of warfare and other serious opposition, flirtation is the play-form of seduction (serious sexual association), etc.[6] The tendency to "play" was seen by Simmel as having an important function in promoting serious associational life. Often our realities are too grim for us to look at them coolly and objectively; by converting them into a "play-form" (by making jokes about our "troubles," for example) we can face these realities without being overwhelmed.

Whatever the functions of sociable behavior for more serious associational life, much of human sociability must be seen as motivated by the desire for association with others for its own sake. The only purpose for sociable behavior is the pleasure of the participants. Simmel noted in this connection that sociable occasions are governed by rules that are inherently democratic, the "principle of sociability" being that "everyone should guarantee to the other that maximum of sociable values (joy, relief, vivacity) which is consonant with the maximum of values he himself receives."[7] From this viewpoint, certain kinds of association are not sociable, although they may have the outward appearance of being so. If one or a few individuals monopolize the "fun" during a sociable encounter, such as when a royal family sometimes uses its "court" to

---

[6] Georg Simmel, "The Sociology of Sociability," *American Journal of Sociology,* 55(1949):254–261.

[7] Ibid., p. 257.

amuse itself at the expense of the courtiers, there is perhaps no more real "sociability" than there is in a situation of a cat amusing itself with a mouse.

HUMAN COMPARED TO NONHUMAN ASSOCIATION

Grouping or association is not unique to the human species. The association of members of an animal species is common. *Pack, school, colony* are a few of the terms to denote the living together of members of an animal species. In these groups may be found all of the characteristics of human association that we have just discussed. The "social insects," for example, have a high degree of shared fate and of species organization. Different members of a beehive make special contributions to the maintenance of the hive, and all members tend to be similarly affected by changes in the environmental conditions of the hive. Members of many animal species appear to be "sociable," showing signs of what humans may call "enjoyment" in the presence of one another and indulging in much playful behavior.

While human association is not unique in any of these respects, it does appear to be unique in some other respects. In the first place, it is unique in the level or type of *consciousness* that accompanies the process of association. Other animals do not, in all likelihood, give any thought to their associations with one another; no "canine relations commission" has ever been formed among dogs to promote harmony among the various breeds. Men, on the other hand, do worry about "whether this marriage can be saved" and they do verbalize their pleasures in "getting to know you." Much of human behavior is influenced by this consciousness of association as persons attempt to initiate and sustain desirable associations and to terminate or avoid undesirable ones.

Another aspect of human consciousness as related to association or group membership is the degree to which association is determined by the *meaning* that persons have for one another. With other animals, living together refers to immediate physical presence. A wolf pack is simply a number of wolves who travel together and the associational rule is probably "out of sight, out of mind." With man, the situation is quite different. Isolation—the absence of association—is by no means synonymous with physical separation. Being "lonely in a crowd" is a recognition of the fact that persons often feel dissociated from the persons immediately around them.

On the other hand, people may feel quite close to loved ones from whom they are far removed physically. A man and woman may be married even though they are separated and communicate only by letter or telephone, or not at all. A person's "associates" may be the writers of books or the characters in them. A person may feel that he "knows" Hamlet or Perry Mason better than he knows someone with whom he works every day. No sociological study of human association can properly avoid a concern with the way people themselves conceive their associations with other persons.[8] Cooley seemed to have this in mind when he observed that "the imaginations that people have of one another are the solid facts of society."[9]

A second contrast between human and nonhuman association is in the *normative* regulation of human association. Many centuries ago, Aristotle made this observation:

Nature, as we often say, makes nothing in vain, and man is the only animal whom she has endowed with the gift of speech. And whereas mere voice is but an indication of pleasure or pain, and is therefore found in other animals . . . the power of speech is intended to set forth the expedient and the inexpedient, and therefore likewise the just and the unjust. And it is a characteristic of man that he alone has any sense of good and evil, of just and unjust, and the like, and the association of living beings who have this sense makes a family and a state.[10]

The exact degree of emphasis that should be placed on the normative element in human association is a matter of controversy in sociology. Talcott Parsons, on the one hand, found that the works of classic writers such as Durkheim, Weber, and Pareto converged on the importance of the normative element,[11] and this redefined classic tradition is carried forward in Parsons' own work. Critics like Dennis Wrong, on the other hand, have argued that too great an emphasis on normative regulation obscures the many ways in which

[8] One way of showing the essentially symbolic character of human association is illustrated in Merton's treatment of "reference groups." A person may associate himself mentally with groups of which he is not actually a member, as when an enlisted man in the army identifies himself with the officer corps rather than his fellow enlisted men. Robert K. Merton, *Social Theory and Social Structure*, rev. ed. (Glencoe, Ill.: Free Press, 1956), Ch. 8.

[9] Charles H. Cooley, *Human Nature and the Social Order* (New York: Scribner's, 1902), p. 121.

[10] Reprinted in Robert Bierstedt (ed.), *The Making of Society* (New York: Random, 1959), p. 24.

[11] Talcott Parsons, *The Structure of Social Action* (New York: McGraw-Hill, 1937).

men are not the "oversocialized" creatures that many sociologists imagine.[12] *Homo homini lupus* ("Man to man is a wolf") may contain more than a grain of sociological truth.

Whatever degree of emphasis the normative regulation of association deserves, we are clearly dealing with an important order of fact about human association. The moral indoctrination of children is liable to be heavily laden with rules related to the formation of group memberships: find yourself a nice Jewish girl, don't go out with hippies, join the Boy Scouts, etc. In choosing his associates and in maintaining relations with them, a person is likely to be made aware continually that he is conforming to or deviating from the expectations of others in these matters.

CLASSIFICATION OF GROUPS

Given the importance of the concept of the *group* to sociological analysis, it is not surprising that sociologists have been much concerned with attempts to refine the analysis by identifying some fundamental forms of the human group. The problem of classifying groups has not been an easy one to solve. If one counts as "groups" such diverse aggregates as the members of a family, the members of an office staff, and the members of the Paducah Batman Fan Club, the variety of different groups in the world is almost innumerable. Each group has its own identity, its unduplicated individuality, and any pigeonholing of groups into categories will necessarily do some violence to this individuality. But the classificatory problem for sociology is not unique to that science. All scientific classifications do some violence to the radical individuality of empirical phenomena, but there is no alternative if the science is to *generalize* about these phenomena. Regarding the study of groups, the question is not *whether* to classify or not to classify but rather *how* to think most usefully about different kinds of groups.

The latter question is still controversial, and one accordingly finds different solutions to the problem of classification in the sociological literature. One solution would place in one category all groups having a common aim or purpose. Thus, one could generalize about religious groups, ignoring some obvious differences between, say, a very small sect of believers in an esoteric divinity

---

[12] Dennis H. Wrong, "The Oversocialized Conception of Man in Modern Sociology," *American Sociological Review*, 26(1961):183–193.

and the huge congregation of an urban nondenominational church. Similarly, one might employ such categories of generalization as political groups, domestic (family) groups, medical groups, work groups, play groups.

Critics of classifications based on a group's purpose or "content" will say that such a set of categories will not allow for uniquely sociological insights to be brought to bear on the understanding of what it means for behavior to be determined by group membership. The economist, for example, may be the specialist required to understand what is unique to work groups and the political scientist could surely tell us most about the behavior of persons in political groups. Many sociologists have followed Simmel's insistence that sociology makes its unique contribution when it classifies social phenomena in terms of similarities in form rather than similarities in content.[13]

To apply this distinction to the current problem, each group has certain form-properties that are similar to those of other groups, only some of which have the same purposes of content-properties. Thus there are the categories "large group" and "small group," and a large religious group is more similar in *form* to a large criminal group than it is to a small religious group. One accordingly finds such special fields of study in sociology as the sociology of small groups or of complex organizations.

PRIMARY AND SECONDARY GROUPS

One of the most fundamental formal distinctions among groups is that which classifies them as *primary* or as *secondary* groups.[14] A close-knit family and a group of close friends are illustrations of primary groups. A large political party and an army are examples of secondary groups. The form-properties that distinguish these two types include the properties of degree or type of intimacy, integration, and formal structure. In the following section we shall examine the distinction between primary and secondary groups in

---

[13] Georg Simmel, "The Problem of Sociology," in Kurt Wolff (ed.), *Georg Simmel, 1858–1918* (Columbus: Ohio State University Press, 1959), pp. 310–336.

[14] The concept of *primary group* traces its influence from the work of Charles H. Cooley. The term *secondary group* as a description of groups with an opposite set of form-properties was not used by Cooley in his early work but became conventional in later works. See Charles H. Cooley, *Social Organization* (New York: Scribner's, 1909).

terms of their differences in relation to these form-properties.[15] Once the distinctions are made, we can begin to see some of the important complications and exceptions that appear when we look at real-life human groups.

Intimacy

The distinction. Relatively intimate interaction occurs among members of a primary group, while impersonal interaction prevails among members of a secondary group. The dimensions of intimacy are twofold, and differentiating between them will help us to understand the distinction between primary and secondary groups.

In the first place, intimacy involves a more *intensive* level of association, a deeper emotional involvement on the part of the participants. Members of a family or a group of friends become attached to one another, a fact that becomes vividly clear when a member of such a group detaches himself or is detached from membership. Losing a husband or friend or child is a serious matter, as anyone who has had this experience knows. However, losing a member of one's political party or a fellow employee is not likely in itself to involve any high degree of emotional trauma.

Second, the association of primary group members is *extensive*. In other words, there is breadth or scope as well as depth to the involvements of primary group members with one another. The association of secondary group members tends to be more specialized or focused on a single topic of interaction. In a secondary group such as a political party or a college classroom, there are always some aspects of each member's life which are none of the business of the other members, such information being outside the scope of appropriate interaction in this kind of group. Among family members or friends it is much harder to define what is not appropriate to the association. A person reveals more different facets of himself to members of his primary group; it is notoriously difficult to keep secrets from one's family and friends.

---

[15] These distinctions will treat primary and secondary groups as "ideal types" in Weber's terms and in his rationale for using them, which is a "heuristic" one; that is, although an ideal type is an exaggeration of empirical reality, it is *useful* in helping us to understand reality and its variations. Max Weber, *The Methodology of the Social Sciences*, trans. by Edward A. Shils and Henry A. Finch (Glencoe, Ill.: Free Press, 1949).

Some complications. Many secondary groups provide some intensive and extensive involvements for their members and many primary groups are relatively lacking in these characteristics. In a secondary group like a political party or a trade union, some members will attach themselves with deep emotion to the group, making a "big thing" out of a group membership that other members treat more casually. Likewise, although a secondary group is supposedly specialized in its activity, there may be pressures by some members to extend the scope of group interaction. For example, a college faculty or a ladies' sewing circle may be urged to go outside its usual realm of activity and "take a stand" on some political issue of the day. The presence of a group "fanatic" and the recurring pressures to extend the scope of secondary group activities are indications of the persistent tendency of primary forms of association to spill over into secondary groups. Human beings are, after all, emotional creatures, and few groups, however hard they may try to minimize emotional attachment or to keep behavior and emotion compartmentalized, can escape these counterpressures.

On the other hand, primary groups tend to have elements of emotional superficiality and specialization that are not anticipated in their definition. Many primary group "involvements" are sustained not so much by deep emotional attachment as by resignation to alliances from which people cannot extricate themselves. It would be a hopelessly idealized view of marriage or friendship or neighborliness that would see these primary relationships as based always on emotional attachments. Marriage may be the "thing to do," particularly if the woman is pregnant or the man is facing military induction, and people may be neighborly, not so much because they like or are attracted to their neighbors but because neighborliness is the "norm" in one's community.[16]

Much of the mystique of primary groups as unions of soul mates can be dispelled by a few sociological observations on the processes by which people come to form primary groups. Marriage, for example, tends to be heavily influenced by situational opportunities and pressures. The rather impersonal nature of mate selection is captured in the popular view that such secondary groups as colleges, work groups, and social clubs tend to be "mar-

---

[16] On the enforced sociability of the suburbanite, see William H. Whyte, Jr., *The Organization Man* (New York: Simon & Schuster, 1956).

riage markets" for their single members (or for those contemplating a change of spouse).[17] The frequency of marriage between "the only singles on that weekend hike," or between bosses and secretaries, or doctors and nurses is sufficient to encourage many people to *select* their secondary group associations with an eye to their potential as sources of primary group formation.

Primary groups also typically involve elements of specialization, the keeping of secrets, and the view that there are some things that are none of the business of other members. A marriage, as Simmel points out, would be essentially impossible sociologically if the marriage partners were completely candid with one another about all their past, present, and contemplated activities.[18] The "right to privacy" in the home that people demand and receive is not only the right of the family as a unit to keep secrets from those outside the family but also the right of a child to keep a diary and of a husband or wife to keep a purse or a desk drawer that is exclusively his own "territory." These observations support Simmel's view that the distance or "reserve" that people maintain in their association with others cannot be effaced completely even in the most intimate of primary groups.[19]

Integration

The distinction. A major problem in the sociological study of groups has been the problem of integration, of that which holds groups together, or accounts for their durability, or for the willingness of people to join them. Rather than a single answer to this question, it appears that a somewhat different answer must be given for the two types of groups—primary and secondary.

Primary group members, perhaps because of the intensive and extensive involvement of themselves with each other, are bound together by a close feeling of identification with the group. The

---

[17] On the use of an outdoor recreation association as a "marriage market," see Joseph Harry, "A By-Product Theory of Primary Behavior," *Pacific Sociological Review,* 13(1970):121–126. For an earlier study of the tendency for primary groups to be formed from among people associated in secondary groups, see Nicholas Babchuk, "Primary Friends and Kin: a Study of the Associations of Middle-Class Couples," *Social Forces,* 43(1965):483–493.

[18] Kurt Wolff (ed.), *The Sociology of Georg Simmel* (Glencoe, Ill.: Free Press, 1950), pp. 326–329.

[19] Ibid., pp. 320–324.

"we-feeling," the sense of oneself as a relatively insignificant member of a larger whole, prevails more strongly in the primary group. Tonnies used the word *Gemeinschaft* to describe the relations between persons bound together by a we-feeling or sense of community.[20] Durkheim wrote of a *mechanical solidarity* in which persons feel bound together by their similarities, expressed in the "collective conscience" of a common moral community.[21]

Secondary groups, since they demand less depth or scope of involvement on the part of members, must depend on other sources of integration to account for their durability. The ties that bind secondary group members to one another are more in the nature of what Durkheim called "organic solidarity."[22] Group members are mutually dependent on one another, somewhat in the way that the different organs of the body are interdependent. This type of integration can coexist with a very weak identification of members with the group, with a greatly lessened we-feeling. Tonnies discussed a *Gesellschaft* kind of social relationship in which the contract between independent persons is the model of social interaction, with all parties getting something out of it.[23] Similarly, secondary groups seem to be sustained largely by the fact that individuals can use membership in these groups for their own purposes.

Complications. Secondary groups quite typically attempt to enlist the we-feeling of their members. A corporation tries to generate a feeling among its employees of being "one happy family"; a college faculty emphasizes the common feeling of colleagueship among its professors. However, there is likely to be an element of strain in these attempts, reflected in the characterization of such efforts as pseudo *Gemeinschaft*. One critic of the attempt to convert would-be individual entrepreneurs into "organization men" comments with some distaste on the tendency of corporations to require their employees to view their company as a kind of benevolent extended family.[24] In a similar vein, Riesman comments on the "false person-

---

[20] Ferdinand Tonnies, *Community and Society,* trans. by Charles P. Loomis (East Lansing: Michigan State University Press, 1957).

[21] Emile Durkheim, *On the Division of Labor in Society,* trans. by George Simpson (New York: Macmillan, 1933), pp. 129–131.

[22] Ibid.

[23] Tonnies, *Community and Society.*

[24] Whyte, *Organization Man.*

alizations" by which other-directed individuals attempt to embue work with an intimate associational atmosphere.[25] The false or pseudo character of such efforts suggests the dominant feeling that secondary groups *should not* attempt to approximate the associational characteristics of the primary group.

Another viewpoint is that of Cooley, who argued that the more formally structured or institutionalized forms of group activity always will and legitimately should involve an attempt to translate such primary group ideals as equality, charity, and brotherhood into complex organizational patterns.[26] Although different value judgments have been made regarding the attempt of secondary groups to elicit a we-feeling, there has been a rather general recognition of the problem of mixing primary with secondary bases of integration.

The *Gesellschaft* or contractual elements in primary group integration cannot easily be dismissed. People may form friendships or love relationships on the basis of perceived similarity and the desire for the formation of a "we" spirit, but they may also make calculations of expediency in considering the formation or retention of these associations. One's friends may be seen as "useful" in advancing an occupational or a political career, and family relationships may be kept in good repair in anticipation of "hard times" when the person may need the aid of his family. Although in Western societies marriages are based on personal compatibility, legally such relationships are treated more as contractual arrangements in which divorce is possible only if one party is not living up to his side of the "bargain"—a husband is accused of nonsupport, a wife of infidelity, etc. Incompatibility per se is not a ground for divorce in many states, and people mutually desiring a separation must often pretend that they are adversaries in a civil suit.[27] Although the term has never become popular, we might suggest that legal attitudes toward marriage and divorce indicate some tendency toward pseudo-*Gesellschaft* integration in primary groups.

Formality

Both primary and secondary groups are *organized* groups in the

---

[25] David Riesman, *The Lonely Crowd* (New Haven: Yale University Press, 1950), pp. 311–314.

[26] Cooley, *Social Organization.*

[27] Ely Chinoy, *Society,* 2nd ed. (New York: Random, 1967), p. 480.

sense that there are highly patterned and predictable forms of association among the members of these groups. But, whereas *formal* organization characterizes the secondary group, *informal* organization is the basis for association in primary groups.

The distinction. For a group to be formally organized means at least two things. First, it means that the group is characterized by a definite and official plan or blueprint which outlines the specific job or office of each member of the group. Formally organized groups are often called *bureaucracies.* Max Weber wrote in detail of a *rational-legal* bureaucracy,[28] and by the "legal" aspect he probably had in mind the division of organizational activity by formal offices. The holder of an office is bound by "the law" or by a set of rules which define precisely what he can and cannot do in that office. The bureaucratic nature of a political organization is expressed in the phrase "a government of laws, not of men." In the United States, presidents are elected and presidents retire (or are retired) but the presidency goes on, and each incumbent of the office swears to "uphold the duties" of that office.

The rules which govern association of people in bureaucracy are, then, rules that define the official relationship between the different offices of that group. "The law" says the president shall nominate, Congress shall advise and consent; the teacher shall make study assignments, the student shall execute those assignments. One way of analyzing further this formal organization is to distinguish between *line* and *staff,* a distinction which indicates that there are two kinds of rules for relating offices.

The *line* refers to the structure of *authority* in an organization. Line defines the chain of command or stipulates which officeholder may legitimately give orders and expect to be obeyed by which other officeholders. The organization of the army by division, regiment, company, platoon, and squad commands is a good example. The *staff* side of an organization refers to those officeholders who are officially designated to give advice and technical assistance to various other specified officeholders. A general staff is a group of technical specialists and advisors who assist an army commander; a similar function is filled by the president's cabinet and by the

---

[28] Max Weber, *The Theory of Social and Economic Organization,* trans. by A. M. Henderson and Talcott Parsons (New York: Oxford University Press, 1947), pp. 329–341.

relatively recently created "specialists" in the enlisted ranks of the American armed forces.

Primary groups are sharply contrasted with secondary groups in the matter of bureaucratic structure. In a family, or in a group of intimate friends or close neighbors, association is based not so much on the members' "offices" as on the personal characteristics of the various members. Association is governed less by a blueprint or "the law" than by mutual interest in one another and mutual gratification because of this interest. If a citizen were to request some service from a bureaucrat, that official would quite appropriately consult a book of regulations telling him whether he could legitimately honor the request. A husband who dealt with his wife's requests by attempting to go by "the book" would probably be seen as violating the spirit of a primary association.

A second dimension of the distinction between formal and informal organization can also be noted. Formally organized groups are those which exist for some specific purpose, and association is closely regulated by the purposes or goals of the group. Every secondary group is an association for the advancement of some interest, although it is not always obvious what that interest may be (as when an apparent candy store is actually a collecting point for gambling bets). Primary groups, on the other hand, are informal in the sense that they are based on no purpose-defining charter, no "we the people, in order to . . ." preamble. The "pledge of allegiance" by which most secondary groups commit their members to loyalty to the special purposes of the group are almost unknown in the primary group realm. Compacts made between lovers or friends, even when "written in blood," are invariably pledges of *personal* loyalty rather than of mutual loyalty to any cause.

Complications. Secondary groups are seldom as completely formal as the foregoing definition would suggest. When we examine bureaucracy with its official blueprint for each office, we invariably find that many things are actually done in a way that departs from "the law" of that organization. Some persons in high official authority actually have little influence on collective decisions while others in lower positions exercise much unofficial influence or *leadership*. Thus, the actual operating line may diverge considerably from the official one.

Individuals may also become "experts" in some areas of organizational activity in ways unanticipated by the official blueprint, so that the formal staff structure is circumvented or supplemented by unofficial channels of technical advice and assistance.[29] A new officeholder in a bureaucracy may find that he must learn much more than is specified in the official job description of his own and other offices in the organization. He must learn the ropes; he must learn the identity of the "Miss Jones" who really "runs things around here." It appears that no bureaucracy adheres to "the book" so strictly that these elements of informality and resistance to legal authority are entirely absent. The holders of offices are more than officeholders, they are persons, and the interplay of personal and impersonal relations in a bureaucracy has been a prime source of sociological interest in this sort of group.[30]

There are several reasons for the typical development of these extralegal elements in bureaucracy. Part of the subversion of formal authority comes from the fact that people who are members of a given bureaucratic organization may have informal associations *outside* the bureaucracy that influence their performance in office.[31] A lower echelon member of a bureaucracy who has a "friend in power" may use his personal influence to gain advantage from that powerful officeholder. Related to this is the effect on an officeholder's performance if he has been *promoted* from an inferior office. Although the rules of his office certainly do not require this behavior, he may see it as his special obligation to "take care of" his former colleagues or of those who have helped him gain the promotion.

Finally, the actual power of an officially inferior member of a bureaucracy may be enhanced by the fact that he enjoys a greater tenure than someone at a higher rank and can use his greater organizational experience to wield unofficial power.[32] An example

---

[29] Peter M. Blau, "Cooperation and Competition in a Bureaucracy," *American Journal of Sociology,* 59(1954):530–535.

[30] For reviews, see Peter M. Blau and W. Richard Scott, *Formal Organizations* (San Francisco: Chandler, 1962), Ch. 4; and Philip Selznick, "Foundations of the Theory of Organization," *American Sociological Review,* 13(1948):25–35.

[31] The extralegal "indulgency pattern" in a factory described by Gouldner was encouraged by the fact that the factory was located in a very small town and workers and managers were well acquainted off the job; managers, therefore, were not inclined to be too strict with workers who were their "friends and neighbors." Alvin W. Gouldner, *Patterns of Industrial Bureaucracy* (Glencoe, Ill.: Free Press, 1954).

[32] David Mechanic, "Sources of Power of Lower Participants in Complex Organizations," *Administrative Science Quarterly,* 7(1962–63):349–364.

is the typical mental hospital, in which such authoritative figures as the medical doctors are likely to be short-term medical trainees serving a required residency in psychiatry, while the low-ranking attendants tend to be old-timers who are well enough acquainted with the local situation to weather out any reforms initiated by authorities who are here today but gone tomorrow. There is a similar situation in many military organizations; the top sergeant of an outfit who is a career soldier may use his greater longevity to attain dominance over the "Lt. Fuzz" who is a junior reserve officer on a short tour of active duty. In many countries, the civil service, protected in their jobs by tenure laws, have been able to subvert the wills of the elected public officials who are technically their superiors.[33]

Another persistent source of tension for formal authority in a bureaucracy is the effect of the *professional* orientation of many of its members. A lawyer who goes to work for a law firm, a psychiatrist for a state hospital, a minister for an army unit may find that his loyalty to the professional standards of his calling are inconsistent with the demands of authoritative people in the bureaucracy. A doctor may be required to release patients before they are "medically" ready, a military chaplain may be expected to propagandize for his country's military operations, a professor in a church-related school may be obligated to support religious values in his teaching, etc.[34] Some professionals—those who have been called "locals"—will resolve this dilemma in favor of loyalty to the employing bureaucracy. Others—the "cosmopolitans"—will resist bureaucratic authority if it is seen as inconsistent with the expectations of professional colleagues.[35] There frequently is conflict between the organizational loyalists and the professionally oriented members of a bureaucracy. Sometimes this takes the form of *staff* people, who tend to be more professionally oriented, chal-

---

[33] Seymour M. Lipset, *Agrarian Socialism* (Berkeley: University of California Press, 1950).

[34] Erwin O. Smigel, *Wall Street Lawyer* (New York: Free Press of Glencoe, 1964); Richard Hall, "Professionalization and Bureaucratization," *American Sociological Review*, 33(1968):92–104; Arlene K. Daniels, "The Captive Professional: Bureaucratic Limitations in the Practice of Military Psychiatry," *Journal of Health and Human Behavior*, 10(1969):255–265.

[35] Merton, *Social Theory and Social Structure*, Ch. 10; Alvin W. Gouldner, "Cosmopolitans and Locals: Toward an Analysis of Latent Social Roles," *Administrative Science Quarterly*, 2(1957):281–306; 2(1958):444–480.

lenging some of the status prerogatives of *line* members, who tend more toward bureaucratic loyalty.[36]

The characterization of a secondary group as a *special-purpose* group is an oversimplified version of actual secondary groups, if it is presumed that secondary group members *always* subordinate their personal goals to the goals of the group. Actually, the problem of securing loyalty to organizational goals is a chronic difficulty of most special-purpose groups. In most groups of this kind, members seem to be less than fully committed to the goals of the group as a whole. *Apathy* and *corruption* are two chronic problems of secondary groups.

Leaders of many groups complain of mass apathy among their members, of a lack of strong commitment among the rank and file.[37] In a complex society a person is typically a member of many secondary groups, and any one of these (e.g., a political club) has the problem of competing effectively with other associations for the person's time, energy, money, and emotional involvement. Providing *incentives* to avoid member apathy is thus a problem generic to secondary groups. These incentives may be in the nature of "bribed cooperation"[38]—the offering of monetary or other material reward for participation (with the understanding that *this* is his full-time job with no moonlighting). Most groups will at least supplement these extrinsic appeals with an appeal to members' sentiments. The goal of the association is represented as a "cause" worthy of devotion apart from the extrinsic rewards. So-called *voluntary associations* depend almost entirely on their ability to induce members to participate for the glory of the cause.

The problem of *corruption* arises from the possibility that individual members of a secondary group may "use" their official positions for their own purposes rather than for those of the group. A policeman may use his power of arrest to extort bribes from law violators in a maneuver which circumvents police responsibility for arresting offenders. The holder of an office may neglect the less dramatic duties of his office to concentrate on those which, if performed with obvious success, will gain him promotion to another

---

[36] Melville Dalton, "Conflicts Between Staff and Line Managerial Officers," *American Sociological Review*, 15(1950):342–351.

[37] Bernard Barber, "Participation and Mass Apathy in Associations," in Alvin W. Gouldner (ed.), *Studies in Leadership* (New York: Harper, 1950), pp. 477–504.

[38] Wilbert E. Moore, *The Conduct of the Corporation* (New York: Random, 1962).

office (the professor neglects his teaching duties to concentrate on the publication or research that will bring him promotion).

The fact that special-purpose groups are made up of men with private goals means that the group goal is always endangered by the corruption of officeholders. Most groups try to avoid such corruption by a system of inspection, often surreptitious. But inspection can fail when the inspectors themselves are implicated in corruption (as is sometimes true of police forces) or when custom within a group forbids close inspection (as is true in teachers' resistance to inspection of their teaching methods under the guise of academic freedom). Many groups depend also on a careful screening of potential members to avoid those who might be corrupt. Another technique is to establish a code of ethics by which individuals will refrain from corruption because it is inconsistent with their professional commitments.

Primary groups are not always, if ever, the purely *informal* groups indicated in the definition. In the first place, there are certain elements of legalism or bureaucracy in most primary groups. To be a member of a primary group—to be a friend or lover or neighbor— is, in some respects, to occupy an "office" with rules of behavior independent of the particular "officeholder." In a given society, it is expected that a "friend" will listen to his friend's troubles, that a "neighbor" will look after one's house while he is on vacation, etc. There are also some bureaucratic elements in the American family. "Laws" do exist, in a sense, which define the "office" of father or mother or child and which tell what the holder of any one of these offices can legitimately expect from other officeholders. But these laws are gross or rudimentary, defining little of the detail of the relations of parents and children and almost totally ignoring certain other relations—the relation of brother and sister or of grandchild and grandparent, for example. There seem to be no legal norms at all governing the obligations of friendship.

The sociologist could hardly safely ignore the special-purpose feature of many primary groups. If primary groups typically do not have *goals* that define their reason for being, they do frequently engage in group *projects*. A family project could include paying off the mortgage, putting a child through college, or nursing a sick member through a long convalescence. Most of the things we have said about the problems of secondary groups in motivating members toward group goals could be said about the ·problems of primary groups in eliciting member loyalty to their projects. The difference between the two kinds of groups is one of intensity and not one of kind. Although a family may fail to complete a project, the failure can be dismissed as less important than the quality of personal relationships achieved because "we at least tried." Secondary groups are evaluated more directly on their productive output, and it is less easy to justify an action which accomplishes nothing except the pleasant "togetherness" of its members. Serious secondary group life is no "picnic."

OTHER FORMAL DISTINCTIONS
In addition to the distinction between primary and secondary groups, some other variations in the formal properties of groups have engaged the attention of sociologists.[39] We shall discuss briefly three such variations here.

Size
Ever since Simmel noted the effect of the "number of members" in determining the nature of association within groups,[40] sociologists have been interested in the sociological consequences of variations in group size. One of the most fundamental variations in the nature of the group occurs, according to Simmel, in the shift from a two-person to a three-person group, from a dyad to a triad. The level of intimacy attainable in a three-person group is much reduced, as expressed in the popular saying, "three's a crowd." Some of the intensity of the dyad is based on the sense of identification it engenders in each member; if one member dies or abandons the dyad, the "group" is broken up. A triad can *survive* the departure of one member by closing ranks and eventually replacing the lost member. Most important, perhaps, is the possibility of subgroup cleavage by the introduction of a third party, since two parties may form an alliance or coalition against the third.[41] The triad is, in short, the smallest size at which many of the distinctively sociological features of *group* association can be seen.

Beyond the dyad-triad distinction, increasing size seems to have predictable sociological consequences, some of which concerned

---

[39] For a long list of "group-properties" which are proposed as worthy of sociological study, see Merton, *Social Theory and Social Structure*, pp. 310–326.

[40] Wolff, *Sociology of Georg Simmel*.

[41] Theodore M. Mills, "The Coalition Pattern in Three Person Groups," *American Sociological Review*, 19(1954):657–667.

Simmel. Beyond a certain size, a group must have a more complicated authority structure, not simply one "boss" with a number of undifferentiated followers. The problem of "span of control" must be faced by every larger group. Although a leader can give orders, he can only insure their execution by the limited number of people under his direct supervision.[42] At this point the *line* structure of a group begins to emerge; the top leader directly controls only a few subleaders, each of whom in turn controls a few members under his command. A large group may accordingly find that its "administrative" structure is greatly elaborated. The "chieftain" of a large family may find that it is impossible to operate a joint enterprise like a family camp-out without some delegation of authority—the "big" children to supervise the "little" ones—or without a great deal of attention to coordinating the various specialized "committees" (wood gathering, clean-up, dish washing, etc.) that may be required.

Modes of Recruitment

Membership in some groups is *ascriptive:* a person is assigned to a family, a military unit, or a school classroom, often without either his advice or consent. Membership in other groups is *achieved:* a person's own effort and volition may determine his membership in a church or a political party. So-called *voluntary* associations seem to have some associational patterns that are influenced by the ability of persons voluntarily to enter or leave them. Such groups must concern themselves rather constantly with their "appeal" to their membership. If an association for the advancement of such-and-such cause finds that the goals of the group no longer interest members, there may be a "goal displacement" process whereby group aims are made more appealing to the membership.[43] Groups which gain their members by essentially involuntary processes—a public school, for example, which is populated by the children who live in an area and must attend that school—may confront some alienation of their members; however, the inability of the members to "leave the scene" if they become dissatisfied with established policy is a factor in moderating concern over the group's appeal to the membership.

---

[42] Moore, *Conduct of the Corporation,* pp. 48–50.

[43] Sheldon L. Messinger, "Organizational Transformation: A Case Study of a Declining Social Movement," *American Sociological Review,* 20(1955):3–10.

Legitimacy

Our discussion earlier of the *normative* character of human association indicated that the formation and maintenance of groups is not a matter of indifference to a wider society. People are expected to join certain groups (marriage, church) and not to join certain other groups (a conspiracy to commit murder or a political party with a "foreign" ideology). Every group is only more or less legitimate from this wider perspective. The more illegitimate the group, the greater will be its "public relations" problems—problems that are generic to human groups but which are exaggerated in certain situations.

The relatively illegitimate kind of group often must provide *security* for itself from hostile regulation emanating from a distaste for its goals among outsiders. A criminal gang must consider the possibility of police suppression; even a relatively "legitimate" business must be concerned about government regulation of its product or its pricing policies.

One common group maneuver in dealing with such external security threats is the device of *co-optation* in which hostile persons are dealt with by including them in the political structure of the group. A university may invite dissident students to join the board of trustees, thereby giving them vested interests in promoting the administration's goals. The Tennessee Valley Authority originated as a program with many utopian goals concerning the reorganization of the overall social life of the Tennessee Valley. But TVA encountered strong local vested interests in the agricultural colleges and the agricultural extension service. This hostility was ultimately dealt with by including more leaders of these opposition groups in the governing structure of the authority.[44]

The dilemma of co-optation as a security strategy was well illustrated in the TVA case. As more of the hostile forces were co-opted into the authority structure, the "organizational character" of the TVA itself began to change: there was a significant accommodation of TVA policies to local vested interests. To save itself organizationally, a relatively illegitimate group may have to "sell its soul."

---

[44] Philip Selznick, *TVA and the Grass Roots* (Berkeley: University of California Press, 1949); for further discussion of co-optation and other "environmental" influences on formal organizational goals, see James D. Thompson and William J. McEwen, "Organizational Goals and Environment: Goal-Setting as an Interaction Process," *American Sociological Review,* 23(1958):23–31.

SUMMARY

Men share with most other animal species the tendency to group or associate with others of their own kind. *Getting together* (association) has a variety of meanings: (1) the sharing of a common fate by a number of people; (2) a joining together to promote some organized activity; (3) a sociable meeting for the mutual enjoyment of the associated persons. Other animals associate with similar motives and with similar consequences, but only human association is symbolic or dependent on the meanings that individuals have for one another, and only man seems to be regulated by any "norms" governing his association.

Although some of sociological analysis is thus interested in human grouping *in general,* much is centered around the attempt to define *types* of groups and to distinguish the patterns of association that are characteristic of each type. The most prominent classification of groups is the distinction between primary and secondary groups. As "pure types," the primary group is based on greater intimacy of members, on their ties to one another through an emotional bond or feeling of "we," and on the informal structure of relations among members, while the secondary group is impersonal, integrated by members' calculations of expediency, and formal or bureaucratic in character. Actually, existing primary groups will display many secondary group features and secondary groups contain primary group elements. Some of the most fundamental problems in the sociological study of groups involve the difficulties of primary and secondary groups in maintaining their "purity" of type in a real world of persistent mixtures of the personal and the impersonal.

Groups are also distinguished by such formal properties as size, mode of recruitment (voluntary or involuntary), and the degree of their legitimacy or moral acceptance by the wider society. Since these are *form* rather than *content* distinctions, the characteristics and problems of a type of group will be common to all such groups even though they have disparate substantive features. A sect of exceptionally pious religious zealots and a gang of pickpockets may both be classified as "illegitimate" or outcast groups and will have similar characteristics and problems of security in dealing with a hostile outside world. However much the layman may wish to contrast these groups because of their diverse contents, the sociologist has a habit of making generalizations about categories that make strange bedfellows in the world of groups.

Social Interaction

Although human association occurs in *groups* of various sizes, most social behavior is ultimately reducible to the interplay of behaviors of two social actors. Although the captain who gives the private his marching orders may represent a vast bureaucracy (the army), the command and the obedience or resistance to it is, in the last analysis, an *interpersonal* event between two people. It is this most microscopic level of analysis, namely, the phenomenon of *social interaction,* that shall concern us in this chapter.

FORMS OF SOCIAL INTERACTION

A study of the *forms* of social interaction is a study of the various ways in which the behavior of one person can influence the behavior of others. There are two fundamental forms, with many variations on each and many borderline situations. If each behaving person is seen as striving toward the satisfaction of certain personal goals, other persons' behavior may be seen as furthering or as hindering the accomplishment of these goals. Thus, social interaction may take various forms of cooperation or of opposition.

Cooperation

There are two dimensions of cooperation in interaction which we shall examine, a consummatory dimension and an instrumental dimension.[1]

---

[1] We saw in chapter 5 that the instrumental-consummatory distinction was part of the background for the definition of functional imperatives of social systems; we might suggest now that social systems as well as individuals require these two kinds of cooperative behavior.

Consummatory. Sometimes the cooperation of another person is required to provide a gratifying response to oneself. Human beings seem to require the approving responses of others to themselves or, at least, a social recognition of their existence. As William James says:

> No more fiendish punishment could be devised, were such a thing physically possible, than that one should be turned loose in society and remain absolutely unnoticed by all the members thereof. If no one turned around when we entered, answered when we spoke, or minded what we did, but if every person we met "cut us dead," and acted as if we were non-existing things, a kind of rage and impotent despair would ere long well up in us, from which the cruellest bodily tortures would be a relief.[2]

Such an interaction situation is by no means impossible; it seems to be approached rather closely in the well-advertised anonymity of life in large cities in which, it is often said, it is almost impossible to elicit the notice of people in public places who are busy with their own affairs.[3] Although some people find such an atmosphere personally liberating, others undoubtedly react with "rage and impotent despair" to being consistently ignored by others.[4]

A great many of our social interactions involve the attempt to elicit the notice of others. The behavior of a young man going through the ritual of courtship is a social behavior of this nature. So is the cry of the child for bottle or mother, and so is the agony of the professor attempting to write a book that will receive good reviews from his professional colleagues.

Instrumental. Sometimes the cooperation of other persons is needed to help the person to attain goals that require the concerted effort of a number of people. Goffman has written of the importance of "teams" of persons cooperating to help one another sustain certain impressions before "audiences."[5] A group of actors on a stage must have this kind of teamwork; likewise, a husband and

---

[2] William James, *The Principles of Psychology*, Vol. 1 (New York: Henry Holt, 1890), pp. 293, 294.

[3] Georg Simmel, "The Metropolis and Mental Life," in Kurt Wolff (ed.), *The Sociology of Georg Simmel* (Glencoe, Ill.: Free Press, 1950).

[4] Ralph Ellison's novel, *The Invisible Man* (New York: Random, 1952) develops this theme, with a racial twist.

[5] Erving Goffman, *The Presentation of Self in Everyday Life* (Garden City, N.Y.: Doubleday, 1959).

wife have to operate as a team to keep their signals straight if they are to give a show of solidarity before such audiences as their children, their friends, and their relatives. This kind of teamwork in "impression management" is, of course, only one special case of a larger class of interactions: all those in which some sort of collective action is accomplished by a division of labor or by the advantages of strength in numbers. Cooperation assumes that individual persons have certain mutual interests that bring them together to accomplish what they could not accomplish as individuals.

Opposition

Social interaction does not always proceed on the basis of mutuality of interest of the participants. There are real differences of interest between persons, and the hostile interaction of two suitors for the same girl is as real and as social as the polite interaction at a social gathering. Politicians organize political campaigns and football teams devise game strategies on the assumption that interaction will involve those who can hinder as well as those who can advance the personal goals of a social actor.

These anticipations of opposition by others lead to the forms of interaction called competition and conflict. In *competition,* the opponents follow a common set of rules which define fair and unfair means of opposition. Thus, in an athletic contest, it is "no fair" to slug; in "ethical" business, it is "no fair" to cut prices below a certain level. In *conflict,* this agreement on rules governing opposition is not present. We say that "all's fair in love and war," although the statement about sexual competition is basically false, and there may even be some rudimentary international standards of "decency" in warfare. Nevertheless, there are areas of social life in which interaction is of the relatively amoral or cutthroat variety.

In the area of business practice under capitalist conditions, there have been two major theories. In Karl Marx's view, economic relations have always involved amoral class struggle and the domination of one class by another.[6] Only with the proletarian revolution and the coming of the classless society would amoral conflict be converted to peaceful competition. Sociologists who are more favorably inclined to capitalism have argued that the anomie (normlessness) that prevails in much of business practice is a result of the newness of large-scale industry and the slowness of standards

---

[6] See *The Communist Manifesto* by Karl Marx and Friedrich Engels.

of decent business behavior to emerge. The argument is that the need for standards of peaceful competition will tend to bring these standards into existence.[7]

Accommodation

The form of interaction called accommodation is a peculiar mixture of the elements of cooperation and opposition. Accommodation has been called "antagonistic cooperation,"[8] meaning that one actor may help another in spite of his hostile feelings toward that other. The uneasy peace that occurs between persons or groups when neither side is willing to carry on the conflict is a good example of accommodation. Wars seldom end with the unconditional surrender of one side and the victory of the other.[9] Rather, persons or groups sometimes prefer the compromises of peace to the heroic exertions of war: "better Red than dead." In the contemporary cold war between East and West or between the Soviet Union and China, the antagonism on both sides is kept from turning hot by a mutual fear of the consequences of the other's military power.

A recent study seems to suggest that much of the interaction between persons can be understood as a subtle form of accommodation.[10] Goffman maintains that interacting persons are somewhat like stage actors in that they are concerned with creating impressions upon audiences. The act is tailored to what the actor imagines will look good to his audience. But audiences are aware of this tendency of persons to play a role, and they often try to look behind the façade of self-presentation to discover the "real" character behind the mask. Otherwise, audiences can be duped to their own harm by actors, such as con men, who assume the pose of respectability to defraud the unwary.

There is always an element of potential conflict, then, between the actor who would like to be impressive and the audience which would like "the truth." Since actors so often create an image of themselves that "the truth" will not sustain, there is always the

---

[7] Charles H. Cooley, *Social Process* (New York: Scribner's, 1918); Emile Durkheim, *On the Division of Labor in Society,* trans. by George Simpson (New York: Macmillan, 1933).

[8] William Graham Sumner, *Folkways* (Boston: Ginn, 1906), Ch. 1.

[9] Georg Simmel, *Conflict,* trans. by Kurt Wolff (Glencoe, Ill.: Free Press, 1955).

[10] Goffman, *Presentation of Self.*

danger to the actor that the audience will gain information that will discredit his performance. Much of Goffman's book is a discussion of how an actor plays the "information game," giving audiences information he wants them to have and concealing discreditable information.

In spite of this potential conflict between actors and audiences, instances of actors being discredited seem rather rare. Social life is so organized that, by and large, people go along with the impressions we try to foster. When one person tells another of one of his exploits, the listener will, in all politeness, accept the story without outwardly challenging it.[11] If a person claims some response from others (respect or trust) to which he is not entitled and if he gets caught in the falsehood, he loses "face," which is one of the most dire things that can happen to one in social interaction in any society, not just in the Oriental.

Perhaps some realization of this by social actors lies behind what Goffman calls the "working consensus" in interaction. This is an implicit bargain among social actors that each will not embarrass the other but will go along with responses that are fundamental to each actor.[12] Such an interaction situation would fit the perceptions of many observers that there is much hypocrisy or expedience in social behavior and that good manners often require the soft-pedalling of one's ideal conceptions of what behavior ought to be. The concept of social interaction as embodying the form of accommodation seems to cover much of what we call polite behavior.

SOCIAL RELATIONSHIPS

Each personal act of mutual influence can be classified as cooperative, competitive, conflicting, or accommodative, or as some other form of interaction. However, the orderliness of social life depends on the important fact that these individual acts tend to occur repetitively. If person A treats person B with respect on one occasion, there is a high probability that this behavior will be repeated whenever A and B have occasion to interact. A *social relationship* exists when there is a pattern of repeated interaction

---

[11] Part of the oppressiveness of "total institutions" such as prisons and mental hospitals is that they typically do not allow this courtesy to the inmates. Erving Goffman, *Asylums* (Garden City, N.Y.: Doubleday, 1961).

[12] Goffman, *Presentation of Self,* p. 11.

between two or more persons or groups; or, as Weber puts it, when there is a high "probability" of a given kind of interaction.[13] A *love* relationship, for example, is defined by many individual interactions involving the mutual devotion of two persons. A relationship of *enemies* is defined by repeated acts of conflict.

From the viewpoint of the interacting persons, a relationship exists when each party can accurately predict what kind of act is likely to be forthcoming from each other person. A husband knows, for example, that if he makes certain praising comments to his wife, she will respond in certain predictable ways. Without this ability to predict the responses of those with whom we interact, we should find ourselves in the sort of psychologically intolerable situation depicted in a Franz Kafka novel.

This knowledge on which predictable interaction is based has its origin in social processes; the individual must learn what to expect from the others with whom he interacts. The question is, How does this knowledge develop? The answer seems to depend on whether the relationship in question is a *personal* relationship or a *status* relationship.[14]

Personal Relationships

Much of our knowledge of other persons is based on our past experience with those particular persons. Through prolonged acquaintance with a woman, a man learns "her ins, her outs, her ups, her downs." The process of becoming acquainted is a process in which each party develops an increasing ability to predict the other's response to a wide range of situations. Interaction between strangers must be especially guarded because one can never be sure, for example, whether a particular comment will offend the stranger. (One might notice the rather guarded and ambiguous remarks of people at a party who, under the "sociability" impulse, must talk with others with whom they are not well acquainted.) Becoming acquainted seems to be a rather delicate operation in which each party makes "guarded disclosures"[15] designed to give

---

[13] Max Weber, *The Theory of Social and Economic Organization,* trans. by A. M. Henderson and Talcott Parsons (New York: Oxford University Press, 1947), p. 118.

[14] In light of the discussion of groups in the previous chapter, this distinction might also be called the difference between *primary* and *secondary* relationships.

[15] Goffman, *Presentation of Self,* p. 192.

the other party hints about what actions will probably bring about favorable reactions.

A major problem for sociological study of personal relationships is the problem of who becomes acquainted with whom. Among the conditions which encourage acquaintance are the factors of propinquity and social equality. Innumerable studies have shown the importance of *propinquity:* the fact that intimate association (friendship, marriage, etc.) tends to follow the lines of least geographic resistance, lines defined by physical closeness.[16] *Equality* is a factor because mutual exchange of information seems to be especially difficult between persons of unequal social standing. As we shall see in chapter 11, a great many kinds of association tend to be restricted to social equals.

Status Relationships

The social order which results from the ability of persons to predict the actions of one another does not depend entirely on personal acquaintance. One can often initiate some line of interaction with a total stranger and be quite confident of the stranger's reaction, provided he knows the *status* of the person. A person's status refers to his membership in a social category: young or old, male or female, doctor or patient, etc., and is *not* limited, as in popular usage, to the "high" or "low" prestige position of the person.

Status relationships involve predictability in interaction arising not from personal acquaintance but from acquaintance with the typical behavior of individuals in a particular status or category. A person gets on a bus, pays his fare, and then confidently expects that his driver will deliver him to the destination announced on the front of the bus. Personal acquaintance with the driver is entirely unnecessary to secure this confidence. It is sufficient for passenger and driver to know that the person with whom he is dealing is a person of a certain category, that drivers *generally* drive to announced destinations, and that passengers *generally* put bona fide money into a token box and quietly take a seat. Of course, there may be "mad" drivers who steal busses and drive them over cliffs and "mad" passengers who are aboard for the purpose of com-

---

16 For a review of earlier propinquity studies with reference to marriage and a report of a study in Oslo, see Natalie R. Ramsoy, "Assortative Mating and the Structure of Cities," *American Sociological Review,* 31(1966):773–786.

mitting a murder. But by and large, persons of the respective categories *don't* act like that, and only an extremely paranoid person would worry much about the possible exceptions. We can, as Thomas has said, carry on social life on the mere "inference" of the behavior of others:

We live by inference. I am, let us say, your guest. You do not know, you cannot determine scientifically, that I will not steal your money or your spoons. But inferentially I will not, and inferentially you have me as your guest.[17]

In thinking of these categorical expectations that people have of one another, we are in the presence of some fundamental sociological concepts, and careful distinctions must be made. The term *expectations* is ambiguous, sometimes meaning an individual's prediction of what will happen (I expect it will rain tomorrow) and sometimes meaning the individual's idea of what ought to happen (I expect you to be here at five o'clock—or else). Our ability to anticipate the actions of people as members of categories depends on our acquaintance with both kinds of expectations, which we shall call existential expectations or *stereotypes* and normative expectations or *roles.*

Stereotypes. A stereotype is an idea about how people in a category usually behave. "Negroes are like that," "boys will be boys," "that's what little girls are made of," "what can you expect from a mere child?"—all of these represent stereotyped judgments about the nature of people in a category. People who think of themselves as liberals may deny that they react to others in terms of stereotypes, but the sociologist will be skeptical of the denial. By operating with stereotypes about how people in a particular category generally will act, we spare ourselves the impossible task of getting personal knowledge about each person with whom we interact. For a great many purposes of interaction, the idiosyncracies of personality can well be ignored.

Roles. People who are members of a given category or status— father, minister, bus driver, American—behave by and large in predictable ways partly because there are social norms that define appropriate behavior for persons in that status. A role is a set of

---

[17] W. I. Thomas, cited in Goffman, *Presentation of Self*, p. 3.

norms attached to a status.[18] Anyone can predict the behavior of persons in a category provided, of course, that he is familiar with the role or set of norms governing that status, and further provided that the person is conforming to those normative expectations.

In chapters 13 and 14 we shall discuss some of the sociological explanations of conformity and nonconformity to social norms. Anticipating that discussion, we can say that persons conform to norms governing their status categories because there are social sanctions (punishments) to deal with nonconformity (an improperly behaving bus driver may lose his job) and because persons become identified with their statuses and conform to role expectations by the operation of their own consciences. To fail to perform the role expectations of a father may subject the deviator to a range of social censures as well as to a guilty sense of his own failure.

DISORDER IN SOCIAL RELATIONSHIPS

Any participant in social interaction knows that relationships do not always run smoothly and according to the expected pattern. The "misunderstanding" and the disagreement about appropriate role behavior are common features of social life, and they are of as much interest to the sociologist as are the more orderly kinds of interaction.

Disorders in Personal Relationships

When people form intimate relationships or become personally estranged, the process is not likely to be wholly anticipated by the interacting individuals. Many relationships are formed by people becoming involved in ways contrary to the intention or understanding of those undergoing these involvements. When a more intimate relation *is* willed, events may occur to frustrate this will; the road to romance is proverbially rocky. Estrangement may also occur by rather incomprehensible processes. The sociologist can, perhaps, make two kinds of contribution to the understanding of these processes.

First, he can try to point out some of the origins of involvement and disinvolvement in the social influences affecting the involved

---

[18] The terms *role* and *status* have, unfortunately, almost as many definitions as there are definers. This one works well for many sociologists because it allows one to think of general problems of conformity and nonconformity to social norms as these relate to people located in different social positions.

persons. He can, for example, show how, once a couple makes a tentative commitment to a closer or more distant relationship (toward, for example, marriage or divorce), other people begin to treat the couple in a way that makes it difficult to retreat from these commitments.[19]

Second, he can try to describe some of the consequences of these uncertain situations for other aspects of social behavior. For example, the themes of popular songs have been analyzed to show how the love song evolves as a device to alleviate the stresses associated with the uncertainty of courtship interactions between men and women.[20]

Another source of disorder in personal relationships is the difficulty persons have communicating to one another precisely what are their mutual expectations. Social psychologists have described a kind of communication disorder in some families as a pattern of "pseudo-mutuality."[21] In this pattern, all members of the family communicate a high degree of personal liking for one another, and the family as a whole maintains a strong front of solidarity. Elements of personal hostility are present but are not permitted to be expressed. There appears to be a relationship between this kind of communication disorder in family life and the incidence of the psychosis of schizophrenia, a functional mental disorder in which confused thought processes are prominent.

Disorders in Status Relationships

We have emphasized the importance to social order of the fact that people can interact with one another on the basis of categorical expectations. But orderliness in social relations will not be the outcome of status interactions if there is significant disagreement among people about the appropriate expectations for people in different categories. What are the expectations of a woman? a congressman? the personal secretary of a political leader? On

---

[19] See Waller's discussion of courtship as a "summatory process" in which the reactions of others to the courting pair tend to maintain the relationship. Willard Waller and Reuben Hill, *The Family: a Dynamic Interpretation,* rev. ed. (New York: Dryden, 1951), Ch. 10.

[20] Donald Horton, "The Dialogue of Courtship in Popular Songs," *American Journal of Sociology,* 62(1957):569–578; James T. Carey, "Changing Courtship Patterns in the Popular Song," *American Journal of Sociology,* 74(1969):720–731.

[21] Lyman C. Wynne et al., "Pseudo-Mutuality in the Family Relations of Schizophrenics," *Psychiatry,* 21(1958):205–220.

these matters there may be many disagreements and many ambiguities. The stereotypes or the roles which apply to an individual may be inconsistent or conflicting. Much attention has been given in sociology to the phenomenon of role conflict, and the same considerations could presumably apply to the problem of stereotype conflict.

The term *role conflict* has come to be used in two somewhat different ways. First, a person experiences role conflict when he finds himself simultaneously occupying two or more statuses, with conflicting norms attached to the various statuses. It is typical in complex societies for the same man to occupy both a familial status (father) and an occupational status (employee). Role conflict is experienced when a person must decide whether to interact on the basis of one or the other of these statuses. A man, for example, who hires workers for a company may have to decide whether to follow the occupational norms which require that he hire the best available worker or the familial norms which require that he look after his son, perhaps to the extent of hiring his son in preference to more qualified applicants. In his conformity to the role expectations of either status he will violate the expectations of the other status. Company rules against nepotism are aimed at avoiding deviance in the familial direction.

A related form of role conflict may arise from the phenomenon of *status succession,* which is the passage of a person from one status to another. Where the roles involved with the successive statuses are conflicting, and where there is a period of uncertain transition between the statuses, serious role conflict may result. For example, there are fairly clear-cut norms which define the appropriate behavior of children and of adults, but there seems to be confusion about the status of the adolescent. He is liable to disappoint the expectations of some persons if he fails to "act his age" and of others if he is too "pushy" or "precocious."

The uncertainty in interaction introduced by status succession is a probable reason for the prevalence in most societies of *rites of passage* for leaving childhood and entering adulthood. In American society there seems to be a notable absence of "puberty rites." Is a boy a man when he is old enough to drive a car? to vote? to fight? We can note more definite rites of passage from bachelorhood to marriage (the wedding), from life to death (the funeral), and from the status of student to that of graduate (the commencement). These ceremonial recognitions of status change tend to ease the tension of role conflict in situations of status succession.

Perhaps we should note here that it may be not so much the actual process of status succession as the *anticipation* of such status changes that introduces problems of role conflict. A person may persistently violate the expectations of others for people of his category if he orients his behavior toward a group to which he aspires to belong. The enlisted man who hopes to become an officer, the teacher who hopes to become a principal—these individuals may, through "anticipatory socialization,"[22] behave in ways that are defined as deviant by their less ambitious colleagues who disapprove of this kind of bucking for promotion.

A person who has recently succeeded to a higher status position also may face a role conflict based on the expectation of his former colleagues that they now have a friend in power who will look after their interests. If the person's behavior is influenced by what might be called "residual socialization"—a continued orientation toward the norms of a group to which the person formerly belonged—he may fulfill these expectations but, in the process, violate the expectations of his new colleagues.

As so far discussed, role conflict involves the same person occupying different statuses either simultaneously or consecutively. But the term role conflict has another meaning which involves conflict within a *single status.* A status occupant—for example, a school-teacher or a policeman—may find that different people demand that he play his role in different ways. The behavior that satisfies the teacher's students may violate the expectations of parents or school supervisors. Consensus or agreement among these various "criterion groups"[23] can never be assumed. Where dissensus prevails, the person may experience as much role conflict in a single status as he would experience as a simultaneous or consecutive occupant of different statuses.

Role conflict of both types is a prominent feature of interaction in all but the most simple and least changing societies. A number of sociologists have shown that the individual, when faced with a

---

[22] Robert K. Merton, *Social Theory and Social Structure,* rev. ed. (Glencoe, Ill.: Free Press, 1956), pp. 265–268.

[23] Melvin Seeman, "Role Conflict and Ambivalence in Leadership," *American Sociological Review,* 18(1953):373–380.

"damned if I do and damned if I don't" interaction situation, learns to adopt maneuvers or mechanisms for resolving these conflicts.[24] He might, for example, evade the expectations of a person by pointing out the consequences to himself of acting in accord with these expectations: "I would love to give you a discount on this merchandise since you are such a good customer, but the boss forbids it and would give me hell." Since these maneuvers are not always completely successful, a great deal of unpredictability in the behavior of persons in different categories still exists, a fact which probably adds color and interest to social life and provides additional employment for the sociologist.

SUMMARY

The interaction of people with one another may take various forms of cooperation or opposition. When opposition occurs, it may be peaceful and normatively regulated competition or it may be a violent free-for-all. Much human behavior, however, involves a delicate compromise or accommodation between outright hostility and genuine cooperation. One of the most pervasive tendencies of people in their dealings with others is their willingness to tolerate and to try to get along with them.

Social relationships are formed when people develop predictable and recurrent patterns of interaction among themselves. Some of this predictability is based on personal knowledge and the rather painful process of getting acquainted, but a great deal of it is based on the fact that people hold certain normative expectations about how people in different categories should behave and predictive expectations about how they generally do behave. Conformity to these role and stereotype expectations is one source of predictability in social interaction.

This conformity does not always exist, however. For one thing, there is often a degree of uncertainty or confusion about the personal or status expectations that people have. For another, the expectations applied to a person occupying one status may conflict with the expectations applied to the same person when occupying another status or in one that he has just left or antici-

---

[24] For a discussion of role-conflict resolutions as well as a review of role-conflict literature, see Neal Gross, W. S. Mason, and A. W. McEachern, *Explorations in Role Analysis* (New York: Wiley, 1958).

pates entering. Even within one status, the role expectations may be conflicting; it is literally impossible, for example, for an author to write a textbook that will please everybody, since there is a lack of consensus on just what subject matter should be covered and how.

INSTITUTIONS

PART FOUR

Throughout the discussion in part three, we referred to the social arrangements that influence human behavior. Nowhere is this social constraint on behavior better seen than in the study of institutions. Writers have commented, sometimes with much pathos, on the discrepancy between behavior based on primary human impulses and behavior demanded when human endeavor is organized at the level of institutions.[1] A man may have, by personal temperament, certain predispositions of religious expression or some strong preference for ways of making his living. He may find, however, that there are no organized religious institutions which support and encourage his religious beliefs, no economic institutions which will accommodate his attitude toward work. To associate with others at all religiously or economically, he may have to join a church whose tenets he does not fully accept and take an unsatisfying job in order to feed himself.

The relationship between individual impulse and institutional form does not always work out this way, of course. What usually happens is that people adapt their impulses to the nature of the existing institutions; as is sometimes said, they make a "virtue out of necessity." Erich Fromm argues, for example, that capitalism has created a kind of "market mentality" among people in capitalist countries, making them amenable to the continual monetary calculations that a capitalist economic institution requires. Perhaps

---

[1] Charles H. Cooley, *Social Organization* (New York: Scribner's, 1909).

every society tends to develop a "social character" to match its institutional forms.[2]

Whatever the relation between institutions and human behavior, we are certainly dealing with fundamental kinds of sociological facts when we attempt to describe and explain institutions. In the following three chapters we examine three basic human institutions: family, religion, and government. Except for space limitations, we might similarly treat such other institutions as the economic institution, education, recreation, science, medical practice. Two major sociological perspectives on the study of institutions will be incorporated in our approach—systems analysis and differential participation.

Social systems or functional-structural analysis. Following Spencer's view of society as an "organism," institutions may be seen as the "organs" or *functional* parts of a society. The problem, then, is to develop a kind of "physiology" of society which will indicate the functions or social-system contributions of each institution. In looking at the functions that have been ascribed to institutions, we shall try to remain sensitive to the problems raised by Merton (see chapter 5), especially the possibilities of "functional alternatives" and "latent functions" in the area of institutions.

A special sociological problem in the study of institutions is the process of *institutionalization* by which institutional functions come to be relegated to specific agencies charged with the performance of those functions. Historically, there was education before there were schools, religion before there were churches, government before there was the state. The sociologist is interested in the social conditions that have led to the emergence of such specialized agencies as schools, churches, factories, recreational associations, etc.

The *structural* side of this analysis will concern itself with some of the many *forms* that a given institution takes in different societies. We shall notice the tendency in the studies of each institution to develop typologies of some of the basic alternative forms of the institution. A major problem in the study of institutions arises when this variation in institutional forms is treated as a dependent variable and questions are raised about the independent variables that determine these variations. For example, under what conditions

---

[2] Erich Fromm, *The Sane Society* (New York: Holt, Rinehart & Winston, 1955).

does one find a democratic rather than an authoritarian form of political institution, a socialist rather than a capitalist form of economy, etc.?

Differential participation in institutional activities. Although we have suggested that institutional forms tend to channel and limit individual behavior, it is obvious that not all persons are equally susceptible to having their behaviors determined by the institutional forms. There are deviating individuals in all societies who attempt to substitute illegitimate forms of behavior for the institutionally sanctioned ones, and apathetic persons everywhere who do not involve themselves to the degree that is institutionally demanded. There are, in other words, individual differences in quantity and quality of *participation* in each of the institutions.

A psychologist would undoubtedly approach the explanation of this participation variability in *personality* terms, treating the participation as one manifestation of general personal tendencies. The sociologist's approach, as we suggested in chapter 1, is quite different. He tends to interest himself in questions dealing with the categories of people who participate at different rates in the social institutions: Why do more women than men go to church? Why do poor people have larger families than rich ones?

With each institution that we examine, we shall consider a few of the many findings of sociological research with reference to the question of what kinds of people participate in what manner and with what degree of intensity in the activities involved in that institution.

The Family

The family is a socially regulated system of cohabitation of men and women, together with the offspring of this cohabitation. The institution of the family is found in all societies.

FUNCTIONS OF THE FAMILY
The family involves a combination of *sexual* and *parental* activities and is society's institution for the regularization of these activities. No society leaves sexual intercourse or the care of children to the spontaneous tendencies of human nature. Although there may be instincts related to these activities, they are not specific enough to guarantee the kind of behavior in these areas that tends to be expected socially.

Sexual Functions
The universality of *marriage,* the sexual aspect of the family, appears to correspond to the biological nature of human beings, although it is not necessary to postulate a mating instinct in order to account for human marriage. The human sexual makeup is such that an orderly system for the regulation of sexual intercourse seems to be a necessity for societal survival.

There is no reason to suppose that the sex impulse is stronger in man than in other animals, but the impulse is a more constant element in human psychology. The alternation of periods of sexual heat and sexual indifference is found in only very attenuated form in man, who has no mating season. The temporary alliances of male and female that one finds in much of the animal world would not suffice for man. Add to this biological reality the fact that opposition for sexual partners can be as hostile among humans as among other animals. Since human society is based on a delicate system of cooperation, a means of precisely regulating sexual relations—giving specific persons legitimate sexual access to specific other persons and strictly denying disapproved kinds of access—would seem a workable solution to the problem of social conflict that potentially exists because of the sexual nature of man. A functional explanation of the universal social regulation of sexual relations tends to follow some such line of argument.

Parental Functions

Reproduction. The first function of the family with reference to children is the simple fact of bringing them into existence, the *reproduction* function. The necessity for biological reproduction for the survival of a society is obvious; what is not so obvious is the societal tendency to expect that children will be born to people who have established the permanent sexual relationship called marriage.

In his "principle of legitimacy," Malinowski articulated what he considered a universal sociological law to the effect that "no child should be brought into the world without a man—and one man at that—assuming the role of sociological father, that is, guardian and protector, the male link between the child and the rest of the community."[1] While Malinowski's "principle" may represent a universal norm, it does not necessarily represent a universal practice; witness the very high rates of illegitimacy in some societies—certain Caribbean societies, for example.[2] This may suggest the weakness in some situations of the norm which restricts reproduction to married people. It has been shown, for example, that the mother of an illegitimate child in the lower social classes is not especially likely to experience social "isolation" as a result of bearing a child out of wedlock.[3]

Further analysis of situations of apparent tolerance for illegiti-

---

[1] Bronislaw Malinowski, "Parenthood—the Basis of Social Structure," in V. F. Calverton and S. D. Schmalhausen (eds.), *The New Generation* (New York: Macaulay, 1930), pp. 129–143.

[2] T. S. Simey, *Welfare and Planning in the West Indies* (Oxford, England: Clarendon, 1956).

[3] Leo G. Reeder and Sharon J. Reeder, "Social Isolation and Illegitimacy," *Journal of Marriage and the Family*, 31(1969):451–461.

macy may, however, show that unwed mothers and illegitimate children suffer many social handicaps. In the case of the Caribbean societies, there is a social condemnation of illegitimacy, and the high rates of illegitimacy seem to be a reflection of the weak bargaining position of many women who cannot demand marriage as the price for sexual privilege.[4] Even in societies in which illegitimacy is common, it is usually widely condemned.

It appears that, given the many ways in which a society depends on the family to perform functions with reference to children, a sociological father as well as a mother is a sociological necessity.[5] No dependence on a "paternal instinct" could suffice to insure the provision of a stable relation between fathers and their biological children.

Maintenance. Families also have a maintenance function with reference to children. The extreme physical helplessness of the human infant, as compared with the relative self-sufficiency of the young of most other animal species, requires that children live with adults who will feed them and supply their other physical necessities. There is, of course, a great deal of cultural variation in the duration of the period of "helplessness" and economic dependency of children. In some societies children marry, go to work, and are otherwise on their own at relatively young ages. In other societies, children delay work or marriage until they complete their education; even after marriage they may depend on the help of their parents in getting started financially.[6] Regardless of cultural variation, there is a biological limit to the definition of children as self-sufficient beings. To the chagrin of some parents, no child has yet been born with a built-in self-feeding or self-diapering mechanism.

With respect to child maintenance, there have been occasional social experiments in constituting some other agency as a functional alternative to the family.[7] In the Israeli kibbutz, the desire to

---

4 William J. Goode, "Illegitimacy in the Caribbean Social Structure," *American Sociological Review*, 25(1960):21–30.

5 Kingsley Davis, *Human Society* (New York: Macmillan, 1949).

6 Marvin B. Sussman, "The Help Pattern in the Middle-Class Family," *American Sociological Review*, 18(1953):22–28.

7 Gillian Lindt Gollin, "Family Surrogates in Colonial America: the Moravian Experiment," *Journal of Marriage and the Family*, 31(1969):650–658.

free women from child-care drudgeries so they can engage in productive communal labor has led to the establishment of communal nurseries that take over most of these maintenance chores.[8] However, the tensions created by this system demonstrate some of the difficulty of establishing a functional alternative in the maintenance area.[9] A less extreme alternative is the day nursery or day-care center found in many societies which makes it easier for mothers of even very young children to work outside the home.

Aside from such purely physical aspects of child care, the family seems to provide the kind of *affection* or emotional response without which the integrity of individual psychology is threatened. The need for affection undoubtedly varies between individuals and is influenced by social conditioning; however, it appears that a certain level of emotional response is necessary to the very life of the infant. The high infant mortality rates (and rates of psychological disturbance) of infants who are raised in institutions cannot, apparently, be explained by any lack of strictly physical care of these children but seems to be related to the inability of hospital or institutional personnel to provide the kind of cuddling and warm emotional response that babies appear to require.[10]

Some kinds of emotional response within the family may, however, become dysfunctional to the individual's psychological integrity. The overprotection of children has frequently been seen as a source of psychological difficulties. Green attempted to show that "neurotic" behavior patterns of middle-class boys are related to a pattern of "absorption" of the boys' personalities by their parents, who have ambivalent attitudes toward their sons but profess a great love for them. Some other children—the children of some Polish-Americans, for example—are treated by their parents with harshness and with little evidence of sensitivity to the children's emotional needs; but because the parents do not absorb their

---

[8] Melvin E. Spiro, *Children of the Kibbutz* (Cambridge: Harvard University Press, 1958).

[9] Joseph Shepher, "Familism and Social Structure: the Case of the Kibbutz," *Journal of Marriage and the Family*, 31(1969):567–573.

[10] Rene Spitz, "Hospitalism," in R. S. Eissler et al. (eds.), *The Psychoanalytic Study of the Child*, Vol. 1 (New York: International Universities Press, 1945), pp. 53–74. The instinctive need for "tactile" stimulation was shown in the experiments with infant apes reported in Harry F. Harlow and Margaret F. Harlow, "A Study of Animal Affection," *Natural History*, 70(1961):48–55.

children's personalities, the children avoid neuroses by a rather complete emotional rejection of their parents.[11]

Socialization. A major requirement of every society is that its young learn to conform to the basic elements of its culture. The family, which has access to the child during his impressionable early years, is perhaps the natural agency for the socialization of children in basic beliefs, ideals, and preferences.

The socialization function is another area in which there are frequent attempts to establish functional alternatives to the family. A revolutionary political regime is likely to feel that parents are too reactionary in their moral and social views to be trusted with the task of creating the "new man" required by the revolution. Accordingly, schools for the indoctrination of the young are established in Communist and other totalitarian societies.

In the Soviet Union, according to some evidence, the Communist regime has carried on a long-term struggle with the family for the hearts and minds of Russian children. The family seems to lose the struggle in most cases, either because the regime punishes political deviation severely and parents are afraid the children will reveal their anti-Communist views, or because parents recognize their own lack of contact with the newer social trends and acquiesce in the view that they are unfit to educate their children for the Communist society in which it is assumed the children will live.[12] Similar resigned attitudes may occur wherever there is an especially severe generation gap. Immigrants from a foreign country may realize that their children cannot grow up in the "old country" ways of the parents and may gladly (or grudgingly) allow the public school teacher and other "natives" to take over the burden of socialization of their children.

Social control. Socialization does not, of course, occur overnight and, during the period of his moral immaturity, the child's behavior

---

[11] Arnold W. Green, "The Middle Class Male Child and Neurosis," *American Sociological Review*, 11(1946):31–41. The more positive side of this class difference in family relations is the finding that middle-class children have more "favorable attitudes" toward their fathers than do lower-class children. Thomas E. Smith, "Social Class and Attitudes Toward Fathers," *Sociology and Social Research*, 53(1969):217–226.

[12] H. Kent Geiger, "Changing Political Attitudes in a Totalitarian Society: A Case Study of the Role of the Family," *World Politics*, 8(1956):187–205.

is likely to be a threat to social order in some ways: he may destroy property, disturb the peace, "innocently" insult handicapped people,[13] etc. Accordingly, there is a pervasive need for the social control of children. Wherever children appear in public places there are likely to be one or more adults along to make sure that the children behave themselves. Because of its frequent physical contact and close emotional relation with the child, the family is in a good strategic position to exercise discipline over his behavior, and the family accordingly tends to be a prime agent of social control.[14]

Status ascription. A less obvious parental function relates to the family's role in the process of status ascription. As noted in chapter 7, a society gains in harmony and orderliness to the extent that each person in that society can be assigned a definite place or status in the social structure. Babies are a problem in this respect, since their "place" cannot be determined by any of their own performances. It is highly convenient for persons who interact with children to know "whose little boy are you?" and to ascribe to the child the status of the parents. While the permanence of these ascriptions is a variable, it seems to be universally true that the status of a child's parents will influence in some degree his own status.

INSTITUTIONALIZATION OF FAMILY FUNCTIONS
The institution of the family in Western society furnishes a good example of the process of institutionalization. In this case, there has been a trend toward the emergence of special agencies to perform functions that were once performed within the family. Schools have taken over many of the socializing (and possibly the status ascription) functions of the family. Churches provide religious indoctrination; insurance companies and governmental welfare departments assure economic security. It has been argued that the family, having lost a great many of its functions, has come increasingly to specialize in one function: the provision of affection or emotional stability to its members.[15] It may be, however, that

---

[13] Fred Davis, "Deviance Disavowal: the Management of Strained Interaction by the Visibly Handicapped," *Social Problems*, 9(1961):120–132.

[14] This fact is recognized in the frequent attempts to hold parents legally responsible for the behavior of their minor children.

[15] Ernest W. Burgess and Harvey J. Locke, *The Family* (New York: American Book Company, 1950), pp. 26, 27; Talcott Parsons and Robert F. Bales, *Family, Socialization and Interaction Process* (Glencoe, Ill.: Free Press, 1955), p. 16.

even these companionate functions of the family are coming to be institutionalized in outside agencies. The marriage counselor, the psychiatrist, even the "advice" columnist of the daily newspaper may be seen as emerging institutionalized forms for dealing with the companionate functions of the family.

STRUCTURAL VARIABILITY IN THE FAMILY

One of the fascinating aspects of human society to even the most casual of students is the great variability in forms of the family among the various peoples of the world. Social scientists have developed a number of typologies to classify different forms of family structure. We shall now examine several dimensions of structural variability in the family. Wherever possible, we shall venture into the difficult area of sociological explanations of *why* the family takes the forms that it does in different societies.

Number of Marriage Partners

The family institution of a society defines the number of persons involved in a marital cohabitation. The dominant form in Western societies is that of *monogamy,* the marriage of one man and one woman. Monogamy is by far the most common form of marriage in the world today.[16] Given an equal number of men and women, it is the form that maximizes opportunities for marriage. Perhaps it would not be too ethnocentric to suggest that this is the "natural" form of human marriage and that it is only the alternative forms that require special explanation.

The generic term for all forms of plural marriage is *polygamy,* i.e., any system of marriage involving the cohabitation of more than two persons. Most polygamy in the world today is in the more specific form of *polygyny,* the marriage of one husband with more than one wife. Societies dominated by Islamic culture permit or encourage polygynous marriage, as did the traditional subculture of the Mormons in the United States. Polygyny seems to be related to the existence of a social structure which features great concentrations of wealth and power in the hands of a few men, with the mass of the population being poor and powerless. A multitude of wives is a status prerogative of the powerful and is, of course, at

---

[16] George P. Murdock, *Social Structure* (New York: Macmillan, 1949).

the expense of wives for the poor.[17] *Polyandry,* the marriage of one wife and more than one husband, is extremely rare in the world today. Where it has been practiced, it has been associated with extreme poverty of a whole population and with female infanticide, which reduces the relatively unproductive female population and produces a surplus of men.

Eligibility for Marriage

Every society, through its family institution, specifies which persons are eligible to marry which other persons. There are invariably rules of *endogamy,* which require that a person marry within a field of eligibles, and rules of *exogamy,* which require that a person marry outside a field of ineligibles. The variability arises from the great diversity of ways in which these fields are defined.

Rules of endogamy. Typical rules of endogamy are those which require marriage within one's own religion, social class, race, or place of residence. Intermarriage is a serious problem from the standpoint of many groups, but the definition of what constitutes mésalliance will vary greatly. Members of certain religious sub-cultures experience greater social disapproval when marrying outside their religious group than when marrying someone of another nationality or race. By contrast, a white Protestant Southerner in the United States would be able to marry outside his religion or nationality with less censure than if he married outside his race, the latter kind of intermarriage being a violation of his state's miscegenation laws.[18]

The relative strength of different rules of endogamy is probably a sensitive barometer of the relative importance to people of various of their social categories. A relatively classless society will

---

[17] Contrary to what we said about monogamy as a "natural" form of marriage, it might also be possible to see polygyny as more consistent in some ways with the instinctive sexual nature of man. Considering the more intense sex drive of the male, complicated by the tendency in most societies to place taboos around sexual intercourse during the period of the woman's menstrual cycle and during (and sometimes for a very long time after) pregnancy, polygyny may be the form that maximizes *male* sexual activity, at least for those males fortunate enough to secure wives.

[18] These laws have now been declared unconstitutional, but the informal social sanctions against racial intermarriage in these states are probably as strong as ever.

not exert much pressure to marry within one's social class. A more rigidly stratified society will demand social class endogamy more stringently. Herberg has shown that the strength of endogamous rules requiring marriage within one's nationality group (Polish, German, etc.) is apparently declining in the United States; at least there is an increasing amount of intermarriage of this type. At the same time, there has been *no* apparent decline in religious endogamy, i.e., the tendency of Protestants, Catholics, and Jews to marry within their own faith. Herberg argues that these facts are a reflection of the decline of nationality as a basis of personal identity and a persistent tendency of Americans to believe that everyone should "belong" to one of the three major faiths.[19]

Rules of exogamy. The most important kind of exogamous rule is that which requires marriage outside the group of one's own relatives, a rule enforced by an incest taboo, some form of which is found in all societies. One plausible sociological explanation of the incest taboo is that it protects the family from the interpersonal conflict that would probably ensue if members of a family were in competition with one another for the sexual favors of other family members. Supporting this interpretation is the evidence that a sort of incest taboo also exists among close friends, for example, a rule against dating the girl or boy friend of one's own best friend.

One study of patterns of sexual relations among homosexuals found that men who constituted a clique of friends did not have sexual relations among themselves but were expected to confine themselves to outsiders for sexual partners. As one of the interviewed homosexuals put it:

As far as I know, people who hang around with each other don't have affairs. The people who are friends don't sleep with each other. . . . It's always easier to get along with your gay friends if there has been no sex. Mind you, you might have sex with somebody you just met and then he might become your friend. But you won't have sex with him any more as soon as he joins the same gang you hang around with.[20]

---

[19] Will Herberg, *Protestant-Catholic-Jew* (Garden City, N.Y.: Doubleday, 1955). For more recent evidence of high religious endogamy in the United States, see Andrew M. Greeley, "Religious Intermarriage in a Denominational Society," *American Journal of Sociology,* 75(1970):949–952.

[20] Maurice Leznoff and William A. Westley, "The Homosexual Community," *Social Problems,* 3(1956):257–263.

An alternative explanation of the incest taboo is the influence of "role inertia" on social relationships. Once people have become accustomed to interacting with one another in one pair of social statuses (e.g., brother and sister), it is difficult to shift to another set of statuses (e.g., husband and wife).[21] An experimental demonstration of role inertia was the finding that children are reluctant to call a woman who marries their father by the title "mother" if they previously knew her on a first-name basis.[22]

Societies vary greatly in their definition of persons who are ineligible to marry one another. The various states of the United States (which, in this legal system, constitute subsocieties for purposes of family legislation) differ rather widely in the degree of relationship that would make couples ineligible to obtain a marriage license. If the sociological explanation that the incest taboo limits conflict is valid, we should expect that the field of ineligibles would be wider in those societies in which kinship is traced carefully through many degrees of relationship.[23] In American society, which is not meticulous in its tracing of distant kin relationships, the exogamous laws can be rather simple and permit marriage between any persons related no more closely, for example, than first cousins.

Patterns of Courtship

The process by which men and women "get together" to form marriages, i.e., the process of *courtship,* is a matter everywhere of social regulation. Other animals—for example, many bird species—have elaborate mating instincts that allow a set ritual of approach and response between male and female; human marriage requires cultural regulation to insure an orderly and predictable process.

Courtship practices show much cross-cultural variability. One important difference is found between those cultures in which persons are allowed to choose their own marriage partners and those in which marriages are arranged by the families of the prospective bride and groom. This variation in procedure tends to

---

[21] Allan D. Coult, "Causality and Cross-Sex Prohibitions." *American Anthropologist,* 65(1963):266–277.

[22] William R. Catton, Jr., "What's In a Name? A Study of Role Inertia," *Journal of Marriage and the Family,* 31(1969):15–18.

[23] For a description of a people (the Kurnai) who elaborate the calculation of kinship relations with resultant stringent rules of incest, see Ruth Benedict, *Patterns of Culture* (New York: Mentor Books, 1959), pp. 42–44.

be accompanied by a difference in the standards applied in defining the desirable spouse. Where marriages are arranged between families, the arrangers tend to consider the economic and social status, and other practical qualifications of the prospective spouse: Is he a good provider? Can she cook? People in societies which permit individual choice in marriage partners tend toward more *romantic* considerations, with less emphasis on objective qualifications of a "good match." The theory in societies with arranged marriages is that "love" is the outcome of long years of living together and is by no means a prerequisite to marriage.[24]

Romantically oriented courtship systems are frequently criticized as being dysfunctional for marital stability and satisfaction.[25] Being in love may be one of the poorer prognosticators of marital satisfaction. Love may involve a great deal of idealization of the object of love, a process that is fairly easy under the romanticized conditions of courtship, but one that tends to lead to disillusionment when people settle down to the more prosaic aspects of daily living together.[26] The high rate of divorce in societies with romantic conceptions of courtship may reflect the limitations of romanticism.

On the other hand, it has been shown that there is much resistance to arranged marriages in some of the countries that have them.[27] Moreover, young people from countries with more romantic courtship systems express a greater interest in marriage and more anticipation of a successful outcome than do those from countries with systems of arranged marriage.[28] The higher divorce rates where romantic courtship is practiced may be misleading, too. Most divorced persons in the United States remarry rather quickly;[29] their disillusionment with a specific marriage partner does not seem to precipitate a more radical disillusionment with marriage per se.

---

[24] For a description of Middle Eastern marriage patterns without the "love complex," see Asghar Fathi, "Expressive Behavior and Social Integration in Small Groups: a Comparative Analysis," *Pacific Sociological Review*, 11(1968):29–37.

[25] For example, see Mabel A. Elliott and Francis E. Merrill, *Social Disorganization*, 3rd ed. (New York: Harper, 1952).

[26] Willard Waller and Reuben Hill, *The Family: A Dynamic Interpretation*, rev. ed. (New York: Dryden, 1951).

[27] J. Henry Korson, "Student Attitudes Toward Mate Selection in a Muslim Society: Pakistan," *Journal of Marriage and the Family*, 31(1969):153–165.

[28] George A. Theodorson, "Romanticism and Motivation to Marry in the United States, Singapore, Burma and India," *Social Forces*, 44(1965):17–27.

[29] Paul C. Glick, *American Families* (New York: Wiley, 1957), p. 139.

Place of Residence

The cohabitation which the family involves means that there is invariably a place at which husband and wife live together. There are social definitions of the appropriate place for married persons to live in every society, but the variability in the ways this place is defined constitutes another source of structural variability in the family.

Perhaps the major problem of a society in defining place of residence for a family is specifying the relationship between an individual's *family of orientation* (the family into which he is born and which includes his parents and siblings) and his *family of procreation* (the family which he establishes upon his marriage and which includes his spouse and children). Since the incest taboo guarantees that families of procreation will never be formed between people in the same family of orientation, marriage everywhere means that one or more of the partners to a marriage must "leave home" when he marries. Family institutions always specify an approved practice in this regard.

Basic forms. The form most familiar to American readers is that of the *neolocal* (or *nuclear*) family, the situation in which husband and wife establish a household away from the families of orientation of either spouse. Opposed to the neolocal family is some form of the *extended family,* in which a married couple establishes residence in the family of orientation of one of the spouses, with the result that several generations of persons may be represented in one household.

Two more specific forms of the extended family are the *matrilocal* and the *patrilocal* family, in which residence is established in the household of the wife's or of the husband's family, respectively. Both the matrilocal and patrilocal forms are fairly common. We expect to find extended family households in societies with agricultural economies or wherever land or other real property is maintained in the hands of a family over several generations. In these situations, marriage is a matter of exchange of persons between households, and the household which loses one of its members is likely to be compensated with a dowry or bride price.

In more industrialized economies, property is more fluid and less a matter of family domination and for this reason, perhaps, the neolocal pattern of separate households for each marriage is more common. The "revolution" in family forms that is occurring today in developing countries is largely a matter of a shift away from extended family forms and toward neolocal forms.[30]

Problems of generation integration. The effect of a neolocal residence pattern on family life has been a frequent focus of sociological interest. One effect is that it tends to isolate older people from close relationship with their married children. These children are seen as having their own lives, and a parent of one spouse who lives with a married child is likely to be a source of in-law problems for the other spouse and an intrusion on the "privacy" of all members of the family. The growth in the use of nursing homes for the aged is partly the result of the difficulty of integrating older people into neolocal households.

The extent of this separation of families of procreation from families of orientation in modern societies may, however, be exaggerated. The parents of a married couple may continue to provide such economic benefits to their children as interest-free loans, free babysitting, and "gifts" of economic necessities and luxuries.[31] A study of the lives of working-class older people in London found an unexpectedly frequent pattern of continued mutual relationship between the elderly and their married children. A married daughter would, for example, tend to "run up to see Mum" daily and Mum might, in turn, help the working daughter by watching the grandchildren or helping with the household chores.[32]

Even when the distance between orientation and procreation families precludes such daily contact, certain practices in modern societies tend to provide for periodic renewals of contact of otherwise separated families. In the United States, Christmas seems to be the time for family get-togethers.[33] Were the world to be destroyed on Christmas day, some future archeologist digging in the ruins would discover the skeletons of many people of various ages

---

[30] William J. Goode, *World Revolution and Family Patterns* (New York: Free Press of Glencoe, 1963).

[31] Sussman, "Help Pattern in Middle Class Families."

[32] Peter Townsend, *The Family Life of Old People* (London: Routledge & Kegan Paul, 1957). A more recent study using a *middle-class* sample found much less influence of the extended family on daily living patterns, although the pattern of periodic visiting with extended family relations strongly prevailed. Jane Hubert, "Kinship and Geographic Mobility in a Sample from a London Middle-Class Area," *International Journal of Comparative Sociology,* 6(1965):61–80.

[33] Mark Benney et al., "Christmas in an Apartment Hotel," *American Journal of Sociology,* 65(1959):233–240.

on the same site and conclude that our family pattern took very much an extended family form.

Patterns of Authority

A family is a miniature government in that decisions have to be made and executed which affect the welfare of each family member. The form of this government may be a *democratic* consensus involving all members of the family, or it may be some kind of *authoritarian* structure in which one person makes and executes decisions. The terms *matriarchal* and *patriarchal* designate a wife-dominated and a husband-dominated household, respectively. Sociological research has cast doubt on the existence of any clear cases of matriarchy in the world. In matrilocal systems of residence, where we might expect to find matriarchal families, we usually discover that one of the wife's male relatives is in fact the authoritative figure.[34] Except possibly in "Blondie" and other comic strip and TV depictions of the wife-dominated family, the husband tends everywhere to wear the pants, if an authoritarian structure exists at all. Most family systems in traditional, agricultural societies have been patriarchal. In Roman law, the power of the father *(patria potestas)* extended to the extreme of a legal right to determine the life or death of members of his family.

There has been a notable shift in forms of the family in Western societies toward a decline of patriarchal authority and toward a democratic, if not a matriarchal, form. Since the turn of the century, women have gained so many "rights" outside the family—to vote, to attend college, to hold jobs, to be active in public life—that it would be surprising if the availability of these alternatives outside the family did not affect the ability and desire of women to resist patriarchal authority within the family. Sociological studies have shown that women who work outside the home tend to have more influence on decision-making within the family than do those who are housewives only.[35]

---

[34] Morris Zelditch, Jr., "Role Differentiation in the Nuclear Family," in Parsons and Bales, *Family, Socialization and Interaction Process,* pp. 307–351.

[35] Andrée Michel, "Comparative Data Concerning the Interaction in French and American Families," *Journal of Marriage and the Family,* 29(1967):337–344; Anette Lamousé, "Family Roles of Women: A German Example," *Journal of Marriage and the Family,* 31(1969):145–152; Robert O. Blood, Jr., and Donald M. Wolfe, *Husbands and Wives: The Dynamics of Married Living* (New York: Free Press of Glencoe, 1960).

The emerging family authority pattern in an era of "emancipated" women seems to involve some combination of (1) a sharing of decision-making between husband and wife, the rule being that decisions must follow adequate discussion of the issues, and (2) a division of authority with the understanding that, for example, the husband will make major decisions about place of residence or occupational employment and the wife will make major decisions concerning the treatment of children. Sometimes, of course, this division is skewed toward an uneven distribution of authority, with one of the spouses having authority only to boss the goldfish.

Role Differentiation Within the Family

Besides these varied definitions of roles in terms of authority, we find in different family systems different cultural definitions of the behavior that is expected of persons occupying different family statuses: husband, grandmother, daughter, nephew, etc. Considering only the roles of husband and wife we find that, in some societies, there is a high degree of differentiation of their separate roles; in others, husbands and wives are partners in most family activities.

In family systems with a differentiation of husband and wife roles, there is frequently a specialization of the husband in "instrumental" activities and of the wife in "expressive" activities.[36] The husband is the breadwinner and the taskmaster for the family; he is expected to maintain a level head at all times and suppress any troublesome emotional expressions by himself or other members of the family. The wife, in contrast, is expected to be the family's social-emotional specialist, maintaining a warm home environment and a more lenient attitude toward children, often being the confidante who listens to their troubles. This is the traditional role differentiation pattern, bolstered by the general cultural definition that "the woman's place is in the home."

As women have acquired education and career aspirations and as men have acquired more leisure time to spend at home, this traditional pattern of role differentiation has begun to break down. Increasingly, men are called upon to help out with household work and are expected to spend time with their children.[37] Increasingly,

[36] Parsons and Bales, *Family, Socialization and Interaction Process*, p. 46.

[37] This seems to be especially true where, for one reason or another, the husband does not perform the breadwinner role. Edward G. Ludwig and John Collette, "Disability, Dependency and Conjugal Roles," *Journal of Marriage and the Family*, 31(1969):736–739.

women are working outside the home, acquiring outside interests, and contributing to family income.[38]

There is considerable evidence, however, that in American society the norms governing the roles of the sexes have not caught up with these changes in actual behavior. Many families are still ambivalent about careers for their daughters, and sometimes urge them to "play dumb" with boys lest they frighten away marriage prospects in a society in which males are still expected to dominate intellectually.[39] Many families display embarrassment when it becomes publicly known that the traditional role differentiation has broken down. Many a husband who cheerfully accepts the task of diapering the baby at home will leave this chore to his wife in a public situation.

Systems for Reckoning Descent

The earlier discussion about status ascription indicated that much of a person's general social status depends on that of his ancestors. But each individual has many ancestors—two parents, four grandparents, eight great-grandparents, etc.—often of variegated social statuses. It would be most difficult to trace status through this ancestry unless some simplification were made in the system of reckoning descent. For example, each of a person's eight great-grandparents had a different family name. If all of these names were preserved to provide the person's family name, his last name would be quite unwieldy. The usual simplification is to designate either the mother's or the father's family of orientation as relevant for this purpose. Thus, we have *matrilineal* and *patrilineal* systems of reckoning descent. With a patrilineal system of naming, a child's paternal grandfather's father would be the only one of these eight great-grandparents whose name would be taken by the child.

To some extent, a family institution may be *bilateral,* allowing status to be ascribed based on both sides of a person's family. The wedding announcements that appear in the society pages of American newspapers are careful to provide information on the lineage

---

[38] On the breakdown of differentiation between instrumental and expressive roles see Robert K. Leik, "Instrumentality and Emotionality in Family Interaction," *Sociometry,* 26(1963):131–145; George Levinger, "Task and Social Behavior in Marriage," *Sociometry,* 27(1964):433–448.

[39] Mirra Komarovsky, "Cultural Contradictions and Sex Roles," *American Journal of Sociology,* 52(1946):184–189.

of both the prospective spouses. When children are asked to name relatives, they correctly name with about equal frequency relatives from both their mother's and their father's family of orientation.[40] In Western societies, however, the family is clearly patrilineal with reference to naming practices. In other respects, Western societies are tending toward a more bilateral system. The inheritance of property, for example, seems to become more bilateral as property has become more fluid and therefore more easily divisible so that it can be bestowed on daughters as well as sons.

Even in naming practices, some interesting patterns of bilateralism can be observed. Although a child takes the family name of his father's family of orientation, his given names may be taken from the family name of his mother's family of orientation. Mary Thomas marries John Jones and their child is named Thomas Jones or Thomasina Jones.

The trend toward bilateralism in naming is shown in a study of the practices of American middle-class families in selecting given names for their children.[41] Children are named for relatives of either the father's or the mother's family of orientation with about equal frequency. This represents a major change in pattern in that, of children born in the 1920s and earlier, there was a strong tendency to name sons for someone in the father's family of orientation and daughters for one of the mother's kin. More recently, bilateralism has become more fully realized, with sons and daughters increasingly being given names from either side of the family. The author of this study attributes this change to the improved relations between married couples and their in-laws; it becomes easier, for example, for a man to name his son for his father-in-law if their relations are friendly. An increasing "social symmetry" between the families of orientation of husband and wife may make the bilateral tracing of descent by their children easier to achieve.

Variations in Kinship Orientation
A final area of variability in the structure of the family concerns the distribution of interest and attention to different aspects of kinship.

---

[40] Millicent R. Ayoub, "The Child's Control of His Kindred in View of Geographic Mobility and Its Effects," *International Journal of Comparative Sociology*, 6(1965): 1–6.

[41] Alice S. Rossi, "Naming Children in Middle Class Families," *American Sociological Review*, 30(1965):499–513.

We might use the terms *filial, conjugal,* and *parental* to designate some of the different kinship orientations that exist in various societies. In a society like that of traditional China, which emphasizes filial relationships, a person's principal domestic obligations are to his parents, and the elderly are treated with great respect.[42] In a conjugally oriented society, the relationship of husband and wife and their mutual happiness takes precedence over other kinship relations. In a parentally oriented or child-centered society, the conjugal, filial, and all other kin relationships are subordinated to what is believed to be the welfare of the children.

Filial piety seems to disappear with the breakup of traditional societies and their tendencies toward extended family households. The idea of a child-centered family is a more recent and still controversial concept. Some observers of American life have seen the upsurge in birth rates and the movement to the suburbs which followed World War II as causally related. Since suburbs tend to be defined as good places to raise children,[43] their popularity may have been related to the increasing willingness of Americans to organize their domestic lives around the presence of children.

PARTICIPATION IN THE FAMILY

Our functional analysis of the family has indicated the necessity for systems of regulation of sexual and parental activities. There is, however, a major limitation of functional analysis in explaining human behavior in familial matters. If society requires that, by and large, people marry, confine their sexual intercourse to spouses, bear children and care for them, it is still clear that a certain amount of variation from the expected pattern is tolerable from the standpoint of a social system which may sustain both the individual who wants a home and family and the one who is altar shy. A few bachelors and a certain amount of extramarital sex will not be likely to threaten the integrity of a society's familial system. Within these limits of functional tolerance there will be much variation in the degree to which different persons or categories of persons participate in the family institution. Several dimensions of this variation will now be discussed.

---

[42] Francis L. K. Hsu, *Americans and Chinese* (New York: Schuman, 1953).

[43] Wendell Bell, "Social Choice, Life Styles and Suburban Residence," in William Dobriner (ed.), *The Suburban Community* (New York: Putnam, 1958), pp. 225–247.

Marital and Nonmarital Sex

The husband-wife relationship does not maintain a monopoly on sexual intercourse in any known society. Indeed, while all societies create special sexual privileges for persons through the institution of marriage, a substantial majority of societies have taken approving or lenient attitudes toward premarital sex and toward occasional indulgence in extramarital sex by married persons.[44]

This observation will suggest that one of the first variables to consider in accounting for the rate of participation of different groups of people in premarital and extramarital sex is the subcultural difference in definition of the degree of expected exclusiveness of marital sex. In groups with puritan sexual standards, a boy or girl is expected to save himself for the future spouse and absolute fidelity to the spouse after marriage is expected. In some other groups, there is a great deal more leniency or understanding of the "human nature" that expresses itself in nonmarital sex. In still other groups there is a positive status premium placed on premarital or extramarital sexual conquests.[45]

This subcultural or normative dimension in sexual behavior is highlighted when one considers the differential rates of participation of men and women in nonmarital sex. Kinsey's studies of American sexual behavior found that some 50 percent of American women are virgins when they marry, but only about 20 percent of American men are in this category.[46] Concerning extramarital sex, approximately 26 percent of married women and 50 percent of married men were estimated to have had this experience by age forty.[47] Perhaps these differences reflect the well-advertised double standard for sexual behavior in this society.[48] Men expect to marry

---

44 Murdock, *Social Structure.*

45 Ira L. Reiss, *The Social Context of Premarital Sexual Permissiveness* (New York: Holt, Rinehart & Winston, 1967); Harold T. Christensen, "Cultural Relativism and Premarital Sex Norms," *American Sociological Review,* 25(1960):31–39; Bernard Rosenberg and Joseph Bensman, "Sexual Patterns in Three Ethnic Subcultures of an American Underclass," *Annals of the American Academy of Political and Social Science,* 376(March 1968):61–75.

46 Alfred C. Kinsey et al., *Sexual Behavior in the Human Male* (Philadelphia: Saunders, 1948); *Sexual Behavior in the Human Female* (Philadelphia: Saunders, 1953).

47 Kinsey et al., *Sexual Behavior in the Human Female,* pp. 436–438.

48 Erwin O. Smigel and Rita Seiden, "The Decline and Fall of the Double Standard," *Annals of the American Academy of Political and Social Science,* 376(March 1968): 18–24.

virgins although they feel little constraint for their own virginity.[49] The expectation that a married man will occasionally play around is not matched by a similar leniency in judging the unfaithful wife.

The Kinsey studies also suggest another major difference in rates of participation in sex outside marriage: social-class differences. Incidence of premarital intercourse for men ranged from 98 percent for those with an eighth-grade or lower education to 68 percent for those having some college education.[50] There was relatively little difference by educational level in the number of men who eventually had extramarital affairs, but men with lower educational levels tended to have their first extramarital relations at a much earlier point in their marriages.[51] In the area of sexual behavior, "middle-class morality" seems to operate less stringently in the American lower classes.

Childbearing

The childless marriage and the only child are indications of the possibility that some couples may underparticipate in parental activities even though they participate in marital sex. The use of contraception has produced a separation between sex and reproduction, and its use is a variable between persons that has interested the sociologist.

There is a normative dimension to the degree of participation in childbearing just as there is to the degree of marital fidelity. Some religious groups proscribe contraception and the norm for a married couple is to "be fruitful and multiply." In other normative systems there is an ethical orientation toward childbearing that argues that people should have no more children than they want or can reasonably care for.

Beyond such normative considerations, it appears that family size is much influenced by expedient considerations. For those engaged in agricultural occupations, a large number of children may be highly rewarding economically. In much of the United States, for example, most agricultural work is accomplished by family labor and the more children a family has, the more hands there are to work. For people in most urban occupations, children

---

[49] William F. Whyte, "A Slum Sex Code," *American Journal of Sociology,* 49(1943): 24–32.

[50] Kinsey et al., *Sexual Behavior in the Human Female,* pp. 330–333.

[51] Kinsey et al., *Sexual Behavior in the Human Male.*

make no important contribution to the family economy; each child is simply an extra mouth to feed.

A more subtle kind of expediency for encouraging large families is the situation found in some societies or groups where a woman's social status depends almost entirely upon her participation in motherhood. In patrilocal societies a wife is a "stranger" in a family dominated by her husband's relatives and, until she bears children, she may enjoy no prestige at all in the household.[52] In a somewhat milder form, many American women may feel out of it socially if they are childless, especially when they observe how the society plays up motherhood in such institutions as Mother's Day.

That considerations of expediency can take precedence over normative values is shown in studies of the differential use of contraception between Catholics and persons of other religious groups that do not proscribe contraception. American Catholic wives are about as likely as non-Catholic wives to use contraception, if one controls for such intervening variables as social class and national origins.[53] The participation of Catholics in a pattern of behavior that is condemned by their church creates, of course, some serious problems of self-definition for those who so participate.

Family Stability

Although marriage in most societies in contracted "until death us do part," some provision for the divorce or separation of married persons is found almost everywhere. In the United States, a country with relatively high overall divorce rates compared with other modern nations,[54] there are great differences in the divorce rates among different categories of people. For instance, the poorer and less educated have higher divorce rates than the wealthier and more educated; urban couples have higher rates than rural ones; blacks have higher rates than whites; those who marry at younger ages have higher rates than those who marry at older ages.[55]

Explanation of these rate differences is likely to involve some difficult problems of causal inference. Take the well-known case

---

[52] Kingsley Davis, "Human Fertility in India," *American Journal of Sociology,* 52 (1946):243–255.

[53] *New York Times,* August 5, 1969.

[54] Alexander Plateris, *Divorce Statistics Analysis—United States, 1963* (Washington, D.C.: National Center for Health Statistics, 1967).

[55] William F. Kenkel, *The Family in Perspective,* 2nd ed. (New York: Appleton-Century-Crofts, 1960), pp. 311–320.

of the supposed instability of marriages among Negroes. Although the difference in legal divorce rates between the races is small, the rate of informal separation of husbands and wives is four to five times higher among blacks.[56] Why?

Part of the explanation undoubtedly relates to the fact that blacks are overwhelmingly members of the lower classes. The material and social-status deprivations of members of these classes tend to create major problems for marital interaction; when money is chronically short, marital discord may focus on such "trivial" matters as the husband's insistence on spending money for cigarettes or beer, or the wife's "extravagance" in buying clothes. The difficulty of lower-class people in holding jobs—they tend toward types of employment where they are susceptible to being laid off—creates an insecurity in the status of the husband in a society where role definitions are likely to demand that he be the family's breadwinner. The instability of Negro marriages may simply reflect the exaggeratedly weak economic and status positions of blacks in the United States.

On the other hand, there may be some factors in Negro family instability that are attributable to the specifically *racial* situation of the Negro in the United States. Frazier, for example, has argued that the lack of stability of the husband-wife relation among blacks harks back to the family situation of Negroes under slavery.[57] Since the "maintenance" of a family was the burden of the slaveowner and not of the Negro husband-father, there was no economic incentive for the owner to encourage the integrity of the marital tie. Indeed, it was the practice among some owners to separate the fathers from their wives and children on the theory that this would help prevent the formation of primary-group conspiracies against the slave condition.

In postslavery times, slaveowner paternalism has been replaced by the "matriarchal" family, in which a woman and her children live with the woman's mother and where the children are the products of the sporadic sexual relations of the woman with a man or a series of men.[58] One study of New Orleans Negro families has

---

[56] Hugh Carter and Alexander Plateris, "Trends in Divorce and Family Disruption," *Health, Education and Welfare Indicators,* September 1963, p. 11.

[57] E. Franklin Frazier, *The Negro Family in the United States* (Chicago: University of Chicago Press, 1939).

[58] Daniel P. Moynihan, *The Negro Family: The Case for National Action* (Washington, D.C.: U.S. Department of Labor, 1965); Joan Aldous, "Wives' Employment

suggested that, among the Negro lower classes, men who are excluded by the matriarchal system from expressing their masculinity in stable families express it compulsively in the all-male gang, with its hell-raising, he-man values.[59]

There is much contemporary criticism of the view that the fatherless family is a product of specifically Negro conditions.[60] These criticisms tend to take the form of showing that the *middle-class* black family fully matches or even exceeds the stability of the white middle-class family. From this critical viewpoint, differences in family stability are products of social-class differences; Negro family instability is a reflection of the disproportionate membership of blacks in the lower classes.

SUMMARY

The institution of the family deals with some of the most emotionally charged of human sentiments, those dealing with sex and the relationships of adults to children. Given the necessity for social order which requires that emotional expression be channeled into forms that are functional for a social system, we can understand the universal preoccupation with the social regulation of these behaviors.

The basic functional requirements are that sexual activity be consistent with harmonious social relationships and that children fit into the scheme of social arrangements that prevails in a society. The family is not the only agency that could perform these functions—indeed, through the institutionalization of family functions, many of these responsibilities have been transferred to other agencies—but it tends to be in a good strategic position to do so.

Social order requires not only that sexual and parental activities be regulated in *some* way, it demands that all the people in a society regulate these activities in approximately the *same* way. Each society represents a selection from a variety of alternative structural forms for the provision of family functions. The American

Status and Lower-Class Men as Husband-Fathers: Support for the Moynihan Thesis," *Journal of Marriage and the Family*, 31(1969):469–476; Robert O. Blood, Jr., and Donald M. Wolfe, "Negro-White Differences in Blue-Collar Marriages in a Northern Metropolis," *Social Forces*, 48(1969):59–64.

[59] John H. Rohrer and M. S. Edmonson (eds.), *The Eighth Generation: Cultures and Personalities of New Orleans Negroes* (New York: Harper, 1960).

[60] Lee Rainwater and William L. Yancey, "Black Families and the White House," *Trans-action*, 3(July/August 1966): 6–11.

middle-class family, for example, is often characterized as being monogamous, bilateral, neolocal, and romantically oriented. Most of the sociological distinctions of family form are "ideal types"—pure forms that are seldom found in all their "purity" in real social life. The American family, for example, while basically patrilineal in naming practices, has important elements of matrilineality as well. The sociologist is alert to the problem of explaining the factors or social conditions that lead to the selection of one family form or another (or a mixture of forms) in a given society.

As with all institutions, different categories of people participate with different levels of intensity in family institutions. Some people do *not* confine their sexual activity to marriage, some do *not* bear children, and some do *not* remain married permanently. For example, persons in the category labeled "lower class" can be shown to have *high* rates of participation in nonmarital sex, and *low* stability of marriage. These participation rates may be explained by the fact that people in this category share a *subculture* which defines the importance to be placed on institutional participation. There may also be considerations of expediency, it simply not being convenient or pleasant for the people in that category to fall in line with an institutionally prescribed mode for dealing with family affairs.

Religion

In Durkheim's classic work, *The Elementary Forms of the Religious Life*,[1] he noted that it is the tendency of men everywhere to divide the world around them into two great and mutually exclusive categories: the *sacred* and the *profane*. The profane world is composed of all those things toward which men take a casual attitude; to Durkheim, the profane was synonymous with the mundane, the everyday. The sacred, by contrast, deals with things that are seen as extraordinary or demanding of special attention and respect in dealing with them; they are, as Durkheim says, "set apart and forbidden."

Religion deals with the world of the sacred. The objects of religious interest represent extraordinary powers; whether evil or good powers, they are superhuman in their strength. The religious life, in dealing with these objects, is constituted by two components: *beliefs* and *rituals*. Beliefs are the ideas that men have about the nature of the sacred powers and about how they operate. The rituals are the actions that men take to try to bring themselves into a desirable relationship to the sacred. The rituals may aim at avoiding harm by malevolent powers or eliciting aid from the beneficent ones.

FUNCTIONS OF RELIGION

Religious belief and ritual are found in all human societies. In explaining this universality functionally, there have been two major

---

[1] Emile Durkheim, *The Elementary Forms of the Religious Life,* trans. by J. W. Swain (Glencoe, Ill.: Free Press, 1947).

tendencies: (1) to look at the correspondence of religion to individual psychological needs and (2) to consider religion in relation to the needs or "functional imperatives" of a social system.

Individual Needs

Our discussion in chapter 5 of tension management as a social-system requirement would indicate that the sociologist is not unconcerned with the problem of the psychological stability of individuals. One way of looking at religious beliefs and ritual functionally is to ask, What kinds of persistent tensions in human thought may religious belief and practice help to manage or control? We shall look here at two frequently asserted peculiarities of human psychology: man's need for rationality and for predictability.

Man's rationalizing need. One observation about the peculiarity of human psychology is that man appears to be the only animal that raises the question, *Why?* He wants the events that he observes around him to make sense and he has little tolerance for a view of life that it is "a tale told by an idiot, full of sound and fury and signifying nothing."

Consider a typical situation in which the question *why* is raised. A man is informed of the unexpected death of a friend; almost before he has finished saying, "Oh no!" he is asking, "What happened?" He wants to know why this death occurred. He may see the results of a scientific autopsy and gain some satisfaction for his questioning when he sees the coroner's verdict on the cause of death.

But the man's questioning may demand further answers: Why did it have to happen to *this* man? The biblical Job, observing that he had obeyed well all God's commandments, could not understand why God had visited numerous afflictions on him. The anthropologist Fortes finds a parallel to the Job story in the religious mythologies of primitive West African cultures.[2] Such stories indicate the human concern with justice and injustice or, as it is sometimes put, the problem of evil, the explanation of unrewarded virtue and unpunished evil.

Weber saw the different major religions of the world as using

---

[2] Meyer Fortes, *Oedipus and Job in West African Religion* (London: Cambridge University Press, 1959).

alternative ways of rationalizing evil.[3] Some religions have a notion of heaven or an afterlife in which each man will get his just deserts, however wronged he may have been in his earthly life. Other religions may insist that what appear to be evil events in the world are in fact part of a grand and benevolent plan of a deity whose ways are inscrutable but "altogether righteous."

The tendency to demand explanations for earthly events, while generally human, apparently varies to a considerable extent among different individuals. Some people are able to live rather well with a perception of life as meaningless in certain respects, perhaps even adopting and enjoying a philosophy such as existentialism, which refuses to rationalize what is seen as a thoroughly irrational human existence.[4] There are other persons—James mentions the writers Bunyan and Tolstoy[5]—who are continually tortured by their perceptions of earthly evil and who demand a religious rationalization.

One other personality type in this regard is described by James,[6] namely, the person whose "sky-blue optimism" leads him quite literally to see no evil, whose natural inclination is to exercise what today is referred to as the "power of positive thinking." Such temperamental differences introduce some important variables of a personality nature, but they do not deny a *general* human tendency to employ supernatural explanations of events on earth.

Man's need for future reassurances. Another major feature of human psychology is the human tendency to anticipate the future and to react emotionally to perceptions of what fate or destiny that future may hold. The future existence of any living thing is highly uncertain; its very life may be terminated by any one of innumerable possible future events. Man is apparently the only animal who anticipates these possibilities, worries about them, and self-consciously takes action to avoid unfavorable futures and to secure favorable ones. No dog, we may assume, has fretted over a question like, Where is my next bone coming from?

---

[3] Max Weber, "The Social Psychology of the World Religions," in H. H. Gerth and C. Wright Mills (eds.), *From Max Weber: Essays in Sociology* (New York: Oxford, 1958).

[4] William Barrett, *Irrational Man* (Garden City, N.Y.: Doubleday, 1965).

[5] William James, *The Varieties of Religious Experience* (New York: Modern Library, 1936), pp. 146–159. First published 1902.

[6] Ibid., pp. 77–121.

Although any man's future is uncertain, there may be some elements of predictability about it and some outcomes that can be controlled to some extent. If a man fears contracting a certain disease or hopes to win a wife, he can employ the technologies available in his culture to influence the future in a direction that he desires: he can get an inoculation or start using a "man's deodorant." He may also be reassured when he hears about the high percentage of men in his society who get married or the low percentage who contract the disease that he fears. Sometimes, too, his optimism about the future will depend on his own tendency toward wishful thinking and the tendency of others to reassure him that "it will work out fine." For example, parents of a child with paralytic polio, worrying about his chances for recovery, will get reassurances from others in the form of a recitation of known cases of quick and successful recovery.[7]

With all these nonreligious sources for predicting and controlling future events, it might seem that man would not need recourse to supernatural help. But notice an important limitation of all these naturalistic aids; their reassurances about the future are only in terms of *probability,* indicating the likelihood of a favorable future. There is still a *chance* that things will not go well, and many people operate with a pessimistic view of "just my luck" if some of those rare misfortunes should befall them. This way of thinking about *luck* highlights a very widespread tendency in human thought: the notion of man's "ill-starred destiny" portrayed so powerfully in the Oedipus myth and other great tragedies of ancient Greece.[8]

If the tendency in popular thinking is to imagine that luck runs against one, we can well understand the tendency to attempt to counteract bad luck or, more positively, to attempt to produce a favorable future by obtaining good luck or Godspeed for one's endeavors.[9] So-called enlightened people tend to label as "superstition" such practices as carrying a rabbit's foot or eating black-eyed peas on New Year's Day to bring good luck. But the same people may "pray for God's blessings" on the leaders of their nation in an attempt to bring peace to the world.

This view of the psychologically reassuring functions of religion

---

[7] Fred Davis, *Passage Through Crisis* (Indianapolis: Bobbs-Merrill, 1963), p. 38.

[8] Fortes, *Oedipus and Job in West African Religion.*

[9] On the employment of supernatural aids to success in game-playing, see James M. Henslin, "Craps and Magic," *American Journal of Sociology,* 73(1967):316–330.

will suggest that the intensity of religious activity will tend to vary with the degree of uncertainty or anxiety about human futures. It will suggest (what is not entirely true) that there are "no atheists in foxholes," no atheists among the very old or very sick or among any group faced with imminent death.[10]

Malinowski's anthropological work also stressed these notions. Among the Trobriand Islanders he studied, there was very little tendency to resort to appeals for supernatural aid for group endeavors when the people were relatively sure of the favorable outcomes of their activity. When hunting in a familiar territory with a known supply of game, men simply sharpened their hunting weapons and largely ignored the supernatural. But if a tribe were about to embark on some uncertain venture, like a war with unknown outcome or a hunt in unfamiliar territory, there would be an effervescence of religious activities.

Malinowski gave a similar interpretation to the highly religious content of most rites of passage, those ceremonial recognitions of major changes of status of persons, such as the puberty rites when a person enters adulthood, marriage rites when he marries, funeral rites when he dies.[11] In Malinowski's view, these status changes are invariably sources of anxiety about the future: Will the boy acquit himself well as a man? Will this marriage work? Will the spirits of the deceased hover around and make trouble for the living? Malinowski saw the rites of passage as helping to alleviate these anxieties by giving future reassurances to the involved persons. Radcliffe-Brown, a colleague of Malinowski, took vigorous exception to this functional interpretation of the rites of passage.[12] However, Radcliffe-Brown had, as we shall shortly see, a different functionalist perspective, tending to see the functions of religion from quite a different angle.

Societal Needs

Social scientists like Weber and Malinowski adopt a functionalist view which emphasizes the necessity to a society of dealing with

[10] Although aging may not produce any generalized increase in religiosity, it does appear to lead to an increase in private prayer-saying and in a concern about immortality. See Rodney Stark, "Age and Faith: a Changing Outlook or an Old Process?" *Sociological Analysis*, 29(1968):1–10.

[11] Bronislaw Malinowski, *Magic, Science and Religion and Other Essays* (Boston: Beacon Press, 1948).

[12] A. R. Radcliffe-Brown, *Taboo* (London: Cambridge University Press, 1939).

problems inherent in human psychology. Ideas like those discussed above are accordingly prominent in their work. Others, like Radcliffe-Brown and Durkheim, launch their functional analysis from a different starting point, i.e., the needs of a society rather than the needs of individuals. Two aspects of such societal needs deserve discussion.

Religious support for social values. One of the functional imperatives of a society that we discussed in chapter 5 was what Parsons calls pattern maintenance: the development of individual members who are committed to uphold and defend the society's fundamental values. Our discussion of the variability of culture among peoples and the variability of the forms of basic social institutions will stress the essentially arbitrary character of the selections that any society makes among the alternative forms. There is nothing in universal human nature that requires a capitalistic form of economy, a monogamous marriage system, premarital chastity, etc. Yet a society that maintains these values and institutional forms requires that its members believe in the rightness of these forms. Otherwise, the alienation of men from the prevailing arrangements in their society would threaten the stability of those arrangements.

As is true of other religious functions, there are nonreligious alternatives to religion as a means of pattern maintenance. There may be quite secular ideological systems that justify prevailing practices. A free-enterprise economy may be justified on grounds that it maximizes economic productivity. Premarital chastity may be justified on grounds that premarital sex will make later marital adjustment more difficult.

However, the attempt to justify social forms on such utilitarian grounds is often frustrated by the discovery that it *is* expedient in terms of personal gain to violate major social values. Honesty may *not* be the best policy if by "best" one means the policy most conducive to personal gain. Furthermore, one can readily find examples of other forms used by other peoples without dire consequences or deprivation—many socialist countries do quite well productively, and several societies permit a great deal of premarital sex and their marriages apparently are none the worse for it.

The integrity of a social pattern may depend on most people's believing that the pattern is right and proper, regardless of the relative expediency of conformity or deviance. At this point, religious belief systems may perform major functions for a society. The supernatural is often conceived as a *judging* being and one whose judgments on human behavior are supported by such momentous sanctions as eternal salvation or eternal damnation. Institutional forms are typically supported by supernatural sanctions: a monarchy by a notion of the "divine right of kings," a monogamous marriage system by the view that marriages are "made in Heaven," a military regime by the belief that "God is on our side" in international struggles.

Radcliffe-Brown, observing the rituals involved in rites of passage,[13] found a fundamental flaw in Malinowski's contention that these rituals tend to relieve the anxieties of the persons involved. This is frequently far from the truth, according to Radcliffe-Brown. Often as not, the rituals seem to *create* anxiety because people become anxious lest they are not performing the rites correctly: Is the deceased actually getting a decent burial? Should one have a church wedding and, if so, should it be intimate or public? Is the dress for one's daughter's First Communion quite proper?

Perhaps a society requires a certain level of anxiety for its members, a continual wondering whether they are living up to the proper social forms. The rites of passage may be strategic points to reinforce these anxieties. At a funeral, for example, the deceased is typically eulogized. While the eulogy may bear little relation to the man's character when he was alive, it may raise in the living enough anxiety about their own moral characters to make them resolve to live more decently. It is also during these rites that the supernatural sanctions in support of social patterns are most directly stated: "What God hath joined, let no man put asunder."

The tendency of religion to support existing social arrangements is a source of complaint by persons attempting to bring about social change. Marx characterized religion as the "opium of the people," a device used by a ruling class to divert people from concern with their exploitation by these rulers.

Some religions, however, have major commitments to values that are imperfectly realized in the social system in which they exist. Christianity, for example, has certain commitments to brotherhood and the advancement of the interest of the poor. In a society that violates the moral equality of men (a racist society, for example) or that exploits the poor at the expense of the wealthy, we

---

13 Ibid.

might expect organized religion to pit itself against some prevailing social practices. To some extent these possibilities have been realized in the "social gospel" of modern Protestantism, which has tended to support programs of social welfare, and in the prominent position in favor of racial integration taken by many religious bodies recently in the United States. But not always do these reforming tendencies become active.

A study of the Protestant ministry of Little Rock, Arkansas, during that community's school integration crisis showed that a majority of ministers took no active position in favor of integration despite the fact that integration was strongly supported by the national governing bodies of the various denominations.[14] These local ministers appeared to respond to the segregationist sentiments of their congregations rather than to the expectations of persons in the hierarchies of their churches.[15] The latter were either powerless to enforce their integrationist sentiments or they encouraged ministers to respond to local pressures, expecting a growth in church membership and local financing. If these churches did not actively support the racial status quo in Little Rock, neither did they challenge in any significant way the prevailing pattern of race relations.

Creation of social solidarity. Durkheim makes the provocative assertion that religion "unites in one moral community" all the persons who adhere to the religion.[16] Through common participation with his fellowmen in religious rituals, the individual develops a sense of solidarity or of "we" as he comes to feel a part of something larger than himself, some society or social group. Viewed in this way, religion is at the very foundation of human society, creating in persons the frame of mind without which social unity would be impossible.[17]

There is much to commend the view that a latent function of group rituals is the promotion of social solidarity or unity among the people who practice them. Throughout the medieval period of

---

[14] Ernest Q. Campbell and Thomas F. Pettigrew, "Racial and Moral Crisis: The Role of Little Rock Ministers," *American Journal of Sociology,* 64(1959):509–516.

[15] For a comparison of official pronouncements of church bodies and the typical attitudes of parishioners, see Yoshio Fukuyama, "Parishioners' Attitude Toward Issues in the Civil Rights Movement," *Sociological Analysis,* 29(1968):94–103.

[16] Durkheim, *Elementary Forms of Religious Life,* p. 52.

[17] Calvin Redekop, "Toward an Understanding of Religion and Social Solidarity," *Sociological Analysis,* 28(1967):149–161.

Western European history, the Christian church maintained a common ritual, and whatever social unity exists today in the West is largely a reflection of this history of religious unity. A political leader intent on creating a stronger social unity—for example, Adolf Hitler in Germany—will find it useful to promote a mystical conception of the "holy" cause of the nation and a set of elaborate rituals to celebrate the national unity.

A sociologically naive person may wonder why groups go to such trouble to organize elaborate rituals. Why, for example, does the government of the Soviet Union bother to hold national elections in a one-party system, or why do the political parties in the United States hold conventions to renominate an incumbent president? One explanation is that these actions are ritual reflections of group solidarity, a celebration of the Communist society or of democratic electoral procedures. Even groups as small as the family may depend on traditional group rituals as a basis for the we-feeling among family members.[18]

Although it is easy enough to assemble such cases in support of the view that religious or secular rituals have a socially integrating effect, it is also possible to find social situations in which religion has the opposite effect, that of dividing people into opposing groups.[19] The religious wars throughout the history of Europe, the struggles between Mohammedans and Hindus in India in the 1940s, the continuing struggle between Jews and Arabs in the Middle East and between Protestants and Catholics in Northern Ireland—these instances are hardly favorable to the view that religion "unites in one moral community." Whatever unity exists may be limited to the unity of one religious group in opposition to other unified religious groups. Durkheim's functional analysis of religion does not seem to account for these dysfunctional consequences of religious belief and ritual.

Before the theoretical view of Durkheim is quite abandoned, however, it might be well to explore the idea of some analysts, namely, that religious practice tends to evolve in the direction of accommodating religious conflicts in order to make it possible for various

---

[18] James H. S. Bossard and Eleanor S. Boll, "Ritual in Family Living," *American Sociological Review*, 14(1949):463–469.

[19] Allan W. Eister, "Religious Institutions in Complex Societies: Difficulties in the Theoretic Specification of Functions," *American Sociological Review*, 22(1957): 387–391.

religious groups to coexist in one social system. Parsons has argued that the separation of church and state in the United States is one reflection of accommodation to religious diversity. Recognizing that no one religious denomination was going to dominate the country, the Founding Fathers forbade all attempts at creating an established church.[20]

Herberg has written an influential account of the effects of this pluralism on the content of religion in America.[21] He argues that there has evolved a single religion which unites Americans in one moral community—a rather secularized belief in an "American way of life." Each of the major faiths is seen by Herberg as having been constrained to soften the dogmatism of its peculiar theology in favor of providing broad ideological support for this "American way." Thus, according to one account, social unity has been encouraged by developments in religion; however, this unity has been achieved at a price in secularization of its appeal that many theologians, including Herberg, find rather distasteful.

INSTITUTIONALIZATION

The process by which religious functions become formalized has excited much sociological interest. It appears that the church as a special agency dealing with religion is a fairly recent historical development. The family has traditionally included religious worship among its many functions, and supernatural powers have frequently consisted of household deities peculiar to each individual family.[22]

Once a church is established as a special religious agency, there may still be important differences in the degree of institutionalization found in different kinds of church organization. Sociologists of religion have used the terms *sect* and *denomination*[23] to refer to these different degrees of institutionalization.

A sect is a religious body without a high degree of formalization of its internal structure. The leaders of sects are not likely to be for-

---

[20] "Some Comments on the Pattern of Religious Organization in the United States," in Talcott Parsons, *Structure and Process in Modern Societies* (New York: Free Press of Glencoe, 1960), pp. 295–321.

[21] Will Herberg, *Protestant-Catholic-Jew* (Garden City, N.Y.: Doubleday, 1955).

[22] Pitirim A. Sorokin, *Sourcebook in Rural Sociology* (Minneapolis: University of Minnesota Press, 1930).

[23] In some discussions, the term *church* is used in the same sense that *denomination* is used here.

mally trained, often basing their leadership qualification on some special "call" to religious ministry. Rank-and-file members of the sect are likely to participate very actively and spontaneously in religious ritual, as when they contribute to the spirit of a sermon by adding their "amens." Religious feeling is close to the heart of the members, and the emotionality or fanaticism of their religious life tends to extend to all phases of their everyday lives.

Denominational churches are more formally organized, with a trained ministry and a minimal role in religious ritual by ordinary members. Members of denominations are more able to treat their religious life as a separate department from that of their routine, nonreligious life.[24]

Much of church history may be understood as a dialectic fluctuation between the poles of sect and denomination on the scale of institutionalization.[25] Churches tend to originate as sects, with little formal organization and an attitude of righteous hostility to the evils of "the world." But, as the emotional fervor that generated the new sect subsides, churches find it increasingly necessary to routinize their activities and make some compromises with the world.[26] Thus, the radical sect of nonconformists becomes the established church, with the institutionalization of a new orthodoxy. However, this routinization may so diminish the church's ability to satisfy the primary religious feelings of its members that a fundamentalist reaction sets in and new sect-like churches are established in separatist movements. The history of Christianity—from persecuted radicalism to established church to Protestant Reformation to established Protestant denominations to fundamentalist revivals— well illustrates the dialectic shift between highly institutionalized denominations and weakly institutionalized sects.[27]

STRUCTURAL VARIABILITY IN RELIGION

The extent of variation in religious practice between societies and over time is probably as great as the structural variation in the

---

[24] Ernst Troeltsch, *The Social Teaching of the Christian Churches,* trans. by Olive Wyon (New York: Macmillan, 1932).

[25] John A. Coleman, "Church-Sect Typology and Organizational Precariousness," *Sociological Analysis,* 29(1968):55–66.

[26] On the "routinization" problems of sect-like social organizations of all types, see Max Weber, *The Theory of Social and Economic Organization,* trans. by A. M. Henderson and Talcott Parsons (New York: Oxford, 1947), pp. 358–373.

[27] Troeltsch, *Social Teaching of the Christian Churches.*

family institution. We shall examine here a few of the distinctions of religious form that have helped to organize sociological thinking about variability in this institution.

Magic and Religion

Many social scientists would distinguish between two forms of religious belief and practice, calling one of these basic forms *magic* and reserving for the other form the term *religion*. Magic is based on the belief that the supernatural operates according to certain mechanical principles and can be controlled by the mastery of definite manipulatory formulas. The dominant attitude toward the supernatural in magical practice is one of *coercion* of these powers. Magic is not typically organized into a "church" but is the special prerogative of an occupational group or cult. Therefore, as Durkheim sees it, magic does not unite people in a "moral community."[28] Magic does not seem to create social solidarity, although it may have any of the other functions of religion discussed above.

Religion differs from magic in that the typical attitude toward the supernatural is more humanized. *Anthropomorphism*—conceiving the nature of the supernatural after the character of man—is perhaps the beginning of religion proper. Gods are seen as having wills like the wills of men, and they can only be appealed to in a *propitiatory* manner, by persuading them of the worthiness of the human beings who seek their favor.

With the growth of this notion of supernatural power as a "judge" of human conduct, as a "significant other" for judging oneself, the *ethical* content of a religious system becomes prominent. A religious ethic is a prescription for the kind of everyday life that an individual is expected to lead. By living such a life, a practitioner of one of the great ethical religions is expected to gain supernatural favor. The "book" of the religion (Bible, Torah, Koran) provides precepts for this good life and sometimes a description of an exemplary life, such as that of Christ or Mohammed. Religious instruction is not, as in magic, the teaching of mechanical formulas; rather, it uses these precepts and examples to develop the religious "character" of the faithful.

Other-Worldly and This-Worldly Religions

If all religions have such an ethical content, the nature of the ethics

---

[28] Durkheim, *Elementary Forms of Religious Life,* pp. 59, 60.

found in various religions differs considerably. This variation has interested several sociologists, most notably Weber, whose comparison of the different ethics of the world religions became the basis for his famous theory of the relation between religious and economic institutions.[29] Weber noted that most religious ethics have an "other-worldly" form that enjoins their followers from thoughts about success or failure in this life and urges them instead to concentrate on living a life that will guarantee immortality. From the viewpoint of this ethic, the work of economic production is at best a "necessary evil," and the laying up of great material wealth is a dangerous incitement to concern with things of this world.

Since they incorporate other-worldly ethics, the prescriptions for the good life as propounded by Catholicism, Hinduism, Confucianism, and even Lutheran Protestantism are seen by Weber as being unfavorable to the way of life or spirit of a capitalist economy, based as it is on the profit motive, hard work, and personal thrift. To encourage capitalism, a more "this-worldly" kind of religious ethic was required, and Weber believed that this incentive was supplied by the "Protestant ethic" or, more specifically, the "worldly asceticism" of the Calvinist version of Protestantism.

The Calvinist, believing in original sin, was highly concerned with the status of his personal soul—whether he was damned or of the "elect" in God's eternal plan for the *predestination* of each soul. He also believed in a *transcendental* God, one who does not communicate with men; God does not answer prayers nor does he give men any revelations about the destiny prepared for them in immortality. The Calvinist is accordingly described by Weber as potentially in an acute state of anxiety about his religious future. Relief from this anxiety is provided by the Calvinist's notion of the *providential* character of God, the notion that he is benevolent or just. Having this character, God surely would not allow one of his "elect" to suffer failure in this world. Conversely, earthly failure was seen as a sure "sign" of eternal damnation.

Bolstered with these reassurances and believing that all social institutions were divinely ordained, the capitalist entrepreneur could exploit his employees and defeat his entrepreneurial rivals with good conscience, being sure that whatever happens is part of "God's plan." He could also view his work as a *calling,* a divine

---

[29] Max Weber, *The Protestant Ethic and the Spirit of Capitalism,* trans. by Talcott Parsons (New York: Scribner's, 1930).

mandate to work without regard to the luxuries derivable from the profits of his work. Thus he could participate in that peculiar "spirit" of modern capitalism, what Weber calls the "sober bourgeoisie" spirit of hard work as an end in itself, with any profits from the work being incidental. The famous Yankee thrift, which glorified hard work, abstinence from luxurious consumption, and a continual drive to reinvest profits to "build up the business," was encouraged by this religious ethic. Some of Weber's favorite examples of men who demonstrated the "spirit of capitalism" were men like Benjamin Franklin.

Weber supports this provocative theory of a causal connection between the Protestant form of religion and the capitalist form of economy in two ways: (1) by showing a "logical affinity" between Calvinist theology and capitalist work ethics, and (2) by comparing the different religions of the world in areas in which capitalism did *not* develop.[30] Weber's strategy here was to show that, in countries like China and India, all the strictly *material* conditions for the rise of capitalism (the evolution of a money economy, for example) had developed long before the advent of capitalism. The one thing that held capitalism back in these countries, according to Weber, was the lack of a religious ethic which would provide moral justification for "sober bourgeois" capitalism.

Weber's work began a long controversy in social science about the validity of his hypothesis.[31] A number of recent studies of economic behavior in the United States have attempted to verify or refute the Weber thesis. Most of these studies involve comparing, in some way, the differential aspirations or achievements of Protestants and Catholics in getting ahead economically. The findings have been sharply contradictory. Lenski's study in Detroit found evidence favorable to Weber's thesis.[32] An analysis of national survey data finds that American Protestants are more likely than Catholics to enter "high status nonmanual occupations."[33] Other studies,

---

[30] *Ancient Judaism,* trans. by H. H. Gerth and Don Martindale (Glencoe, Ill.: Free Press, 1952); *The Religion of China,* trans. by H. H. Gerth (Glencoe, Ill.: Free Press, 1951); *The Religion of India,* trans. by H. H. Gerth and Don Martindale (Glencoe, Ill.: Free Press, 1958).

[31] An early review and critique is found in Richard H. Tawney, *Religion and the Rise of Capitalism* (New York: Harcourt, Brace, 1926).

[32] Gerhard Lenski, *The Religious Factor* (Garden City, N.Y.: Doubleday, 1961).

[33] Elton F. Jackson, William S. Fox, and Harry J. Crockett, Jr., "Religion and Occupational Achievement," *American Sociological Review,* 35(1970):48–63.

measuring economic behavior in different ways and controlling for such important intervening variables as the national origins of persons, have found contrasting evidence. Catholics may be as much or more influenced by the Protestant Ethic as are Protestants,[34] and even Lenski's study suggested that American Jews are the most economically ambitious and successful of the three major religious faiths.[35]

To some extent, such studies are really irrelevant to the validity of Weber's argument. Weber insists that he is describing the situation in the very early history of capitalism, when it was still a deviant form of economic activity and appeared to require a great deal of religious conviction to withstand the general disapproval of business conducted in this new "spirit." Once capitalism becomes the *dominant* economic form, Weber admits, it no longer requires religious justification; capitalism will generate its own justification through, for example, some of the free enterprise ideology mentioned above. Perhaps fairer tests of the Weber thesis would be to study the relative aspirations or achievements of Protestants and Catholics in countries where capitalism is *not* the dominant form (in some of the socialist or welfare state societies in Europe, for example).

RELIGIOUS PARTICIPATION

Functional analysis of religion, like that of the family, will not explain all the variations of intensity and style of religious activity of different persons. For one thing, even given a prevailing form of religious structure—the secularized religion of Americanism described by Herberg, for example—there will be a number of churches that provide alternatives for expressing this religious style. For another thing, a social system may tolerate a number of religious nonbelievers even if it demands that most people most of the time adhere to the prevailing religion.

There are two kinds of variability in religious participation that the sociologist is interested in describing and explaining: (1) variation in the *quantity* or intensity of participation by different people, and (2) variation in the *quality* or style of participation by different

---

[34] Earlier evidence is cited and new critical material is presented in Norval D. Glenn and Ruth Hyland, "Religious Preference and Worldly Success: Some Evidence from National Surveys," *American Sociological Review,* 32(1967):73–85.

[35] Lenski, *The Religious Factor,* pp. 113, 114.

people. As always, the independent variables tend to be *category* differences in participation *rates:* men versus women, young versus old, etc. Here we shall consider only one basis of group differentials in participation rates—the factor of social class.

Nature of Religious Participation

A major problem for the sociological analysis of religious behavior has been the development of a clear understanding of what is meant by "religious participation." In contrast with familial participation, where a person either is or isn't married, is or isn't a virgin, there are no clearcut criteria to determine whether a person is or isn't a religious person. In everyday life we often find controversies arising around just this question: Is so-and-so religiously pious, apathetic, or hypocritical? The sociologist, who is interested in studying religious behavior as a variable correlated with other kinds of social behavior, is faced with the same problem of devising valid measures of religiosity.

Durkheim's definition of religion as involving *belief* and *ritual* is a first step toward the analysis of the meaning of religious participation. A person can conceivably believe very strongly in the theological notions of a given religious persuasion but, for whatever reason, may be a very marginal participant in the worship services and other collective rituals of the church. In Glock's terms, such a person is high on the *ideological* component of religious participation but is low on the *behavioral* component.[36]

The reverse situation is also frequently observed: the person who attends "religiously" all the rituals of the church but who shows a low level of ideological commitment to any of its beliefs. Church attendance may be the thing to do in this person's social circle and the thing is done when he has daydreamed through another sermon or has attended, at least bodily, the monthly meeting of the governing council of the church.

Glock's analysis of participation indicates two other dimensions of the phenomenon. One, a *consequential* dimension, distinguishes degrees of religious involvement by comparing those whose daily lives are closely affected by their religion with those for whom religious practice has little effect on their secular activities. Related

---

[36] Charles Y. Glock, "The Religious Revival in America?" in Jane C. Zahn (ed.), *Religion and the Face of America* (Berkeley: University of California Press, 1959), pp. 25–42.

but not identical with this distinction is an *experiential* dimension of religious participation. Some people experience or "feel" their religion very deeply; others are like Freud, who says that, if there is such a thing as an "oceanic feeling" that many people call religious, he, for one, has never had it.[37]

Given these various dimensions of religious participation or non-participation,[38] it may be necessary to indicate the kind of participation one is trying to explain. Several of the studies of religious participation discussed below do attempt to define the kinds of participation involved in the study or to suggest that there may be different variables correlated with religious participation, depending on the kind of participation in question.

Influences of Social Class on Religious Participation

One of the most persistent and provocative hypotheses in the sociology of religion is the assertion that religious participation is strongly influenced by social-class position. Much of the interest in this hypothesis goes back to Weber's assertion that each of the major world religions, at its historical origin, expressed the interest of a specific status group. "Early Hinduism was borne by a hereditary caste of cultured literati";[39] "Christianity began its course as a doctrine of itinerant artisan journeymen"[40] and became a "religion of the disinherited."[41]

Weber's view suggests not so much that the *quantity* of religious participation is a variable between classes but that different classes tend to associate themselves with different religions that express their separate class interests. However, it is easy enough to move from this position to the view that some social classes show more intense religious participation than do others. If a given religion becomes dominant, as Hinduism is in India, Mohammedanism is in the Middle East, Christianity is in Europe and the Americas, it should follow, according to Weber's thesis, that those classes

---

[37] Sigmund Freud, *Civilization and Its Discontents,* trans. by Joan Riviere (London: Hogarth, 1930), pp. 1, 2.

[38] For a more detailed study of the various dimensions of religious participation, see Morton King, "Measuring the Religious Variable: Nine Proposed Dimensions," *Journal for the Scientific Study of Religion,* 6(1967):173–190.

[39] *From Max Weber,* p. 268.

[40] Ibid., p. 269.

[41] H. Richard Niebuhr, *The Social Sources of Denominationalism* (New York: Holt, 1929).

whose interests are least represented by the dominant religion would be least likely to participate religiously. If they do participate, we should expect them to participate in deviant religious movements directed against the conservatism of the established religions.

The relationship between social class and participation in Christian religion has been of particular interest to sociologists, most of whom hail from so-called Christian countries. A very prominent idea is that Christianity as a whole has moved away from its identification with the "disinherited" and has taken on a strongly middle-class flavor as it has moved from the status of persecuted *sect* to that of established *denomination*.[42] There are apparently two major consequences of this trend, corresponding to our two fundamentally different ways of looking at differentials in religious participation.

Association of different classes with different churches. The first such consequence is that this trend has been a powerful impetus toward the well-known schismatic tendency within the Christian religion, the splitting of the religion into many separate church organizations.[43] As Christianity as a whole has evolved toward support of middle-class social interests, the "disinherited" have split off from the parent religious body and formed churches whose rituals and beliefs were more congenial to their lower-class interests.

An examination of the social-class distribution of membership in American Protestant denominations will strongly support this view. Whether "social class" is measured by such criteria as educational level, income, or occupation, there is a high degree of specialization of the different denominations in the social-class composition of their membership. Baptist and Methodist churches tend to have predominantly lower-class memberships, Episcopal and Presbyterian churches predominantly higher-class memberships.[44] These figures probably underestimate the degree of social-class homogeneity of the individual churches that people attend. While the Methodist Church, for example, has a substantial minority of relatively upper-class members, it is probably true that these persons

---

[42] Ibid.

[43] Ibid.

[44] Glenn and Hyland, "Religious Preference and Worldly Success."

are highly segregated in congregations that cater to wealthy Methodists.

The student may well exercise some caution in interpreting the sociological meaning of these correlations. The fact that a given denomination is predominantly lower class in membership *may* mean that religious participation promotes the social interest of that class, but not necessarily. One study of religion in a North Carolina community found a pattern of "social control" by which even the pastors of "mill churches" (with a working-class congregation) were led to exercise constraint against any radical questioning of the activities of the dominant business class.[45]

Three aspects of this social control may be of general significance for American Protestantism. First, the control was exercised by the economic power of the dominant classes; mill owners typically furnished church buildings and gave other financial aids to the mill churches. The holder of a church's purse strings may influence greatly the social message of that church.[46] Second, many of the mill churches were "mission" churches sponsored by the "uptown" churches with their middle-class congregations, and the parent religious bodies were able to control to some extent the behavior of mission pastors. Finally, there was a predominantly "other-worldly" style of religious ritual in the lower-class churches that Pope observed. Marx, in characterizing religion as an "opium of the people," had assumed that working-class people would participate religiously in a capitalist society but that this religion would promise salvation in the next world and divert attention from their exploitation in the capitalist system. The exciting—sometimes called "orgiastic"—character of church rituals in lower-class churches may be seen as a compensation for earthly misery. With all these considerations in mind, one must approach cautiously any assumption that lower-class churches promote the status interests of lower-class persons.

Churches with relatively upper-class memberships may, on the other hand, take positions on social issues that are favorable to

---

[45] Liston Pope, *Millhands and Preachers* (New Haven: Yale University Press, 1942).

[46] This factor may explain partially the often-noted fact that Negro churches have tended to exercise the main leadership in Negro civil rights movements. Negro churches have also been notable for their financial independence of white support and the heavy financial burden that black Americans have placed on themselves to maintain their own churches.

the interests of the lower classes. The ancient ethic of *noblesse oblige,* the obligation of charitable treatment of the socially unfortunate, is well represented in the Christian view of man as his brother's keeper. The National Council of Churches, an affiliation of American denominations largely white, Protestant, and middle class in composition, has been a prime supporter of racial desegregation. The liberalism of these national religious organizations has not, however, filtered down to local church activity in many cases.[47] It may be entertained as a sociological hypothesis that, the more closely church officials must work with a congregation with a specific social-class composition, the more directly must they deal with the interests of the dominant social class in that church. The local pastor may pay lip service to the charitable ideals of his denomination, but his very survival and effectiveness as a leader may require that he temper his religious messages with an awareness of which local toes are being stepped on.

Social-class influence on religious participation or nonparticipation. These various accommodations by all Christian denominations to middle-class social interests provide a background for the second major hypothesis about the effects on religious participation of the evolution of Christianity toward a middle-class social orientation. If middle-class interests have dominated in the operation of Christian religion, we might expect that the "disinherited" have tended to abandon Christianity altogether.

Studies of differential religious participation have supported this expectation, if participation is defined at the *behavioral* level and is measured by such criteria as church membership, frequency of church attendance, and involvement in the governing of church bodies.[48] The unchurched, in the United States and elsewhere in the Christian world, are largely members of the lower classes, who tend either not to affiliate with churches at all or, if they do, to limit attendance to "weddings and funerals."

The lesser participation of the lower classes in formal church rituals is a matter of well-established fact; the interpretation of this fact is still highly controversial, however. One view, which has some empirical support, is that the lower classes are no less reli-

---

[47] Campbell and Pettigrew, "Racial and Moral Crisis."

[48] This evidence is reviewed in N. J. Demerath III, *Social Class in American Protestantism* (Chicago: Rand McNally, 1965), pp. 4–12.

gious than the higher classes but are less likely to express their religiosity through participation in the formal activities of churches.

In a study of religious behavior in several large American cities, Demerath found that, if you distinguish between a church-like and a sect-like form of religious participation, a higher-class position is conducive to church-like religious involvement and a lower-class position to sect-like involvement.[49] Church-like involvement entails such *behavioral* measures as church attendance, while sect-like involvement deals with the degree to which church members see their religion as relevant to their daily lives—the extent to which their friendships are confined to fellow church members, for example.

Demerath's sample of Protestant church members showed that lower-class persons tended toward greater religiosity in the *consequential* component of religious involvement. Other studies have indicated that lower-class persons are likely to be more fundamentalist in their religious beliefs (e.g., believing in heaven and hell), more involved in what Glock calls the *ideological* component of religious involvement.[50]

If such findings are meant to show that lower-class persons are equally as religious as higher-class ones (though with different "style" tendencies), the interpretation can be criticized. It has been suggested that studies like that of Demerath deal only with church members, only with those "lower-class persons who are sufficiently involved in religion to belong to a congregation"[51] and that such persons may not be a representative sample of lower-class religious attitudes generally. Glock and Stark show that, if one uses data derived from surveys in which total populations rather than church members are sampled, higher-class persons are more likely than lower-class ones to hold to some of the basic beliefs of Christianity (life after death, etc.).[52]

According to Glock and Stark, the low religious participation of the lower classes reflects a pervasive alienation of the lower classes from the established religious system. Some evidence for this view is produced by showing that lower-class people tend to define

[49] Ibid., p. 66.
[50] Ibid., pp. 44–45.
[51] Charles Y. Glock and Rodney Stark, *Religion and Society in Tension* (Chicago: Rand McNally, 1965), pp. 189–190.
[52] Ibid., pp. 197–199.

politics as more relevant to their lives than religion, while the higher classes see religion as more relevant.[53] European and American data show a rather striking correlation between low religious participation (in ritual and in belief) and a tendency to affiliate with a radical political party. These authors conclude that "there is excellent empirical support for supposing that religious involvement and radicalism tend to be mutually exclusive."[54] Where "status politics" becomes relevant (as it is, for example, in Europe and Latin America), it may be that the relevance of "status religion" to sociological analysis tends to decline.

There are many other differences in rates of religious participation by different categories of people that sociological research has established. For example, by most measures of religious participation, in the United States blacks participate more actively than whites, older adults more than young adults, women more than men, rural dwellers more than urban dwellers, third-generation immigrants more than second-generation immigrants.[55] All these facts are grist for the mill of sociological interpretation; we leave the reader with just the one example of analysis and controversy on the matter of social-class differences in religious participation.

SUMMARY

The universality of religious beliefs and rituals is fully consistent with the psychological nature of man and with some of the requirements of viable societies. Religion provides the individual with rationalization for or explanation of puzzling situations and with reassurance about the future. For society, religion tends to give ideological support to the existing social values and institutional forms and to provide a basis of solidarity or unity for a people. With all these functions, major questions arise concerning the possibility of functional alternatives to religion; can religion be replaced, for example, by a more adequate science and technology, or by a more secular ideology like communism or humanism?

Religious life is only more or less socially organized or institutionalized in church activity, and the sociologist concerns himself

---

[53] Ibid., pp. 196, 197.

[54] Ibid., p. 226.

[55] Differences between generations of immigrants are indicated in Herberg, *Protestant-Catholic-Jew.* For other group differences, see Michael Argyle, *Religious Behavior* (London: Routledge & Kegan Paul, 1958).

with those processes which lead to the greater institutionalization of religion as formal *denominations* or to the greater responsiveness to human emotion of the *sect* form of religious organization.

All the major world religions have developed an ethic to guide the daily lives of their members. This ethic may enjoin other-worldly concern with life in the next world or a this-worldly concentration on affairs in this life. The latter kind of ethic was seen by Weber as incorporated in the Protestant Ethic and as a major contributor to the rise of capitalism—a highly controversial view, with evidence pro and con.

Finally, we have considered social class as one of many sociological variables associated with variations in religious participation. The best evidence seems to be that Christianity, beginning as a lower-class church, has evolved toward a middle-class orientation which has resulted in: (1) a splitting off of lower-class elements from established religious bodies, and (2) a rather general alienation of lower-class people from Christian religion in its more organized aspects. Although lower-class people may be personally pious, they tend not to express this piety in any systematic participation in organized church activity.

Political Institutions

DEFINITIONS

In sociology, a number of terms to describe political institutions are used in ways that differ from some of the popular usages of these terms. We begin, therefore, with a discussion of four key terms of political analysis: power, authority, government, and the state. With most of these definitions we shall follow the direction of analysis provided by Max Weber.

Power

Power is a feature of interpersonal relations of all kinds. Power exists whenever one person is able to exercise his will in determining the behavior of another person.[1] The professor who gives assignments to his students has power; the mother who controls a child's access to the cookie jar has power. In virtually every social relationship there is power, although it may not be all on the side of one party to the relationship.[2]

Authority

Authority is *legitimate* power, the ability to command by virtue of the recognition of the *right* of certain persons to give commands

---

[1] Max Weber, *The Theory of Social and Economic Organization,* trans. by A. M. Henderson and Talcott Parsons (New York: Oxford, 1947), p. 152.

[2] Simmel insists that few, if any, relationships involve a level of subordination so complete that the subordinate party has no power at all. Georg Simmel, *Conflict,* trans. by Kurt Wolff (Glencoe, Ill.: Free Press, 1955), pp. 113, 114. A similar point is made in Dennis Wrong, "Some Problems in Defining Social Power," *American Journal of Sociology,* 73(1968):673–681.

and the *obligation* of others to obey them. Not all power is of this kind, of course. The bully who intimidates small children, the professor who exacts the execution of an assignment on pain of failing the student—these are among the numerous examples of power which those subject to it may define as *illegitimate.* A major theme of Max Weber's sociology was the problem of how social forms, including prevailing distributions of power, become legitimated as authority; how, for example, the economic power of the capitalist entrepreneur was legitimated by the Protestant Ethic.[3] The problem of authority in political systems will concern us throughout this chapter.

Government

Power and authority exist at the interpersonal level wherever there is interaction between persons. But the power of one friend over another or the dominance of a person at a social party are not usually defined as *government.* This term is reserved for those situations in which power and authority are exercised at the level of some group or society: the government of a family, a trade union, or of the United States. Although specific individuals may make and enforce decisions on all members of the group, the power is exercised on behalf of the group as a whole and is usually legitimated by reference to some notion about the welfare of the group as a whole.

As we indicated in the discussion of the functional imperatives of social systems (chapter 5), there are two ways of describing the nature of the power which is exercised on behalf of a social system. When government is conceived as *polity,* power represents the process of deciding upon and enforcing *policies* of the system as a whole. A family decides to take its vacation at a specific time and place, a nation to commit its military forces at a specific time and place. When government is conceived as a *legal system,* governmental power refers to the enactment and enforcement of *laws* which regulate the behavior of each member of the social system. Policies and laws are the products of political activity at the governmental level, and the question of *how* laws and policies are arrived at and enforced is a prime question of sociological interest.

---

[3] Max Weber, *The Protestant Ethic and the Spirit of Capitalism,* trans. by Talcott Parsons (New York: Scribner's, 1930).

The State

Government, we have just seen, is found in groups of all kinds and sizes. However, it is the government found among people who occupy a given geographic territory that is usually involved in the studies of "governments" made by political scientists and sociologists. *The state,* which is the agency that performs governmental functions, has been defined as having a "monopoly of the legitimate use of physical force within a given territory."[4] By this definition, the state embraces a wide variety of political jurisdictions, including those agencies that exercise the power of government in a city, a county, a nation, or what is popularly called "the state."

FUNCTIONS OF GOVERNMENT: USES OF POWER

Our following discussion of the functions of government will focus on the problem of why these power monopolies within territories appear to be functional requirements for societies. Later in the chapter we will deal with the question of the historical emergence of the state as a special agency for the performance of governmental functions.

Social Control

Our first observation about the functions of governmental power brings us back to the view of government as a legal system. The law and the "legal violence" that stands behind the law appear to be necessary, given the various ways in which people may be tempted to behave, ways that are subversive to social order. The possibility of being spanked, imprisoned, or even executed may be powerful factors in deterring socially disapproved behavior although, as we shall see in chapter 13, legal punishments may be a relatively minor part of the total array of mechanisms of social control that a society uses to produce conforming behavior.

An organized society without weapons-carrying policemen is probably a contradiction of the nature of human association under modern conditions. Even when the police themselves are equipped with a minimum of weaponry, as is the gunless London bobby, there is behind those policemen a structure of prisons and other penal institutions that may be designed to strike terror in the minds of

---

[4] H. H. Gerth and C. Wright Mills (eds.), *From Max Weber: Essays in Sociology* (New York: Oxford, 1958), p. 78.

citizens. Some countries carry to an extreme the social-control possibilities of their police forces, putting police in plain clothes so that the would-be law violators are never sure which observer might be empowered to initiate legal violence against them.

There is, however, a well-developed notion in popular thought to the effect that legal violence may encourage rather than inhibit law violation. The policy of imprisonment is often criticized for creating an embittered man who comes out of prison both more determined and more technically equipped (through learning from other experienced criminals in prison) to carry on a life of crime than he was before he entered prison.[5] Similarly, it is frequently alleged that police use their weapons extralegally and excessively, and that this "police brutality" simply stimulates greater hatred for the "pigs" and for the laws that they enforce.

One sociological study has reported on some of the motives for police violence.[6] First, police tend to justify extralegal violence if they feel it is necessary to get a confession from a suspect. The feeling among many police is that, once an accused criminal enters the formal prosecution procedure, with all its legal safeguards of his "rights," there is relatively little chance of his being convicted. Since police are judged professionally on the basis of their ability to make a "good pinch" (an arrest that leads to a conviction), there is a temptation to use extralegal violence to obtain incriminating evidence.

Second, the study showed that police tend to condone violence if the victim of the violence has somehow publicly humiliated or brought harm to a member of the police force. A "cop killer" is seen as deserving no mercy, and a person who openly resists arrest casts doubt on the potency of the police, an implication which the policeman may feel impelled to refute by an overly violent reaction.[7] Perhaps the recent widespread police repression of the Black

---

[5] Donald P. Clemmer, *The Prison Community* (New York: Rinehart, 1958).

[6] William A. Westley, "Violence and the Police," *American Journal of Sociology*, 59(1953):34–41.

[7] This may be especially true if the policeman is of the same minority group as the person being arrested and the latter tries to play on the policeman's minority-group sympathy to avoid being arrested. A black policeman, faced with a civilian who makes this appeal, may feel that he "must repress the offender by force in order to maintain his initial definition of the situation" (his definition being that race is irrelevant to the episode). Nicholas Alex, *Black in Blue: A Study of the Negro Policeman* (New York: Meredith, 1969), p. 151.

Panther Party, a militant organization of gun-carrying blacks devoted to "protecting" black communities from police, is largely explained as a reaction to the killing of policemen by members of the group and the public ridicule against established authority that the organization carries on. Whether police brutality or black militancy began this cycle of violence and counterviolence is, of course, a matter of controversy.

Defense

The same monopoly of weaponry that insures domestic tranquility when exercised by police forces may be employed to defend the people of a territory against the military ambitions of external enemies. The affinity between the social-control and defense functions of government is shown in the tendency for the same men and weapons to be used interchangeably for the two purposes, as when the governor of a state calls out the National Guard to deal with a domestic riot, or when the local constabulary is impressed into military service on the occasion of an imminent foreign invasion of a territory. The ease with which military personnel can be used to deal with problems of domestic order is, however, a variable between different political systems. In countries in which military and civilian powers are not so clearly separated, it is relatively easy to employ military forces to deal with emergency domestic situations.[8]

This functional interchangeability of military and police forces creates a major problem for the stability of government in a society. In many countries, the military coup or takeover of the domestic political apparatus is an ever-present possibility. In the United States there is a vigorous attempt to separate civilian from military, and a tendency to lament any evidence of a power elite in which civilian and military leadership is interchangeable[9] or the threat of an industrial-military complex which could exert undue influence on the society. In a cold war era, when so many of the policy decisions to be made by a government involve military considerations, a special strain is placed on this traditional separation of the defense and social-control functions.[10]

---

[8] William A. Anderson, "Social Structure and the Role of the Military in Natural Disaster," *Sociology and Social Research,* 53(1969):242–253.

[9] C. Wright Mills, *The Power Elite* (New York: Oxford, 1956).

[10] Morris Janowitz, *Sociology and the Military Establishment* (New York: Russell Sage, 1959).

Welfare

The federation of the United States was established to, among other things, "promote the general welfare," and this aim is typical of the concern of government to establish programs or policies for the benefit of the residents of a territory. Many of the conditions that people define as beneficial to themselves are not easily attainable by their individual actions or by any combination of individuals that they can arrange.

The schooling of children, for example, requires more organization and a larger accumulation of facilities than most individuals can muster. The largely futile attempts of white parents to produce "homemade" school systems to replace the public schools that were closed to avert racial integration are symptomatic of the problem. Some of the earliest efforts toward large-scale government were influenced by the need to evolve complex and bureaucratic organizations to deal with such massive problems as flood control and the irrigation of land.

In discussing these welfare activities, we are again concerned with the view of government as a policy-making mechanism. In each society decisions must be made concerning the priorities of need in terms of welfare and the appropriate tactics for fulfilling these needs. Furthermore, these decisions must be made binding on all members of the society, lest the implementation of policies fail for lack of public support.

It is apparently here that the *power* element comes into play again. A decision to commit the society to a poverty program may, for example, be repugnant to many people who may work for repeal of the decision in favor of other policies more to their liking. While most political systems tolerate such protests and agitations against established policy, no system apparently tolerates widespread refusal of people to pay taxes or otherwise support the policy decisions so long as they stand. The well-publicized decision of a popular American folk singer to withhold from her federal income tax payment an amount proportionate to the country's expenditure for military policies that she opposes is a behavior that would be tolerated in no political system if widely practiced. The full power of "legal violence" will, if necessary, be brought to bear to enforce the expectation that every citizen, regardless of his personal will, shall provide a degree of support to the decisions made by the polity.

INSTITUTIONALIZATION

The emergence of *the state* as a special agency to make and enforce law and policy for the people of a territory is another instance of the process of institutionalization. It is frequently asserted that power was used for collective purposes before there were special agencies established to exercise political functions. In relatively simple societies it may be that the formal machinery of the state is not required to maintain social control. In a rural community where "everybody knows everybody," it is possible for persons to exercise discipline over the behavior of one another without resort to legislatures, police, and courts. In primitive societies, as MacIver puts it, "custom serves to regulate many things that in a less primitive system are determined by law or decree."[11]

Along with this notion of the informality of primitive forms of government, it is often thought that there was a lack of a territorial basis for whatever instruments of government may have existed in primitive societies. Sir Henry Maine writes that "the idea that a number of persons should exercise political rights in common simply because they happened to live within the same topographical limits was utterly strange and monstrous to primitive antiquity."[12] What was not "strange and monstrous" to the primitive, according to this view, was the idea that the family or clan should serve as the unit of political organization.

At least one anthropologist, Robert Lowie, has taken vigorous exception to this view of primitive societies as lacking in territorially based government.[13] He believes that students of primitive government, in their emphasis on the exercise of political authority within kinship units, have systematically ignored the political activities of those territorially based groups, the membership of which cuts across family lines. In many societies there are, for example, "men's societies" and "old people's societies" made up of persons from various families living in a region, and Lowie sees the political power of these nonfamilial groupings as the germ from which the modern state has grown. Even Lowie says, however, that "it must

---

[11] Robert M. MacIver, *The Web of Government* (New York: Macmillan, 1947), p. 156.

[12] Quoted in Robert Lowie, *The Origin of the State* (New York: Russell & Russell, 1962), p. 51.

[13] Ibid.

be conceded that the blood tie is frequently the overshadowing element in the governmental activities of primitive peoples."[14]

Whatever may be the truth about the character of primitive forms of political institutions, it seems clear that the growth of the modern state has resulted in a reorganization of political activities in at least three respects.

First, there in an increasing dominance of territorially based political organization, with the modern nation-state replacing the family, the church, or other functional alternatives to the state as a monopolist of political power. The family, the church, and the voluntary vigilante committee are clearly subordinate to the state in the sense that law made at the level of the state binds members of these groups, often against their collective will. The futile struggles of Mormons to maintain a polygamous marriage system or of some parents to refuse to send their children to officially accredited schools are lessons in the relative omnipotence of the state under modern social conditions.

Second, there has been an expansion of the size or geographic extent of the territory within which a single political system is operative. Some of this expansion in the size of the modern nation-state is undoubtedly a consequence of international wars. War has typically resulted in the incorporation of the territory of a conquered people into the area dominated by their conquerors.

Although warfare is thus often seen as a major force in creating the modern nation-state, war can also be viewed as a "great divider,"[15] producing schisms that make political union impossible. Under conditions of modern warfare, in which extensive military alliances are formed among combatant nations, victory in warfare is often the occasion for the division of territories which are then dominated by different members of the victorious alliance. Eastern Europe was carved up as a result of World War I, and World War II resulted in the apparently permanent creation of two Germanys.

Under such conditions, warfare can probably no longer be treated as a major factor in the expansion of the size of the state. Rather, the force that apparently now most influences the movement toward enlarged states is the increasing economic interdependence of the nations of the world. The European and other "common

---

[14] Ibid., p. 73.
[15] MacIver, *Web of Government*, p. 36.

markets" have begun to evolve tariff regulations that apply in an area wider than the territory of any one nation, and aspirations are still being entertained that a more complete federation or a United States of Europe might develop from these beginnings.

Finally, the modern state represents a movement toward a more *permanent* territorial organization of power. The earliest ventures in collective government were probably stimulated by such special contingencies as warfare or a group hunting expedition, and the earliest forms of authority represented submission to the leadership of persons who could organize these special activities. The authority of such "state" organizations tended to expire with the end of the crisis.[16] Where economic activity becomes more routine and less sporadic, as happens in the movement from a hunting to an agricultural society, the need for more permanent political organization becomes apparent. The ad hoc political organization of the hunting tribe would not suffice to satisfy political needs under more routinized social conditions.

VARIABILITY IN POLITICAL INSTITUTIONS

An interest in the variation of forms of political structure is at least as ancient as the writings of Aristotle and Plato. A classic expression of this interest is Montesquieu's comparative study of political forms, *The Spirit of the Laws* (1748). The modern political sociologist is heir to a long line of speculation about the conditions that encourage one or another form of political structure.

Authority

One dimension of variability of political forms concerns the degree and type of *legitimacy* of the prevailing political order in different situations. As we have seen, legitimate power or authority is that power which is willingly accepted as right and proper by the people who are subject to its exercise. Two major kinds of variation in political institutions concern political sociologists: (1) the extent to which the prevailing order is a legitimate or authoritative one, and (2) the basis for the authority of a legitimate political regime.

Degree of authority. One major tradition in political sociology emphasizes the near inevitability with which people accept as

---

[16] Lowie, *Origin of the State.*

legitimate the political system that prevails among them. MacIver, a proponent of this view, asserts that:

Men obey because they are social beings—or, if you prefer it, because they are socialized beings, trained and indoctrinated in the ways of their society. . . . Law-abidingness is the pragmatic condition of response to the whole firmament of social order.[17]

This response may be reinforced by the devices available to rulers to impress their subjects with the majesty of the state. Merriam distinguishes two such devices: *credenda,* or things to be believed, and *miranda,* or things to be admired.[18] Credenda consist largely in the "myths" that grow up around an existing political order: the myth, for example, of the "divine right of kings" or of the power of government derived from a "social contract" such as a constitution.[19] Miranda tend to center around the elaborate ritual that a state employs to emphasize its majesty: the coronation of a king, the inauguration of a president, the pomp of a state dinner or a state funeral. These tend to impress the citizen with the dignity of his political institutions. The man who stands at the center of an inauguration pageantry and says, "I, Richard Milhous Nixon," appropriates to his person some of the awesome dignity of the state, and this dignity no doubt gives his words the "authority" of irresistible command to many citizens of his country.

In contrast, some political orders are based on a minimum of willing obedience and a maximum of terror tactics or raw power to enforce conformity. A so-called police state is a form of government in which the suppression of disobedience is carried to an extreme. Perhaps the key to a successful exercise of power in a police state is what Neumann calls the "institutionalization of anxiety."[20] Although rulers cannot suppress every instance of disobedient behavior, they can sometimes create an atmosphere of uncertainty as to when and how the police may strike against suspects. The unexpected midnight raid, the use of paid informers, random punishments of people whether innocent or guilty (every tenth man in

---

[17] MacIver, *Web of Government*, p. 77.

[18] Charles E. Merriam, *Political Power* (Glencoe, Ill.: Free Press, 1950).

[19] Ernst Cassirer, *The Myth of the State* (New Haven: Yale University Press, 1946).

[20] Franz Neumann, "Anxiety and Politics," in Eric and Mary Josephson (eds.), *Man Alone: Alienation in Modern Society* (New York: Dell, 1962), p. 259.

the village will be shot)—these are a few of the infinitely various devices to keep people submissive to a set of rulers who possess neither favorable credenda nor miranda with the people. George Orwell's fictional account of a police state in *1984* illustrates some of these devices. The pervasive sense that "Big Brother is watching" tends to suppress any potential movements toward disobedience.

The totalitarian political regimes of recent years, the control exercised over prisoners in concentration camps,[21] and even the control exercised by staff over inmates of such benevolently conceived "total institutions" as mental hospitals[22] are illustrations of the possibilities of the exercise of control without there being any high degree of authority or perceived legitimacy of the power.

Sources of authority. Having given police-state forms of political power their due, we return to the central sociological problem of the nature of authority in political systems. Given the difficulty of maintaining unlegitimated power, it is not surprising to observe a tendency for naked power to clothe itself with legitimacy and be transformed into authority. But there are a number of quite different styles of this "clothing." The most influential typology of the forms of authority is that of Max Weber.[23] We shall review the forms of authority defined by Weber and then assess the usefulness of this typology in understanding the nature of political authority in one country, the United States.

First, there are political systems in which the authority of governors is *traditional* in its origins. A purely monarchical government is of this type, the reigning monarch's authority being guaranteed by the belief of his subjects in the legitimacy of the ruler as the heir of a legitimate line of rulers. This line may be thought to extend back to a heroic "founder" of the society, as exemplified in the theory of government of the Roman Catholic Church, which teaches that the current Pope is the present representative of a line of authority extending back to Saint Peter.

Second, a ruler may gain authority through his personal *charismatic* quality, his ability to make people believe in his personal mission, often one which contradicts the established and tradi-

---

[21] Edgar H. Schein, *Coercive Persuasion* (New York: Norton, 1961).

[22] Erving Goffman, *Asylums* (Garden City, N.Y.: Doubleday, 1961).

[23] Weber, *Theory of Social and Economic Organization,* p. 328.

tional political structure. Weber placed a great deal of emphasis on charisma as the source of social innovation, including new forms of political structure. Revolutionary governments tend toward the charismatic form, with a Cromwell, Washington, Mao Tse-tung, or Castro as the magnetic personality who holds together the diverse elements of a successful revolution.

The third type of authority Weber called *rational-legal.* Rulers acquire legitimacy from the belief that they were duly elected or duly appointed in accordance with the society's rules for the selection of officeholders and that their performance of official duties follows the due process of law in that society. This form of government might also be called *constitutional,* if we think of a constitution as a set of basic rules for political activity. A constitutional government is "of laws, not of men," and a ruler in such a system benefits from the belief of all citizens in his legitimate right to hold and exercise the power of his office.

These types of authority are ideal types in the sense that no existing political system will be a complete embodiment of any one type; however, these types are useful for analyzing and comparing political systems. Using Weber's typology, we might ask how one could characterize the nature of political authority in the United States. On the surface, the system is almost completely a rational-legal one. The constitution of the country prescribes a set of rules for the election of officials and a set of limitations on the powers that they may legitimately exercise. The Supreme Court has evolved as the principal agency for exercising restraint against extraconstitutional uses of power by any of the branches of government.[24]

The strength of constitutional restraint on political power is shown in the willingness of the public to submit to an electoral-college mode of presidential selection that is constitutionally prescribed but contrary to the preferences of most political leaders and most citizens. Further, there is a broader strain of *legalism* in the political attitudes of people in the United States. Once a piece of legislation becomes the law of the land it tends to be submitted to regardless of personal attitudes. The compliance of the Southern states with unpopular desegregation decisions of the Supreme

---

[24] The degree of restraint that is appropriate for the Court to exercise is a matter of disagreement among jurists. Justices of the type of Hugo Black argue that the Court should carefully restrain any extraconstitutional exercise of power of any branch of government, while those like Felix Frankfurter have favored more flexibility of interpretation to adapt to the times.

Court is the most frequently cited example.[25] Other examples include the finding that, while most American doctors and the American Medical Association opposed public medical insurance for the aged (Medicare) before the program was instituted, most doctors have cooperated rather fully with the program and have even developed attitudes favorable to it.[26] The constitutional and legal conservatism of the American political system seems to be well established.

On the other hand, there may be important traditional and charismatic elements in political authority in the United States. In the direction of traditional authority, it is interesting to note an apparent tendency of the public to accept certain ideas about "legitimate heirs" to political power. There have been "political families" throughout the country's history—the Adamses, the Roosevelts, the Kennedys—in which the presumption is that any adult male is an heir to the family's tradition of political leadership.

We may also be developing certain ideas about legitimate heirs on a basis other than family lineage. Consider the vice-presidency of the United States, historically ridiculed as a dead-end political job (a cartoon published while Lyndon Johnson was vice-president carried the following caption—First man: You know, you never hear much about Lyndon Johnson these days. Second man: Lyndon who?). There seems to be an increasingly common presumption that the current vice-president will receive his party's presidential nomination when the incumbent president is ineligible or unavailable for renomination. Although there is nothing in the American constitution that supports this presumption, it may be emerging as a political tradition to accompany more established political axioms such as the old saw that the governors of New York and California are good presidential timber.

The role of personality or charisma in American political authority is frequently commented upon. A favorite popular expression used by people to express their political independence is their assertion that they vote for "the man," not "the party." Voting for

[25] Arthur Earl Bonfield, "The Role of Legislation in Eliminating Racial Discrimination," *Race*, 7(1965):108–109.

[26] John Colombotos, "Physicians and Medicare: a Before-After Study of the Effects of Legislation," *American Sociological Review*, 34(1969):318–334. On a similar theme, see William K. Muir, Jr., *Prayer in the Public Schools: Law and Attitude Change* (Chicago: University of Chicago Press, 1967).

"the man" seems often as not to come down to voting for the most likable candidate or the one with the best physical appearance. In one recent presidential election a woman was quoted as saying that, in deciding how to vote, she always pictured a wall of oval picture frames with pictures of all the American presidents; the last frame is empty and she mentally places each candidate in the oval frame to see which looks best and she votes for that man.

David Riesman attributes the recent emphasis on "glamour" in political leaders to a general change in American "character."[27] The increasingly "other-directed" person has no clear-cut personal goals of any kind, and he does not really know what he *wants* from his political leaders in terms of support for given laws or policies, but he knows what he *likes* and he "likes Ike" or "detests Nixon." According to Riesman, what the American really likes in his political candidates is the appearance of sincerity (a rather dangerous criterion, since sincerity can so easily be faked). This view touches a persistent theme in social criticism of American political life: the view that political candidates are too carefully "packaged" in the image-making style of Madison Avenue.[28]

Influence

A different way of looking at variations in political structure is a consideration of the distribution of political *influence*. While the problem of authority refers to the problem of securing compliance to a *given* set of enacted laws and policies, the problem of influence refers to the ability of different people to determine the nature of the laws and policies that are enacted by a government. At one extreme we have a *dictatorial* form of political structure in which one man imposes his will in the making of laws and policies. At the other extreme we have a purely *democratic* form in which all persons within a social system have influence on political decisions. Close to the dictatorial form is that of an *oligarchy* or an *elite* political structure in which political influence is concentrated in the hands of a very few persons.

Dictatorial and oligarchic forms. The more concentrated forms of political influence have excited much sociological interest. One

27 David Riesman, *The Lonely Crowd* (New Haven: Yale University Press, 1950).

28 Vance O. Packard, *The Hidden Persuaders* (New York: McKay, 1957).

tradition in political sociology holds that oligarchy is an inevitable tendency in political structure. Michels' "iron law of oligarchy" is a typical statement of such an elitist conception of politics.[29]

Michels bases his "iron law" on his observation of the internal political structure of European socialist parties. It was his view that, if one were to find anywhere a democratic structure with a large degree of rank-and-file influence on group decisions, one ought to find it in those political parties that supposedly represent the interests of the common man. In fact, Michels found these parties to be highly oligarchic; a few men make the decisions for the party and select its leaders and rank-and-file views seldom have much weight.

The oligarchic tendency that Michels describes is based on two major characteristics of the mass of members of an organization: (1) their incompetence, and (2) their apathy. Rank-and-file members are incompetent in the sense that they can have no adequate grasp of the technicalities involved in political administration. Ordinary citizens seem quite incapable, for example, of understanding the fiscal intricacies involved in the international balance of payments. For the administration of their affairs people must depend upon "experts." As the distance between the expert's and the ordinary citizen's understanding of the technicalities of government widens, it becomes less and less possible for the general public to judge the merit of the handling of their affairs by these experts, who tend to detach themselves from the masses and become part of the ruling oligarchy.

Michels notes also the frequently lamented indifference or apathy of the rank-and-file member: "There is no exaggeration in the assertion that among the citizens who enjoy political rights the number of those who have a lively interest in public affairs is insignificant."[30] The low rate of membership turnout at a business meeting of a union or social club or at the primary election of a political party is an often-cited symptom of this "mass apathy."[31] Even when people participate in activities such as labor unions,

[29] Robert Michels, *Political Parties: A Sociological Study of the Oligarchical Tendencies of Modern Democracy*, trans. by Eden and Cedar Paul (New York: Collier Books, 1962). First published in 1911.

[30] Ibid., p. 85.

[31] In a Democratic Party primary in New York to select candidates for governor and United States senator, in June 1970, only some 30 percent of the registered voters went to the polls. *New York Times*, June 28, 1970.

they may be more motivated by primary-group considerations (the satisfaction of "belonging" to a congenial group of peers, for example) than in actively promoting their political interests.[32]

When people are asked what is "worrying" them, they tend to cite such private troubles as financial insolvency and only very infrequently do they express much concern with the political issues of the day.[33] The leaders of parties or nations, on the other hand, tend to be highly committed or interested in the group because, being leaders, they have invested more of their own fates in the success of their organization.[34] With a highly committed leadership and an indifferent mass, the stage is set for a take-over of control by an oligarchy. "Though it grumbles occasionally, the majority is usually delighted to find persons who will take the trouble to look after its affairs."[35] Although Michels does not personally despair of the "desperate enterprise" of combatting this oligarchic tendency, he does emphasize in his work this "pessimist aspect of democracy."[36]

This "pessimist" viewpoint has colored sociological studies of the structure of political influence in nations, communities, and formal organizations. One investigation which aimed to examine the validity of the "iron law of oligarchy" was a study of the politics of the International Typographical Union.[37] In this union there was, contrary to the situation in most labor unions, a great deal of rank-and-file participation and influence on the decisions of the union leadership. But the ITU had some rather unusual features for a labor union.

First, there was a long tradition of conflict of interest between different kinds of printers, and there existed in the union an unusual kind of "two-party" system in which each party had to compete

---

[32] Eugene C. Hagburg, "Correlates of Organizational Participation: An Examination of Factors Affecting Union Membership Participation," *Pacific Sociological Review,* 9(1966):15–21.

[33] Samuel A. Stouffer, *Communism, Conformity and Civil Liberties* (Garden City, N.Y.: Doubleday, 1955).

[34] In his study of Mobilization for Youth, Brager finds a higher "commitment to values" of the organization among leaders than nonleaders. George Brager, "Commitment and Conflict in a Normative Organization," *American Sociological Review,* 34(1969):482–491.

[35] Michels, *Political Parties,* p. 88.

[36] Ibid., pp. 367, 368.

[37] Seymour M. Lipset, Martin Trow, and James Coleman, *Union Democracy* (Glencoe, Ill.: Free Press, 1956).

continuously with the other for rank-and-file support.[38] Second, printers as a group are highly skilled workers in a high-status occupation. These authors suggest that one source of union oligarchy is the high status enjoyed by the typical union leader by virtue of his leadership position. If he loses an election, he falls a long way in social status; therefore, he is highly motivated to maintain his leadership at whatever cost. If the rank-and-file members also have high status, however, there is less distance for the leader to fall and the more gracefully he can accept the democratic decision against his leadership.

These observations on the ITU suggest some important conditions that seem to affect the tendency toward oligarchy in other kinds of organizations. We might expect less oligarchy in a two-party political structure or in a professional society or other group of persons with high social status. Like all "iron laws" in sociology, this one may not be quite so "iron" as to preclude a concern for the independent variables associated with more or less of the tendency that was supposedly inevitable.

Democratic forms. Democracy is the form of political structure in which influence on governmental decisions is widely dispersed among the members of a society. Government is a reflection of public opinion, the "public" whose opinion has weight constituting all or a major part of the total population. This weight of opinion may or may not be exercised through the direct participation of masses of people in decision-making.

The *referendum*—a direct popular vote for or against new laws or policies—is one device by which the "will of the people" is made to prevail on government decisions. In a *representative* form of democracy, the tendency is to leave direct decision-making to public officials: prime ministers, members of Parliament, etc., and for the popular will to be exerted through universal suffrage, i.e., the right of all citizens to participate in voting for these representatives. The democracy of the Greek city-states of antiquity and that of the New England town meeting are illustrations of the more direct

---

[38] It has been suggested that it is "close elections" (regardless of whether there are one or more "parties") that counters oligarchy in a union. J. David Edelstein, "Countervailing Powers and the Political Process in the British Mineworkers' Union," *International Journal of Comparative Sociology*, 9(1968):256–288.

expressions of popular will; most modern states maintain the form if not the substance of a representative democracy.

Sociological perspectives will tend to raise different questions about these two kinds of democracy. The direct participation by masses of people in political decisions will raise the "competency" question that arose in connection with the "iron law of oligarchy." Are the masses able to participate *competently* in decision-making? This is a troublesome question in the many situations in which certain masses are asserted *not* to be competent: for example, in the faculty argument against the professional competence of students to participate on a one-man-one-vote basis in the governing of a college.[39]

Direct participation of the referendum type may also have some of the features of *crowd behavior,* as we shall discuss that concept in chapter 16. To anticipate that discussion, the behavior of people in referendum voting tends toward the naysaying or negative spirit that is often attributed to crowds; the rule seems often to be, if in doubt, vote no.[40] Another crowd-like feature of the referendum is the tendency for voters to be swayed by emotional considerations. The defeat by referendum of a plan for a civilian review board to deal with alleged cases of "police brutality" in New York City was widely attributed to the successful "scare" campaign conducted by a politically oriented association of policemen, the Policemen's Benevolent Association.[41] All of this is not to say that direct political participation always or necessarily involves incompetent or irrational political action, but only that these tendencies are persistent problems for democracy of this type.

Representative democracy raises questions about whom the lawmaker actually represents in his decision-making activity. Supposedly, in most political systems, he represents a local constituency that elected him to office, but a member of Parliament, for example, may find that there are several conceptions of his

<hr>

[39] James M. Buchanan, "Student Revolts, Academic Liberalism and Constitutional Attitudes," *Social Research,* 35(1968):666–680.

[40] This negativism is rather selective, however, operating especially when taxes are being levied or when the issue involved is very complicated. For one study, see Joseph G. La Palombara, *The Initiative and Referendum in Oregon, 1938–1948* (Corvallis: Oregon State University Press, 1950).

[41] Jerome K. Skolnick, *The Politics of Protest* (New York: Simon & Schuster, 1969), pp. 279–281.

constituency and these may come into conflict.[42] If he is a member of a conservative political party or comes from a higher-class background, he may find that on some issues he is torn between loyalty to one of these group memberships and loyalty to his local constituency.

The British parliamentary system places a premium on the legislator's loyalty to the policy of his party. Party discipline is stronger than in the United States, where it is understood, for example, that a congressman from a district that would suffer from a piece of tariff legislation will not be bound by the ideological commitment of his party in favor of that legislation. Even in the United States, however, a legislator is sometimes admired if he takes a stand on moral grounds contrary to the prevalent opinion in his constituency. During the 1970 campaign for the United States Senate in New York State, one candidate—an incumbent congressman—emphasized that he had opposed the war in Vietnam at a time when most of the people in his congressional district supported it. The adoption of such a campaign appeal is perhaps symptomatic of the ambiguity of public expectation for representation of their viewpoints by their elected officials.

Democratic society can be further categorized according to whether it is a *pluralist* or a *mass* form of society. In a pluralist society most political activity of ordinary men takes place at the local or small-scale level. People are primarily interested in political issues that arise in their local communities, their trade unions, their chambers of commerce, etc. Government at higher levels is largely a matter of interaction among these smaller political groups. An old tradition in American political thought holds that widespread participation in government is most effective when it is mediated by such "intermediate" groups.[43]

Where these smaller-scale groups are weak, a mass society is said to exist, one in which masses of people are directly involved in national politics. Recent critics of the mass society have argued that the lack of such small-scale groups to absorb the political interests of the masses has led to a situation in which it is easy for demagogic leaders (like Hitler) to exploit these masses in radical

[42] William D. Muller, *The Parliamentary Activity of Trade Union MP's, 1959–1964.* Unpublished Ph.D. dissertation, University of Florida, 1966.

[43] Alexis de Tocqueville, *Democracy in America,* trans. by George Lawrence (New York: Harper & Row, 1966).

political movements that eventuate in political dictatorships.[44] In this vein, C. Wright Mills has argued that the increasing dominance of a "power elite" of business, government, and military leaders in the United States is promoted by the weakness of small-scale political groups.[45]

Such pluralist critiques of "mass" democracy may overlook some of the nondemocratic features of those "small-scale" organizations whose declining influence is so much lamented. Given the oligarchic tendencies of groups such as trade unions, chambers of commerce, and professional associations, the rank-and-file member may still find his voice muffled at the national level, despite the so-called mediation of his views by the organizations to which he belongs.

The assertion of greater democracy at the local level of government is also debatable. The very homogeneity of human types at the local level may make it easier for a political boss to emerge here than at the national level, where the political leader must attempt to respond to a great variety of political pressures. Also, there are many minorities whose political interests can be expressed only at a higher level. The Negro in a deep Southern town can support only national political leaders if he takes a position opposed to the racist ideas of the local majority. A segregationist in a northern American city can likewise not expect to find many local candidates to support his political interest; he may have to support a George Wallace for the presidency to make any effective political expression. The "tyranny of the majority" seems to be a chronic problem for democracy everywhere, but it may grow especially acute as one moves toward the local or "intimate" level of political action.

POLITICAL PARTICIPATION

A structural-functional analysis of political institutions, such as the type just presented, ignores consideration of two problems that have been of prime interest to the political sociologist. First, a

---

[44] William Kornhauser, *The Politics of Mass Society* (Glencoe, Ill.: Free Press, 1959); Robert A. Dahl, *Pluralist Democracy in the United States* (Chicago: Rand McNally, 1967). For critical treatments of the mass society view of politics, see Maurice Pinard, "Mass Society and Political Movements: a New Formulation," *American Journal of Sociology,* 73(1968):682–690; and Joseph R. Gusfield, "Mass Society and Extremist Politics," *American Sociological Review,* 27(1962):19–30.
[45] Mills, *Power Elite.*

political system usually allows people some freedom of choice between alternative styles of political action. In most systems there are several *political parties,* and the sociologist is interested in the conditions that lead people to affiliate with and support one or another of these parties. Second, different people have different degrees of influence on the making of political decisions. Even in a democratic polity, with an ideology that "all men are equal" politically, it will appear, on examination, that some men are "more equal" than others. Who has the power? is a major kind of sociological question, demanding answers which tell us *what kinds* of people participate most actively in the decision-making process.

Political Affiliation

Different political parties tend to draw their support from different groups of people. A party is frequently understood to represent the interest of, for example, the common man or of the Eastern establishment. Sociologists can thus make certain predictions about the political affiliations and the voting behavior of people on the basis of a knowledge of their memberships in different social categories.[46]

In an early study of voting behavior in the United States, Lazarsfeld and his associates constructed an "index of political predisposition" for their study of voting patterns in the 1940 presidential election in Erie County, Ohio.[47] Their findings showed that Protestants, rural dwellers, and persons of higher socioeconomic status were more likely to vote for the Republican candidate than were Catholics, urban dwellers, and persons of lower socioeconomic status. By and large, these group differences in party alignment have continued to the present in the United States.[48] In more recent elections the additional factor of *race* has strongly differentiated voters: blacks overwhelmingly support Democratic candidates, while a majority of whites in many parts of the country support Republican candidates.[49]

The tendency of people of a given class to support a given

---

[46] For an example using European election data, see Herbert Tingsten, *Political Behavior* (Totowa, N.J.: Bedminster, 1963).

[47] Paul F. Lazarsfeld, Bernard Berelson, and Hazel Gaudet, *The People's Choice,* 3rd ed. (New York: Columbia University Press, 1968).

[48] For voting patterns in the 1968 election, see *Congressional Quarterly Weekly Report,* November 29, 1968, p. 8.

[49] Ibid.

political party is a tendency showing considerable variation between different political systems. A study of a number of "Anglo-American democracies" found that class voting is much more frequent in Great Britain and Australia than in the United States and Canada.[50] In Britain, for example, the Labour Party is closely affiliated with the trade union movement, and few persons outside the working classes would support that party. The "working man's party" in the United States (the Democratic Party), on the other hand, draws substantial support from throughout the social structure. The lack of ideological "purity" of the parties in the United States is reflected in the ambiguity of national party platforms, in their attempts to be "all things to all people," and in the strong sense of tolerance between people of different parties.

In countries like Italy and France, with their multiparty systems, each party tends to be more ideologically oriented and to draw its support from a more narrow range of social groups.[51] One symptom of the greater social cleavage accompanying political party affiliation in these countries is the fact that, in the United States (and even in Britain), most people would have no objection to a family member's marrying someone from another major political party, while people in a country like Italy would strongly object to such a marriage.[52] (Recall the argument presented in chapter 8 that a society's rules of endogamy are a sensitive barometer of the relative importance that people of that society place on the various kinds of social differences.)

In addition to this variation in the class base of political affiliation between societies, it appears also that the relationship of class and political affiliation varies within a society, depending upon the situation. If working-class people in the United States normally vote Democratic, a very substantial minority of them *may* vote for a highly popular Republican such as Eisenhower.[53] If the business classes generally support Republican candidates, there may be

[50] Robert R. Alford, *Party and Society* (Chicago: Rand McNally, 1963). For other studies of class voting, see Seymour M. Lipset and Stein Rokkan, *Party Systems and Voter Alignments: Cross-National Perspectives* (New York: Free Press, 1967).

[51] Lawrence E. Hazelrigg, "Religious and Class Bases of Political Conflict in Italy," *American Journal of Sociology,* 75(1970):496–511.

[52] Gabriel A. Almond and Sidney Verba, *The Civic Culture* (Princeton: Princeton University Press, 1963), pp. 135–137.

[53] Herbert Hyman and Paul B. Sheatsley, "The Political Appeal of President Eisenhower," *Public Opinion Quarterly,* 17(1953):443–460.

serious defections from a candidate such as Goldwater, who is seen as unsound on other than economic grounds.[54] Two sources of situational variation may be suggested.

First, an individual is likely to be influenced in his political affiliation by his membership in a number of social categories. As a member of a higher social class, he might tend to vote for a Republican, but as a Catholic or a Polish-American he might vote for a Democratic candidate who is a fellow Catholic or Pole. The presidential candidacy of John F. Kennedy tended to blur class differentiation in voting at the same time that it emphasized religious differentiation, i.e., many higher-class Catholics voted for him and many lower-class Protestants voted against him.[55]

The introduction of religious factors into an election will not necessarily have such an effect; it depends on the manner in which issues become defined in the course of a political campaign. The religious issue may be neutralized by a candidate's appeal to the electorate's sense of fair play or nondiscrimination against members of his religion. On the other hand, the issue may be accentuated by incidents and statements during the campaign. These contingencies illustrate one source of the situational character of group difference in affiliation with political parties.

Second, a political leader with charisma or personal likability may attract a following that cuts across usual lines of differentiation of voters. A candidate like Richard Nixon may have a sort of wholesome American appeal that attracts people from all groups who happen to admire this trait and repels those from all classes who are suspicious of this personal trait.

We have already noted Riesman's view that American political behavior is determined more by the *likes* of people than by their *wants*. Perhaps group affiliation (by class, sex, race, age, etc.) is more closely correlated with differentiations in *wants* than in *likes*. If Riesman is correct, we may expect a diminishing relation between group affiliation and political party support as we move further into the era of "other direction."

---

[54] John H. Kessel, *The Goldwater Coalition* (Indianapolis: Bobbs-Merrill, 1968), Ch. 8.

[55] For a discussion of the influence of religion and ethnic group membership on voting, see Edward C. Banfield and James Q. Wilson, *City Politics* (Cambridge: Harvard University Press, 1963).

Intensity of Political Participation

Like religious participation, political participation is found with all degrees of intensity among different persons. Just as an individual may attend church only for weddings and funerals, his political participation may be limited to a desultory vote for president every four years, or it may be nonexistent. Political scientist Lester Milbraith has suggested that, in thinking about variations in intensity of political participation, it is possible to construct a "hierarchy of political involvement" with several degrees of intensity of involvement.[56] Beginning with the most intense level of participation, Milbraith has ranked these activities as follows: (1) *gladiatorial activities,* including running for public office, actively participating in political campaigns, holding a party office; (2) *transitional activities,* such as contributing money to a political party or candidate, attending a political rally; (3) *spectator activities,* requiring minimal involvement such as wearing a campaign button, voting in an election; and (4) *apathetics,* completely nonparticipating.[57]

A sociologist might ask what kinds of people tend to participate more frequently toward the gladiatorial end of the hierarchy; or he might, beginning with a given kind of political involvement such as voting or officeholding, ask which kinds of people tend most frequently to participate in that activity. In fact, voting and officeholding have been the most frequently studied forms of political participation, and we shall now consider these.

Voter turnout. A frequently employed measure of the intensity of political participation is the percentage of eligible voters who turn out to vote in a given political election. The low percentage of eligible voters who actually vote in most school district elections or who appear at the annual meetings of the stockholders of a company are usually taken as measures of public apathy about the political process at these levels.

In most elections in the United States, men are more likely than women to vote, the middle aged more likely than young adults, the better educated more likely than the less educated, the urban dweller more likely than the rural dweller.[58] One explanation of

---

[56] Lester W. Milbraith, *Political Participation* (Chicago: Rand McNally, 1964), pp. 5–38.

[57] Ibid., p. 18.

[58] Ibid., pp. 110–141.

these group differences in voter turnout is the idea that people located near the *center* of a social system—those in frequent contact with many other people—are more likely to vote than those located on the *periphery* of association: the relatively isolated.[59]

Another interpretation of these differences is that they reflect differing intensities of interest in the outcome of political controversies. People who are more involved in affairs in which political decisions will immediately affect them are more likely to vote.[60] In the Ohio study it was shown that there was a high correlation between people's intention to vote and the degree of concern they expressed over the outcome of that election.[61]

One major caution on this interpretation may be suggested. Voting behavior may reflect a person's concern with whether or not one kind of law or policy becomes established, but it may also be that a person votes because it is the thing to do, one of the responsibilities of respectable citizenship and a right for which men have fought and died. The greater voting frequency in some groups may be a reflection of the fact that this obligation to vote is felt most heavily by people in *responsible* positions.

In the Ohio study, there was an interesting difference between men and women in voting interest and voting behavior. Among those *men* who were indifferent about the outcome, 83 percent planned to vote anyway, while only 44 percent of the indifferent *women* planned to vote.[62] This finding might not be repeated today when women have moved so far toward equality with men in participation in worldly affairs, but the result in 1940 seems to reflect the greater sense of obligation of men to get out and vote as an expression of good citizenship.

In contrast to analyses that compare the political participation of people in two or more social categories, there is another line of analysis of the origins of political apathy as expressed in nonvoting.

---

[59] Robert E. Lane, *Political Life: Why People Get Involved in Politics* (Glencoe, Ill.: Free Press, 1959).

[60] Glenn and Grimes show that, contrary to much earlier analysis, people continue to increase their political activity as they move into old age and that this increased participation fits an "involvement" model of political behavior (old people are directly affected by legislation) better than it fits a "center-periphery" explanation of political participation. Norval D. Glenn and Michael Grimes, "Aging, Voting and Political Interest," *American Sociological Review,* 33(1968):563–575.

[61] Lazarsfeld et al., *People's Choice,* p. 46.

[62] Ibid., pp. 48, 49.

When a person is a member of two or more groups with differing political orientations, he may be subject to a kind of "cross-pressure" that leads him to retreat into a state of political indifference.

Consider the situation of a higher-class Catholic in the United States who, on the basis of his class affiliation, would tend to vote Republican but who, on the basis of religious affiliation, would tend to vote Democratic, if he followed the example of most of his co-religionists. Voters in the Ohio study who were subject to such cross-pressures made their decisions on how to vote much later in the campaign (if they ever decided); they also were less likely to indicate an intention to vote than were those not subject to such cross-pressures.[63]

This notion about the political effects of cross-pressures has been applied in an attempt to explain the intensity of political interest (the moderation or radicalism of politics) found in different countries. In the United States, most people are cross-pressured in some way; they include higher-class (Republican tendency) people who live in the Solid South (Democratic tendency), blacks (Democratic tendency) who live in small towns (Republican tendency), blue-collar workers (Democratic tendency) who move to suburbs (Republican tendency), etc. There are many ways in which an American's loyalties are likely to be torn in an election, and perhaps these conflicts serve to neutralize the intensity of his political convictions.

Other societies (most European ones, for example) seem to show less of this cross-pressuring tendency, perhaps because most of the people in a given area belong to one religion, one social class, one race. Where different group affiliations reinforce rather than counter the political tendencies derived from other affiliations, more radical forms of political involvement seem to prevail.[64]

Officeholding. Variations in officeholding and other kinds of "gladiatorial" political participation tend to be related to the same group differences that influence variations in voting turnout. Most officeholders in most countries and social organizations are men; the

---

[63] Ibid., pp. 56–64; Bernard R. Berelson, Paul F. Lazarsfeld and W. N. McPhee, *Voting* (Chicago: University of Chicago Press, 1954), p. 200.

[64] Seymour M. Lipset, *Political Man* (Garden City, N.Y.: Doubleday, 1960), pp. 88–90; Morris Janowitz and David R. Segal, "Social Cleavage and Party Affiliation: Germany, Great Britain and the United States," *American Journal of Sociology*, 72 (1967):601–618.

less educated and poorer citizens are less likely to be involved in the more intensive forms of political participation.[65]

The variable of social class as related to political leadership is especially interesting. Given the fact that different parties tend to support the interests of different social classes, we might expect that, for example, a party with working-class support would choose working-class people as nominees for public office, as chairmen of their party organizations, etc. Studies of the social backgrounds of officeholders have shown that in Britain, for example, the Labour and Conservative Parties have differed in the kinds of men (in terms of class) who have been elected to Parliament or who have assumed cabinet leadership in a government dominated by one of the parties. As expected, the Labour Party elevates more working-class men to positions of political leadership. However, a very substantial minority of Labour Party officeholders have higher-class backgrounds.[66] In the United States, persons of higher-class background—Roosevelt, Harriman, Kennedy, etc.—have become dominant in the affairs of the so-called party of the common man, the Democratic Party.

The explanation of the prominence of higher-class persons in the leadership of working-class parties is an interesting problem sociologically. One explanation is that political leadership requires the leader of even a popular party to operate in relatively elite social circles, and there may be a feeling among the working classes that a higher-class person sympathetic to their interest may do more for them than one of their own who would be too gauche to operate effectively in sophisticated "Washington" or "Albany."

Another possibility is that political leadership requires a greater expenditure of one's own time and money than most working-class people can afford. The frequently cited extreme is the situation of a U.S. ambassador to a foreign country. Given the relatively low salary and high expense of these positions, only persons who are independently wealthy can afford to hold them, and Democratic as well as Republican administrations must choose relatively wealthy people for those posts.

---

[65] In the Ninety-first Congress of the United States, which convened in January, 1969, there were 11 women and 524 men; there were virtually no members from lower-class occupations. *Congressional Quarterly Almanac, Ninety-first Congress, First Session, 1969* (Washington, D.C.: Congressional Quarterly Inc., 1970), p. 40.

[66] Donald Matthews, *The Social Background of Political Decision Makers* (Garden City, N.Y.: Doubleday, 1954).

Another fact about group differences in political leadership should be mentioned here. There are some middle and upper-class *occupations* that are much more likely than other occupations of equivalent class ranking to produce political officeholders. In the United States House of Representatives, for example, there is a predominance of *lawyers,* a lesser representation of *businessmen,* but virtually no representation of such respected occupations as physicians and clergymen.[67]

In explaining such occupational differences, Milbraith suggests that the occupations most favorable to producing political office-holders are those which permit flexibility of work schedule and those in which a career can be advanced through a successful political career.[68] Doctors with busy practices can seldom arrange time off even to serve, say, in a state legislature with relatively short sessions. Furthermore, the political experience would not be productive to his medical career when the doctor returned to practice. Lawyers, on the other hand, do have flexible schedules, and the contacts they make while officeholders are often invaluable in the advancement of their later legal careers.

SUMMARY

Political sociology is interested in the various dimensions of the exercise of power on behalf of a group or society. Power is used for several purposes: to insure domestic tranquility, to deal with external enemies, and to cope with problems of public welfare that require concerted group efforts. This power may be exercised by a special agency (the *state,* at the level of territorial government), but it may also take less formal or less institutionalized forms.

The way in which political influence is distributed in a society is a variability in political form that is of interest to the political sociologist. An oligarchy concentrates decision-making in the hands of a relatively few persons while the several forms of democracy distribute participation in decision-making more widely. The social conditions that encourage oligarchy or democracy have been

---

[67] *Congressional Quarterly Almanac,* p. 40. In countries with higher voter turnout, this predominance of lawyers and businessmen is less pronounced and other professionals are more frequently involved, although usually more often at the parliamentary rather than at the higher cabinet levels. Rosalie Wences, "Electoral Participation and the Occupational Composition of Cabinets and Parliaments," *American Journal of Sociology,* 75(1969):181–192.

[68] Milbraith, *Political Participation,* p. 125.

much studied and several theories of explanation have been advanced.

Another focus of interest in the study of political forms concerns the variation in devices used to secure conformity to the decisions of rulers, in other words, the basis of political authority. In a police state, terror is the usual basis of political control, and legitimate power (authority) is minimized. In more legitimate systems, authority may derive from such sources as tradition, charismatic qualities of the leader, or from a legal instrument such as a constitution.

Individuals vary in their intensity and style of political participation, and the sociologist is interested in correlations between this participation and such sociological variations as age, sex, and social class. Different categories of people affiliate with different political parties and exhibit different degrees of interest in political affairs. To identify these group correlates of political participation, to explain them, and to describe their consequences for the political processes of a society are major problems of sociological interest.

SOCIAL DIFFERENTIATION

PART FIVE

One aspect of that *status interaction* that we discussed in chapter 7 is the tendency for people to distinguish themselves and others as being certain kinds or categories of people, and to treat one another accordingly. The sociological study of *social differentiation* is the study of these categorical interactions, their social origins and social consequences. There are as many bases of social differentiation as there are distinctions and names for kinds of people. Men and women, young and old, rich and poor, married and single, healthy and sick, white and black—any of these bases of differentiation may become the focus of sociological interest.

In this section we discuss two kinds of differentiation: social class and ethnic group. The discussion will typify the kinds of problems that might be anticipated when any other set of categories of social differentiation is being studied. Several varieties of problems in the sociological study of social differentiation will now be outlined.

Category-consciousness. The characteristics that people notice about one another and that become the basis for social interaction vary greatly from one social situation to another. People in some societies are class-conscious, race-conscious, age-conscious, or sex-conscious and make that kind of consciousness a fundamental basis for social organization. In other situations the same kind of consciousness may be ignored or minimized. The main sociological problem is that of understanding what conditions lead people to emphasize or de-emphasize a given kind of category-consciousness.

Criteria of differentiation. A person is not born with the categorical label "boy" or "Negro" or "upper class" or "mentally ill" stamped upon his brow. Rather, certain traits of the individual are taken as *symbolic* of his categorical identification. His skin color, his manner of speaking, his material possessions, etc. may be used to determine his classification. Since the criteria employed vary from one situation to another, an important determination in the study of any particular form of social differentiation is the criteria used in categorizing individuals.

Consequences of differentiation. Once a person is labelled a Caucasian or a male or a criminal, what are the effects of this labelling on his relations with other persons? Four general categories of effects may be suggested: (1) *segregation,* the tendency for people to limit, voluntarily or involuntarily, their associations with other people to those of their "own kind"; (2) *discrimination,* the operation of processes of exclusion of people of certain categories from the enjoyment of privileges that are enjoyed by members of other categories (a *minority group* is a category of people which experiences systematic discrimination); (3) the formation of *subcultures* or special ways of life among the people who occupy a given social category; (4) the possibility of organized *conflict* between the members of different categories: class conflict, parent-youth conflict, the battle of the sexes, etc. All of these are *possible* consequences of a given kind of differentiation, but each shows much variability in different situations, and the sociologist's main problem is that of accounting for these variations.

Mobility. Persons sometimes change their categories: a country hick becomes a city slicker, a maiden becomes a wife, a sick person becomes well. The sociologist's interest in these processes is largely a matter of observing the *rates* at which people in different societies are experiencing a given kind of mobility, and of attempting to assess some of the causes and consequences of these variations of mobility rates.

Social Stratification

FORMS AND FUNCTIONS OF INEQUALITY

Some of the distinctions that people make among themselves involve the ranking of one another in some sort of hierarchy. A *stratum* is a category of people who are similarly ranked (high, middle, low) and the making of such distinctions is called *social stratification.* How much is he worth? is an extremely common question in everyday life, and the judgment of a person's worth will determine many aspects of his social life, as we shall discuss later in the chapter.

Universality of Structured Inequality

The invidious distinction between categories of "worthy" and "unworthy" people appears to be a universal aspect of human society. Even in societies that are supposedly equalitarian or "classless," close examination will show that there are high and low social strata, although the criteria of stratification may not be the ones we have come to expect in modern industrial societies. On an Israeli kibbutz, invidious distinctions are made between the old-timers and the newcomers to the kibbutz,[1] and in the Soviet Union, membership in the Communist Party and access to the governmental bureaucracy make some Russians "more equal" than others.[2]

The ubiquity of social stratification has called forth different

---

[1] Eva Rosenfeld, "Social Stratification in a 'Classless' Society," *American Sociological Review,* 16(1951):766–774.

[2] Alex Inkeles, "Social Stratification and Mobility in the Soviet Union, 1940–1950," *American Sociological Review,* 15(1950):465–479.

sociological explanations, depending on the theoretical viewpoint that is brought to bear on the problem. One *functional* explanation of social stratification has asserted the necessity of structured inequality for the survival of a society. The view is that a society requires that certain kinds of valued work must get done. Some of this work requires the development of skill and an arduous process of training, and people can be motivated to undertake these responsibilities only if they are appropriately *rewarded* for their efforts in money, prestige, or other special privileges.[3] In the language of Homans, "distributive justice" demands that the rewards that people receive shall be commensurate with their costs.[4] This viewpoint has been criticized by pointing out that the rewards that accrue to a favored social position are often far beyond any objectively determinable "sacrifice" that people are called upon to make to qualify themselves for these positions.[5]

Another functional perspective on social classes is that of Parsons, who asserts that every society is characterized by a *value* system, and that these values are upheld by the public's honoring of people whose activities show outstanding performance in terms of the society's values. This idea is useful in explaining some of the variation between societies in the definition of high and low social strata.[6] For example, the rating of honorability of a soldier's or a cleric's occupation seems to vary with the value that a society places on military or religious values. The "outcaste" status of the Jew in Europe during the Middle Ages seems to be related to his willingness to undertake the mercantile occupations that were thought to be beneath the dignity of a pious Christian.[7]

From a *conflict* perspective on social reality, social stratification is seen as an inevitable though often dysfunctional consequence of human nature. Men everywhere strive for dominance, and the inevitable system of inequality that results represents simply the

---

[3] Kingsley Davis and Wilbert E. Moore, "Some Principles of Stratification," *American Sociological Review,* 10(1945):242–249.

[4] George C. Homans, "Social Behavior as Exchange," *American Journal of Sociology,* 63(1958):597–606.

[5] Melvin M. Tumin, "Some Principles of Stratification: A Critical Analysis," *American Sociological Review,* 18(1953):387–394.

[6] Melvin M. Tumin, *Social Stratification: The Forms and Functions of Inequality* (Englewood Cliffs, N.J.: Prentice-Hall, 1967), p. 10.

[7] James W. Parkes, *An Enemy of the People: Anti-Semitism* (Harmondsworth, England: Penguin Books, 1946), pp. 64, 65.

current balance of power between the contending forces. This is, of course, the Marxian view of the origin of social stratification. It is also rather close to Weber's view that dominant groups tend to *impose* their superiority on the rest of the society and only gradually to legitimate their power as "authority."[8]

Forms of Stratification

When worth is being judged, various standards may be employed, yielding rather different kinds of social strata. In a famous essay on social stratification, Weber defines three kinds of power and, correspondingly, three different bases for the classification of people from high to low.[9] First, people differ in their degree of *economic* power, their command of productive resources and their buying power in the market. Weber used the term *class* to refer to a category of people with similar economic position. Second, some people enjoy more esteem, honor, or *social* power than others. Some are looked up to, treated as "sacred" persons (those "set apart and forbidden"),[10] while others are more "profane" or less respected and more approachable. Weber used the term *status group* to refer to a category of people who are high or low in social honor. Third, people may be differentiated in terms of their *political* power, distinguishing between those who are influential in political decision-making and those who are politically impotent; a *party* is a stratum of the politically powerful or the politically weak.

Weber made these distinctions largely for the purpose of examining the relationship between the rankings of people in terms of these different kinds of power. One obvious possibility is that one kind of power tends to support the other kinds. The wealthy man may use his wealth to gain election to public office or otherwise to exert political influence (for example, by contributing to a political party's campaign fund); and there may be a certain amount of esteem that people enjoy merely because they are wealthy. It is sometimes observed with irony that wealthy gangsters are the objects of a degree of public admiration. The politically powerful may exert their political influence to make decisions that will en-

---

[8] Tumin, *Social Stratification*, p. 7.

[9] Max Weber, "Class, Status, Party," in H. H. Gerth and C. Wright Mills (eds.), *From Max Weber: Essays in Sociology* (New York: Oxford, 1958), pp. 180–195.

[10] Emile Durkheim, *The Elementary Forms of the Religious Life*, trans. by Joseph W. Swain (Glencoe, Ill.: Free Press, 1947), p. 62.

hance their personal wealth, and the "dignity" of public office may create esteem for a man who was nobody when he entered the office.

Another important possibility is that people who are highly placed in terms of one kind of power are weak in terms of another kind. Some wealthy people are less respected than others who are no more wealthy, and political power may be gained by parties dominated by people from lower status groups (the Irish dominance of politics in Boston, for example). Weber was especially interested in the power positions of the higher status groups or aristocracies who are often precluded from gaining great wealth by the fact that the honor which they are concerned to protect forbids them to engage in certain activities that, while remunerative, would be beneath the dignity of persons of their status.[11] The economic plight of such persons is a favorite literary theme; it is expressed, for example, in Tennessee Williams' plays emphasizing the pathos of the bankrupt Southern American aristocracy. Persons outside these aristocracies may take a measure of pleasure in their aristocratic discomfort, as when we are amused to hear that financially embarrassed British nobles have been forced to open the ancestral castles to tourists to get the money to make ends meet.

In the remainder of this chapter we shall deal with only one of these three kinds of power differentiation: that involving distinctions between the more and less respected or socially esteemed strata of people. Contrary to Weber's usage, the term *social class* has come to be used in sociology to designate distinctions between the respected and the unrespected. All the problems that we deal with in this chapter will involve, in one way or another, the element of respectability in social life.

CLASS CONSCIOUSNESS

The people of a social class are in the same boat socially in that they share a certain level of social prestige. It is quite another question, however, whether or how they are aware of their fellow passengers. Two possibilities are: (1) that people will not think of themselves and others in class terms, preferring to stress such other identities as their age, sex, community of residence, or religious affiliation, all of which identities cut across class lines; and

---

[11] A similar analysis of aristocratic status tendencies is found in Thorstein Veblen, *The Theory of the Leisure Class* (New York: Random, 1931).

(2) that, although they identify themselves with others in class terms, they have a "mistaken" conception of who are their class peers. Such persons are victims of what Marx called "false consciousness." It has been asserted that both these possibilities have been realized by people in the United States, although there is controversy on both points.

An early study of class consciousness by Centers found Americans reluctant to admit that they were members of the lower classes; given the choice of self-identification as upper, middle, or lower class, Americans overwhelmingly classify themselves as middle.[12] Later studies have shown that a somewhat larger percentage of Americans will classify themselves as working class, but the dominant image of the country as an essentially classless one has not yet entirely disappeared from popular thought.[13] One symptom of low class consciousness is the finding that, when people are asked to give a series of answers to the question, Who am I? they more frequently give answers that reflect such other identities as age and sex rather than self-identifications in terms of social class.[14]

Some other studies suggest not so much low class consciousness as "false consciousness." White-collar employees have a tendency to identify themselves with the management of the company rather than with their fellow employees with blue collars.[15] A study of janitors found that most of these men recognized the lowly status of janitors as a category and shared the negative evaluation, but that each tended to see himself as "different and better" than other janitors, emphasizing the highly "professional" attitude that he takes toward his work.[16]

One frequently asserted source of middle-class identification of the worker is his belief in a "tradition of opportunity" for class

---

[12] Richard Centers, *The Psychology of Social Classes* (Princeton: Princeton University Press, 1949).

[13] For a review of research on class-consciousness, see Thomas E. Lasswell, *Class and Stratum* (Boston: Houghton Mifflin, 1965), pp. 190–201. Evidence for lack of class-consciousness in the Los Angeles riots of 1965 is shown in Richard T. Morris and Vincent Jeffries, "Class Conflict: Forget It!" *Sociology and Social Research,* 54(1970):306–320.

[14] Unpublished research by the author on self-evaluations as related to social identifications.

[15] C. Wright Mills, *White Collar* (New York: Oxford, 1951).

[16] Ray Gold, "Janitors Versus Tenants: a Status-Income Dilemma," *American Journal of Sociology,* 57(1952):486–493.

advancement in this country and his tendency to hold in some way to the American ideal of "getting ahead"[17] and to blame himself and not the system for any personal failure. A criticism of this interpretation of the American worker is found in a recent study showing that poor people much more frequently than rich ones will deny that "a boy whose father is poor and a boy whose father is rich have the same opportunity to make the same amount of money if they work equally hard."[18] The authors of this study suggest that there may be less "false consciousness" among American workers than most sociologists have assumed.

CRITERIA OF SOCIAL CLASS

We shall discuss a number of frequently used *indicators* of social-class position. With each indicator, there are problems concerning the standards used for the status placement of people. When we consider later the confusions arising from the fact that *several* of these indicators are used and that different ones are used by different people, the complexity of the problem of the criteria of social-class differentiation should become very clear.

Social-Class Indicators

Wealth. One popular way of distinguishing "upper" and "lower" social classes is the distinction between the wealthy and the poor. It is not entirely clear, however, what the concept "wealth" designates in popular terms. Clearly it denotes a favorable monetary evaluation of a person, but it is not so clear whether the judgment is made in terms of how much the person is worth (the value of his bank accounts, real estate, stocks, and other unexpended resources) or whether the judgment involves an estimate of how much the person makes (the value of his *income*). A person with a lower income who is thrifty or has a minimum of familial obligations may obviously have a larger savings than another who enjoys a higher income but has a much larger outgo. Who is the "higher" class person economically, as between these two persons?

---

[17] Ely Chinoy, *Automobile Workers and the American Dream* (New York: Random, 1955).

[18] Joan Huber Rytina, William H. Form, and John Pease, "Income and Stratification Ideology: Beliefs About the American Opportunity Structure," *American Journal of Sociology,* 75(1970):703–716.

Sociologists have tended to use income as the basis for attributing class position. Perhaps this is because many thrifty people keep the size of their accumulated assets secret, as do banks and other agencies that have this information. On the other hand, most people derive their incomes from occupations which pay wages the size of which is more or less a matter of public knowledge. (There are some interesting exceptions. Few people have much idea of the amount collected in fees by physicians or lawyers, in tips by waitresses and bartenders or, for that matter, in royalties by textbook authors; hence the apologetic "I don't want to appear nosey" questions of one's friends.) Since social class is largely a matter of the person's public image, the more public nature of information about income may lead people in everyday life as well as the sociologist to emphasize the income dimension in calculating monetary worth.

Occupation. Evaluations of people are very frequently based on a knowledge of what the person does for a living, his full-time occupation, often defined as his "job" but perhaps a broad enough term to cover the full-time playboy or philanthropist as well as the full-time "nonemployed" student or housewife. One sociologist has argued that a social class is *essentially* a category of people engaged in various occupations with a similar degree of social respectability,[19] and almost no sociological study will ignore the occupational dimension in social-class differentiation. It has been found that the American public shows a rather high degree of consensus about which occupations rate as more and as less respectable,[20] that there has been a remarkable consistency of these ratings for a number of years,[21] and that there is considerable similarity between different industrialized countries in the rating of occupations.[22]

---

[19] Bernard Barber, *Social Stratification* (New York: Harcourt, Brace, 1957), p. 20.

[20] National Opinion Research Center, "Jobs and Occupations: a Popular Evaluation," in Reinhard Bendix and Seymour M. Lipset (eds.), *Class, Status and Power* (Glencoe, Ill.: Free Press, 1953).

[21] Robert W. Hodge, Paul M. Siegel, and Peter H. Rossi, "Occupational Prestige in the United States, 1925–1963," in Bendix and Lipset, *Class, Status and Power,* 2nd ed. (New York: Free Press, 1966), pp. 322–334.

[22] Alex Inkeles and Peter H. Rossi, "National Comparisons of Occupational Prestige," *American Journal of Sociology,* 61(1956):329–339; J. Michael Armer, "Intersociety and Intrasociety Correlations of Occupational Prestige," *American Journal of Sociology,* 74(1968):28–36.

When we ask about the standards that people use in making these judgments of respectability of occupations, we ask a difficult question. One approach to some suggested answers would be a look at those occupations whose incumbents are given the honorific name of "professionals": lawyers, physicians, professors, etc. What makes an occupation a worthy profession rather than a mere job?

First, there is likely to be a sense that the performance of duties in a profession is more *fateful* for more people or in a more radical way. A supervisor who consistently neglects his duties is likely to produce more disruption in an office than would be produced by the work delinquency of a more subordinate staff member. A surgeon who bungles an operation produces a more radical effect (e.g., the death of a patient) than a repairman who bungles the repair of a lawn mower.

Second, professional duties are likely to be seen as involving esoteric skills that require long training and a highly competent worker. Professionals require degrees and certificates which attest to their mastery of these special skills.[23] Although the graduate of a beautician's school may, like a physician, display her diploma, few people believe that the physician's and beautician's certificates attest to a similar amount of technical training, and the physician's occupation is much more highly honored.

Third, the professional is seen as more highly *committed* to his work; he sees it more as a calling than as a task to be accomplished in a nine-to-five workday. Frequently associated with this moralistic conception of the occupation as a cause is a code of ethics that forbids behaviors seen as damaging to the professional's work.[24] But a nonprofessional like an assembly-line worker in an airplane factory may be condoned in the illegal use of an instrument called a "tap" which can speed up production but which can also weaken the airplane part.[25] The professional would be seen as having a moral responsibility for the integrity of the products of his labor, and his code of ethics would forbid behaviors which are illegal but used if the worker can get by with it.

Finally, and related to the foregoing characteristics, the organi-

---

[23] On the role of the "licence" in creating a professional occupational climate, see Everett Hughes, *Men and Their Work* (Glencoe, Ill.: Free Press, 1958).

[24] William J. Goode, "Community Within a Community: the Professions," *American Sociological Review,* 22(1957):194–200.

[25] Joseph Bensman and Israel Gerver, "Crime and Punishment in the Factory," *American Sociological Review,* 28(1963):588–598.

zation of the professional's work life is likely to be less rigid. If he arrives late for work in the morning or takes an "executive lunch" of two-hours duration, he will not, like the jobholder, have his pay docked for the delinquency.[26] The assumption is likely to be that the professional "takes his job home" and his physical presence during the workday may be less rigidly expected. This lack of close surveillance of the professional's work is also justified on the grounds that his professional sense of responsibility is sufficient to insure proper execution of his work. The professor's stout defense of his "academic freedom" and his tendency to feel that any attempt by university officials to supervise his teaching or research is an insult to his professional integrity provide an example of the professional's demand for autonomy in exercising his professional judgment in doing his work.

Education. Formal education is not only a requisite to employment in some of the more esteemed occupations; the completion of educational programs is likely to be a source of prestige in its own right. The care with which, in some colleges, one must distinguish between those professors who hold Ph.D. degrees and those who do not hold them (*Mr.* Jones but *Dr.* Smith) is symptomatic of the honorific implications of formal education.

The prestige value of formal education is certainly determined by more factors than the number of years of schooling completed or the title of the degree that has been earned. On many college campuses invidious distinctions are made between those students who major in "tough" curricula and those who are pursuing "mickey mouse" majors; in high schools, between students in vocational and in college prep programs of study. Also, distinctions are made on the basis of the school attended: a Harvard B.A. is considered more prestigious than a B.A. degree from a state teacher's college. Some interesting cases of status confusion arise when the prestige of, say, an M.A. from a "second-rate" university is being compared with a holder of a B.A. degree from an Ivy League university.

Life style. In the fleeting encounters that occur in everyday life, it is often impossible for people to locate one another by such social-

---

[26] One symbol of higher status of an occupation is that its incumbents are not paid on an hourly basis but usually on an annual basis paid in monthly installments.

class indicators as wealth, occupation, or education, simply because these involve facts about persons that are not always readily known. Rather, there is a tendency to use style, manner, or appearance as a basis of inference about class position. A Briton who speaks with a cockney accent is probably working class; one who has a "public school" accent is probably upper class. A man riding a subway to work carrying a lunch box and wearing an open-necked colored shirt is probably working class; one who stands with attaché case in hand and wearing a business suit as he hails a taxicab to go to work is probably a higher-class person.

These stylistic criteria of class differentiation seem especially prominent in urban social settings, where the anonymity of people guarantees that the persons with whom urbanites interact are unlikely to know much about one another's education, occupation, or income.[27] Many people may, of course, take advantage of this situation to affect a manner that reflects a higher (or lower) class status than other criteria will sustain. The Cockney flower girl Eliza Doolittle is carefully trained to "pass" as a duchess by learning to behave in the style of a member of the aristocracy. Some people attempt to pass intermittently, indulging in "status cycles" in which they live in poverty for most of a year to save the funds to go to a resort hotel or on a ship's cruise and live for a week or so in a sumptuous style to which they are *not* accustomed during the rest of the year.[28]

The problem of Professor Higgins in sustaining the image of Eliza as a "lady" is symptomatic of the problem of all people who adopt the manners of a class other than their own: he must try to prevent people from discovering who Eliza "really" is. Similarly, when a person whose manners suggest that he is a nobleman is discovered to be in fact a servant by occupation, people are likely to feel that they were misled by a person who is really lower class. This suggests that occupation, education, and wealth are, in popular thinking, the more *substantial* indicators of class position; stylistic criteria are used only provisionally, pending the person's validation of his status position by demonstrating his standing on these more substantial indicators.

[27] William H. Form and Gregory P. Stone, "Urbanism, Anonymity and Status Symbolism," *American Journal of Sociology*, 62(1957):504–514.

[28] Mills, *White Collar*, pp. 257, 258.

Ambiguities in Social-Class Placement

We have seen some of the problems that arise when there is an attempt to apply any one criterion of social-class placement. Some further complexities will now be examined by way of suggesting the richness of this area of social behavior as a source for the generation of sociological problems.

Lack of consensus on criteria. Many sociological discussions of *the* class system of a given society or community imply a high degree of consensus among people concerning the criteria to be applied in making status judgments. In fact, many communities are marked by major conflicts on just this question; some persons have pretensions to high social status that are rejected by others. One interesting feature of modern social life is the tendency of large bureaucracies to locate some of their activities in small communities; a small town is dominated by the presence of a large factory, prison, or university, for example. The arrival of such bureaucratic activities in a small community tends to bring with it a cosmopolitan population of employees who are unfamiliar with and often disdainful of the traditional local social-class structure, with its "old family" upper class and its middle classes represented in the local chambers of commerce.

On the basis of income and occupation, many of these cosmopolitans can claim status superiority, and they derogate the life style of the natives, who are criticized for rolling up the sidewalks at night and for their indifference to the more sophisticated tastes of the cosmopolitans. From their side, the locals reject the life style of the cosmopolitans as being too libertarian. We thus seem to have different groups of people employing different criteria of status judgments and a lack of that consensus on criteria that has so often been assumed.[29]

Different perspectives on the class system. Another frequent assumption about criteria of social-class differentiation is that the same criteria are used regardless of people's own positions in the

---

[29] For two studies of communities with such conflicts, see Gregory P. Stone and William H. Form, "Instabilities in Status: the Problem of Hierarchy in the Community Study of Status Arrangements," *American Sociological Review,* 18(1953):149–162; William M. Dobriner, "The Natural History of a Reluctant Suburb," *Yale Review,* 49(1960):399–412.

social-class structure. We find, in fact, that many of the status distinctions that are made among people of approximately equal status are ignored by those of very different status. Among professors, the distinction between an assistant professor and an associate professor may be rather important; the general public and perhaps even students are likely to lump all professors together in one status category.

A study of the social perspectives of people in "Old City," Mississippi, found that members of the highest social class make many fine distinctions in various gradations of upper-class status and think of all those below the median level of status as an undifferentiated group of "poor whites."[30] Members of the lowest classes reverse the perspective, seeing many gradations of lower status and viewing those above a median level as a single group called "society" or "folks with money." The middle classes, situated so they can look both ways, make more distinctions overall than either the higher or the lower classes.

Inconsistency of status by different criteria. Status placement can be ambiguous because many people rate differently on the different criteria of social-class placement. There are, for example, persons in highly respected occupations who receive minimal incomes (clergymen and public school teachers in many places) or there are those who have relatively high incomes although they are engaged in less respectable occupations (highly paid "celebrities" such as baseball players and movie stars may fall into this category). Sociologists use the term *status crystallization* to refer to the degree of consistency or inconsistency of a person's ranking on different criteria.[31] High status crystallization means that the person is rated consistently by all criteria, whether the rating is high or low; low status crystallization refers to inconsistency of rating by different criteria.

Low status crystallization has some interesting consequences for persons who experience this condition. One effect is the creation of a dilemma in their interactions with others: Does the enlisted man from a wealthy family interact as a superior or a subordinate

---

[30] Allison Davis, Burleigh B. Gardner, and Mary R. Gardner, *Deep South* (Chicago: University of Chicago Press, 1941), p. 65.

[31] Gerhard E. Lenski, "Status Crystallization: a Non-Vertical Dimension of Social Status," *American Sociological Review,* 19(1954):405–413.

with the officer from a poor family? Does the janitor who earns a higher income than many of the tenants of the apartment building where he works interact with them as a superior on the basis of his income or as an inferior on the basis of his "dirty" occupation?[32]

A study of recent changes in the status of the working classes in Britain suggests that just such a dilemma may become increasingly common for people in these classes.[33] The *embourgeoisment* of the working classes, their movement toward status equality with the middle classes, is almost entirely in the area of narrowing the *income* gap between themselves and the middle classes. In terms of such other criteria of status as life style and respectability of their occupations, working-class people tend to retain their lower-class orientation.[34]

The same process of income equalization between the lower and middle classes has occurred in the United States and has tended to create much tension between blue-collar and white-collar workers.[35] However, the recent increasing migration of blue-collar workers to the suburbs of American cities has apparently led to the lessening of this dilemma as lower-class people have taken on the life styles as well as the income levels of the middle classes.[36]

Another effect of low status crystallization is that it may lead to a general dissatisfaction that is conducive to participation in radical political movements. Lenski found in a sample of Detroit residents that liberal voting and attitudes on social issues were associated with low status crystallization.[37] On the basis of these findings, he suggests a common explanation in low status crystallization of four groups of Americans: Jewish businessmen, Hollywood actors, college professors, and the Protestant clergy.[38] In some respects, the consistency or inconsistency of a person's

---

[32] Gold, "Janitors Versus Tenants."

[33] John N. Goldthorpe and David Lockwood, "Affluence and the British Class Structure," *Sociological Review*, 2(1963):133–163.

[34] For a critical treatment of the *embourgeoisment* thesis with a case study of a special working class subculture, see Otto Newman, "The Sociology of the Betting Shop," *British Journal of Sociology*, 19(1968):17–33.

[35] Mills, *White Collar*.

[36] Irving Tallman and Ramona Morgner, "Life-Style Differences Among Urban and Suburban Blue-Collar Families," *Social Forces*, 48(1970):334–348.

[37] Lenski, "Status Crystallization."

[38] Ibid.

status based on different criteria may be a better predictor of his social behavior than the level of status based on any one criterion.

CONSEQUENCES OF SOCIAL-CLASS DIFFERENTIATION

Much of the discussion of the sociological consequences of social-class differentiation has been undertaken in the preceding three chapters, wherein we have examined the variable of social class as related to familial, religious, and political participation. However, it will be instructive to examine some further consequences for human social behavior of the uneven distribution of esteem or honor among people, using the categories of consequence outlined in the introduction to part 5.

Segregation

Many forms of association tend to be restricted to social-class equals. In intimate kinds of interaction like friendship and marriage, social distance is often maintained even in a largely egalitarian society like the United States. This was a major finding of Hollingshead's study of the dating and courtship practices of the high school students of "Elmtown."[39] In choosing their buddies and their dates, these young people were highly sensitive to the class positions of the families of these prospective intimates.

Similar findings are made when one studies that most intimate of associations, marriage.[40] Especially in the upper classes and especially with women, the rules of social class endogamy are very strong. The "loss" of one of its daughters through a "bad" marriage is a calamity in many upper-class families. Marriage of a son to a woman from the lower classes can be more easily sustained, but even young men from the higher classes experience many pressures, both direct and subtle, to select appropriate wives.[41]

Social-class *commensalism* (people of the same class eating together) is also prominent. The author would mildly disagree with the observation that eleven o'clock on Sunday morning is the most segregated hour in America. This may be true of racial segre-

---

[39] August B. Hollingshead, *Elmtown's Youth* (New York: Wiley, 1949).

[40] Lee G. Burchinal, "The Premarital Dyad and Love Involvement," in Harold T. Christensen (ed.), *Handbook of Marriage and the Family* (Chicago: Rand McNally, 1964), pp. 653–655.

[41] Marvin B. Sussman, "Parental Participation in Mate Selection and Its Effects on Family Continuity," *Social Forces,* 32(1953):76–81.

gation, but in terms of social class the lunch hour during a workday is probably the most segregated hour. Work organization may require persons of various classes to work closely together, but lunch time (and coffee break) tends to separate them by social class: the secretary meets fellow secretaries for lunch, the boss goes to lunch with other bosses. The ubiquity of social-class commensalism may be seen in such situations as hospital or factory cafeterias which cater to all classes but in which one finds particular areas "staked off" as separate eating territories for doctors, nurses, patients, etc.

Social gatherings tend to have guest lists comprised largely of people from the same social class. Simmel explained this form of segregation as a result of the fact that the spirit of sociability requires all participants in a party to treat one another as social equals, a difficult feat if there is much discrepancy in class status of the guests.[42] The discomfiture, as portrayed in much popular literature, of a family dinner in which the father's "boss" is a guest, is an illustration of Simmel's point. The distaste of many people for the annual office party which throws people of various statuses into a sociable situation may provide another illustration.

Less intimate kinds of association may also be segregated by social class. Although in theory public transportation and public entertainment may be open to all classes by custom and by law, in fact one usually finds a rather homogeneous social-class group at most affairs and on most forms of transportation. Baseball games and operas draw the bulk of their customers from different social strata, as do the operators of bus and taxicab companies.

Even in situations where all social classes are represented, there tend to be different "classes" of participation corresponding to the general social classes. Thus, there are first class and tourist seats for air travelers, orchestra and balcony seats for concert goers. The price differential of these participation classes may suggest that this kind of segregation is related to nothing more fundamental than the differential life chances of various social classes, people from each social class participating in the best style that they can "afford." But there may also be subtle pressures of class consciousness that lead members of each class to assume their appropriate "place" in public gatherings, even when they have the financial resources to assume another place.

---

[42] Kurt Wolff (ed.), *The Sociology of Georg Simmel* (Glencoe, Ill.: Free Press, 1950).

Discrimination

The disadvantages or restrictions of life chances that accompany lower-class membership tend to be fairly obvious. Some of these disadvantages include lower income, higher rates of mortality (especially infant mortality), higher divorce rates, and greater frequency of unwanted children born to lower-class persons.[43] There are, however, less apparent ways in which social-class position seems to determine one's social opportunities. One of these is in the area of health.

A study of mental illness in New Haven, Connecticut, found that the lower classes have a disproportionate number of members having *psychoses,* the more serious mental disturbances. On the other hand, the higher classes are much more likely to get effective treatment for mental illness, including treatment for the less severe forms of mental disturbances, the *neuroses.*[44] Many other studies in medical sociology have shown higher rates of a number of kinds of diseases among lower-class people.[45]

A critic of these studies, Kadushin, presents evidence to suggest that it is not so much that lower-class people experience higher rates of illness as that they more frequently *complain* about their medical symptoms.[46] The suggestion is that, having less access to regular preventive medicine or to effective treatment when ill, lower-class people are more fearful than higher-class ones about their personal medical conditions. Whichever of these viewpoints one takes, it seems clear that lower-class people tend to be a minority group with reference to health considerations.

One interesting idea about the life-chance correlates of social class is that there may be, in some respects, a *reverse* relationship between class position and privilege. There are "advantages to the disadvantages," and we should, in some ways, pity the poor little rich boy. For a long time it was accepted as a truism in sociology that lower-class children enjoy the psychological advantage

---

[43] A number of differences in life chances between social classes are reviewed in Tumin, *Social Stratification,* pp. 56–65.

[44] A. B. Hollingshead and Frederick C. Redlich, *Social Class and Mental Illness* (New York: Wiley, 1958); Jerome K. Myers and Lee L. Bean, *A Decade Later: A Follow-Up of Social Class and Mental Illness* (New York: Wiley, 1968).

[45] A number of these studies are cited in Charles Kadushin, "Social Class and the Experience of Poor Health," *Sociological Inquiry,* 34(1964):67–80.

[46] Ibid.

of more lenient discipline by their parents and that lower-class persons in general have the privilege of greater freedom in expression of their aggressive and sexual impulses. Middle-class morality was thought to be one of the burdens of respectable social status.[47]

More recent research has cast much doubt on the view of greater lower-class childrearing leniency; many lower-class parents seem to be more demanding of their children's good behavior than many middle-class parents.[48] Even if this greater leniency of lower-class discipline did exist, the relationship of it to the alleged greater "freedom" of the lower classes may be disputed. The question seems to be, Does the removal of limits on a certain behavior produce greater satisfaction in the exercise of that behavior? At the risk of arguing like a social-contract theorist, we suggest that the removal of restraint on aggression leads to a kind of "jungle" social situation in which one individual's aggression is checked only by the greater strength of others who have likewise had *their* aggressive impulses freed from moral constraint. The "tough guy" orientation that one finds among lower-class boys may reflect not a freeing of aggressive impulses from inhibition but a survival technique in a frightening environment in which the aggressions of others against the self are an ever-present possibility. The general social-philosophical problem of freedom without limits is here involved. The earlier explosion of the myth of the "happy savage" is akin to a process that is currently going on: a skeptical review of the stereotype of the lower-class man as "freer" than the responsibility-burdened man of the middle classes.

Subcultures

The upper, middle, and lower social classes of a society may represent different subcultures or life styles. We have had much to say already about class "styles" of familial, religious, and political participation. Much of sociological research has been concerned with descriptions of life-style differences in such matters as cloth-

---

[47] Allison Davis and Robert J. Havighurst, "Social Class and Color Differences in Child-Rearing," *American Sociological Review,* 11(1946):698–710; Arnold W. Green, "The Middle Class Male Child and Neurosis," *American Sociological Review,* 11(1946):31–41; Frederick Elkin, *The Child and Society: the Process of Socialization* (New York: Random, 1960), pp. 79–82.

[48] Melvin L. Kohn, "Social Class and the Exercise of Parental Authority," *American Sociological Review,* 24(1959):352–366.

ing, speech, artistic taste, home furnishings, etc.[49] A highbrow preference for wine, classical music, and tennis may be contrasted with a lowbrow taste for beer, pop music, and pool.[50]

The sociological interest in class subcultures is likely to involve an attempt to define contrasting general value-orientations or cultural "themes" of the different classes. One large generalization would hold that the upper-class way of life is *past-oriented,* the middle-class way is *future-oriented,* and the lower-class way is *present-oriented.*

The upper-class child is born into a family with a traditionally respectable position in the community, and the child is taught to behave in ways that uphold the family tradition. When he goes to school, for example, it must be the right school, and "right" tends to mean a school with traditional prestige—an Ivy League school in the United States, a "public" school in Great Britain. The house which he occupies as an adult is likely to be one which has belonged to the family for several generations, and it is filled with "sacred" relics of the family's valued past.[51]

The middle-class child is born into a different environment, one which emphasizes personal achievement and social recognition. In the middle-class way of life the future is all-important, "past is prologue," and present gratifications are deferred in order to concentrate on building the instruments of future success.[52] This future-orientation may be of an optimistic or a pessimistic variety. As described by Zborowski, the future-oriented pessimism that is typical of Jewish-Americans leads to a great deal of worry about the future, while the optimism of "Old Americans," their belief in progress, leads them to assess the future very hopefully.[53] In either case, the emphasis of middle-class future orientation is on getting ahead of one's peers,[54] and schools are selected for children on the basis

---

[49] See Lasswell, *Class and Stratum,* pp. 207–266.

[50] Russell Lynes, "Highbrow, Lowbrow, Middlebrow," *Harper's Magazine,* 198 (February 1949):19–28.

[51] W. Lloyd Warner, *The Living and the Dead* (New Haven: Yale University Press, 1959).

[52] Louis Schneider and Sverre Lysgaard, "The Deferred Gratification Pattern: a Preliminary Study," *American Sociological Review,* 18(1953):142–149.

[53] Mark Zborowski, "Cultural Components in Responses to Pain," *Journal of Social Issues,* 8(1952):16–30.

[54] The result of this kind of socialization is shown in Turner's finding that a group of college students report they are "satisfied" with their status only when they

of whether they are believed to be schools which will help them to get ahead; the preferred schools may or may not be the traditional prestige schools.[55]

The lower-class person has no reputable past to uphold and little realistic opportunity of attaining conventional success in the future. The practical philosophy of live for today may prevail. The taking of "no thought for the morrow" is undoubtedly related to a number of consequences, including a high birth rate and the difficulty of future mobility out of the lower classes.

A major qualification on this view of social-class life styles has been suggested by Gans.[56] The working-class Italian Americans of Boston whom he studied seemed to be divided between an "action-seeking" group who live for the present, especially for the "thrills" therein, while a "routine-seeking" group attempts to gain security for itself at the expense of excitement. This division is reminiscent of Warner's distinction between an "upper-lower" class of self-styled "poor but honest folk" and a "lower-lower" class which is rejected by all others as immoral, shiftless, and criminalistic.[57] The alleged security-consciousness of much of the lower class brings out another major sociological theme in the attribution of life styles to social classes. Lower-class people have been found to be more oriented to seeking security in their employment than are middle-class individuals. Faced with a choice of a job of low but certain income and one with uncertain but potentially high income, the lower-class person is more likely to choose the limited but safe occupation.[58]

A final complication on the matter of social-class life styles should be noted. That very security-consciousness, which is supposedly an element of lower-class life styles, has been found to be appearing with increasing frequency in segments of the American middle classes. William H. Whyte describes with some nostalgia

---

consider it superior to that of their peers. Ralph Turner, "The Reference Groups of Future-Oriented Men," *Social Forces,* 34(1955):130–136.

[55] For a description of the attempt of "elite" American colleges to shift from a status-elite to a talent-elite basis, see Gene R. Hawes, "America's Upper Class Colleges," *Saturday Review,* 46(November 16, 1963):68–71.

[56] Herbert Gans, *The Urban Villagers* (New York: Free Press of Glencoe, 1962).

[57] W. Lloyd Warner, *Yankee City,* abridged ed. (New Haven: Yale University Press, 1963), pp. 260–265.

[58] Herbert H. Hyman, "The Value Systems of the Different Classes," in Bendix and Lipset, *Class, Status and Power,* pp. 488–499.

the decline of motivation for individual entrepreneurship in the United States.[59] One symptom of this decline is the fact that many young business school graduates are not looking for opportunities to make a fast buck by venturing into areas of undeveloped business activity; rather, they want to work for a big company with an established and predictable career laid out for them and a comfortable retirement pension at the end of the career. Once in such a company, they will find that the pervasive obligation of the business executive to subordinate his personal interests to those of the company will tend to eliminate any lingering tendencies toward economic individuality. Analyses like Whyte's suggest that we may find important areas of "routine seeking" in the middle classes as well as in the lower ones.

Conflict

"Inevitable" class conflict. "The history of all hitherto existing society is the history of class struggles."[60] Marx and Engels, with these famous words, present one of the most provocative of sociological hypotheses. Struggle or conflict is seen as inevitable, and this argument is supported by a *dialectic* theory of class struggle to the effect that a dominant social class always "calls out" the class that will destroy it (compare this to Dahrendorf's dialectic view of change discussed in chapter 5). Just as the feudal nobility created conditions that called out a disgruntled bourgeois or mercantile class, so the iron necessities of a capitalist system call out the proletarian class that will produce the final revolution and the "classless society."

The view of Marx concerning the inherent and fatal contradictions of a capitalist society will bear some examination. Capitalist conditions are seen as creating a proletarian class that develops in three respects:

1. *Increasing size.* As capitalism matures, there is an increasing concentration of the "instruments of production" into the hands of fewer and fewer people. The class of petty bourgeoisie—small shopkeepers and small-scale craft producers—are destined to be ground under by competition with larger and more efficient

---

[59] William H. Whyte, *The Organization Man* (New York: Simon & Schuster, 1956).
[60] Karl Marx and Friedrich Engels, *The Communist Manifesto.*

economic units. These displaced persons will fall into the proletariat and swell its ranks.

2. *Increasing misery.* Marx adapts Ricardo's "iron law of wages" to the effect that the wages of labor tend to be driven down to the bare subsistence level. Marx felt this "iron law" was a law peculiar to the operation of capitalism, i.e., the monopoly of the instruments of production owned under capitalism makes it necessary for workers to contract their labor on terms dictated by the owners. A rather different aspect of proletarian misery was emphasized in some of Marx's early work: the view that capitalism produces an *alienation* of the worker from the products of his labor.[61] The mass production techniques that mass capitalism requires tend to make the worker an "appendage of the machine,"[62] with the result that the worker cannot identify the product of his labor with himself. The feudal craftsman, by contrast, could take personal pride in the pair of shoes or the horse harness that was entirely the product of his individual labor.

3. *Increasing unity.* "Workers of the world, unite!" was the Marxian call for a proletarian revolution on a unified world level. Marx saw the formation of this world proletariat as inevitable, corresponding to the development of capitalism on a unified world level; as the national and other barriers to a "world market" break down, any barriers that divide members of the proletariat from one another would similarly be eliminated. The rallying song of the Communist movement is the "Internationale."

Some conditions of class struggle. Like other "iron laws" in sociology, that which postulates the inevitability of class conflict seems to ignore variations in the intensity of this conflict and the influence of conditions or independent variables related to these variations. Advocates of proletarian revolution have been disappointed that the revolution has not occurred as rapidly or as completely as expected; opponents have sought ways to avert the revolution.

From either of these perspectives, there has been an interest in some of the social conditions that seem to retard this "inevitable"

---

[61] For a collection of excerpts from Marx and an editorial comment that emphasizes this theme, see T. B. Bottomore (ed.), *Karl Marx: Selected Writings in Sociology and Social Philosophy* (London: Watts, 1956).

[62] Marx and Engels, *Communist Manifesto.*

struggle between the classes. One way of analyzing such conditions would be to look again at the three arguments of Marx about the inevitable development of the proletariat under capitalist conditions: its increasing size, misery, and unity. An analysis in these terms of some of the reasons for the retardation of proletarian revolutions in capitalist societies will suggest some general points about conditions that encourage or inhibit class conflict.

Size. The increasing concentration of the instruments of production has proceeded very much along the lines indicated by Marx. The petty bourgeois class—the class of small businessmen and small farmers that was seen as the backbone of Jeffersonian democracy —has indeed suffered at the hands of larger-scale capitalist enterprises. This "old middle class"[63] diminishes in size as the corner grocer or the independent craftsman finds himself unable to compete with the economies of scale possible to the grocery chain or the mass-production factory. The percentage of the labor force in the United States classified as "farm owners and managers" declined from 24 percent in 1870 to 3.7 percent in 1960.[64] Most Americans, like most citizens of capitalist countries, are today proletarians in the sense that they do not own the instruments of their production (the machines that produce automobiles, the classroom in which the professor lectures), but sell their labor for wages to those who do own these productive instruments.

Misery. The increasing misery of the proletariat is a more doubtful development. In several respects it appears that proletarians have become reasonably satisfied with their status, or at least that their dissatisfaction has not reached the level of violent action in support of their class interests.

In purely economic terms, proletarian misery has not developed in accord with the iron law of wages. Through a combination of trade union organization—the power of collective bargaining— and the political influence of working men in the direction of government policies favorable to themselves—minimum wage laws, for example—workers have been able to participate in the profits of a capitalist system. Trade unions in the United States have taken a form that Bell calls "market unionism" which is aimed at the

---

[63] Mills, *White Collar.*

[64] Ely Chinoy, *Society,* 2nd ed. (New York: Random, 1967), p. 189.

elimination of wage competition among workers and at gaining a larger share of the profits of capitalist entrepreneurship.[65] Workers thus develop an economically vested interest in capitalism and become susceptible to the "industrial democracy" appeal of Walter Reuther, the late head of the United Automobile Workers, who argued that workers and owners have a mutuality of interest in capitalism. A symptom of the nonrevolutionary character of the American labor movement appeared a few years ago when the UAW agreed to forego wage demands on an automobile company that was already having difficulty competing in the automobile market.

Questions may also be raised about the *alienation* of workers from their work under modern capitalist conditions. For one thing, there has been an upgrading of the level of skill required of workers under conditions of industrial automation.[66] The complex machines of modern industry require technicians to keep them in operation, and the worker may take some pride in his ability to master the operation of the machine and thus feel himself anything but an "appendage" of that machine.

More important, perhaps, is the suggestion that men invest less of themselves in their work than they did under craft-work conditions; their employment is seen as simply a job which pays the wages to allow them to buy the economic goods and services that they want. In such a shift from a "production-oriented" to a "consumption-oriented" society,[67] the worker's pride comes to be invested more in the possession of a color television set, an automobile, etc. than in the product of his work. As long as the wages for the work are adequate, the alienation from the product may be a matter of indifference in terms of overall happiness or misery.

Finally, it is sometimes observed that workers on mass production assembly lines do seem to take a measure of pride in the finished product. An automobile worker may feel "there goes one of *my* Ford's" even though his contribution to its making may have involved the assembly of one minute part. Marx might castigate such attitudes as "false consciousness" or as "commodity fetish-

---

[65] Daniel Bell, *The End of Ideology* (New York: Free Press of Glencoe, 1960), Ch. 10.

[66] Talcott Parsons and Winston White, "The Link Between Character and Society," in Seymour M. Lipset and Leo Lowenthal (eds.), *Culture and Social Character* (New York: Free Press of Glencoe, 1961), p. 110.

[67] John Kenneth Galbraith, *The Affluent Society* (Boston: Houghton Mifflin, 1958).

ism," but they still seem to be part of the psychology of the modern industrial worker.

Unity. The Marxian image of a unified bourgeois class in open conflict with a unified proletariat turns out to be a considerable oversimplification of a complex situation. Dahrendorf, although basically favorable to a class-conflict theory, points out the failure of Marx to foresee the *decomposition* or the breakdown of unity of both the proletarian and the bourgeois classes under modern capitalist conditions.[68] We shall look now at several of these sources of disunity among proletarians and among capitalists.

First, there has developed a chronic cleavage between different sectors of the proletariat. Most of the recent expansion in the size of the proletariat has been in the area of the "new middle classes" or the white-collar workers who are employed by bureaucratic organizations. Much of this new proletariat is engaged in so-called professional occupations, and professionals may be more concerned to distinguish themselves from blue-collar workers than to identify themselves with the interests of wage workers. One symptom of this cleavage within the proletariat is the difficulty in organizing white-collar workers in trade unions. Collective bargaining and the strike as a weapon in that bargaining are seen by many white-collar workers as inconsistent with the special moral commitment or "calling" of the professional to his work.[69] Mills describes a kind of "status panic" among many white-collar workers as they see the traditional sources of their claims to superiority of status (higher wages, for example) eroded by the recent status rise of blue-collar workers.[70] Such "panic" has hardly been conducive to general proletarian solidarity.

Second, there has developed a parallel cleavage within the bourgeois ranks. One aspect of this is the development of a "managerial revolution," in which there has been a separation between persons who *own* business enterprises and those who *manage* them

---

[68] Ralf Dahrendorf, *Class and Class Conflict in Industrial Society* (Stanford: Stanford University Press, 1959), Ch. 2.

[69] Teachers and other professionals *have* engaged in strikes in recent years, but it appears that only the relatively "desperate" professionals (e.g., *men* supporting families) have very frequently participated. Stephen Cole, "The Unionization of Teachers: Determinants of Rank-and-File Support," *Sociology of Education*, 41 (1968):66–87.

[70] Mills, *White Collar*.

and who have the power to make decisions about such matters as wages and working conditions.[71] This new class of managers may be actuated by motives other than those of pure profit-making. Business management has become professionalized, and the manager may respond as much to the standards he learned at the graduate school of business as to those of the owners of the enterprise. The so-called human relations school of management, with its emphasis on promoting the morale of workers,[72] may encourage a benevolent administration of business enterprise that is not easy for workers to get mad at. The managerial revolution may well be related in a negative way to the possibilities for a proletarian revolution.

Third, the unity of *both* the bourgeois and proletarian groups may be compromised by the kind of *cross-pressure* that we discussed in chapter 10. We saw that "radical" political action is inhibited by people's membership in a variety of groups that draw support from throughout the social structure. This idea may have special applicability to the problem of class conflict. Any potential toward class struggle may be overshadowed by the fact that class does not divide people in quite the same way as do other criteria of differentiation. Even if the owner and the employee face one another as class enemies by virtue of their different industrial roles, they may be allies in other group struggles: they are members of the same American Legion post fighting together the "Communist menace," they are members of the same church, they are identified as inhabitants of the same region—Southerners, for example, standing together against "outside interference" with their racial customs.

One kind of cross-pressure that has been of particular interest to the Marxist is that of national identification. Patriotic considerations may lead people to subdue their conflict of class interests; especially during wartime or national emergency, industrial strikes may be rejected as unpatriotic and business owners are shamed if they try to pursue profits in a business-as-usual manner. In these and other kinds of cross-pressures we have many suggestions for sociological hypotheses about social conditions that inhibit class struggle.

---

[71] Adolph A. Berle and Gardner Means, *The Modern Corporation and Private Property* (New York: Macmillan, 1932).

[72] The bible of the human relations school is Elton Mayo, *Human Problems of an Industrial Civilization* (Cambridge: Harvard University Press, 1945); see also Fritz J. Roethlisberger and William J. Dickson, *Management and the Worker* (Cambridge: Harvard University Press, 1959).

Finally, the fact or even the hope of *mobility* of people from a lower to a higher class may disrupt the unity of the working classes. The proletarian may tolerate the "misery" of his working condition if he sees his proletarian status as only temporary or as a stepping-stone to "something better" for himself. The college student working summers or part-time in a manual job may have this kind of attitude toward his work. The assembly line worker may entertain ambitions for a business of his own.[73] These attitudes are not conducive to class unity since, in a process of "anticipatory socialization," the ambitious person tends to take the attitudes of a class to which he aspires to belong rather than the one to which he currently belongs.[74] These ambitions may, of course, be highly unrealistic and anticipate a status move that will never occur. The unreality of these mobility expectations may be irrelevant, however, to their effects on class conflict. Willie Loman, in *Death of a Salesman,* remains the exploited wage earner while he continues to entertain fantasies of himself (or, even more, of his sons) "striking it rich" in the mode of Uncle Ben, the Alaskan entrepreneur.

SOCIAL MOBILITY

Social mobility refers to the passage of persons from one social class to another; such movement may be upward or downward. This status movement of persons can be accomplished in two different ways. First, the occupation or other group of which one is a member may be reevaluated in the society so that one's standing moves up or down with that of the group. Second, a person may achieve social mobility by moving out of groups with one level of social status into groups with another level. We shall now discuss the *group* and the *individual* levels of social mobility.

Group Mobility

Caste societies—those which do not permit individual social mobility—still may allow mobility on a group basis. In India, for example, although the individual cannot move out of the caste into which he is born, the relative status of the different castes is sometimes

---

[73] Chinoy, *Automobile Workers and the American Dream.*

[74] W. Clayton Lane and Robert A. Ellis, "Social Mobility and Anticipatory Socialization," *Pacific Sociological Review,* 11(1968):5–14.

reevaluated so that whole castes of people move up or down in prestige.[75]

Group mobility is often instigated by the effort of some oppressed group to improve its collective social status. The effort to promote mobility on a group basis seems to be stimulated by a lack of opportunity for individual mobility. There is evidence that the French and other revolutions have occurred when a society which was once open to individual mobility was closing the mobility opportunities of large groups of people.[76] The impetus for revolution has frequently come from status groups who were experiencing such a situation of "revolutionary cramp."[77]

The observer of society can always see instances of groups of people quietly or noisily going about the business of attempting to improve their collective social standing. The activity of occupational groups is a good place to observe this phenomenon. A major device for improvement of occupational status is the "professionalization" of the occupation, on the theory that a profession is more socially impressive than a mere "job" in several of the ways outlined above.

One example is that of the public school teacher. Teachers would like to improve their collective status by showing that teaching is a profession. There is much discussion about the necessity for a self-enforced code of ethics for teaching which would demonstrate the high moral commitment of teachers. Public school teachers have resisted unionization, perhaps because union demands for the private interests of teachers do not seem consistent with the view of teaching as a public service occupation. Similar processes of public image-making could be seen in any occupational group that is on the make socially: janitors who would like to be considered as custodians or building superintendents,[78] anesthesiologists who would like to be considered as doctors, not as nurses,[79] etc.

[75] Henry Orenstein, *Gaon: Conflict and Cohesion in an Indian Village* (Princeton: Princeton University Press, 1965), pp. 136–149.

[76] Elinor G. Barber, *The Bourgeoisie in 18th Century France* (Princeton: Princeton University Press, 1955).

[77] George Pettee, "Revolution—Typology and Process," in Carl J. Friedrich (ed.), *Revolution* (New York: Atherton, 1967), pp. 10–13.

[78] Gold, "Janitors Versus Tenants."

[79] Dan C. Lortie, "Anesthesia: from Nurses' Work to Medical Speciality," in E. Gartley Jaco (ed.), *Patients, Physicians and Illness* (Glencoe, Ill.: Free Press, 1958), pp. 405–412.

Individual Mobility

The class systems of various societies are more or less open to individual social mobility, and social-class systems vary between the extremes of being completely *open-class* systems and completely *caste* systems. The sociologist, in his usual perspective, has been interested in the *rate* or frequency of these individual behaviors in various societies and in both the causes and the consequences of relatively high or low rates of mobility.

Causes. The explanation of variation in individual social mobility involves a combination of the factors of *opportunity* and *aspiration* for social mobility. The opportunity for social mobility is related to the existence of an expanding occupational system with adequate room at the top for mobility. There is also a related factor, the existence of a base of persons available to fill the lower social positions that are vacated by the upwardly mobile. The operation of this factor can easily be seen in the history of immigrants to American cities. Each new wave of immigrants has tended to move into the least desirable occupational positions, occupy the poorest parts of the city, and push the last previous wave of immigrants up into higher occupational positions and out from the most congested residential areas.[80]

The decline in individual social mobility in the United States that some observers have seen[81] may be explained partly by the decline of both these sources of mobility opportunity. Not only have the geographic frontiers of expansion closed in this country, but the opportunities for individual entrepreneurship have tended to disappear with the growth of a corporate economy. Also, the waves of foreign immigration to furnish the "bottom" of the class structure have disappeared since the institution of repressive immigration quotas, beginning in the 1920s.[82] To some extent, urbanization has

---

[80] W. Lloyd Warner and Leo Srole, *The Social Systems of American Ethnic Groups* (New Haven: Yale University Press, 1945); William R. Aho, "Ethnic Mobility in Northeastern United States: An Analysis of Census Data," *Sociological Quarterly,* 10(1969):512–526.

[81] For a review of the complex and contradictory evidence on changing amounts of social mobility in the United States, see Bernard Barber, *Social Stratification,* pp. 422–471.

[82] The "liberalized" Immigration Act of 1965 will not change this situation since the act, while ending discriminatory quotas for people of different national origins, substituted a discrimination in terms of selection of only more talented applicants

replaced immigration in this respect. Recent rural migrants to cities in the United States and elsewhere have tended to perform this bottom-filling function for urban class structures.[83] But the possibilities for continued influence of rural-urban migration seem to be diminishing as the rate of urbanization declines in already highly urbanized countries like the United States and the nations of Western Europe.

The aspiration or motivation for social mobility is also influenced by social conditions. A caste system like that of India tends to eliminate mobility aspiration by a religious system which teaches the desirability of accepting one's caste position and measuring one's prospects for favorable reincarnation by how well he fulfills the duties of his caste. Some evidence suggests, however, that Western scholars may have overestimated the degree of complacent acceptance of their position by members of the inferior castes.[84]

Some observers argue that American society has undergone a recent change in the direction of less emphasis on personal mobility. Whyte asserts that the Protestant Ethic which urges the importance of personal achievement has been replaced by a social ethic which urges people to "belong" and "get along" with others.[85] Riesman argues that today's "other-directed" man is too sensitive to the disapproval of his peers to formulate the bold and aggressive plans that were features of the "inner-directed" character of the nineteenth-century man.[86] McClelland discovered that, while "achievement motivation" is on the rise in some countries, most notably the Soviet Union, Americans are increasingly characterized by a high level of "affiliation motivation."[87] Assuming the validity of

for immigration. Any subsequent immigration can hardly fulfill the demand for an "unskilled" class of workers. For a discussion of the philosophy and the political process involved in this act, see Edward M. Kennedy, "The Immigration Act of 1965," *Annals of the American Academy of Political and Social Science*, 366 (1966): 137–149.

[83] Seymour M. Lipset and Natalie Rogoff, "Class and Opportunity in Europe and the United States," *Commentary*, 18(1954):562–568.

[84] Gerald Berreman, "Caste in India and the United States," *American Journal of Sociology*, 66(1960):120–127.

[85] Whyte, *Organization Man*.

[86] David Riesman, *The Lonely Crowd* (New Haven: Yale University Press, 1950).

[87] David C. McClelland, *The Achieving Society* (Princeton, N.J.: Van Nostrand, 1961).

these asserted changes, they may require a sociological rethinking of the forces that encourage or retard social mobility in the United States.

Consequences. We have earlier in this chapter suggested two possible sociological consequences of a high rate of social mobility in a society: (1) to break up the unity of a social class as many people anticipate moving out of that class into another one; (2) to hold down the revolutionary fervor of a class by removing the more ambitious members who "desert" it to make a personal status move. In addition to these possibilities there are at least two other kinds of consequences of mobility that are often asserted and that we shall briefly discuss.

Dislocating effects of mobility. Numerous studies of social mobility have suggested that mobility is disruptive of the social relationships of people who experience mobility and that sometimes mobility is a precipitating factor in mental illness or other disturbed individual behavior.[88] Vorwaller calls this the "dissociation hypothesis" and summarizes it as follows:

> Vertical movement through social space is seen as a precipitant of social isolation, separating individuals from nonmobile peers who remain in their status of origin, as well as from peers in their status of destination. The social distance resulting from vertical mobility effectively reduces the integrative effects of shared norms, values, beliefs, and presses for conformity. Social mobility in this view is a disruptive experience, generating anxiety, alienation, insecurity, and other forms of dissociative behavior.[89]

Actually, Vorwaller's study is critical of the dissociative hypothesis and finds that only the *downwardly* mobile seem to suffer the effects of disaffiliation from ordinary social contacts.

A related assertion is that social mobility tends to produce highly conservative social attitudes. The evidence for this hypothesis is rather contradictory. One review suggests that attitudinal conserva-

---

[88] R. Jay Turner, "Occupational Mobility and Schizophrenia: an Assessment of the Social Causation and Social Isolation Hypotheses," *American Sociological Review,* 32(1967):104–113; Robert A. Ellis and W. Clayton Lane, "Social Mobility and Social Isolation: A Test of Sorokin's Dissociative Hypothesis," *American Sociological Review,* 32(1967):237–253.

[89] Darrel J. Vorwaller, "Social Mobility and Membership in Voluntary Associations," *American Journal of Sociology,* 75(1970):481–495.

tism tends to be true of the *downwardly* mobile but is less true of the *upwardly* mobile.[90]

Mobility and skeptical outlooks. Karl Mannheim makes the provocative assertion that social mobility is a major explanation of the intellectual skepticism that he sees as so prominent a feature of contemporary Western mentality.[91] This skepticism takes the form of a tendency to view truth as highly relative and to debunk a man's beliefs by seeing them as "ideologies" that justify some vested interest of his. Having lived in at least two social-class worlds and having experienced in himself the contrasting ideologies associated with these classes, Western man is ready to take the viewpoint of the "sociology of knowledge" that a man's social position is likely to determine his mode of thought.

The empirical tests of this notion are a little difficult to imagine. If the viewpoint is correct, perhaps we should expect, as Mannheim seems to do, that our professional skeptics, such as scientists and other "intellectuals," will be people who have experienced the disillusionments of social mobility. If *professors* are a fair sample of intellectuals, the evidence seems to go against the hypothesis. Lazarsfeld and Thielen found something of a predominance of family backgrounds of solid upper-middle-class standing among American academic men.[92]

Even those intellectuals who do experience mobility may simply carry their background attitudes with them into their middle-class careers. This was the viewpoint of Mills, who identified a category of men from rural (perhaps lower-class) backgrounds who encountered urban life from the biased perspective of their backgrounds, emphasizing the "disorganized" aspects of urban life.[93] Mannheim seems to assume that movement from one social category to another will give the individual full exposure to the "ideologies" of each category. Analyses like that of Mills show that, at very least, such assumptions can be challenged.

[90] Tumin, *Social Stratification*, pp. 93–97.

[91] Karl Mannheim, *Ideology and Utopia*, trans. by Louis Wirth and Edward Shils (New York: Harcourt, Brace, 1946).

[92] Paul F. Lazarsfeld and Wagner Thielens, Jr., *The Academic Mind* (Glencoe, Ill.: Free Press, 1958), p. 7.

[93] C. Wright Mills, "The Professional Ideology of Social Pathologists," *American Journal of Sociology*, 49(1943):165–180.

SUMMARY

People make various ratings of the "worth" of their fellows, including ratings of political power, economic standing, and social respectability. Sometimes these various dimensions of rating place a person consistently as high or low; sometimes there is variance from one dimension to another. Social-class differentiation refers to differential ratings of *respectability*.

Class consciousness cannot be assumed from the fact that people are "objectively" members of the same class, since they may ignore or minimize their class identities in favor of other identities. Where class consciousness does prevail, there may be some problem of confusion or disagreement on the appropriate criteria for social-class placement. With a variety of criteria and disagreement on how to apply any one of them (e.g., occupational rating), there are many occasions for "status inconsistency" with a number of important behavioral effects.

Social-class membership tends to affect the general social life of the individual in a great many ways. To varying degrees his intimate associations with others, his opportunities to enjoy scarce privileges, and his general way of life will be determined by his class position. Under certain conditions, more involved than Marx had realized, members of a class may join together to carry on organized conflict with other classes.

Given these multiplying consequences of class position, we can well understand the motivation of some people to attain social mobility and the disruptive consequences of downward mobility. The conditions that encourage or inhibit mobility (analyzed as motivational and opportunity factors) interest the sociologist, as does the possibility that social mobility may produce some predictable effects on the attitudes and behaviors of people who experience it.

Ethnic Groups

DEFINITIONS

The concept of *ethnic group,* although variously and loosely defined in sociological writing, involves one of the most basic of categorical distinctions for both the layman and the sociologist. A first approximation to a meaning of the term is that it denotes a "people," a number of individuals who see themselves and are seen by others as having an ancestral tradition and a "consciousness of kind"[1] that sets them off from members of other ethnic groups. Thus, according to Shibutani and Kwan, "an ethnic group consists of those who conceive of themselves as being alike by virtue of their common ancestry, real or fictitious, and who are so regarded by others."[2] The Jewish "people," American Indians, the black "community"—these are a few examples of ethnic groups.

Some of these peoples may include all the members of a given *society*—the American people, the Japanese people, etc.—in which case the variability of peoples and the interaction between them involve problems we have already defined under the headings of "society" and "culture." But, often enough, these peoples have memberships that transcend societal boundaries. The Jews in a state of diaspora are found in societies throughout the world. Also, there tend to be a number of ethnic groups coexisting *within* a given society; the Soviet Union, for example, contains under the broad

---

[1] Franklin H. Giddings, *Inductive Sociology* (New York: Macmillan, 1901), pp. 91–110.

[2] Tamotsu Shibutani and Kian M. Kwan, *Ethnic Stratification* (New York: Macmillan, 1965), p. 47.

umbrella of Soviet society a great many ethnic peoples—Byelo-russians, Ukrainians, etc.

Perhaps it is because of the potential divisiveness of ethnic group membership—the tendency to think of oneself not simply as American but as Italian-American or Afro-American—that the sociologist takes so strong an interest in ethnic groups. Hardly any modern society has escaped the problem of trying to reconcile the interests of ethnic groups with differentiated "consciousnesses of kind": English and French ethnic groups in Canada; Anglo and Mexican-Americans in the southwestern United States; Japanese, Chinese, "Hawaiians," and Europeans in Hawaii, etc. The relations of these ethnic groups with one another constitute one of the major problems of social organization in virtually every modern nation.

ETHNIC CONSCIOUSNESS

Like social class, sex, age, or any other category of differentiation, ethnic ancestry provides only one possible basis for people's personal identity. A person may think of himself primarily as a *man* or as a *professor,* and the fact that he is a *Negro* man or a *Jewish* professor may be of relatively little significance to himself and those with whom he interacts. The sociologist has an interest in finding those social conditions that encourage high or low levels of ethnic consciousness.

One basic notion, which can be derived from social psychological considerations of the type we shall discuss in chapter 13, is that those people develop a strong consciousness of kind who are treated as ethnically similar by people in the larger society. The self-identity of an ethnic group may be a kind of looking glass or mirror image of the way they are seen in the larger society. A fairly familiar notion is that people who are singled out for discrimination or persecution—as Jews have been so frequently—are likely by virtue of their common persecution to develop an enlarged consciousness of similarity among themselves.

One piece of evidence for this notion is the finding that members of minority ethnic groups—Catholics in the United States, for example—are more likely than members of more dominant groups to mention their ethnicity very early in a list of answers to the question, Who am I?[3] For such people, their ethnic consciousness may

---

[3] Manford H. Kuhn and Thomas S. McPartland, "An Empirical Investigation of Self-Attitudes," *American Sociological Review,* 19(1954):68–76.

take precedence over other and alternative consciousnesses. It is reported that Negroes in an upstate New York community identify themselves so thoroughly with the total "Negro community" of the United States that, in a ball game between their hometown team and a visiting team with black players, the local Negroes will often root for the visitors rather than for the home team.[4]

A related source of increased ethnic group consciousness is the experience of a group in moving from a situation in which they are the dominant group to one in which they are subordinate members of a larger society. With many groups immigrating to the United States, for example, people entered the country without a strong sense of themselves as being Germans or Norwegians or Poles. Rather, their identities were in terms of a particular region of a country or even a particular village in that country.[5] Like many Americans, who think of themselves as Californians or Southerners or Chicagoans and have their sense of being American stimulated when they go abroad and find that, to the foreigner, "you Americans are all alike," so the foreign immigrant to America may not "discover" his national origin until he finds himself faced with the American perception that "you Italians are all alike."

In the area of ethnic groups, it is well to remind ourselves that group consciousness is not necessarily highly correlated with the solidarity or mutual helpfulness of members of a group. In many ethnic groups, especially those that are discriminated against, there is a kind of "self-hatred" in which many people, highly conscious of their membership in a group, still experience dislike for other members of their group.[6]

In a study of Jewish residents in an upper-middle-class Midwestern suburb, Ringer finds that established Jewish residents of the community share with their Gentile neighbors a distaste for the newer Jewish immigrants to the community, some of their distaste being based on the view that the newcomers give a bad name to the whole Jewish group.[7] Another study finds a pattern of "disaffection" between Mexican-Americans in a Texas community, manifested in the fact, for example, that another Mexican (but never an

---

[4] Robin M. Williams, Jr., *Strangers Next Door* (Englewood Cliffs, N.J.: Prentice-Hall, 1964), p. 238.

[5] Will Herberg, *Protestant–Catholic–Jew* (Garden City, N.Y.: Doubleday, 1955).

[6] Kurt Lewin, *Resolving Social Conflicts* (New York: Harper, 1948), pp. 186–200.

[7] Benjamin B. Ringer, *The Edge of Friendliness* (New York: Basic Books, 1967).

"American") is seen as the source of the *mal puesto* (an illness induced by someone's ill will) in which the people believe.[8]

CRITERIA FOR ETHNIC DIFFERENTIATION

We have said that common ancestry, real or fictitious, is the sociologist's criterion for placing people as members of an ethnic category. The meaning of ancestry, especially of the "fictitious" kind, is uncertain enough to justify some special examination.

Although, as we shall see, an ethnic group tends to have some level of endogamy or marriage within the group, these rules are violated frequently enough, and the results can present some interesting complications about "ancestry." Throughout the world there are "mixed-breed" peoples, often called *mestizos;* there are, for example, the Anglo-Indian descendants of the natives and the English colonizers of India,[9] and the "Cape Coloured" descendants of a variety of the ethnic groups that have inhabited South Africa.[10]

Much of the conflict within such an ethnic group and between the group members and outsiders may focus on the definition of the relative importance of different components of the ancestry. In a study of various American Indian peoples with mixtures of white and Negro ancestry, Berry found much uncertainty whether to classify a group of people as Indians or as Negroes.[11] In Southern areas, many Indian mestizo groups are classified as Negroes by the whites, much to the indignation of group members, who insist that, whatever they are, they are emphatically *not* Negroes.

In these and other mixed ancestry situations, the popular understanding is likely to be that blood determines ancestry and that one drop of blood (i.e., any discernible ancestry coming from that group) is sufficient to classify the mestizo as a member of that group.[12] The miscegenation laws (forbidding interracial marriage)

---

[8] Arthur J. Rubel, *Across the Tracks: Mexican-Americans in a Texas City* (Austin: University of Texas Press, 1966).

[9] Noel P. Gist, "Conditions of Inter-Group Relations: the Anglo-Indians," *International Journal of Comparative Sociology,* 8(1967):199–208.

[10] David L. Niddrie, *South Africa: Nation or Nations?* (Princeton, N.J.: Van Nostrand, 1968), pp. 40–45.

[11] Brewton Berry, *Almost White* (New York: Macmillan, 1963).

[12] This popular notion is sometimes given official sanction in the manner in which people are classified for census-taking or other administrative purposes. In Hawaii, for example, a person is officially given the ethnic label of "Part-Hawaiian" if he has any discernible ancestors from among the native population. Andrew W. Lind, *Hawaii's People* (Honolulu: University of Hawaii Press, 1967), p. 23.

of the Southern states of the United States[13] have been applied on the ruling that one is legally a Negro for purposes of marriage regulation when he has "one drop" of Negro blood, that is, when he has a single Negro ancestor. The musical drama *Showboat* ridiculed this conception by posing a situation in which a white man, engaged to a Negro woman, evades the local miscegenation laws by cutting his fiance's finger and imbibing a drop of her blood, claiming thereby to be himself a Negro planning to marry another Negro. The success of this ruse with the local sheriff suggests something of the irrationality of popular thought about "blood" as a basis of ethnic ancestry.

The practical consequence of this popular notion of an ancestral trait that does not show up in actual physical appearance especially interests the sociologist. In such situations, one is never sure on the basis of physical inspection whether the person with whom he is dealing is a member of a stigmatized race. Everyone is suspect in the same way that, in a society in which no one knows for sure who is or is not a homosexual, any friendship of male with male or female with female is suspect. A marriage of two persons is likely to be the occasion for an extensive "background investigation" of the ethnic origin of the intended spouses. The failure to conduct these checks results occasionally in a newsworthy story about an unfortunate victim of a mistaken identity: for example, the white supremacist who is suddenly jailed for having married a woman who, as it turns out, had one great-great grandmother who was black.

CONSEQUENCES OF ETHNIC DIFFERENTIATION

Segregation

Ethnic segregation is among the most easily observable of social phenomena. A tour of any metropolis like New York City inevitably involves a journey through its various ethnic "sections": its China-towns, its Yorkvilles (German-American), Little Italys, Spanish Harlems (Puerto Rican), Bedford-Stuyvesants (Negro), etc.

A major sociological question about ethnic segregation of a given type is whether it corresponds to the wishes of the segregated

---

[13] These laws have been declared unconstitutional, but the informal social sanctions against racial intermarriage continue.

peoples or whether it is the result of the refusal of other groups to associate with them. *Social distance scales* have been developed to measure tendencies toward involuntary segregation, based on the distaste for association with members of a given ethnic group. Typical questions are: Would you allow a member of this group to enter your country? your neighborhood? your social club? your family through marriage?

Research using social distance scales has tended to yield two different kinds of findings: (1) the showing that a group of people is much more approving of association with some groups than with others, with less approval of association with groups whose members are highly dissimilar and whose ways of life stimulate the ethnocentrism of those who enforce segregation;[14] (2) the finding that people tend to be more tolerant of association with members of most ethnic groups when the association is less intimate in nature.[15] Members of a group may be "all right in their place" but the place is often defined so that a line is drawn against some more intimate kinds of association.

Some of the intimate associations discussed in chapter 11 as the bases for social-class segregation—friendship, marriage, commensalism, sociability—also tend to be strongly segregated along ethnic lines. In the United States, a country that has rapidly desegregated many of its social institutions in recent years, the frequency with which members of many ethnic groups marry outside the group is still very low.[16] "Public" situations may allow or require ethnic intermingling; "private" situations tend to become more exclusive. A typical finding is that many more white people are willing to tolerate association with blacks in public situations, such

[14] Emory S. Bogardus, "Comparing Racial Distance in Ethiopia, South Africa and the United States," *Sociology and Social Research,* 52(1968):149–156.

[15] For example, a study of racial attitudes in an upstate New York community finds that objections by whites to association with Negroes vary from 33 percent objecting to Negroes in "your work group" to 77 percent objecting to Negroes in "your social group." Robert B. Johnson, "Negro Reactions to Minority Status," in Bernard E. Segal (ed.), *Racial and Ethnic Relations* (New York: Crowell, 1966), p. 254.

[16] For a review of studies on ethnic intermarriage, see George E. Simpson and J. Milton Yinger, *Racial and Cultural Minorities,* 3rd ed. (New York: Harper & Row, 1965), pp. 365–373. For a later study of one ethnic group see Frank G. Mittelbach and Joan W. Moore, "Ethnic Endogamy: the Case of Mexican Americans," *American Journal of Sociology,* 74(1968):50–62.

as work, than they are in more private situations, such as the neighborhoods in which they live.[17]

One by-product of the insistence on residential segregation is that it tends to produce de facto segregation in such areas as school attendance, where people are willing to accept desegregation. The recent opposition to bussing minority-group children from segregated residential areas to desegregated schools suggests that this readiness for school desegregation is not strong enough to offset the sense of inconvenience in having to put one's children on school busses.

One surprising fact about involuntary segregation of an ethnic group is that this segregation is not necessarily found to be practiced most fully in situations in which the group is most openly discriminated against. American Southerners sometimes justify Southern racial segregation by pointing out that the Negro is just as residentially segregated in the North as in the South. Sociological research supports this contention: the larger Southern cities are no more segregated racially than are cities of equivalent size in the North.[18] Further, there is in much of the rural South a pattern of residential intermingling of the races: white and black families are quite likely to be "neighbors." This apparently does not mean, as many Southerners seem to think it means, that the Negro is less discriminated against or has a more sympathetic relation with whites in the South than in the North. A well-defined discriminatory system of racial etiquette may make it possible for Southern whites and blacks to intermingle physically without any dropping of the social barriers between them.[19] When citizen White calls citizen Black "Tom" while the latter calls him "Mr. White," it is possible for Tom and Mr. White to live closely together without challenging the white supremacy system.

Voluntary segregation is another matter, sociologically. Persons may choose to associate with others of their own ethnic group for

[17] Dietrich C. Reitzes, "Union v. Neighborhood in a Tension Situation," *Journal of Social Issues,* 9(1953):37–44.

[18] Karl Taeuber, "Trends in Negro Residential Segregation," *Social Problems,* 12 (1964):42–50.

[19] Charles S. Johnson, *Patterns of Negro Segregation* (New York: Harper, 1943). For a generalization of the point that low segregation may coexist with a rigid caste system, see Pierre L. van den Berghe, "Paternalistic versus Competitive Race Relations: an Ideal-Type Approach," in Segal, *Racial and Ethnic Relations,* p. 56.

reasons of ease and economy of effort. Especially when groups of people simultaneously face the situation of living in an unfamiliar environment, there may be a voluntary association with those of their "own kind." Many ethnic groups seem to traverse a kind of natural history of segregation and desegregation in the course of their collective existence. Immigrant groups to the United States have tended to settle in ethnically segregated ghettos in American cities where they attempt to maintain the old country ways and to establish "parallel institutions"—churches, welfare agencies, etc. that cater only to members of that ethnic group.[20] As the Americanization process goes on, immigrants begin to experience the social disadvantages of their segregated existence and, as they acquire the facilities to do so, they begin to disperse throughout the community. Various studies of *population succession* in American cities have shown this tendency, which is expressed in the finding that the most segregated ethnic groups are those which have migrated most recently to the United States.[21]

Many ethnic groups with a strong *racial* identification have experienced residential segregation that *does not* disappear as their members acquire the motivation to disperse. An *index of segregation* applied to large American cities shows that most of these cities were as highly segregated racially in 1960 as in 1950.[22] The usual interpretation is that race, being a highly visible trait, represents a special barrier to desegregation. It has been argued, however, that the slow rate of desegregation of Negroes in American cities is a result of the *recency* of the Negro immigration to the cities and the lack of a favorable condition for social mobility such as existed in the earlier periods of heavy foreign immigration.[23] At any rate, it is only in very recent years that the black has begun to join the

[20] Oscar Handlin, *The Uprooted* (Boston: Little, Brown, 1951).

[21] Paul F. Cressey, "Population Succession in Chicago, 1898–1930," *American Journal of Sociology*, 44(1938):59–69; Ying-Cheng Kiang, "The Distribution of the Ethnic Groups in Chicago, 1960," *American Journal of Sociology*, 74(1968):292–295.

[22] Karl E. Taeuber and Alma F. Taeuber, "The Negro as an Immigrant Group: Recent Trends in Racial and Ethnic Segregation in Chicago," *American Journal of Sociology*, 69(1964):374–382. One study suggests that there has been an actual *increase* in racial segregation in American cities. Theodore G. Clemence, "Residential Segregation in the Mid-Sixties," *Demography*, 4(1967):562–568.

[23] James M. O'Kane, "Ethnic Mobility and the Lower-Income Negro: a Socio-Historical Perspective," *Social Problems*, 16(1969):302–311.

white in very great numbers in the move to the suburbs,[24] and even a black suburban movement may not mean desegregation if the races continue to be segregated in the suburbs.

Not in all situations do racially based ethnic groups experience permanent segregation. In Hawaii, the Chinese, Japanese, Filipino, and other immigrant groups settled initially in ghettos in the central part of Honolulu, but these populations quickly dispersed so that, for example, the "Chinatown" that is so prominent in several American cities is not so sharply defined in Honolulu.[25] The Hawaiian situation may reflect the relatively equalitarian relations between the races there. When the social distance between races is greater, we may expect that it requires vigorously enforced open-housing legislation to eliminate residential segregation.

The question of the voluntary or involuntary character of a given kind of segregation is often a controversial one. In many cases of forced segregation, the official version of the dominant group is that segregation is voluntary. White Southerners in the United States have maintained that the bulk of black Southerners are not interested in desegregation, although public opinion polls have shown overwhelming Southern Negro support for the Supreme Court decision invalidating segregated school systems.[26] The fact remains that, in many areas in which desegregated activities are legally open, many Negroes do not avail themselves of these opportunities.[27] It may be, in fact, that much segregation involves a subtle combination of the voluntary and involuntary. Members of an ethnic group may indeed prefer to "keep their place," but this preference may be based on a fear of the injury, humiliation, or inconvenience that might result if barriers to association were breached.

Discrimination
Most of the forms of ethnic discrimination are familiar to the reader; they represent the publicized grievances of a minority group and,

---

[24] Reynolds Farley, "The Changing Distribution of Negroes Within Metropolitan Areas: the Emergence of Black Suburbs," *American Journal of Sociology,* 75(1970): 512–529.

[25] Lind, *Hawaii's People,* pp. 54–61.

[26] Melvin M. Tumin, *Segregation and Desegregation: a Digest of Recent Research* (New York: Anti-Defamation League of B'nai Brith, 1957), p. 109.

[27] Eugene A. Weinstein and Paul N. Geisel, "Family Decision Making Over Desegregation," *Sociometry,* 25(1962):21–28.

sometimes, become the focus of legislation requiring fair treatment of ethnic-group members. Charges are frequently made that members of an ethnic group are denied employment opportunities, access to education, the right to vote, etc. One classic study of racial discrimination in the American South analyzed discrimination in terms of three kinds of "gains" of the whites in that community:[28]

1. *Economic gain.* Whites tend to be landowners, Negroes to be tenants. The income differential of the races produces many inequalities of access to consumer goods.
2. *Sexual gain.* The white man gains sexual access to the Negro woman while he ruthlessly suppresses any flirtation of Negro men with white women.
3. *Prestige gain.* The Negro is humiliated by being called derogatory names like "boy" or "nigger" while the white man must be called "sir" or "mister."

Except possibly for the sexual gain, these forms of discrimination are experienced by a great many ethnic groups. Mexican-Americans, for example, have a per capita income in the United States that is far below that of the "Anglos" in the country generally or in the communities where the Mexican-Americans live.[29] Also, many of them suffer the humiliation of being treated in terms of Anglo-American stereotypes of them as being "unclean," "deceitful," "immoral," etc.[30]

The explanation of discrimination is an important sociological problem. One major explanation would hold that discrimination is the behavioral expression of intergroup *prejudice.* There are various conceptions of the nature of prejudice, but most of them can be reduced to *cognitive* and *affective* forms. Cognitively, prejudice refers to negative stereotypes or beliefs about the characteristics of the members of an ethnic group: Negroes are smelly, Jews are pushy, Poles are dense, Italians are hot-tempered, etc. Affectively, prejudice refers to dislike or distaste for the members of an ethnic group; it is akin to the notion of *social distance.*

The relation of either kind of prejudice to discrimination is fairly obvious. If negative stereotypes are held, discriminatory behavior

---

[28] John Dollard, *Caste and Class in a Southern Town* (New Haven: Yale University Press, 1957).

[29] Herman P. Miller, *Rich Man, Poor Man* (New York: Crowell, 1964), pp. 113–120.

[30] Ozzie G. Simmons, "The Mutual Images and Expectations of Anglo-Americans and Mexican-Americans," *Daedalus,* 90(1961):286–299.

can be justified as "only natural." If Negroes are childish and irresponsible, the denial of the right to vote is quite logical; if Jews are pushy, it may make sense to deny them the "inch" that will allow them "to take a mile." Dislike for members of a group may lead to the denial of privileges, if the granting of the privilege would throw prejudiced people into unwanted social contact with them. The reluctance of some hotels to give room reservations to people with Jewish names[31] reflects the Gentile "exclusiveness" of their clientele, a desire to avoid being put in an equal status with someone of an "inferior" group.

This essentially commonsense view—that our discriminatory actions are the consequence of our prejudiced attitudes—can be criticized from several angles. Merton has discussed two kinds of discrepancy between intergroup attitude and action.[32] One is the nonprejudiced discriminator or "fair-weather liberal" who discriminates in spite of his lack of personal prejudice. The motel owner or barber who says to the Negro, "I would like to serve you but it would ruin my business if I did," is responding to the inconvenience to himself of practicing his personal liberality. The second kind is the prejudiced nondiscriminator or "fair-weather illiberal" exemplified by the Southern political leader, a racist by inclination, who yields to the law of the land and permits the enrollment of a Negro in a "white college" or publicly upholds black voting rights. Like the fair-weather liberal, the prejudiced nondiscriminator is discouraged from expressing his convictions by an unfavorable political climate or social situation. The existence of these types provides a useful lesson in the power of society to constrain actions against the wills of individuals. The practical implication of the idea of the fair-weather illiberal is probably obvious; his existence suggests that, if given sufficient "teeth," antidiscriminatory laws *can* be effective even though nondiscrimination goes against the convictions of local populations where the policy is being enforced.[33]

Another possibility is that prejudice may be not so much a cause of discrimination as an effect of it. We noted in chapter 10 how the

[31] Gordon W. Allport, *The Nature of Prejudice* (Garden City, N.Y.: Doubleday, 1958), p. 5.

[32] Robert K. Merton, "Discrimination and the American Creed," in Robert M. MacIver (ed.), *Discrimination and National Welfare* (New York: Harper, 1949), pp. 99–126.

[33] John P. Roche and Milton M. Gordon, "Can Morality Be Legislated?" *New York Times Magazine,* May 22, 1955, p. 10.

naked power of one individual over another tends to become "clothed" in the garments of legitimate authority. The privilege that one ethnic group enjoys at the expense of another typically demands such rationalization of the privilege: *we* deserve the privilege; *they* (members of the minority group) do not.

In the Southern town studied by Dollard, there were a number of "defensive beliefs" about the nature of Negroes by which whites rationalized their gains at the Negroes' expense.[34] One of these, a justification of the sexual gain of whites, is the belief that Negro men are sexually aggressive toward white women and that their sexual potency is so great that the very lives of Southern women would be threatened if the Negro man were ever once allowed to "take liberties" with the white woman. Another belief is the stereotype of the Negro as "happy," the view that Negroes are by nature childlike in their naiveté and their behavioral irresponsibility, and that they happily accept the paternalistic relation of themselves with whites.

The reader can readily see the self-justifying components in these beliefs; they rationalize a discrimination that would perhaps exist without the rationalization. Where a privilege monopoly exists for a long period of time, some form of the "white man's burden" kind of justification of privilege and underprivilege tends to emerge, but there is little reason to assert that prejudicial ideas of this sort are a *precondition* to the establishment of a system of discrimination.[35]

Somewhere between these two competing explanatory formulae (prejudice leads to discrimination versus discrimination leads to prejudice) there are other views which hold that there is a relation of mutual dependency of these two variables. This is one aspect of Myrdal's "principle of cumulation" to the effect that the various aspects of underprivilege of the American Negro are causally interrelated.[36]

A somewhat more familiar statement of this notion is the idea of a vicious circle or self-fulfilling prophecy which exists in ethnic as

---

[34] Dollard, *Caste and Class in a Southern Town*, Ch. 16.

[35] A book which articulates this view with reference to the American Negro's situation is Oliver C. Cox, *Caste, Class and Race: a Study in Social Dynamics* (Garden City, N.Y.: Doubleday, 1948).

[36] Gunnar Myrdal, *An American Dilemma* (New York: Harper, 1944), pp. 1065–1070.

in other kinds of human relations. We do sometimes act on the basis of our prejudicial attitudes toward persons. Residents of a neighborhood may try to institute some kind of gentleman's agreement to prevent the sale of houses in the neighborhood to members of ethnic minorities. The explanation is likely to be that the excluded people could not or would not take care of their property and their negligence would spoil the neighborhood and lower property values if they were permitted to own houses there. The effect of such housing discrimination is to limit ethnic group members to slum residential areas in which the facilities and motivation to take care of housing are lacking. As the suburban white drives to work and observes the very real dirt and disorder of slum dwellings, he may take comfort in the cleanliness and order of his own all-white residential area and thank his stars that "that kind" of people have been kept out. He tends to see how the behavioral deficiencies that he observes justify the continued discrimination; he is less likely to see the character of his own prejudicial attitudes as an element of the "racist society"[37] which produces this kind of behavior.

The effect of a discriminatory system in creating the very derogated qualities that are part of the discrimination-justifying stereotype generates some of the liveliest controversies in contemporary ethnic relations. Minority group members and their friends are likely to argue that, given the disadvantages accumulated by generations of discrimination, the minorities are entitled to special treatment in several respects: special educational programs like Head Start, for example, or admission to college even though such students lack the requisite high school academic credentials. Fair employment rules may require that a certain number of minority group members be employed, and less than fully qualified persons may have to be hired to meet this requirement. In some academic circles, the demand for nonwhite teaching personnel is very high relative to the supply. Every academic department would like to have a "Negro or two" as a demonstration of nondiscrimination; the scarcity of black Ph.D.'s may give some competitive advantage to those who do hold them. Reflecting the ironic effects of policies to eliminate racial and sex discrimination, one chairman of a university department of sociology, responding to a questionnaire

---

[37] National Advisory Commission on Civil Disorders, *Report* (New York: Bantam, 1968).

designed to indicate the extent of academic discrimination against women, wrote, "Our department will look better next year; I just hired a black woman assistant professor!"[38]

Opponents of special treatment for minority group members are likely to denounce it as "discrimination in reverse" or to deplore the "lowering of standards" that may be necessary when a quota for educational, employment, or other kinds of participation by minority group members must be filled. Although a white person may see well enough the abstract principle of justice in allowing Negroes special privilege to compensate for previous discrimination, he may feel nothing but injustice if his own child is denied admission to a college which grants admission to less academically qualified members of "disadvantaged" groups.

These last observations will suggest an appropriate kind of sociological frame for the phenomenon of ethnic discrimination. Durkheim argued long ago that the "work" of modern society is a "work of justice," aimed at the elimination of all inequalities of privilege that are not based on the unequal distribution of personal talents.[39] The moral flavor of controversies about ethnic discrimination tends to emphasize disagreements concerning which discriminations are justified and which are not. The "prejudiced" person tends to see these discriminations as justified by the inferior quality of the persons who are discriminated against. The "liberal" person refuses to clothe the power of a dominant group in legitimacy. The granting of a privilege to an ethnic group member is seen by the prejudiced as unjust since "he doesn't deserve it"; the denial of a privilege is seen by the liberal as unjust since "he *does* deserve it." Anger, resentment, and moral indignation are the emotions most frequently aroused when issues are raised about the justice or the injustice of a given distribution of privileges.

Life Styles

In many respects, the discrimination against or segregation of an ethnic group and its relationships with other groups will be influenced by the particular way of life that is lived by people in that group. This being the case, there have been many attempts by

---

[38] Alice S. Rossi, "Status of Women in Graduate Departments of Sociology, 1968–69," *American Sociologist*, 5(1970):1.

[39] Emile Durkheim, *On the Division of Labor in Society*, trans. by George Simpson (New York: Macmillan, 1933), p. 387.

sociologists to describe the life styles or subcultures of different ethnic groups.

An example of such studies is an examination of the different value-orientations of several ethnic groups in a small geographic region of New Mexico.[40] The authors describe a number of neighboring communities, each dominated by one ethnic group: Mormons, Mexican-Americans, Zuñi Indians, Navaho Indians, and "Texans." Although people in each community faced the common problem of scratching a living from a meagre environment, their general values or outlooks on life reflected quite different ethnic traditions.

For example, the Mexican-American residents of "Atrisco" lived an essentially present-oriented way of life and practiced a fatalistic acceptance of conditions in a manner reminiscent of the lower-class subcultural style described in the last chapter.[41] "Texans" (those who came from Texas and Oklahoma), by contrast, showed a future-oriented way of life with the typically middle-class emphasis on getting things done and getting ahead; but the extreme *individualism* of their subculture often made it difficult to achieve any goals at the community level. The Mormon community, although sharing most of the characteristics of the Texans, were less extremely individualistic and more successful in accomplishing a group project such as the building of a school for the community.

One major sociological perspective on the study of ethnic life styles would emphasize the impact of discrimination against a minority group on the ways of life adopted by members of that group. The "future-oriented pessimism" that Zborowski describes as typical of the Jewish-American subculture may be seen as a response to the actual experience of persecution of Jews.[42] The "amoral familism" (a pervasive sense of apathy about civic affairs) that Banfield found to be typical of the life style of people in certain

---

[40] Florence R. Kluckhohn and Fred L. Strodtbeck, *Variations in Value Orientations* (Evanston, Ill.: Row, Peterson, 1961).

[41] This view of Mexican-American passivity has been criticized by Steiner, who finds a pattern of strong latent anger or "silent violence" among these people. The notion of the passive acquiescence of the Mexican is called a "dream" of social scientists as well as of Anglo-Americans generally. Stan Steiner, *La Raza: the Mexican Americans* (New York: Harper & Row, 1970).

[42] Mark Zborowski, "Cultural Components in Responses to Pain," *Journal of Social Issues,* 8(1952):16–30.

regions of southern Italy[43] (and that Gans found to carry over into the life styles of Italian-Americans in Boston[44]) may be seen as responses to the restriction of political participation for these people. In learning to live with the fact of discrimination, minorities may have to learn to live in such a way as to minimize the pains of discrimination.

This line of analysis will suggest an important kind of sociological variable which determines variations in ethnic life style. One typically finds variations in life style *within* an ethnic group, and these variations may partly be accounted for by the way in which different members of the group experience discrimination. There are a variety of ways for adapting to minority group status, and one usually finds a number of "social types" within a minority which define different life styles.[45]

The life-style patterns of American Negroes have been much studied in this way. In slavery times, "house" servants enjoyed status and other privileges at the expense of "field" servants,[46] and it was the house servants who specialized in developing a servile "white-folks manner" which has more recently been castigated as an "Uncle Tom" life style. A study of the "personalities" of New Orleans Negroes provides case studies of a variety of life-style adaptations to racial discrimination.[47] These include (1) a middle-class orientation: a life style marked by superrespectability in terms of the standards of middle-class morality; (2) a matriarchal orientation: a life style developed especially among lower-class women in which men are defined as objects of scorn but also fair targets of exploitation while family life is organized around the mother-daughter relationship; (3) "marginality": essentially the life-style counterpart for men of the matriarchal style among women. Men, excluded from any adequate expression of their masculinity in the role of husband and father, involve themselves in the super he-man cultural orientation of the lower-class street gang.

---

[43] Edward C. Banfield, *The Moral Basis of a Backward Society* (Glencoe, Ill.: Free Press, 1958).

[44] Herbert J. Gans, *The Urban Villagers* (New York: Free Press of Glencoe, 1962).

[45] Samuel M. Strong, "Social Types in a Minority Group: Formulation of a Method," *American Journal of Sociology,* 48(1943):563–573.

[46] Wilbert E. Moore and Robin M. Williams, "Stratification in the Ante-Bellum South," *American Sociological Review,* 7(1942):343–351.

[47] John H. Rohrer and M. S. Edmonson (eds.), *The Eighth Generation: Cultures and Personalities of New Orleans Negroes* (New York: Harper, 1960).

Ethnic Relations

We noted at the start of this chapter the tendency for a number of ethnic groups to coexist in the same society. We shall now look more closely at ethnic coexistence and consider some of the variety of ways in which ethnic groups may react to the presence of one another in the same social system. Ethnic coexistence may take any of the forms of interaction discussed in chapter 7: cooperation, competition, conflict, and accommodation. The sociologist is mainly interested here, as elsewhere, in finding out what conditions or factors are associated with these variations in intergroup relations: Why do members of two ethnic groups get along with such tranquility in some places and with so much tension in others?

Competition as a source of tension. One of the most famous sociological propositions about a condition promoting conflict within a social system is Durkheim's notion that "moral density" leads to conflict.[48] By *moral* density Durkheim had in mind the intensity of social interaction between people, including the situation in which a great many people are competing for the same scarce privileges: many people, for example, competing as applicants for one job or as suitors for one woman. Durkheim saw the division of labor (occupational specialization) as a "mellowed denouement" of potential conflict arising from moral density. Rather than competing for the right to perform a task, men tend to divide a task into functional specialties and give each person a special "part" to perform.

Such ideas are frequently applied to the problem of the relation between ethnic groups. The coexistence of two or more ethnic peoples may lead them to struggle between themselves for access to privileges.[49] Irish, Italians, and Poles compete for control of the Catholic church in America (with the Irish generally winning[50]); Mexican-Americans and Anglo-Americans in New Mexico compete for the use of land, the Mexicans wanting grazing land for their sheep and the middle-class Anglos wanting public forest reserves for vacation use.[51] In our discussion of discrimination we cited one

---

[48] Durkheim, *On the Division of Labor*, p. 270.

[49] For a discussion of some of the varieties of ethnic-group rivalry, see Shibutani and Kwan, *Ethnic Stratification*, Ch. 14.

[50] Herberg, *Protestant–Catholic–Jew.*

[51] Steiner, *La Raza.*

possible outcome of this competition: the formation of dominant and minority groups composed of those who habitually succeed and fail in this competition. The angry feelings of minority groups and perhaps the guilty feelings of dominant groups may give a strong hostile coloration to the interaction between members of dominant and minority ethnic groups.[52]

The same hostility may prevail between two minority ethnic groups. Contrary to what might be expected, that two minority ethnic groups such as Jews and Negroes will have much sympathy for one another by virtue of their being in the same boat, we may find many situations similar to the teachers' strike in New York City in which Negro anti-Semitism and Jewish hostility toward Negro-dominated "neighborhood schools" were major sources of tension.[53] The competition of these two groups for control of the schools was evidently a factor in this situation.

The "mellowed denouement" by which interethnic tension is sometimes avoided is some sort of caste-like differentiation of functions between members of the different ethnic groups. Each group knows its "place" in the hierarchy of privilege, and members make a psychological adjustment to their inferior or superior status. This kind of interethnic accommodation frequently takes the form of a "paternalistic" system,[54] since part of the arrangement is the understanding that members of the superior groups will look after members of inferior groups, just as a good father looks after his children. American race relations in the South, as described by Dollard[55] among others, have been strongly paternalistic in this sense, with the white man assuming the "burden" of responsibility for the Negro and the Negro assuming at least the outward appearance of a happy acceptance of his childlike social status.

Having identified two types of relations between ethnic groups in terms of competition for life chances, we can suggest more explicitly the kind of situation in which tension and conflict is most likely to occur. It may be that the least tension occurs when the

---

[52] van den Berghe, "Paternalistic versus Competitive Race Relations."

[53] For studies of hostility and prejudice between Negroes and Jews, see Richard L. Simpson, "Negro-Jewish Prejudice: Authoritarianism and Some Social Variables as Correlates," *Social Problems*, 7(1959):138–146; and H. Lever and O. J. M. Wagner, "Ethnic Preferences of Jewish Youth in Johannesburg," *Jewish Journal of Sociology*, 9(1967):34–47.

[54] van den Berghe, "Paternalistic versus Competitive Race Relations."

[55] Dollard, *Caste and Class in a Southern Town.*

form of interaction between groups either is very nearly purely competitive or is rigidly caste-like.[56] In a fully developed competitive system, in which everyone fully accepts the right of everyone else to compete on an equal basis without regard to "race, creed or color," there should be no occasion for hostility based on the observation that one ethnic group is "getting ahead" in the struggle for advantage. In a fully caste-like system, minority ethnic group members know and keep their place and, again, tension should be minimized.

It is only when a previously caste-like situation is breaking down, and the question of the "place" of different ethnic groups becomes problematic, that minority groups will act in ways that others will define as "pushy" and the dominant groups will suppress these minority group ambitions in ways that the latter define as "unfair." Here is the modicum of truth in the white Southerner's contention that race relations in the South were amicable until the Negro was stirred to question his inferior place by "outside agitators." Interracial conflict has been intensified at just those periods when minority races have begun to challenge the traditional conception of their inferior place. Civil rights demonstrations by minority groups and such extralegal repressive activities as the Ku Klux Klan, the White Citizens Councils, and the lynching mob have developed at those points of transition between a purely paternalistic and a purely competitive interracial situation.

Out-group conflict and in-group solidarity. Another applicable proposition from general sociological theory is the idea that the conflict of one society with another tends to conciliate any differences within each of the societies.[57] People in wartime are urged to put aside partisan conflicts "for the duration." Winston Churchill's ruling governments in Britain during World War II were coalition governments that included members from the various parties, and such governments symbolized the unity of the nation under emergency conditions.

This idea can be applied fairly directly to interethnic situations. Considering the relatively harmonious relations of ethnic groups in the United States throughout most of its history, it may be that

---

[56] Shibutani and Kwan, *Ethnic Stratification*, p. 378.

[57] Lewis A. Coser, *The Functions of Social Conflict* (Glencoe, Ill.: Free Press, 1956), pp. 87–95.

the recurrent crises and wars in which the country has been involved have had a periodic unifying effect. Ethnic conflict, like class conflict, has typically been muted during wars. More important, perhaps, the dramatic contributions of members of different ethnic groups to the country's war effort have served to remove any legitimacy from the denial of privileges for minority ethnic groups. Given the equality of sacrifice to the war efforts of Americans of Negro, Indian, Mexican, and European heritage, the sensibleness of discrimination against members of these groups becomes increasingly questionable.

A usual observation about the effect of war service on members of minority groups is that it makes them increasingly resentful of discrimination when they return to civilian life. An American Indian who has been a full peer of other soldiers may find it especially difficult to return to the restrictive life of the Indian reservation.[58] From this perspective, the country's wars have tended to intensify interethnic antagonism. But the other viewpoint is that these differences have undermined the legitimacy of existing discrimination and hastened the movement toward a state of intergroup harmony based on the conditions of a fully competitive system.

The other side of the proposition that we are discussing is the apparent fact that interethnic hostilities will be *intensified* if it is suspected that ethnic groups within a society have special loyalties to an external "enemy" of the society. German-Americans in the United States experienced increasing antagonism from their fellow Americans during World War II, and Japanese-Americans on the West Coast excited enough fear and antagonism that they were eventually evacuated to "relocation centers" which were basically concentration camps. Many Americans shared the attitude of the syndicated columnist who wrote in 1942:

I am for the immediate removal of every Japanese on the West Coast to a point deep in the interior. . . . Let 'em be pinched, hurt, hungry. Personally, I hate Japanese. And that goes for all of them.[59]

The recent bitter strife between Protestants and Catholics in Northern Ireland is apparently related to the fact that the dominant

[58] Evon Z. Vogt, "Navaho Veterans: A Study of Changing Values," *Papers of the Peabody Museum of American Archaeology and Ethnology.* No. 41, Cambridge, Mass., 1951.

[59] Harry H. L. Kitano, *Japanese Americans: the Evolution of a Subculture* (Englewood Cliffs, N.J.: Prentice-Hall, 1969), p. 32.

Protestants see the Catholic minority as aligned in some collusive way with the Catholic-dominated Irish Republic to the south, a country that is, in many ways, the "enemy" of Northern Ireland.[60] Much of the anti-Semitic incitement in the American South is based on a propensity to associate Jews with a tendency toward Communist or "Northern" sympathies.

ETHNIC ASSIMILATION

Ethnic differentiation, like social-class differentiation, has its dynamic side. The degree of segregation, discrimination, and subcultural variation associated with different ethnic groups will change over time, as will the prevailing modes of relationship between the various ethnic groups. We have discussed above some of these changes, especially those involving segregation and changing patterns of interethnic relations. In this section we examine more closely the changing or dynamic aspect of the discrimination experienced by ethnic groups and the degree of cultural variation between ethnic groups.

The terms for this analysis are set largely by Gordon's discussion of assimilation of ethnic groups in the United States.[61] Although the term *assimilation* has had a great variety of usages in social scientific writing,[62] we can use the term meaningfully provided we define it precisely. Assimilation here refers to the process by which the distinctiveness of ethnic groups disappears and members of those groups become merged into a society without clear ethnic boundaries.

As Gordon notes, there are *cultural* and *structural* aspects of assimilation.[63] Culturally, a people are assimilated when the subcultural ways of life that distinguish them disappear: the Jew gives up his distinctive style of dress, food consumption, and religious practice; the Indian gives up his tribal ways of life. Structurally, assimilation has occurred when people from an ethnic group have been fully accepted as equal participants in the general social life of the society, one in which there is not a differential distribution of the roles and statuses to members of different ethnic groups. The

---

[60] Timothy Patrick Coogan, *Ireland Since the Rising* (New York: Praeger, 1966), pp. 297–303.

[61] Milton M. Gordon, *Assimilation in American Life* (New York: Oxford, 1964).

[62] Ibid., pp. 61–68.

[63] Ibid., Ch. 3.

measure of structural assimilation is the ability of ethnic group members to move freely through the society, joining clubs, marrying, and selecting places of residence without any hindrance because of their ethnic names or their known ethnic backgrounds.

Gordon distinguishes between cultural and structural assimilation because he, like many other sociologists, wants to point out that these two kinds do not necessarily go together. Jews and Gentiles might work side by side in a factory or office (structural assimilation), but when they open their lunch boxes each may take out food that is peculiar to the life style of his ethnic group (lack of cultural assimilation). Or, although members of an ethnic group are fully assimilated culturally, they may be denied the opportunity of joining an "exclusive" social club or of being elected president of the United States.

Different ethnic groups will display all degrees of structural and cultural assimilation at any given time. The explanation of this variation is the problem of the rest of this chapter. Since ethnic groups also vary in terms of whether they themselves are attempting to promote or inhibit assimilation, it seems advisable to discuss variations in assimilation separately for ethnic groups with these two kinds of intentions.[64]

Groups Promoting Assimilation

We start by noting an interesting kind of assymetry that may exist between the assimilation intentions of people of an ethnic group and the intentions for them of people outside the group. Members of many ethnic groups favor structural assimilation: they want themselves and their children to enjoy all the opportunities that are available to members of other ethnic groups. At the same time, they may hope that this structural assimilation can be achieved without compromising an ethnic way of life that they value and would like to maintain. On the other hand, persons outside that ethnic group may be willing, even eager, for members of that group to assimilate to their own way of life: the Americanization of immigrant groups is heartily approved of. However, at the same time, dominant group members may be unwilling to relinquish any

---

[64] There is some problem in adhering to this distinction since, for many ethnic groups, there is controversy within the group about the desirability of assimilation. Still, as "ideal types," it is quite possible to distinguish between the problem of an ethnic group that wishes to retain its ethnic identity resisting assimilation and one that wishes to reduce its distinctiveness resisting the barriers to its assimilation.

of their advantages in participation opportunities to members of these groups.

Perhaps a more usual attitude of dominant group members is that they are willing to permit the structural assimilation of minority ethnic group members, but *only* if they are willing to accept the way of life of people in the dominant groups. Merton has said, in another context, that frequently conformity is demanded as the price of acceptance as a full-fledged member of a group.[65] Gordon notes a predominant attitude among Americans of expecting "Anglo-conformity"—the adoption of the English language and Anglo-Saxon political values—as the price of acceptance of the immigrant as a full participating member of the society.[66] Similarly, the Anglo residents of a south Texas town are reported to be willing to accept on a nondiscriminatory basis only the "high" type of Mexican-American resident—the one who has most fully assimilated Anglo cultural ways.[67]

In the struggle of an ethnic group for equality of opportunity coupled with the maintenance of the integrity of an ethnic tradition, the dominant group's demand for "Anglo-conformity" (or an equivalent attitude) has frequently prevailed. Herberg argues that people of all national origins and of Protestant, Catholic, and Jewish religious persuasions have all had to adapt themselves culturally to American social conditions.[68] However, these adaptations have a strong "Anglo" flavor; American society has acted as a "transmuting pot" whereby ethnic groups have had to assimilate themselves to an essentially Anglo-Saxon Protestant cultural world.

The extent of Anglo-conformity of Jewish-Americans was well demonstrated in a study of Jews on the "frontier" of contemporary American life, namely, the suburbs.[69] Sklare found that, in this sample of upper-middle-class Jews, the practice of traditional religious ritual was much neglected by most of the subjects and that there was a significant decline in ritual observance by

---

[65] Robert K. Merton, *Social Theory and Social Structure,* rev. ed. (Glencoe, Ill.: Free Press, 1956), Ch. 8.

[66] Gordon, *Assimilation in American Life,* Ch. 4.

[67] Simmons, "Mutual Images and Expectations of Anglo-Americans and Mexican-Americans."

[68] Herberg, *Protestant–Catholic–Jew.*

[69] Marshall Sklare, *Jewish Identity on the Suburban Frontier* (New York: Basic Books, 1967).

the present generation compared with the previous generation. There were a few exceptions to this rule: for example, the continued and even increased observance of Hanukkah, a relatively minor holiday traditionally. This is one exception, however, that *does* seem to prove a rule. American Jews have found that Hanukkah observance allows them to assimilate their ritual observances to the parallel Christmas observances that so predominate in the United States. (One can send the same greeting card that says "happy holidays" to both Jewish and Gentile friends at Christmas-Hanukkah time.) Otherwise, the Jewish-American finds that the traditional religious ritual is a burden on his mobility aspirations. (It is difficult, for example, to have a kosher meal with a Gentile colleague at a "businessman's lunch.")

A somewhat earlier study of third-generation Jewish-Americans found that, by this point in the assimilating process, Jewish children had rather fully assimilated the general middle-class American trend toward a consumption-oriented rather than a work-oriented way of life and had rejected the "money-grubbing" life styles of their mobility-conscious parents.[70] (These parents are described as having "devoted twelve hours a day to work and the other twelve to worry.") This study also reported that young Jews reported little or no restriction of their life chances by virtue of their Jewishness, suggesting a thorough structural assimilation but apparently at the price of a rather complete cultural assimilation as well.

Another viewpoint about the relation between cultural and structural assimilation is that many ethnic groups, although promised structural assimilation as the reward for giving up their "un-American" ways, have not in fact been rewarded in the promised fashion. This is Gordon's viewpoint when he points out that Jewish-Americans, for example, have adopted Anglo-Saxon ways and manners only to discover that the exclusiveness of the "Protestant establishment"[71] will ultimately exclude them from the top positions of power in the society.[72]

These two studies of Jewish-Americans also find elements of incomplete structural assimilation of Jews in certain respects. Suburban Jews, even those highly acculturated to Anglo-Saxon ways,

---

[70] Judith R. Kramer and Seymour Leventman, *Children of the Gilded Ghetto* (New Haven: Yale University Press, 1961).

[71] E. Digby Baltzell, *The Protestant Establishment* (New York: Random, 1964).

[72] Gordon, *Assimilation in American Life,* pp. 111–113.

report that nearly all their friendship associations are with other Jews with whom they "feel comfortable."[73] Apparently Jewish-Gentile intimate association is still tinged by the hint of Gentile exclusiveness, and this may help explain the tendency of Jews of all degrees of acculturation to look for a "nice Jewish girl" for a wife. Kramer and Leventman find that there is still some understanding that Jews do not enter certain lines of work, such as executive management of corporations, and that there are "Jewish businesses," retail merchandising, for example, that are seen as faintly unrespectable *because* they are "Jewish."[74]

This involuntary restriction on structural assimilation or social-mobility opportunities has apparently led some ethnic groups to adopt avenues of mobility that differ from the conventional ones. Bell has shown that organized crime as an illegitimate mobility opportunity in lieu of legitimate avenues was adopted by immigrant ethnic groups shortly after they first arrived in America in great numbers.[75] First Jews, then Irish, then Italians have controlled organized crime in U.S. cities. Weinberg and Arond have similarly shown that careers in boxing were used as a mobility opportunity by ethnic groups in their early attempts at structural assimilation; professional boxing has been successively dominated by Irish, Jewish, Italian, and Negro fighters.[76] Finally, Banfield and Wilson have shown how ambitious members of ethnic groups have forged successful political careers by building their support around an ethnic constituency.[77] However, Anglo-Saxon Protestants and Jewish-Americans have tended to look on city politics as "dirty" and, possessing alternative avenues of mobility, they have not supported political leaders of their own ethnic groups in the same way.

Groups Resisting Assimilation

Probably most ethnic groups, at some point, have actively resisted cultural assimilation, even at the price of continued discrimination against themselves. Early Jewish religious leaders decried the

---

[73] Ringer, *Edge of Friendliness.*

[74] Kramer and Leventment, *Children of the Gilded Ghetto.*

[75] Daniel Bell, "Crime as an American Way of Life," in Daniel Bell, *The End of Ideology* (New York: Free Press of Glencoe, 1960).

[76] S. Kirson Weinberg and Henry Arond, "The Occupational Culture of the Boxer," *American Journal of Sociology,* 57(1952):460–469.

[77] Edward C. Banfield and James Q. Wilson, *City Politics* (Cambridge: Harvard University Press, 1963).

Americanization tendency that we have been discussing and argued that what the Jewish immigrant really needs is not Americanizing but "Judaising."[78] Members of dissenting religious groups like the Amish have hoped to retain the integrity of their special way of life and have been quite willing to accept a modest social-status position in return for being able to maintain their highly valued way of life.[79]

The strength of outside pressures for assimilation is well illustrated in the case of the Amish. Members of this religious group are predominantly farmers, and they have not seen the necessity or desirability of having their children attend school beyond a few years. To provide this limited schooling they have hoped to maintain their own schools with Amish teachers and with a curriculum suited to their life style rather than to those of the people who make laws governing required elementary school curricula. There have been serious brushes with the law and with the informal opinion of people in surrounding communities on the issue of the education of Amish children.[80] In a similar way, Mormons trying to maintain a polygamous way of life and, more recently, hippies trying to develop their separate peoplehood with a distinctive life style have encountered the assimilating expectations of the law or of their neighbors.

The external pressures for assimilation on Amish and other ethnic communities are shown in the schismatic tendencies of such communities. Among the Amish there is a continual process of families splitting off and founding new communities, and these schisms typically result from some controversy about the acceptability of some accommodation to the "worldly" ways of the people from the outside world.[81] The experience of discrimination against unassimilated members of such an ethnic group in this outside world is undoubtedly a major factor in precipitating these assimilation crises within a separatist ethnic group.

SUMMARY

An ethnic group is a number of persons who see themselves as a "people" with a common ancestry. Among different people there

---

[78] Sklare, *Jewish Identity on the Suburban Frontier*, pp. 4–6.

[79] John A. Hostetler, *Amish Society*, rev. ed. (Baltimore: Johns Hopkins Press, 1968).

[80] Ibid., pp. 193–208.

[81] Ibid., pp. 259–262.

are varying degrees of consciousness of being members of an ethnic group, and many ambiguities surround the question of who is or is not a member.

Ethnic group membership tends to have multiple consequences for the social lives of the members. People tend to segregate themselves or be forced into segregation by the social distance of those who find it distasteful to associate with them, especially at the more intimate levels of association. Members of ethnic groups frequently experience discrimination or restriction of life chances. Whether this discrimination is based on the prejudicial attitudes of others toward them or whether the prejudices are simply rationalizations for the discrimination is a moot question. Ethnic groups tend to develop distinctive life styles, often as adaptations to the fact of discrimination against them, and life-style variations within an ethnic group reflect variations in modes of adaptation to discrimination.

The relationships between members of different ethnic groups show various degrees of harmony and tension, being perhaps most tense when traditional understandings about the inferior "place" of some ethnic group are beginning to break down. Ethnic differences tend to disappear in the process of assimilation, which ethnic group members may promote or resist. When they promote assimilation, they often are more interested in fuller participation in the general group life than in the effacement of their subcultural traditions. What they frequently find, in contrast, is that they must either give up their cultural traditions as a condition for acceptance on an equal basis or, in the face of more persistent barriers to the elimination of discrimination, make use of "deviant" opportunity structures such as crime, athletics, or city politics. Groups actively resisting cultural assimilation may experience many pressures from outside to assimilate and this pressure tends to be reflected in internal disagreements about the desirability of assimilation.

SELF AND SOCIETY

So far we have given relatively little attention to the situation of the individual person confronted with the necessity of living within an organized society. It is this problem to which we turn our attention in this section.

One way to approach this relation between individual and society is to observe that the individual's behavior more or less conforms to or deviates from the expectations of other persons. We saw in the discussion of social relationships in chapter 7 that orderly social relations depend on the fact that, by and large, people conform to the expectations that others have of them. But "by and large" may leave much room for individual variation in conformity, and the sociologist is interested in understanding those social conditions that promote either conformity or its opposite, deviance. Some of the determinants of this variability will be discussed in chapters 13 and 14.

Chapter 15 aims to acquaint the reader with an increasingly prominent approach to the study of human behavior. If people are sensitive to the impressions that other people have of them, they may "present themselves" as conformists or as deviants, sometimes concealing from others the conforming or deviating character of their actions. A criminal may hide his criminal acts, and a boy in a "hip" gang may need to conceal from his gang fellows any adjustments he has made to the expectations of the "square" world. Once we recognize the fact of the manipulation of impressions of self, we can look at many of the long-standing problems in the relationship of individual and society from a new perspective.

Conformity
and Social Control

CHAPTER
13

CONFORMITY IN PERSPECTIVE

In examining the behavior of members of any animal species, we can notice that there is a "typical" kind of behavior found in that species. To mention a few human stereotypes about animal behavior: lions are ferocious, cattle are docile, ants are industrious. The popular, even the biological attributions of properties to an animal species are generalizations about the typical or average behavior; some lions may be tamed and some cattle are wild, but these are exceptional traits in each species. The instinctive biological equipment of each species guarantees that behavior will vary only within limits set by these instincts; no whale will ever fly, no eagle will swim under water.

Social Control

Human behavior, as we indicated in chapters 3 and 4, is not closely limited by instinctive tendencies. The discovery of the range of variations in human behavior from one cultural context to another has virtually demolished the notion of a universal "human nature" to which the behavior of each member of the human species must conform. This fact does not, however, support any contention that human behavior is ultimately free or unconstrained by any tendency toward uniformity. People in a given region tend to speak the same language, eat the same foods, dress similarly, have similar religions and political ideas. These uniformities have very little to do, however, with instinctive tendencies. It is simply that, wherever men have *culture* (that is to say, wherever men live together), they share a set of ideas about *valued* or right and proper forms of human behavior. Conformity to the social type defined by these values is a matter of *social control:* the pressure that men can bring to bear on their fellows to bring them in line with social expectations.

Empirical Studies of Social Control

A number of experiments have demonstrated the effects of group pressures on human behavior. Sherif conducted studies on the "autokinetic effect," i.e., the illusion that a pinpoint of light in a totally dark room seems to be moving.[1] Subjects asked to describe this movement will tend to make judgments approximating the group norm of judgments that emerges when groups of subjects are exposed together to the autokinetic effect. Asch developed similar findings in experimental situations in which subjects were asked to make perceptual judgments about relative lengths of lines, etc.[2] The experiments were conducted with small groups of subjects of whom all but one were the paid confederates of the experimenter. The confederates were instructed to express perceptual judgments in the presence of the "naive" subject which would contradict the subject's own sensory impression. The finding was that, in most cases, the naive subject would yield to the pressure of a group opinion.

Studies in more real-life situations have produced similar findings. Newcomb found that most of the girls who entered Bennington College, Vermont, came to college with political attitudes formed in the conservative Republican backgrounds of their wealthy families. At the college, however, there was a pervasive atmosphere of political liberalism, especially among the faculty, and most girls yielded to this climate of opinion and became more liberal politically.[3] Numerous sociological studies of the effects of "reference groups" have elaborated on this view of the tendency of a person's

---

[1] Muzafer Sherif, "An Experimental Approach to the Study of Attitudes," *Sociometry*, 1(1938):90–98.

[2] Solomon E. Asch, *Social Psychology* (New York: Prentice-Hall, 1952).

[3] Theodore M. Newcomb, "Attitude Development as a Function of Reference Groups: the Bennington Study," in Guy E. Swanson et al. (eds.), *Readings in Social Psychology* (New York: Holt, 1952), pp. 420–430. For a more recent study of this type using a population of students at the University of Georgia, see William J. Crotty, "Democratic Consensual Norms and the College Student," *Sociology of Education*, 40(1967):200–218.

behavior to conform to the expectations of his peers.[4] High school students, for example, frequently experience the pressure from an adolescent subculture to conform to values of their fellow students, often values which emphasize popularity or athletic prowess at the expense of academic achievement.[5]

Explanation of Conformity

The *fact* of social influence on individual behavior has been well established by studies like those we have just reviewed. The problem of *explanation* of conformity involves another question: *Why do people conform to the expectations of others?*

Durkheim provides the starting point for a discussion of social control with his view that, from the viewpoint of the individual, society is an entity which is *exterior* to the individual and which continually *constrains* his behavior.[6] It is easy to adapt this idea to the analysis of social organization developed in the preceding chapters. None of the social arrangements that make orderly social life possible can be thought of as "belonging" to the individual; they belong to society, and their functioning is in the interest of maintenance of a society. The culture, the forms of interaction, the array of social groups, the institutions, the sets of categories in social differentiation—these are social facts to which the individual must adapt himself.

Although he may exert himself to deviate from the expected pattern of behavior in a few directions, the individual can hardly hope to escape the constraining power of social arrangements generally. As Cooley says, "either to be exceptional or to appreciate the exceptional requires a considerable expenditure of energy, and no one can afford this in many directions."[7] With his very first encounters with society in the form of his parents, siblings, and nursery school peers, the child learns that others expect him to conform to the rules and regulations that sustain a social order. As

---

[4] For a general statement, see Tamotsu Shibutani, "Reference Groups as Perspectives," *American Journal of Sociology,* 60(1955):562–569.

[5] James S. Coleman, *The Adolescent Society* (New York: Free Press of Glencoe, 1961).

[6] Emile Durkheim, *The Rules of Sociological Method,* trans. by Sarah A. Solovay and John H. Mueller (Chicago: University of Chicago Press, 1938).

[7] Charles H. Cooley, *Human Nature and the Social Order* (New York: Charles Scribner's, 1902), p. 296.

he moves into wider circles of group affiliation, he discovers everywhere a preexisting set of social arrangements into which he must fit: when he joins a club or occupies an office, for example. Wherever there are social expectations that the individual's behavior will fit into the social organization, there are mechanisms to constrain his behavior and make it costly of his "energy" to be "exceptional."

The remainder of this chapter will deal with various mechanisms of social control. One's conception of the process by which conformity is accomplished is apparently determined largely by which of several alternate basic models of human psychology one might choose to emphasize.

SOCIAL CONTROL: IMITATION

In the first place, human behavior may be seen as fundamentally *imitative* in character. People conform to the prevailing ways because they "never see anything else" and it is highly expensive of energy to act in ways for which there are no models for imitation.

The American psychologist Baldwin was an early developer of the notion that human behavior is essentially imitative in character. He asserts that "all that is characteristic of the race or tribe or group or family—all this sinks into the child and youth by his simple presence there in it, with the capacity to learn by imitation."[8]

Cooley expands on this viewpoint by insisting on the major role of suggestion in human behavior.[9] Cooley feels that some psychologists have tended to overestimate the degree of imitation engaged in by children (for example, he does not believe that the smiles of babies are imitative of the smiles of adults; babies smile, Cooley thinks, because they are happy, and an exceptionally mobile face, whether smiling or grimacing, may appeal to their active nature).[10] What is called imitation may involve a great deal of strenuous effort by the child.

On the other hand, Cooley feels, the role of suggestion or imitation in adult life is frequently underestimated. We may think of the tendency to idolize and emulate heroes as childish behavior, but adults, too, seek rather constantly for model persons to imitate. Ethical religions capitalize on this tendency, promoting religious values by putting forth examples of religiously perfect lives (Christ

---

[8] James Mark Baldwin, *The Story of the Mind* (New York: Appleton, 1898), p. 207.

[9] Cooley, *Human Nature and Social Order,* Ch. 2.

[10] Ibid., p. 83.

or Mohammed, for example) for the religiously faithful to imitate.

Such more or less conscious imitative processes could be matched with many examples of situations in which people accept unthinkingly the ways of the groups in which they live. A striking example is language. Adults who struggle to learn a foreign language sometimes show a tinge of jealousy in observing, for example, the fluent French of a six-year-old Parisian, who has grown up with that language and has learned it quite spontaneously in the course of his social life. Some adult language-learning programs try to reconstruct the child's situation by surrounding the learner with other persons speaking the language, making it impossible for him to avoid that language if he would communicate at all.

In another realm, that of ideology, it is sometimes observed that people do not choose their basic ways of thinking about and evaluating the world. The basic values and structural arrangements of a society are incorporated in the behavior of every person with whom the person associates, and he breathes Puritan or democratic or authoritarian ways of life as he would breathe the air itself. As the German sociologist Mannheim puts it, "Strictly speaking, it is incorrect to say that the single individual thinks. Rather, it is more correct to insist that he participates in thinking further what other men have thought before him."[11] Much of this social domination of thought depends on a monopoly of the ideas to which the individual is exposed. Accordingly, groups desiring to preserve a way of life through the mechanism of imitation may feel the need to draw an iron curtain of isolation around their members to keep them from competing thought-ways.

A person often finds, of course, that there are many and competing models for his imitation. A girl contemplating a career for herself may be encouraged to be like "Aunt Sarah" who went to college and became a successful lawyer or, alternatively, like "Cousin Agatha" who married right out of high school and started raising a family. In such situations persons must exercise some *choice* of models—and suffer all the agony that people go through in the process of making decisions. Such agonies become the basis for frequent criticism when new social influences are introduced into previously isolated places. The tribal native may be confused by the juxtaposition of the new model of the good life introduced

---

[11] Karl Mannheim, *Ideology and Utopia,* trans. by Louis Wirth and Edward Shils (New York: Harcourt, Brace & World, 1963), p. 3. First published in 1936.

by the Christian missionary with the models familiar to him from his native culture. Once the "cake of custom" has been broken by exposure to alternative ways of life, it may be impossible to reconstruct the blissful ignorance that has been lost.[12]

SOCIAL CONTROL: RATIONAL CALCULATION

Another idea about human psychology that enjoys a long and honorable history is the notion that human behavior is motivated by tendencies toward pleasure-seeking and pain-avoidance. These tendencies are probably unique to *human* psychology, not because other animals do not experience pain and pleasure, but because they seem not to *anticipate* these experiences before they occur and to plan ways and means to attain pleasure and avoid pain.[13] Only men, it appears, are truly susceptible to the influence of promises and threats.

Directly Interpersonal Controls

A major adaptation of this conception of human psychology to sociological problems is the observation that the reactions of other people in social interaction are painful or pleasurable, and that the anticipation of these reactions will tend to influence the behavior. People can "reward" and "punish" one another in a variety of ways; indeed, literary works like Sartre's *No Exit* express the view that "hell" consists in the tendency for people to make life painful for one another.

The ability of one person to punish another depends, of course, on the sensitivities of the person being punished. Most people appear to want to be liked by others (in *Death of a Salesman,* the frequently mentioned desire is to be *well-liked*). James has commented on the uniquity of this approval-seeking tendency in human psychology: "We are not only gregarious animals, liking to be in sight of our fellows, but we have an innate propensity to get our-

---

[12] For a study of the impact of the "modern" on "traditional" ways of thought, see Daniel Lerner, *The Passing of Traditional Society* (Glencoe, Ill.: Free Press, 1958).

[13] This statement is made with full awareness of experiments in animal "problem-solving" in which, for example, apes put together sticks in order to secure some nearby food. Although animals can certainly adjust present behavior to anticipated future rewards, there is no evidence that any animal can be threatened with a cutoff of food supplies "if you do that again."

selves noticed, and noticed favorably, by our kind."[14] There are some people who are so preoccupied with "favorable notice" that, it is often said, their behavior in a decision-making situation will depend on the attitudes that were expressed by the last person who tried to influence them.

It might seem that wherever a number of people have relationships with one another, each party would be able to control rather closely the behavior of each other party to the relationship. Actually, in a small group like a family or a friendship pair or clique, one person's influence may dominate over that of others, often because one person is relatively independent of the others for his rewards and punishments. In some families, a husband may displease his wife and still anticipate a favorable balance of approval because of the favorable reactions to him at his place of work, while a housebound wife may depend so completely on her husband's approval that she must consistently yield to his wishes.[15] Similar notions have been used to explain the existence of *exploitation* in interpersonal situations like dating and courtship. The party who is least involved emotionally in the relationship (that is, has potential alternative relationships available to him) may be in the best position to dominate the other.[16]

Normative Controls

Sociological analysis will insist on another factor in behavior as determined by pain-pleasure balances, namely, the factor of the *legitimacy* of the expectations that are fulfilled or frustrated. People sometimes treat others well not because they *want* to do so or because they expect something in return for their kindness, but because this treatment is someone's *right* to receive and their own *obligation* to give.[17] A president of the United States is *entitled* to be called "Mr. President" or to a twenty-one-gun salute; a wife is

---

[14] William James, *The Principles of Psychology,* Vol. 1 (New York: Holt, 1890), p. 293.

[15] For an extended discussion of power relations between people as they are influenced by alternatives to the relationship, see John W. Thibaut and Harold H. Kelley, *The Social Psychology of Groups* (New York: Wiley, 1959), pp. 100–125.

[16] Willard Waller and Reuben Hill, *The Family: A Dynamic Interpretation,* rev. ed. (New York: Dryden, 1951), pp. 190–192.

[17] On the relation between rights and obligations, see Vilhelm Aubert, *Elements of Sociology* (New York: Scribner's, 1967), pp. 21–24.

entitled to economic support by her husband, etc. A society has normative expectations for people's behavior and will bring *sanctions* (punishments and rewards) to bear to encourage conformity to those expectations.

Sociologists have commented frequently on the pervasiveness of the obligatory element in people's treatment of one another even in some areas that are not commonly thought to be regulated by social rules. We often think of gift-giving as acts that are from the heart and not constrained by any obligation to give them. But Gouldner suggests the universality of rules defining obligations with reference to gift-giving, such as the rule that a gift should be repaid by another gift of equivalent value but not the identical thing (the exchange of ten-dollar bills as Christmas presents would strike most people as in rather bad taste) or the rule that gifts should be repaid in a reasonable time but not too promptly (the latter offense suggesting too baldly that the debtor is unwilling to be obligated for a time to his benefactor).[18] These rules may be useful in promoting the stability of social relationships. Since they leave the definition of fulfillment of obligation rather vague and enforce a time interval between contracting and repaying a debt, they tend to leave people in a chronic state of having obligations to people that they might otherwise desert.[19]

The importance of rules or norms in regulating human behavior has led sociologists to become interested in distinguishing in several ways between different types of norms. We shall now review some of these distinctions.

Scope. Norms differ, first, in the degree of generality in the scope of their coverage. Some norms are expectations of *all* persons by virtue of their membership in a society. In most of the thou-shalts and the thou-shalt-nots of social expectations, the thou refers to any and all members of the society: adultery and blasphemy are "sins" no matter who commits them.

Some other norms, by contrast, define expectations only for certain categories of persons, constituting the *roles* that accompany different social statuses. The norms governing the behavior of

---

[18] Alvin W. Gouldner, "The Norm of Reciprocity: a Preliminary Statement," *American Sociological Review*, 25(1960):161–178.

[19] Ibid. See also Barry Schwartz, "The Social Psychology of the Gift," *American Journal of Sociology*, 73(1967):1–11.

a student are somewhat different from those governing the behavior of a professor. Professors, but not bricklayers, are expected to be scholarly; children, but not adults, are expected to be dependent on their elders. There is a double (or multiple) standard demanding different behaviors of different categories.

An important feature of these more differentiated norms should be noted. While they are limited in the scope of persons to whom they apply, differentiated norms tend to be general in the respect that all people hold to these differentiated expectations. Professors and students share the expectation that professors will behave in one way, students in another. Although the medical code of ethics represents only a moral obligation on the part of professional medical practitioners, the code is enforced by the community's general expectation that professionals will conduct themselves according to its stipulations.

This point could easily be overstated, however. We find that many specialists develop a set of standards for their special activities that are unfamiliar to the community at large or are even in conflict with the wider expectations of what a specialist should be. The academic community establishes a more or less autonomous set of standards for judging the professional behavior of professors, often resisting the pretensions of professionally "unqualified" people, such as students and boards of trustees, to have a major voice in determining what is competent academic performance.

Sometimes the motivation for developing autonomous standards is the fear that, if the specialists don't police themselves, they will be policed by the general public in ways distasteful to the specialist. The production code adopted by the Motion Picture Association of America represents an attempt at self-censorship as an alternative to censorship by legislatures and local political agencies. It is generally a sign of the maturity of a specialty that its practitioners have a set of self-enforced professional standards. At such a mature stage, for example, art or science does not pander to popular demands; the artist applies the judgments of his artistic colleagues to his own work; the scientist resists the temptation to oversimplify his work by popular scientific writings in favor of more scholarly work.[20]

---

[20] For a discussion of the evolution of a "group spirit" among artists and other specialists, see Charles H. Cooley, *Social Organization* (New York: Scribner's, 1909), pp. 162–166.

Intensity. If people base their behavior on calculations of probable reward or punishment for conformity or nonconformity to rules, they clearly must take into account the different levels of intensity of the sanctions attached to different norms. There are some rules which people can get by with violating because the rules are not considered significant enough to warrant severe punishment for deviance. Sociologists have used the terms *folkways* to refer to the less severely sanctioned norms and *mores* to refer to those norms which represent "doctrines of group welfare,"[21] the violation of which are seen as harmful in some basic way to the society.

A woman who violates current fashion norms by wearing a skirt two inches longer or shorter than the fashionably prescribed length has violated a folkway and will be punished by the mild disapproval or derision of her peers. If the same lady were to choose to go "topless" or "bottomless" to a social gathering, she would be likely to shock the sense of decency of others, having violated one of the mores that define those body parts that may be exposed without harm to public morals.

The cultural relativity of these judgments of seriousness of norms should be apparent. In cultures with a strict regulation of dress, the slightest deviation may be a source of severe public condemnation, while the standards of a nudist colony or a "swinging" social set may tolerate or even require the same bodily exposures that are severely condemned elsewhere.

Formal and informal. A final distinction among types of norms is in the mode of enactment and enforcement of the sanctions attached to them. *Customs* are those norms that grow up spontaneously as the result of the living together of a group of people and that are enforced *diffusely,* that is, by the sanctioning behaviors of members of the society at large. *Laws* are those norms that are enacted as the result of formal discussion and deliberation (How shall the legislature handle this problem?) and that are enforced by such specific agencies of law enforcement as police, courts, etc.

A long tradition in sociological analysis has emphasized the overwhelming importance of *custom* in the regulation of human behavior.[22] It may be, however, that wherever people are highly interdependent on one another, they are highly self-conscious

---

[21] William Graham Sumner, *Folkways* (Boston: Ginn, 1906), p. 30.
[22] Sumner, *Folkways.*

about the rules regulating their behavior; as a result, there is a proliferation of legal norms. The use of intoxicating drugs, which in some situations merely exposes the user to the diffuse disapprovals of his relatives and neighbors, becomes in other situations a "drug problem" requiring regulatory legislation. The "pollution" of the atmosphere, in some situations merely a nuisance to those who must smell or see the "unseemly" practices of a neighbor, comes to be viewed in a tightly interdependent community as a threat to "our environmental heritage" and, again, becomes the focus of formal legislation.

The distinctions between customs and laws and between folkways and mores are easily confused. We may be tempted to think that laws represent the same areas of social regulation as do mores, since people will not bother to go through the deliberation and controversy of legislative process unless the norms in question are of sufficient moment to warrant the trouble. The exactly contrary view is that law is a kind of last resort for the enforcement of norms that are receding from strength in the consciences of people in the community at large.

Actually, the identification of law with either folkways or mores seems to be misguided. Many of our most emotionally charged norms—those forbidding murder or incest, for example—are institutionalized in the form of laws with teeth. But there are many mores that are not enforced by legal sanctions; indeed, the legal rights of persons to behave in certain ways may expose those who so behave to diffuse punishment. It is not against the law, in many places, for a white to marry a black or for a Catholic to marry a Protestant, for an unwed mother to retain custody of her illegitimate child, for consenting adults to engage privately in homosexual acts, or for persons who were once members of the Communist Party to hold jobs. But, in these same places, customary standards of decent behavior may visit heavy sanctions on a person who is exercising a legal right.[23]

On the other hand, some behaviors that are legally prohibited are not met with any sense of outrage in the community at large. Failing to file one's income tax on a certain date or driving forty miles per hour in a thirty-five mile per hour zone is against the law, but it is

---

[23] For a study of popular tendencies to punish accused Communists and other unofficially proclaimed "deviants," see Samuel A. Stouffer, *Communism, Conformity and Civil Liberties* (Garden City, N.Y.: Doubleday, 1955).

not likely that a violator of one of these laws will be very severely condemned by people at large.[24]

The lack of general community support for the law may have some interesting effects on the enforcement of the law itself. Public apathy about speed limits, for example, may lead to informal understandings by legal officials that "speeding" refers only to speeds ten or more miles in excess of the limit, or that the limits may be stretched to accommodate faster speeds late at night. However, some dramatic event, such as a traffic accident, or the need of public officials running for reelection to demonstrate through an augmented arrest record that they are doing their job may result in a crackdown on speeders.

The moral outrage of a victim of a crackdown (Why *me* when everybody else is doing it?) is one symptom of the frequent discrepancy between legal norms and the informal understandings concerning which laws should be obeyed under what circumstances. Although there may be this sense of outrage, the vigorous enforcement of a hitherto neglected law may still have the effect of curbing a prohibited behavior. A crackdown on drinking drivers in Britain did, for example, have the effect of reducing traffic accidents in that country.[25]

Limitations of Pleasure-Pain Calculation

The reward-punishment view of human psychology has yielded some useful ideas about the mechanisms of social control, but there are some problems with this sort of explanation. If social control were based *entirely* on such mechanisms, it would be subject to some limitations.

Considering the exchange or directly interpersonal model of reward-punishment (in which the withholding of a favor is a device for insuring control), the model seems to deal inadequately with

---

[24] For studies of the discrepancy between legal punishments and the customary morality of people, see Arnold M. Rose and Arthur S. Prell, "Does the Punishment Fit the Crime? A Study in Social Valuation," *American Journal of Sociology*, 61 (1955):247–259; Robert V. Sherwin, "The Law and Sexual Relationships," *Journal of Social Issues*, 22(1966):109–122; Don C. Gibbons, "Crime and Punishment: a Study of Social Attitudes," *Social Forces*, 47(1969):391–397; B. Eugene Griesseman and Charles H. Proctor, "Law and Custom: a Study of the Enforcement of Forest Fire Laws in Two Rural Communities," *Sociological Focus*, 2(1969):145–158.

[25] H. Laurence Ross, Donald T. Campbell, and Gene V. Glass, "Determining the Social Effects of a Legal Reform: the British Breathalyser Crackdown of 1967," *American Behavioral Scientist*, 13(1970):493–509.

the possibilities for *exploitation* in human relations. A powerful person may control a weak person because of the latter's fear of his reactions, but it is not so clear how the powerful person's behavior would be controlled. What prevents a parent from mistreating a child, or a professor from abusing a student, so long as the exploitation remains within the bounds of legality? Although such abuses obviously do occur, they quite typically do not, and their infrequency cannot easily be explained by the dominant person's fear of retaliation by the weaker. Who governs the governor? has been a perennial question in human history; frequently, it can be answered only by reference to the consciences of the governors themselves, their adoption of some form of the ethic of *noblesse oblige.* The regulation of human behavior by such ethical considerations involves another model of human psychology, some features of which we shall take up in the following section.

The view that norms are enforced by punishment or the threat of punishment also has its limitations. Such views assume that punishments for violations will be quickly and certainly administered and, further, that the potential offender is *aware* of this prospect and takes it into account when he considers some deviant act. A typical criticism of the idea of such hedonistic calculations is reflected in the controversy surrounding the efficacy of capital punishment.[26] Many capital crimes are highly tempting in terms of what the offender might gain from them: a very lucrative robbery may require the killing of obstructors, a husband denied legal recourse may be tempted to secure a divorce "Italian style" (by murder). Capital punishment is justified on grounds that potential offenders will stop and think of the extreme penalties for such tempting acts.

Critics of capital punishment have pointed out, however, that: (1) in fact, the rate of conviction and execution is relatively slight compared with the number of known offenses; (2) even if the potential offender were aware of a *general* danger of committing criminal acts, he may minimize the danger in his own case, believing that he, at least, can commit the "perfect crime"; (3) capital offenses

---

[26] Thorsten Sellin, *Capital Punishment* (New York: Harper & Row, 1967), pp. 135–138. For an examination of the more general issue of the relation between punishment severity and crime rates, see John C. Ball, "The Deterrence Concept in Criminology and Law," *Journal of Criminal Law, Criminology and Police Science,* 46(1955):347–354; Charles H. Tittle, "Crime Rates and Legal Sanctions," *Social Problems,* 16(1969):409–423.

tend to be "crimes of passion" in which offenders do not indulge in any rational calculation of future rewards and punishments. All these points could be applied in varying degrees to other kinds of criminal offenses as well as to violations of customary norms.

Perhaps the most basic flaw in a social-control system based entirely on the application of sanctions is that it assumes the close surveillance of human acts by sanctioning agents. A child whose conformity to rules is based on a fear that "mama will spank" is obviously not controllable out of her sight or in the presence of people whom he perceives as having neither the right nor the will to spank him or who will not "tell on him" to his mother. Likewise, any lapses of discipline by his mother may encourage him to believe that he can get away with those very acts for which he previously has been punished. A child (or adult) who cannot be trusted out of sight represents a difficult problem in social control. Even the elaborate monitoring devices of Big Brother in Orwell's *1984* were insufficient to prevent a conspiracy against the regime from hatching in a corner of a room which somehow evaded the surveillance of the electronic monitor.

Finally, social control based on sanction application is limited by the reactions of those being rewarded or punished. A parent often observes that the more a child is punished for some deviant act the more stubborn he becomes in his insistence on that act. The psychologist thinks of "reaction formation" as a tendency to reject patterns of behavior to which one has been severely trained. A sociologist writes of "compulsive alienation" as one deviant reaction to social control.[27]

Perhaps this resistance to control is one aspect of a general tendency of human nature, a kind of naysaying tendency which, according to Simmel, is found in a person who "cannot maintain himself except by means of opposition . . . . [The] first instinct with which the individual affirms himself is the negation of the other."[28] With such powerful motivations to resist the influence of another's ideas, human behavior is understandably recalcitrant in the face of attempts to manipulate behavior by the carrot-and-stick method of rewards for conformity and punishments for nonconformity.

---

[27] Talcott Parsons, *The Social System* (Glencoe, Ill.: Free Press, 1951), pp. 254–256.

[28] Georg Simmel, *Conflict,* trans. by Kurt H. Wolff (Glencoe, Ill.: Free Press, 1955), p. 29.

SOCIAL CONTROL: SELF-CONSCIOUSNESS

A final approach to the understanding of social control is that which begins with a model of human psychology as characterized by *self-consciousness*. Man, we are told, is the only animal who thinks in any basic way about himself; according to Mead, a human self is an "object to itself," something reflected upon and emotionally reacted to as one might react to such external objects as trees or microscopic organisms.[29]

Precisely *what* a person is conscious of when he is conscious of himself is a matter of some disagreement. When people are asked to answer the question, Who am I? their answers reflect a variety of ways in which people think about themselves.[30] In research using this question there has emerged, however, a typical pattern of responses. When asked to write twenty answers to the question, Who am I? most people begin listing categorical or status designations such as man, student, boxer, Negro, etc. When they have exhausted the categories of which they can readily think, they begin writing statements about personality characteristics: "I am a happy person" or "I am deeply religious." Not all subjects follow this pattern of answers, but nearly all include answers of the two types. This research suggests that, in thinking about themselves, people *identify* themselves with some of the categories of social differentiation of which they are members and also that they *evaluate* themselves as rating high or low on personal characteristics.

Self-Consciousness and Socialization

The relation of this human self-consciousness to the problem of social control should now be made clear. We have just noted certain limitations of social control based upon the sanctions that others can bring to bear on a person, especially the problem of maintaining constant surveillance of the behavior of the person being controlled. If, however, the person can be brought to apply normative standards in examining his own behavior, the surveillance problem is largely solved since, we assume, the person lives

---

[29] George H. Mead, *Mind, Self and Society* (Chicago: University of Chicago Press, 1934).

[30] Manford H. Kuhn and Thomas S. McPartland, "An Empirical Investigation of Self-Attitudes," *American Sociological Review,* 19(1954):68–78; Manford H. Kuhn, "Self Attitudes by Age, Sex and Professional Training," *Sociological Quarterly,* 1(1960):39–55.

constantly and intimately "with himself."[31] The process of *socialization* aims at instilling in the internal psychology of the individual the desire to act in socially acceptable ways. As Parsons and Shils put it, socialization produces individual *motives* which match socially established *values*.[32]

Relating this to the research on self-identity, it might be said that the person acquires motives to *identify* himself with categories of people that are socially recognized as important bases of personal identity and to *evaluate* himself in terms of standards that he learns from others. The self or "social character"[33] of a person will accordingly vary from society to society. In a race-conscious society or a religiously pious community, people will be encouraged to identify themselves by race and evaluate themselves in terms of their personal piety. Another society with other cultural values and other significant criteria of distinction between kinds of people will produce persons with quite different selves.

Socialization Process

A fully socialized identity is not acquired overnight. Children born into a society come without any standards for thinking about themselves, and the moral education of a child is an involved process. Even fully socialized adults may find themselves thrown into new situations in which "resocialization" is the order of the day. Recruits from civilian life enter a military situation and find that they are expected to think of themselves exclusively as soldiers.[34] Prisoners of war sometimes find that their captors are interested in their political reeducation and will subject them to a vigorous program of brainwashing.[35] Goffman has described a typical process of "stripping" by which entrants to total institutions such as mental hospitals, prisons, and nunneries are required to divest themselves of their noninstitutional identities; the standard institutional haircut

---

[31] This assumption may not always be correct, however. There is a line in an Ingmar Bergman screenplay, *The Seventh Seal,* in which one character says to another, "You're lucky, you can believe in your own twaddle." This suggests that some people do not know themselves a great deal better than others know them.

[32] Talcott Parsons and Edward A. Shils (eds.), *Toward a General Theory of Action* (Cambridge: Harvard University Press, 1959), Part 2.

[33] Erich Fromm, *The Sane Society* (New York: Rinehart, 1955).

[34] Sanford M. Dornbusch, "The Military Academy as an Assimilating Institution," *Social Forces,* 33(1955):316–321.

[35] Edgar H. Schein, *Coercive Persuasion* (New York: Norton, 1961).

and the uniform clothing issue are symbolic of these assaults on previously acquired identities.[36] These resocialization processes, like the processes of socialization of children, are likely to be fraught with many difficulties and to meet with much resistance by the people who are being socialized.

The end product of the socialization process is a person who practices self-regulation of his behavior, who is familiar with and voluntarily observes the rules of good behavior that prevail in his society. When we look at the behavior of people in various social situations we find, however, all degrees of development of this level of socialization. The behavior of some people is "good" only because they fear the punishment that others may inflict on them if their behavior violates social expectations.

The movement toward more complete socialization seems to involve two stages. At the first stage, people begin to examine their own behavior and judge it to be acceptable or unacceptable, depending on how they imagine it appears to the other people with whom they are involved. In the language of Mead, people "take the attitudes of others" toward themselves, seeing their behavior from the perspective of the viewpoints of others.[37] A child refrains from a behavior of which his mother would disapprove, an adolescent boy avoids behaviors that would be rejected by his gang. This level of socialization is clearly an advance beyond the level at which behavior is controlled by fear of punishment. It no longer assumes that others must maintain constant surveillance over one's behavior; the mere imagination of what the other's attitude *would* be is sufficient to deter disapproved behavior.

This level of socialization is not always so easy to achieve, however. It assumes the *sensitivity* of the person being socialized to the attitudes of the socializing agents. With a young child there may be no great problem, since we can usually assume the child's rather complete identification with his parents, beginning at an early age, and his acute sensitivity to their expressions of disapproval. In some of the resocialization situations mentioned above, this sensitivity may be more difficult to achieve. Political prisoners in a concentration camp, for example, are unlikely to identify themselves emotionally with their captors in the same way, although it is sometimes suggested that there *is* a tendency of abused pris-

---

[36] Erving Goffman, *Asylums* (Garden City, N.Y.: Doubleday, 1961).

[37] Mead, *Mind, Self and Society.*

oners toward "identification with the aggressor."[38] A drill sergeant with a group of recruits, a professor with a group of students taking a required course—these are examples of socializing agents who cannot always assume that those whose behaviors they try to control will "take the attitude" of the socializing agent toward their behavior in the situation.

Apart from the problem of *motivation* to take other people's attitudes toward oneself, there is the technical problem of how it is *possible* for people to imagine the attitudes of others toward themselves. Mead believed that people learn to take the attitudes of others largely through the activity of *play*.[39] A young girl learns to take her mother's attitude toward herself by imaginatively putting herself in the place of her mother and reacting to her doll as she imagines that her mother reacts to her. Much of childhood play involves playlike situations in which children pretend that they are all sorts of other people: schoolteacher, fireman, housewife, soldier, etc. Adults do not seem to play very much in this way, but what they perhaps do as an alternative is to *daydream* themselves in the roles of other persons: their wives, bosses, children, etc., or else, as Mead emphasized, they hold internal conversations wherein they try out various ways of acting toward others and respond to themselves with the anticipated reactions. Without the ability to play or, at least, to imagine, it may be difficult for a person to know and make allowances for the attitudes of various other people toward himself.

There is one major limitation of this level of socialization. People take the attitudes of others selectively, being especially sensitive to the attitudes of "significant others" and ignoring or minimizing the attitudes of those persons about whose opinions they do not happen to care. There is no particular problem for the general social order if these significant others (or, as they are sometimes called, *reference groups*) have attitudes that reflect general social norms and values. But it may well be that the reference groups of a person are composed of people whose personal standards are less than acceptable from the viewpoint of the wider society. A teen-ager may be motivated primarily by what his school-

---

[38] Bruno Bettelheim, "Individual and Mass Behavior in Extreme Situations," *Journal of Abnormal and Social Psychology*, 38(1943):417–452.

[39] Mead, *Mind, Self and Society*, pp. 364, 365.

mates will think about some behavior, and if these other adolescents share an adolescent subculture that devalues academic achievement, this sensitivity may lead to the ignoring of studies in a way that violates the general societal expectations that children go to school in order to learn.[40] Sensitivity to the attitudes of members of a hippie community may lead to behaviors in the areas of drug-taking and sexual relations that are decidedly deviant from the wider societal perspective.

A more mature or fully socialized self is one who takes the attitude toward the self of the "generalized other," which Mead defines, somewhat mystically, as "the attitude of the whole organized social community."[41] He makes this point clearer by his suggestion that the *game* is the prototypical experience for learning the attitudes of generalized others, just as play is the basic activity for the learning of attitudes of significant others.

Games have some features that play does not have. Most fundamentally for Mead, a game has an organized structure, an articulation of roles of different individuals in the cooperative action of the "team." A baseball player, one of Mead's favorite examples, must take the attitudes of all other members of his team simultaneously and must understand where his particular function fits into the overall organizational scheme. For example, a pitcher must know that if a ground ball is hit to the left of the first baseman, the baseman must move so far from first base that he cannot field the ball and arrive at first base with it ahead of the batter; it is therefore the pitcher's obligation to cover the base by running to it and receiving the throw of the first baseman. The first baseman must, of course, share this set of role definitions if the defensive team is to achieve an "out" in this situation. It is not sufficient for organized social participation for each to know only his own status and its role requirements; he must be able to see the behavior of other people in the context of their roles.

There is another critical feature of games as microcosms of general social life. Games have rules or norms, as opposed to "just playing" in which there is more spontaneity and style in the play (this is not to deny that there is style or flair in game playing as well). To play a game, one must be willing to adhere to these

---

40 Coleman, *Adolescent Society.*
41 Mead, *Mind, Self and Society,* p. 154.

rules. Rules or norms may be thought of as community "attitudes," defining behavior as right or wrong not because mother says or even because the umpire says, but simply because the rules of the game prescribe this behavior, and anyone who would play the game must adhere to them.

Young children cannot play games primarily because they lack the ability to respond to depersonalized and abstract rules. The child seems to live in a rich and almost exclusively personal world (as do some adults), and it is nearly impossible to prevent his "cheating" by violating abstract rules.[42] The process by which people come to judge their own behavior from the perspective of abstract principles of right behavior may be a difficult one to understand, and the experience of game playing as a socializing experience may have been overemphasized. But, clearly, a society requires that by *some* process or other the person come to regulate his behavior in this fashion.

SUMMARY

Sociologist Peter Berger has suggested that the message of sociology, at least at the outset of its study, is that men are "imprisoned" by the various constraints on their behavior.[43] Berger seems to have in mind not the "tyranny of custom," that is, the tendency of people to imitate ways of behavior that they see all around them, but rather the great variety of sanctions, from gentle ridicule to ostracism and capital punishment, that a society can bring to bear on recalcitrant individuals. But "to deepen the gloom a little more" before presenting the escapes that he later suggests, Berger indicates that social control is heightened by the tendency to put "society in man," the propensity of men to internalize social expectations and enforce them through the dictates of conscience.[44]

In this chapter we have dealt in a similar way with the view of society as containing a number of mechanisms to control the behavior of its members. These include the tendency to adopt imitatively the prevailing patterns of behavior around oneself, the tendency to avoid behaviors that others will punish if they find them unacceptable, and the tendency to internalize the attitudes of

---

[42] Jean Piaget, *The Moral Judgment of the Child*, trans. by Marjorie Gabain (New York: Free Press, 1965).

[43] Peter Berger, *An Invitation to Sociology* (Garden City, N.Y.: Doubleday, 1963).

[44] Ibid., p. 93.

others toward oneself and to make them the basis for one's self-regulation. With all these mechanisms of social control, it may seem a wonder that individual or collective acts of deviance ever occur. In the next chapter we shall dispel this wonder by looking systematically at situations in which there is a failure of social control.

Deviant Behavior

NATURE OF DEVIANT BEHAVIOR

Deviant behavior is that behavior which does not conform to social expectations. When the sociologist labels a kind of behavior as deviant, he is not, contrary to popular conception, condemning that behavior as bad or harmful. From some perspectives deviance might be morally the most defensible kind of behavior. A man's deviation may be a violation of social expectations that are, in fact, unwise or unjust; civil disobedience of laws that are seen as immoral is often advocated from a lofty ethical position. The sociologist's problem is not to approve or to disapprove human behavior, but to understand the basis on which people disapprove one another's behavior, and to understand some of the causes and consequences of this kind of behavior.

To begin the analysis, there are many complications and ambiguities in the way people arrive at the judgment that an act or a person is deviant. The judgment is always based on a sense that the person's behavior falls short of a standard provided by some ideal conception of what behavior ought to be. We shall now examine several of the kinds of ambiguities in social definitions of deviance.

Tolerance

Typically, there is a certain area of public tolerance for the failure of persons to live up to ideal standards. If the standard requires that employees arrive at work or that students arrive at a classroom at an appointed hour, only a martinet of an employer or professor would severely censure as deviant the action of a person in arriving a half-minute late on one occasion.[1]

Expectations of Deviance

In some situations, the behavior of people is disapproved if it adheres too rigidly to the ideal. A perfectionist tends to make others uncomfortable in comparison with themselves. The well-coiffured lady who "never has a hair out of place" is likely to be disparaged as being *too* neat, and the unfailingly articulate conversationalist is accused of being glib. Blau has suggested something of this reaction to the overly perfect person when he argues that a person, to be well integrated into social relations, must demonstrate not only that he is a *respectable* person (that he measures up well to ideal standards) but that he is *approachable,* one who, after all, has his "little foibles and faults like the rest of us" and can therefore be treated as something of an equal.[2]

Another source of rejection of the "compulsive conformist" is the fact that a person can be so overly concerned about letter-perfect adherence to one norm that, in the process, he violates another one. The person who prides himself on his honesty in an extreme way might, for example, insist on having a cashier at a restaurant correct a waitress's error of five or ten cents in his favor when she computed the bill. A less compulsively honest person might realize that, in insisting on the letter of adherence to one norm, he is violating another fundamental norm, namely, that "you don't get people in trouble" over minor matters, as the waitress might well get into trouble in this situation.

Conflict of Norms

The definition of a given act as deviant is always relative to the standards of the people doing the defining. What is deviant from one perspective may be the essence of approved behavior from another. Cohen illustrates this fact in his demonstration of the nature of the "culture" of the lower-class street gang.[3] Approved

---

[1] Courtland C. Van Vechten, "The Toleration Quotient as a Device for Defining Certain Social Concepts," *American Journal of Sociology,* 46(1940):35–44.

[2] Peter M. Blau, "A Theory of Social Integration," *American Journal of Sociology,* 65(1960):545–556.

[3] Albert K. Cohen, *Delinquent Boys: the Culture of the Gang* (Glencoe, Ill.: Free Press, 1955).

behavior here includes vandalism, truancy, disrespect for police, indeed any kind of behavior that makes trouble for respectable authorities and is treated by them as deviant.

Many sociologists tend to suspect that, wherever behavior is seen by members of the dominant society as chronically deviant, the behavior, in fact, conforms to the expectations of some subgroup. The "promiscuous" sexual behavior of the young lower-class male in the slums is shown, on analysis, to be regulated by a rigid code that defines appropriate and inappropriate sexual partners and a set of conditions that determine when it is proper to "take advantage" of a female.[4] The discovery that many "deviants" are, in fact, conforming to the norms of some social group leads to the caution that deviance must always be defined by indicating precisely *whose* expectations are disappointed by the deviant behavior.

Overlooking of Deviance

It is not clear whether deviance as it is popularly conceived involves primarily the *act* of deviance or the fact of *being caught in the act* of deviance. A great deal of deviance may be tolerated so long as it is done quietly and without calling the deviance to the attention of those responsible for administering sanctions.[5] Gouldner wrote of the existence in a factory of a "mock bureaucracy" in which a set of rules (for example, the no-smoking rule) are, in a sense, made to be broken and that may be broken with impunity so long as it is done discreetly, that is, in a way that does not put supervisors in the position of openly condoning the violation.[6] In the area of sexual relations, it is commonly understood that unmarried adults are "not children," and that their heterosexual or homosexual relationships are their own affairs so long as they do not openly violate laws or embarrass others by flaunting their behavior. A single girl who becomes pregnant may be condemned not so much because of the sexual relations that led to her condition but because she was so careless as to allow herself to be put in a condition that forces others to deal with her problem.

Reflecting the tendency to overlook deviance as much as possi-

[4] William F. Whyte, "A Slum Sex Code," *American Journal of Sociology*, 49(1943): 24–32.

[5] Bronislaw Malinowski, *Crime and Custom in Savage Society* (Paterson, N.J.: Littlefield, 1959).

[6] Alvin W. Gouldner, *Patterns of Industrial Bureaucracy* (Glencoe, Ill.: Free Press, 1954).

ble, officials charged with policing deviant behavior frequently develop a subtle understanding or kind of bargain with deviants in their jurisdiction. For example, there is a deal that the policeman on the beat will not interfere with the law violators who operate on his beat: the prostitutes, gamblers, narcotics pushers, etc. The popular understanding is that the policeman who turns his head on deviance is "on the take" (paid off by deviants to leave them alone); however, the bargain may be more subtle than a simple payoff. In return for immunity to carry on his deviant activity, the deviant may repay the policeman by "keeping it quiet" and not indulging in major or violent crimes that would bring the policeman's dereliction to the attention of his supervisors.[7]

It appears that, while the popular demand is for the policeman to maintain "law and order," in fact, the policeman is primarily expected to maintain order by preventing noisy or violent deviance in his area of jurisdiction, and that a permissive attitude toward law violation may be a necessary condition for maintaining this kind of order. Viewed in this way, we can understand why much "police brutality" is directed against *disorderly* persons such as street demonstrators and rioters whose actions focus public attention on the inability of the police to maintain public order.[8] These responses suggest rather strongly that there is tolerance for deviance only so long as it occurs surreptitiously and outside the spotlight of wider publicity.[9]

Justifications for Deviance
The sharp edge of moral disapproval of deviance is often blunted by what has been called "neutralizations" of deviance.[10] Although

---

[7] For a description of a covert pattern of acceptance of the deviance of prison inmates by prison guards, see Richard A. Cloward et al., *Theoretical Studies in Social Organization of the Prison* (New York: Social Science Research Council, 1960), pp. 20–48.

[8] On the highly negative attitudes of police toward most street demonstrators, see Jerome K. Skolnick, *The Politics of Protest* (New York: Simon & Schuster, 1969), pp. 258–268.

[9] To many of the respectable citizens of "Yankee City," the antics of a clownish politician, Biggy Muldoon, who was elected mayor of the town, were disapproved not so much for the despicability of his acts as for the unfavorable national publicity that the election campaign focused on Yankee City, "making fools of us all." W. Lloyd Warner, *The Living and the Dead* (New Haven: Yale University Press, 1959).

[10] Gresham M. Sykes and David Matza, "Techniques of Neutralization: a Theory of Delinquency," *American Sociological Review*, 22(1957):664–670.

certain acts are technically violations of norms, the violation may be seen as fully justified by the situation. Sometimes these neutralizations represent generally accepted ideas about the special circumstances that make behaviors acceptable that would otherwise be judged deviant. For example, an unwritten law excuses the killing of a man who is found to be taking sexual liberties with the killer's wife. The principle of self-defense permits aggressive actions that would not be permissible if done offensively.

As Matza points out, however, there is often a difference between a legal justification for deviance and some of the notions about justifiable deviance that prevail, for example, in a delinquent gang.[11] On the matter of self-defense, the law tends to hold that this is a justifiable excuse only if there is no path of retreat open to the physically endangered person. But to the gang member, any path of retreat may be viewed as a coward's way out. From the moral perspective of the gang, a person has a right to defend a piece of "turf" against hostile invasion, and the gang member may define as self-defense what officials will define as delinquent acts of public disorder. This situation illustrates an important point about neutralization: like deviance itself, the justification of deviance is relative to the moral standards of those who are making judgments on behavior. Those people who lack the political power to impose *their* moral standards on the enforcement mechanisms of the state are likely to live with a chronic sense of the injustice of their treatment by "society."

FORMS OF DEVIANT BEHAVIOR

Sociological generalizing about deviant behavior has been characterized by the tendency to distinguish between different forms of deviance, with somewhat different causes and consequences being attributed to each form. The general term *deviance* is likely to be considered too inclusive a category of acts to permit any generalizations about such diverse behaviors as alcoholism, treason, extramarital sex, embezzlement, and vagrancy. The impulse, therefore, is to lower the level of abstraction by one notch and to identify *types* of deviance and to develop different explanations for each type.

An early example of this tendency was Durkheim's study of

---

[11] David Matza, *Delinquency and Drift* (New York: Wiley, 1964), Ch. 3.

suicide,[12] which argued that suicide is not a unitary phenomenon but includes three different forms: (1) *altruistic* suicide, committed under the impulse of conformity to group norms—for example, suttee, the ritual in which a Hindu woman willingly gave herself for cremation with her husband on the occasion of his death, or the more recent example of the Japanese kamikaze pilots who flew their planes to certain death as heroic military acts; (2) *egoistic* suicide, committed as the result of a rational calculation that the pains of living are not compensated by its rewards, a type of suicide most often committed by persons who are not in positions of responsibility for the welfare of others or who follow the ethic of individuality or "looking out for number one"; (3) *anomic* suicide, a behavioral response to a person's frustration with his situation in the social world (see the further discussion of *anomie* below).

Many other theories of deviance begin with the idea that some fundamentally different sociological properties attach to different kinds of deviance. Henry and Short, for example, try to show that homicide and suicide are two forms of "aggressive" deviance that represent alternative responses to similar kinds of frustrating experiences.[13] Following Emile Durkheim's notion of egoistic suicide, they argue that suicide-prone persons are the relatively socially isolated, those who literally have only themselves to blame for their troubles. The homicidally inclined, by contrast, are those persons who are heavily involved with other persons and who more easily find a target for their extreme aggression among these others. Single people have higher suicide rates than the married, the married have higher homicide rates than the single, and the spouse is the victim in a large proportion of the cases of homicide.[14]

Clinard and Quinney have argued that there are different *behavior systems* associated with different kinds of crime, and the generalizations that hold for one kind of crime will not necessarily

---

[12] Emile Durkheim, *Suicide,* trans. by John A. Spaulding and George Simpson (Glencoe, Ill.: Free Press, 1951).

[13] Andrew F. Henry and James F. Short, Jr., *Suicide and Homicide* (Glencoe, Ill.: Free Press, 1954).

[14] On homicide victims, see Marvin Wolfgang, *Patterns in Criminal Homicide* (Philadelphia: University of Pennsylvania Press, 1958). On marital status differences in suicide, see Marshall B. Clinard, *Sociology of Deviant Behavior,* 3rd ed. (New York: Holt, Rinehart & Winston, 1968), p. 511.

hold for another type.[15] An extended illustration of this point was Cressey's study of embezzlement which showed the peculiarity of embezzlement as a form of crime compared with most other types.[16] For one thing, the embezzler typically does not learn his criminal technique from other criminals; he simply applies his expert knowledge of accounting to juggle the books to his own benefit. For another, the embezzler tends not to see himself as a criminal in the way that a professional burglar, for example, might see himself. Embezzlements are rationalized as "borrowings" that will be paid back, and when the embezzler is caught it may be a distinct shock to find himself treated as a criminal.

In contrast with such typologies that are developed for a limited purpose or to analyze the forms of a given kind of deviance (like crime or suicide), there have been a few attempts to develop more general classifications that will embrace all of deviant behavior. Merton's typology is probably the most familiar.[17] In it he specifies four alternative modes of behavior that would constitute deviance: innovation, ritualism, retreatism, and rebellion.

The *innovator* violates social expectations by using illegitimate means to accomplish socially approved goals. A pickpocket or a cheater in a game is oriented toward such approved goals as the acquisition of wealth or the winning of a game; only his *methods* are rejected.

The *ritualist* is the opposite of the innovator in certain respects. He is so overly concerned to act only legitimately in every situation that he willingly permits the failure of socially approved goals rather than stray from the narrow path of proper behavior. The fussy bureaucrat, who insists on operating strictly by the book, encourages the bureaucratic red tape which often makes it impossible for the bureaucracy to accomplish its aims.[18]

The *retreatist* is one who has withdrawn from concern with either

---

[15] Marshall B. Clinard and Richard Quinney, *Criminal Behavior Systems* (New York: Holt, Rinehart & Winston, 1967).

[16] Donald Cressey, *Other People's Money: a Study of the Social Psychology of Embezzlement* (Glencoe, Ill.: Free Press, 1953).

[17] Robert K. Merton, *Social Theory and Social Structure,* rev. ed. (Glencoe, Ill.: Free Press, 1956), pp. 139–157.

[18] Robert K. Merton, "Bureaucratic Structure and Personality," in Merton, *Social Theory and Social Structure,* pp. 195–206. For a discussion of some of the "deviances" by which red tape in bureaucracies is circumvented, see Charles H. Page, "Bureaucracy's Other Face," *Social Forces,* 25(1946):88–94.

socially approved goals or adherence to standards of good behavior. Retreat involves the various ways in which people withdraw from the rat race of everyday life: vagrancy, bohemianism, alcohol, drugs, mental illness, and (the ultimate withdrawal) suicide. Merton suggests that retreatists tend to be a special threat to a society because their withdrawal suggests the unworthiness of the race that others are running.[19] Missionaries of various kinds may attempt to reclaim the retreatist but, failing this, the conventional world tends to reject most vehemently those long-haired hippies and skid row derelicts who seem to be living socially unproductive lives.

The *rebel* also rejects conventional goals and means but attempts to carry through a revolution that will establish new standards of right behavior. Merton thus identifies rebellion with the revolutionary promotion of deviant causes and seems to leave no room in his typology for those rebels *without* a cause who act defiantly and provocatively but without any clear notion of a substitute social order of which they approve.

All the studies reviewed here converge on a single point of view: that deviance is a "many-splendored thing" and that no one general theory of deviance can explain its existence without taking into account some of the variety of its forms. We shall try to keep this kind of caution in mind as we proceed to an analysis of some of the causes and consequences of deviant behavior.

SOURCES OF DEVIANT BEHAVIOR

There is a well-known situation in which a client of a prostitute says to her, "What's a nice girl like you doing in a place like this?" The sociologist, too, is interested in knowing how, given all the constraints on people to behave "nicely" in various ways, some of them get into a place like a brothel, a mental hospital, or the drunk tank in the local jail. The naive wonderment about what causes some people to "go bad" is matched by the sociologist's professional interest in the conditions that encourage high or low rates of deviant behavior.

Sociological explanations of deviance came rather late to an already crowded arena of alternative explanations. Theologians had for centuries attributed errant ways to supernatural forces operating through the bedeviled individual. More recently, biolo-

---

[19] Merton, *Social Theory and Social Structure*, p. 154.

gists came into the arena with explanations attributing deviance to genetic deficiencies in the deviating person. The Italian criminologist Lombroso, for example, believed that the criminal is an unfortunate victim of an *atavistic* heredity, a throwback to the physical and moral constitution of primitive man, who was supposed to be inherently criminalistic.[20] In the twentieth century, psychologists, inspired by the immense popularity of Sigmund Freud's psychoanalytic theory, have advanced explanations which emphasize the psychological abnormality of people who "go bad."[21]

Against such interpretations of the causes of deviance, the sociologist has kept his eye fairly consistently on the major article of faith of those who indulge in sociological explanations: the insistence that deviant behavior is an inherently social act and, following Durkheim, that "social facts" of any kind should be explained by other social facts and not by psychological, biological, or any other nonsocial facts.[22] The sociologist has, in other words, approached the problem of explaining deviance by studying the correlation of rates of deviance of various kinds with variations in conditions of social organization.[23]

Beyond this simple but fundamental agreement to explain deviance in terms of variations in social conditions, we find striking disagreement among sociologists about the best models or general orientations to employ in explaining deviance. We shall consider now three fundamentally different approaches to the explanation of the social factors that encourage or inhibit deviant behavior.[24]

---

[20] Cesare Lombroso, *Crime, Its Causes and Remedies,* trans. by H. P. Horton (Boston: Little, Brown, 1912).

[21] For a review and criticism of such approaches, see Albert K. Cohen, *Deviance and Control* (Englewood Cliffs, N.J.: Prentice-Hall, 1966), pp. 54–62.

[22] Emile Durkheim, *The Rules of Sociological Method,* trans. by Sarah A. Solovay and John H. Mueller (Chicago: University of Chicago Press, 1938), p. 110.

[23] For a formulation of sociological explanations as demonstrating a correlation between a *state* of society and a *rate* of behavior, see Alex Inkeles' statement in Robert K. Merton et al. (eds.), *Sociology Today* (New York: Basic Books, 1959), pp. 249–276.

[24] Matza distinguishes between approaches which emphasize the factors of affinity, affiliation, and signification. David Matza, *Becoming Deviant* (Englewood Cliffs, N.J.: Prentice-Hall, 1969). Since these terms (except possiblly the term *affiliation*) are still rather idiosyncratic to Matza, they have not been employed as headings for the following sections. However, the three terms designate exact equivalents for the three approaches discussed, and the reader is referred to Matza's discussion for a detailed analysis of the history and the logic of each of these approaches.

The Anomie Approach

One major orientation in the explanation of deviance is the notion that social conditions may be so frustrating to some people that they are driven in desperation to deviant ways of behavior. Deviant behavior is seen as a personal adjustment or adaptation to these frustrating conditions.

Much of the inspiration for the anomie approach to deviance goes back to Durkheim's study of suicide, first published in 1895.[25] Among the variations in suicide rates that interested Durkheim was a peculiar kind of correlation between the rates of suicide in a country and the fluctuations in level of economic prosperity of the country.[26] The increase in suicides during periods of economic depression is fully understandable, since frustration or misery is stimulated by the disappointment of hopes that were built up in more prosperous times. Common sense would seem to predict a decline in suicide rates during very prosperous years when people come closer to satisfying their economic wants. In fact, suicide rates also rise in periods of extreme prosperity, and it was largely in the explanation of this fact that Durkheim's conception of *anomie* and anomic suicide was developed.

Anomie is a state of dissatisfaction arising from a sense of discrepancy between the *aspirations* of a person and the *means* that he has available to realize these ambitions. It is not so much the magnitude of a person's means—his wealth and political power, for example—that determines his level of satisfaction; rather, it is his feeling of abundance or deprivation relative to what he desires.[27] In boom periods of economic prosperity, people may generally have more wealth, but the excitement of the boom—a prevailing spirit of "the sky's the limit"—may mean that people are actually less contented at a higher economic level because they have escalated the scale of their personal ambitions.[28]

---

[25] Durkheim, *Suicide.*

[26] For a more recent verification of this relation between suicide rates and business cycles, see Albert Pierce, "The Economic Cycle and the Social Suicide Rate," *American Sociological Review,* 32(1967):457–462.

[27] As James puts it, our self-esteem is determined by a ratio between our pretensions or ambitions and our success in achieving the ambitions. Increased satisfaction or self-esteem may come *either* by greater achievement or by scaling down the pretensions. William James, *The Principles of Psychology,* Vol. 1 (New York: Holt, 1890), p. 310.

[28] For a literary account of the restlessness accompanying a land boom in a town, see Thomas Wolfe, *You Can't Go Home Again* (New York: Harper, 1940), Ch. 7.

The idea of anomie or closely related notions have been used to explain a great many of the varieties of deviant behavior.[29] Merton set the tone for this application in his essay on anomie as related to deviant behavior in the United States.[30] Merton observes a tendency toward anomie in the society as a whole; the American success theme which holds, for example, that every boy can be president leads to a greater emphasis on getting ahead than on the normative regulation of the means to achieve success. In such a society, it's not how you play the game but whether you win or lose that is really important.[31]

Given this emphasis on success, people are frequently tempted to cheat a little if necessary to achieve their ambitions. Children who experience heavy pressure from their parents for academic achievement are especially likely to cheat on school examinations.[32] If a young woman's sex appeal is somewhat limited by less than spectacular natural endowments, she may employ wigs, cosmetics, and padded undergarments to help her "win" the game of physical attractiveness. In another padding operation, a man in need of extra income may claim income tax deductions for charitable contributions that he never actually got around to contributing.

Although all persons in a society feel this pressure to cheat, it seems to fall most heavily on those with the fewest opportunities to achieve success by legitimate means: members of the lower classes, for example, who lack the capital and the social know-how to acquire education and the other symbols or prerequisites of social success. Criminal deviance may be seen as a typical lower-class response to the general societal anomie and to the poor's disadvantaged position in the race to get ahead. Many criminal acts—e.g., robbery, extortion, bootlegging, purse snatching—are aimed at obtaining wealth or power by illegitimate means. Denied

---

[29] For essays which apply this approach to different areas of deviant behavior, see Marshall B. Clinard (ed.), *Anomie and Deviant Behavior* (New York: Free Press of Glencoe, 1964).

[30] Merton, *Social Theory and Social Structure,* pp. 132–139.

[31] Lerner notes the anomic tendency in America in his statement that "the whole impulsion of American culture is to raise hopes and claims in the individual and spur him on to fulfill the hopes and nail down the claims." Max Lerner, *America as a Civilization* (New York: Simon & Schuster, 1957), p. 665.

[32] Leonard I. Pearlin, Marian Radke Yarrow, and Harry A. Scarr, "Unintended Effects of Parental Aspirations: the Case of Children's Cheating," *American Journal of Sociology,* 73(1967):73–83.

legitimate opportunities, the lower-class person is more likely to resort to illegitimate means, according to Merton's reasoning.

Cohen gives a similar account of the anomic pressure on lower-class people but describes a quite different response to the frustration.[33] Like Merton, Cohen finds that lower-class people experience a discrepancy between their ambitions and their perception of their realistic legitimate opportunities, but the response Cohen noted was not a criminalistic response of the kind described by Merton. Rather, he saw anomie as culminating in the peculiar "culture" of the gang, a positive evaluation of acts of defiance of gang members against respectable authorities. The lower-class boy experiences "status frustration" and he is encouraged by his gang to take out his aggression on that world of middle-class respectables—teachers, policemen, etc.—who represent the society that produces these frustrations. The attitude is one of alienation and disenchantment with the "American dream" of unlimited opportunity for all. This kind of alienation was well expressed in a recent cartoon showing a black child trying to sell for a nickel his chance of becoming president of the United States.

The anomie theory of deviance, while useful in explaining some kinds of lower-class delinquency, makes some questionable assumptions about the situation of lower-class people. It assumes, first, that people from the lower social classes develop about the same level of aspiration for themselves as do people from the more favored classes. Numerous studies of lower-class subjects show that this is not the case, that lower-class people tend to develop a fairly realistic assessment of their lowered life chances and accept the situation grimly if not gladly.[34]

Another apparent assumption of the anomie theory is that people who are thwarted in the realization of their ambitions by legitimate means will be *able*, once they are motivated to do so, to use illegitimate means to achieve their aspiration. Actually, as Cloward

---

[33] Cohen, *Delinquent Boys*. There is a similar explanation of lower-class gang delinquency in Martin Gold, *Status Forces in Delinquent Boys* (Ann Arbor: University of Michigan Press, 1963).

[34] Robert A. Gordon, James E. Short, Jr., Desmond S. Cartwright, and Fred L. Strodtbeck, "Values and Gang Delinquency: A Study of Street-Corner Groups," *American Journal of Sociology*, 69(1963):109–128; William H. Sewell and Vimal P. Shah, "Parents' Education and Children's Educational Aspirations," *American Sociological Review*, 33(1968):191–209.

and Ohlin point out, there are also differences in people's command of illegitimate means for achieving success; not everyone who is desperate enough to rob a bank has the organizational facilities to do so.[35] Lower-class people, even though they are the most frustrated segment of the population, may not be well situated in terms of illegitimate opportunity structures. A company accountant, however, while probably in a fairly good economic position legitimately, is also likely to be in a highly tempting illegitimate opportunity situation. It would be relatively easy for the accountant to steal from a company; the blue-collar employee of the same company might run a greater risk of detection since he would have to carry company goods home with him.

Cloward and Ohlin also acknowledge the notion of illegitimate opportunity structures in their observation that not all deviant gangs take the form of the defiant, negativistic, hell-raising, rebel-without-a-cause orientation of the gangs described by Cohen. Some gangs are criminalistic in nature, using their gang activities to enrich themselves by rackets and other illegitimate means. Other gangs are organized around the pursuit of forbidden vices such as drug use and illicit sexual activity. Whether the response to anomie takes one or another of these forms may depend on the chance factor of whether in a given community one or another of these lines of illegitimate activity is relatively open.[36] In wide-open communities in which crime is not vigorously suppressed and in which activities like narcotics pushing, gambling, and prostitution are more or less openly practiced, we might expect that disadvantaged people, frustrated by their failure to attain success legitimately, will resort to the most easily available alternate to legitimate success-striving.

The Subculture Approach

A second approach to the explanation of deviance emphasizes the view that deviant behavior is *normal* behavior both psychologically and sociologically. Supporters of this view (who tend to be critical

---

[35] Richard A. Cloward and Lloyd B. Ohlin, *Delinquency and Opportunity: A Theory of Delinquent Gangs* (New York: Free Press of Glencoe, 1960).

[36] For a study of different types of lower-class gangs as they are influenced by illegitimate opportunity structures, see Irving Spergel, *Racketville, Slumtown, Haulberg* (Chicago: University of Chicago Press, 1964).

of the anomie theory) contend that deviant behavior is normal psychologically because the deviant is no more likely than conforming persons to be psychologically "disturbed." The behavior is normal sociologically because, although deviant from the viewpoint of the wider society, it conforms to the behavior in the more narrow social circle or subculture in which the deviant lives and from which he draws group support for his deviant activity.[37]

Some justification for this view of deviance can be realized by examining the results of some of the modifications of the Asch experiments on group pressure described in the last chapter. Asch and others have found that providing the naive subject with a single "deviant" ally, who is instructed to agree with the subject's "wrong" opinion, has the effect of reducing drastically the extent to which the subject will yield to majority opinion.[38] These experiments seem to suggest that an individual can sustain a general social rejection of himself as "different" provided he can find other persons who are different in the same way and who can supply him with a moral justification for his deviant behavior.

This perspective on deviance obligates the sociologist to consider quite different deviance-generating social conditions than those to which the anomie theorist is sensitive. The key variable in determining who becomes deviant is the differential exposure of people to the influence of deviant subcultures. According to this view, slum dwellers tend to have higher rates of several kinds of deviance, not because of the frustrating conditions of slum life (often decried as "miserable" by outsiders who fail to appreciate some of the gratifications available in this way of life, says Gans),[39] but because of the number of deviant subcultures that tend to flourish as the result of the relative "social disorganization" (e.g., the failure of law enforcement) found in such areas. "Delinquency areas" are parts of a city that offer more frequent exposure to deviant influences.[40] The subculture approach, therefore, empha-

---

[37] Clinard, *Sociology of Deviant Behavior*, pp. 52–55.

[38] For a recent study and a bibliography of earlier experiments, see Vernon L. Allen and John M. Levine, "Social Support, Dissent and Conformity," *Sociometry*, 31(1968):138–149.

[39] Herbert Gans, *The Urban Villagers* (New York: Free Press of Glencoe, 1962), pp. 3–16.

[40] Clifford R. Shaw and Henry D. McKay, *Juvenile Delinquency and Urban Areas* (Chicago: University of Chicago Press, 1942).

sizes the factor of "differential association" of different people with the influence of deviant subcultures.[41]

A number of refinements on the meaning of *association* have been made by way of trying to fit this theory to the reality of differential rates of deviance. The mere fact of residence in a delinquency area is not sufficient to produce deviance, since most people in areas with high crime rates are *not* criminals. Many families in such areas, concerned about their children's exposure to bad companions, make vigorous efforts to keep their children off the streets and in school or church or in other forms of nondelinquent association.[42] Given the fact that people may choose to associate with various groups with varying degrees of delinquency proneness, the important factor in determining deviance may not be differential *association* in any physical sense of closeness, but differential *identification* of people with various of the groups or social influences around them.[43]

Subcultural explanations of deviance have been criticized in several ways; two kinds of criticism will be mentioned. One criticism suggests that the causal relation between deviance and association with other deviants is actually the reverse of the one suggested in the theory. People become deviants, or become socially recognized as such, and thereby are rejected as "outsiders"[44] and forced to seek the company of other outsiders if they are to have any agreeable social relations at all. From this perspective, a delinquency area like a slum is not so much a delinquency-generating area as a collecting point for persons already committed to deviant careers.[45]

This idea is obviously applicable in some situations. "Skid row," as the term implies, is an urban area in which persons who have been unable to make it elsewhere congregate where there are

---

[41] Edwin H. Sutherland and Donald R. Cressey, *Principles of Criminology,* 7th ed. (Philadelphia: Lippincott, 1966), pp. 75–78.

[42] Walter C. Reckless, Simon Dinitz, and Ellen Murray, "The Good Boy in a High Delinquency Area," *Journal of Criminal Law, Criminology and Police Science,* 48(1957):18–25.

[43] Daniel Glaser, "Criminality Theories and Behavioral Images," *American Journal of Sociology,* 61(1956):433–445.

[44] Howard S. Becker, *Outsiders: Studies in the Sociology of Deviance* (New York: Free Press of Glencoe, 1963).

[45] For a discussion of the cause and effect relationship between schizophrenia and slum residence, see H. Warren Dunham, *Community and Schizophrenia: an Epidemiological Analysis* (Detroit: Wayne State University Press, 1965).

physical facilities and some subcultural support to sustain a vagrant way of life.[46] Wherever there is a correlation between deviant acts and association with people in deviant subcultures, it is always highly appropriate to ask which came first, the deviance or the association.[47]

Matza has offered a second criticism of the subculture perspective. Contrary to most of the theorizing from this perspective, he contends that deviants do not give much moral support to one another by approving deviant acts.[48] Most delinquents share with nondelinquents the view that their behavior and that of their peers is wrong; the rapist does not believe in rape, the child molester does not believe in child molesting.[49]

Although the deviant subculture does not generally give moral approval of the deviant behavior, it serves a very important alternative function: it acquaints the deviant with a socially acceptable vocabulary of excuses by which he can neutralize his deviance so that he can act in deviant ways without committing himself to the moral rightness of that behavior. In the case of child molesters, for instance, a subcultural explanation that people may do things when drunk that they would not do when sober enables the molester to "excuse" himself by explaining that he was drunk when he committed that act, thereby preserving a self-presentation of himself as a "good" person, at least when sober.[50]

Societal-Response Approach

A final perspective is that which asserts that the effort of society to avert or control deviance is, rather ironically, a factor in producing deviance.[51] This viewpoint runs somewhat against commonsense understandings of deviance, which tend to see social-control efforts as an effect rather than a cause of deviant behavior. But an increas-

---

[46] Donald J. Bogue, *Skid Row in American Cities* (Chicago: Family Study Center, University of Chicago, 1963).

[47] For a study which suggests that associations with other delinquents is more a consequence than a cause of deviance, see Leroy C. Gould, "Juvenile Entrepreneurs," *American Journal of Sociology*, 74(1969):710–719.

[48] Matza, *Delinquency and Drift*.

[49] Charles H. McCaghy, "Drinking and Deviance Disavowal: the Case of Child Molesters," *Social Problems*, 16(1968):43–49.

[50] Ibid.

[51] On the strong sense of "irony" expressed by proponents of the societal-response approach, see Matza, *Becoming Deviant*, pp. 80–85.

ing number of sociologists have taken what may appear to be a perverse point of view, expressed by Becker in his assertion that:

Deviance is *not* a quality of the act that the person commits, but rather a consequence of the application by others of rules and sanctions to an "offender." The deviant is one to whom that label has successfully been applied: deviant behavior is behavior that people so label.[52]

The inspiration for this viewpoint derives largely from Lemert's analysis of the process by which people become secondary or career deviants, those who practice some line of deviance on a regular and sustained basis.[53] The term "secondary deviance" is used to distinguish the career deviant from the person who practices "primary deviance," i.e., the occasional and isolated deviant act engaged in by almost everyone.[54]

Primary deviance is often never discovered by others. If it is discovered, we may find ways to excuse ourselves from the act. We say that we were not ourselves, that we had a temporary lapse or a bad day. Primary deviance can remain primary so long as it is not observed or so long as the audiences respond favorably to these attempts by the offender to excuse himself. Crucial phases in the making of a deviant career occur when the deviant is caught and publicly recognized, and when others refuse to accept his excuses. At this point the person becomes labelled as deviant, making it difficult for him to excuse himself to others and also making it difficult for him to play any role other than a deviant one.

Goffman illustrates the process of deviant-career development among mental patients.[55] Many come to the hospital convinced that they are not mentally ill; they have many alternative explanations (some of which may be quite true) for their presence in the hospital. The staff of the hospital, as well as many patients, see it as their

---

[52] Becker, *Outsiders*, p. 9.

[53] Edwin Lemert, *Social Pathology* (New York: McGraw-Hill, 1951). For a more recent statement by Lemert on the matter of secondary deviance, see Edwin Lemert, *Human Deviance, Social Problems, and Social Control* (Englewood Cliffs, N.J.: Prentice-Hall, 1967).

[54] The frequency with which the "law-abiding" citizen violates laws is documented in James S. Wallerstein and Clement J. Wylie, "Our Law-Abiding Law-Breakers," *Probation,* 25(1947):107–112.

[55] Erving Goffman, "The Moral Career of the Mental Patient," in *Asylums: Essays on the Social Situation of Mental Patients and Other Inmates* (Garden City, N.Y.: Doubleday Anchor Books, 1961).

duty to disillusion the patient so that he will see himself as, in fact, mentally ill. To this end, the patient's rationalizations, his "sad tales," are systematically derogated and the patient must, at least outwardly, accept the prevailing definition of himself as mentally ill. (A typical derogating statement to a self-excusing patient: "If you're so smart, how come you got your ass in here?")[56] Even the person who is released from the hospital as cured may find that the public knowledge of his prior hospitalization will stigmatize him with the prevailing view of others that he is just a bit suspect in terms of his mental stability. Goffman's view comes very close to the idea that a career of mental illness is, at least partly, the result of mental hospitalization. Critics of penal institutions are likely to argue, similarly, that the experience of imprisonment is a major force in the production of the criminal career.[57]

Goffman and others have emphasized that it is necessary to consider the contingencies that lead some people to exposure to these deviance-defining societal responses. If persons become career deviants largely through their exposure to a kind of social response to primary deviance, it may be important to know whether different categories of persons are differentially susceptible to this exposure. It may be that one of the life chances associated with being a woman or a Caucasian or an upper-class person is the privilege of avoiding exposure to social reactions that tend to label one as a career deviant. We know, for example, that a lower-class person who commits a crime is more likely to be arrested and tried (given publicity) and convicted (have his excuses disbelieved) than is an upper-class person who commits a crime. Other differentials in susceptibility to arrest and conviction favor women at the expense of men, whites at the expense of blacks.[58] We know, also, that persons from the upper classes with mental disturbances are more likely to get treatment from private psychotherapists and

---

[56] Ibid., p. 154.

[57] Donald Clemmer, "Observation on Imprisonment as a Source of Criminality," *Journal of Criminal Law, Criminology and Police Science,* 41(1950):311–319; Paul W. Tappan, *Crime, Justice and Correction* (New York: McGraw-Hill, 1960).

[58] Austin T. Turk, *Criminality and Legal Order* (Chicago: Rand McNally, 1969); William M. Kephart, *Racial Factors and Urban Law Enforcement* (Philadelphia: University of Pennsylvania Press, 1957). For somewhat contradictory evidence on discrimination in police enforcement, see Steven Spitzer, "An Exploratory Study of Police Attitudes as a Factor in Criminalization," *Sociological Focus,* 2(1969):45–60.

less likely to be exposed to the personal humiliation of admission to a public mental hospital.[59]

There may, however, be an upper limit of social positions within which it is possible to hush up or avoid public notice of primary deviance. The goldfish bowl character of the lives of many prominent persons may make it difficult for them to enjoy the privilege of no publicity. At any rate, it is clear that who one is sociologically has a great deal to do with one's chances of being considered as deviant by others and by himself.

The societal-response perspective, like the other viewpoints discussed, is subject to a number of criticisms. One criminologist, Gibbs, suggests that the approach is defective in that, in its radical form, it tends to deny the existence of deviance as any reality apart from the process of social adjudication of deviance.[60] Gibbs believes that this approach is unproductive in that it cannot tell us why one person rather than another commits deviant acts. "The fact that the reaction to armed robbery may involve incarceration hardly explains why some but not all persons commit the act."[61] He feels that the usefulness of the approach is in its understanding of the societal response to deviance, while the deviance itself is left unexplained.

It is also possible to criticize the societal-response perspective for reasons exactly opposite those suggested by Gibbs. Sociological explanations almost never explain why some but not all persons behave in a given way; if the sociologist can understand rates or frequency of behavior he has accomplished something. It seems to be well demonstrated that the social-control efforts of society in dealing with deviance are a factor in producing career deviance, and this approach can certainly say something about the process by which a given person becomes increasingly likely to enter a career of, say, armed robbery.

Where the approach falls short may be, contrary to Gibbs' view, its inability to explain the societal response itself. A sociologist

---

[59] August B. Hollingshead and Frederick C. Redlich, *Social Class and Mental Illness* (New York: Wiley, 1958).

[60] Jack P. Gibbs, "Conceptions of Deviant Behavior: the Old and the New," *Pacific Sociological Review,* 9(1966):9–14. For a statement in defense of this approach against the criticisms of Gibbs and others, see Edwin M. Schur, "Reactions to Deviance: a Critical Assessment," *American Journal of Sociology,* 75(1969):309–322.

[61] Gibbs, "Conceptions of Deviant Behavior," p. 12.

might, for example, raise the question of why prostitution is considered reprehensible by society, given the fact that the prostitute shares with the "respectably" married woman the understanding that her economic security is related to the quality of her sexual relations with men. What "quality" is there in the prostitute's behavior that leads to the institution of social control?[62] The societal-response perspective cannot provide any help on this question. Perhaps it should not be expected to do so, since the approach really aims to explain deviance and not the response to deviance. It is certainly forgivable and probably even necessary for the scientist to put on blinders to focus his attention on the rather narrow path of explanation that he is travelling. He is less than generous, however, if he attempts to argue that his is the only path and the only appropriate set of blinders.

FUNCTIONS AND DYSFUNCTIONS OF DEVIANCE
The popular assumption about deviant behavior is likely to be that it is harmful or dysfunctional in some rather obvious way to some group of which the deviant is a member. Mores, the more seriously held norms, are, as we have seen, "doctrines of welfare," and the violator of the mores is likely to be condemned as an enemy of the common welfare. The sociological study of deviance, on the other hand, tends toward a concern with the *latent* functions and dysfunctions of deviance: those consequences that laymen do not usually recognize as effects of deviant behavior.

Functions
A sociological viewpoint that departs very far from popular notions about deviance is the idea that deviant behavior may, in some respects, be beneficial or contribute to the stability of the social system within which it occurs. Durkheim argued thus in asserting that crime is a "normal" phenomenon, by which he meant that it is found in every society and is a necessary element of a viable society.[63] The most familiar explanation of this normality is that criminal acts reinvigorate the "collective conscience" of a people: the violation of a norm gives people the occasion to reassert the

---

[62] The question of reasons for condemnation of prostitution is raised by Kingsley Davis in "Prostitution," in Robert K. Merton and Robert Nisbet (eds.), *Contemporary Social Problems* (New York: Harcourt, Brace & World, 1961), p. 264.

[63] Durkheim, *Rules of Sociological Method*, p. 65.

importance of the norm.[64] Frequently we do not know how much we care about some value until it is challenged. The value of academic freedom is likely to be reasserted in response to someone's attempt to curtail that freedom. Deviance, from this viewpoint, serves a vital function of reviving group sentiments that would slide into group indifference without these reinforcements.

Durkheim mentions a second function of deviance, namely, the impetus it provides for the social change which social systems must sometimes experience if they are to adapt to changed conditions:

Crime implies not only that the way remains open to necessary changes but that in certain cases it directly prepares these changes. Where crime exists, collective sentiments are sufficiently flexible to take on a new form, and crime sometimes helps to determine the form they will take. How many times, indeed, it is only an anticipation of future morality—a step toward what will be! According to Athenian law, Socrates was a criminal, and his condemnation was no more than just. However, his crime, namely, the independence of his thought, rendered a service not only to humanity but to his country. It served to prepare a new morality and faith which the Athenians needed, since the traditions by which they had lived until then were no longer in harmony with the current conditions of life.[65]

The innovator in all times and places is likely to be treated as a deviant. If innovation is necessary to a social system, it may be necessary that someone suffer the "slings and arrows" reserved for those persons who are born before their time.[66]

A more recent study has approached the functions of deviance from a slightly different angle.[67] Dentler and Erikson found that, in small groups such as Quaker work camps and small Army units, the group is loathe to rid itself of deviant members even though they may dislike them or find them annoying. One explanation of this is that the deviant (e.g., a shirker in a work camp) becomes the focus of a problem for the group and puts some life and sense of urgency into what might otherwise be a rather dull group. Almost as if they

---

[64] Emile Durkheim, *On the Division of Labor in Society,* trans. by George Simpson (New York: Macmillan, 1933), Bk. 1, Ch. 2.

[65] Durkheim, *Rules of Sociological Method,* p. 71.

[66] Lewis A. Coser, "Some Functions of Deviant Behavior and Normative Flexibility," *American Journal of Sociology,* 68(1962):171–181.

[67] Robert A. Dentler and Kai T. Erikson, "The Functions of Deviance in Groups," *Social Problems,* 7(1957):98–107.

recognized the morale-building functions of their deviants, groups shield their "rotten eggs" from outsiders such as Army psychiatrists, who might remove a schizophrenic member and recommend a medical discharge or commitment to a hospital.

A deviant member of a group may also serve a useful function as a scapegoat for group members. A study of family interaction patterns has suggested that there is a kind of family with chronic interpersonal tensions which maintains its stability through the ability of all family members to vent their hostilities on one child.[68] A person whose behavior is chronically deviant is a fairly obvious target for the displacement of intragroup hostilities upon himself.

Dysfunctions

Although the sociologist may agree with the view that deviant behavior threatens the existence of some social systems, he will still attempt to articulate more systematically than does the layman some of the ways in which deviance can be dysfunctional. One effort of this type is an application of Parsons' four "functional imperatives" of social systems—adaptation, goal attainment, integration, and pattern maintenance—to the study of deviant behavior.[69] If these imperatives define "necessary conditions" for the existence of a social system, an act of deviance may be seen as the failure of persons to make appropriate functional "contributions" in one of these functional areas.

Consider a social system such as a family. A family requires *adaptive* contributions by some or all of its members; someone has to be the breadwinner and provide the income necessary for the family's survival. Deviations like alcoholism, mental illness, and suicide have at least this functional consequence: they let down family members who had depended on the deviant for adaptive support.[70] Any kind of *incapacitation* of family members for productive roles—even the inability of a small child to perform his

[68] Ezra F. Vogel and Norman W. Bell, "The Emotionally Disturbed Child as the Family Scapegoat," in Norman W. Bell and Ezra F. Vogel (eds.), *Modern Introduction to the Family*, rev. ed. (New York: Free Press, 1968), pp. 412–427.

[69] The following discussion is based on the typology of deviance discussed by Jesse R. Pitts in Talcott Parsons et al. (eds.), *Theories of Society*, Vol. 2 (New York: Free Press of Glencoe, 1961), pp. 701–706.

[70] For the problems of adjustment of a family to an occupationally "handicapped" member, see Howard E. Freeman and Ozzie G. Simmons, *The Mental Patient Comes Home* (New York: Wiley, 1963).

accustomed chores—may have serious effects on the ability of the family to operate as a unit. One shirker in a large family, as in a work camp, may stimulate family solidarity by giving it a focus of concern; an epidemic of shirking would be a threat to the family's survival.

With reference to the *goal-attainment* requirement of a social system, a family requires that there be a dependable mechanism for making decisions about how family resources will be deployed. Serious disagreements between persons making these decisions represent system problems. One kind of deviant, for example, is the wishy-washy authority who cannot make up his mind. Even assuming harmony and decisive action, the decision-maker or decision-makers may commit serious *errors* of judgment in deciding how to expend resource. The recently purchased car turns out to be a lemon or an unnecessary luxury; the family discovers that it erred when it decided to send one of its sons to college. Although error may be forgiven as "only human," errors must be lived with by the people in the social system whose members commit them.

The failure of people to *integrate* their behaviors with the interests of other members of their social system is a form of *crime:* a taking advantage by one member at the expense of another. The child who hoards the family's candy supply by hiding it away for his own use is guilty of such a "crime." The important consequence to the system of such an act is likely to be the interpersonal alienation that results from such deviant acts. Any social system is based on at least a modicum of harmony, and the attitude of every man for himself is likely to generate severe conflict between members of the system.

Finally, deviant behavior may be a violation of the *pattern-maintenance* imperative of a social system, an act that challenges the moral consensus on which a social system is based. This kind of deviance can be called *sin*: the failure of a person to develop a properly socialized character or a set of behavioral motives that are consistent with fundamental group values. A child who shows disrespect for the family rituals (e.g., the family's gathering for Thanksgiving) on which many families depend[71] is treated as threatening the basic values that are incorporated into the family's life.

---

[71] James H. S. Bossard, *Ritual in Family Living* (Philadelphia: University of Pennsylvania Press, 1957).

Although it is possible to categorize types of deviance in terms of their dysfunctional consequences to the system, we should note that the question of the harm done by a deviant act is often a matter of social controversy. Each of these functional types of deviance carries with it a theory about the causes of deviance of that type. Consider the behavior called alcoholism. Is Mr. X an alcoholic primarily because he is an incapacitated or weak person ("alcoholism is a disease") or primarily because he is a kind of sinner who "just doesn't give a damn" about his family obligations?

The outcome of such controversies often determines the kind of social control of deviance that is instituted. If illness is the problem, some kind of therapy or rehabilitation is called for (if child molesters are really only sick people, they should be treated, not locked up). If error is the problem, some kind of education or on-the-spot supervision or correction may suffice to control the deviance (if young people only realized the effects of alcohol on their bodies, they would not drink it). If a crime is involved, punishment is often suggested to make it disadvantageous to take advantage of others (if more teeth were put in narcotics laws, there would be fewer pushers of drugs). If sin is the cause, moral education or reeducation or perhaps even brainwashing may be attempted to convert the deviant to the true way of life (if young people truly "knew Jesus," they would not be delinquents).

In a society in which many people are engaged professionally or avocationally in "helping people" or in "improving society," we can well understand why there are frequent clashes between those interested in treating deviants in different ways. The educator, the psychotherapist, the judge, and the priest may be competitors for the right to exercise social control, each trying to treat the deviant as a student, a patient, a legal case, or a soul.[72]

SUMMARY

The analysis in this chapter should serve as something of a counterbalance to the "oversocialized conception of man"[73] that an exclu-

---

[72] Even among professionals of a given type, there are frequently controversies about appropriate ways of treating deviants: custodial versus therapeutic approaches to prison administration, for example. For a dissent by one psychotherapist from the tendency of his colleagues to treat mental illness as a disease, see Thomas S. Szasz, *The Myth of Mental Illness* (New York: Dell, 1967).

[73] Dennis H. Wrong, "The Oversocialized Conception of Man in Modern Sociology," *American Sociological Review*, 26(1961):183–193.

sive concentration on conformity and the mechanisms of social control would suggest. Earlier we alluded to the prisonlike constraints of society on its members. But the analogy between the member of society and the prisoner turns out to be incomplete. Perhaps a greater understanding of the covert and tolerated deviances of prison inmates should also be made a part of the sociologist's model of the behavior of men in society. We have suggested, at least, that there are numerous societal recognitions of the "all too human" behavior of humans and many occasions when deviance is overlooked or the deviant is allowed to excuse himself for his behavior.

Sociological analysis of deviance sometimes begins with the view that deviant behavior is too broad a concept to permit unitary generalizations; there have, accordingly, been a number of attempts to define types of deviance. We have examined a few of these typologies.

Because of these ambiguities in social definition of deviance and because of the diversity of characteristics of different types of deviance, the sociologist finds himself dealing with a rather shifty subject matter when he comes to explain the causes and consequences of deviant behavior. With reference to causation, the sociology of deviant behavior is in a state of controversy. Three theoretical perspectives for the explanation of deviance have been presented: (1) an *anomie* approach, which suggests that deviance is a response to the frustrating discrepancy between socially induced ambitions and socially instituted restrictions on the means of achieving these ambitions; (2) a *subculture* approach, which argues that deviance is the result of association with persons whose values differ from the approved values of the wider society; and (3) a *societal-response* approach, which contends that deviance is the end result of publicly defining or labeling persons as deviant, thereby establishing them in stable deviant careers. Each of these approaches has been severely criticized, often from one of the alternative theoretical perspectives.

Sociological study of the consequences of deviance has tended to emphasize the latent functions and dysfunctions of deviant behavior. A moderate amount of deviance may be "normal" or functional for a social system in a number of ways. The dysfunctional quality of given kinds of deviance may be examined by starting with some set of systemic requirements like the Parsonian "functional imperatives" and attempting to define the various ways in which individual behavior can fail to fit the needs of a social system. However, there is much controversy about the nature of the harm done by a given deviant act and, accordingly, much disagreement about the appropriate mechanisms for control of that deviance.

Self Presentation

NATURE OF HUMAN MOTIVES

Most of traditional social psychology has dealt in one way or another with the *motives* of human behavior, attempting to understand behavior in terms of the desires of individuals and introducing the *social* element only as an explanation of the origins of motivated conformity or motivated deviance. This view, implicit in both the previous chapters, leads to the search for those social factors which tend to frustrate individuals or which make it possible for them gladly to accept their social condition.

One sociologist, C. Wright Mills, criticizes the view of human motives as the "springs of action" and suggests a radically different and perhaps, at first glance, a rather strange conception of motives.[1] Mills asks us to think of motives as the linguistic devices that persons use to explain their actions to other persons who observe that behavior. A motive is, in this view, not so much an instigator of behavior as an explanation of it (although Mills suggests that a behavior for which one cannot anticipate an explanation when needed tends not to be instigated).

A perfect motive is an "ultimate in justificatory conversation," an answer to a question like, Why the hell are you doing that? that satisfies all possible questioners about the reasonableness of the behavior being questioned. Mills takes an essentially *pragmatic* view of human motives. We tend to act unthinkingly until a problem arises in pursuing a line of behavior; at that point we begin to

---

[1] C. Wright Mills, "Situated Actions and Vocabularies of Motive," *American Sociological Review*, 5(1940):904–913.

think about the reasons for our actions and to articulate them to others. Fortunately for people in such troubled situations, their culture tends to provide them a ready-made "vocabulary" of motives that will be understandable and palatable to their questioners. In some cultures, a failure to perform some duty is most easily excused by explaining that the delinquent person is "sick," and some action, such as an unscheduled vacation, is justified for its therapeutic value. In another culture, delinquency may be ascribed to human "sin," and a person can square his failure most directly by using the vocabularies of confession and the plea for forgiveness.[2]

These ideas contain most of the elements of a model of human behavior as involving a "presentation of self." In this model, people are seen as *actors* performing their acts before *audiences* which may approve or disapprove those acts. The concern of human beings as actors with the "appearances" they make to audiences will be the focus of analysis in this chapter.[3]

SOME CLASSIC ORIGINS OF THE MODEL

Contemporary views on self presentation follow rather directly from the work of William James and Charles H. Cooley, two American social psychologists writing at the turn of the twentieth century.

The chapter on self-consciousness in James's psychology textbook, published in 1890, is one of the first treatments of the self from a sociological perspective. James, whose psychological system emphasizes the role of *attention* and selective perception in human thought, notes that everyone tends to give special interest and attention to his own affairs. The words "his own" are used advisedly, since James emphasizes the sense of appropriation involved in the self:

In its widest possible sense, however, a man's Self is the sum total of all that he can call his, not only his body and his psychic powers, but his clothes and his house, his wife and children, his ancestors and friends, his reputation and works, his lands and horses, and yacht and bank-account.

---

[2] Vilhelm Aubert and Sheldon Messinger, "The Criminal and the Sick," *Inquiry*, 1(1958):137–159.

[3] The major impetus to this kind of analysis came with the publication of Erving Goffman, *The Presentation of Self in Everyday Life* (Garden City, N.Y.: Doubleday, 1959).

All these things give him the same emotions. If they wax and prosper, he feels triumphant; if they dwindle and die away, he feels cast down—not necessarily in the same degree for each thing, but in much the same way for all.[4]

Like James, Cooley identifies the self with the feeling of possession of objects. To evoke this feeling in himself, the reader is enjoined to think of himself reflecting on some object and gloating "mine, mine, mine with a pleasant warmth of feeling."[5] Cooley also recognized that not all self-consciousness involves gloating, though it always does involve "warmth of feeling." In some ways a shy person himself, Cooley was quite aware of the possibility of "mortification" in the contemplation of "mine, mine, mine." I may, for example, think with an uncomfortable warmth about my foolish behavior at a party or my publication of a book not professionally up to snuff.

Among the more prominent of the objects of appropriation by the self, according to James, is a man's *social self* or the "recognition which he gets from his mates."[6] Depending on whether this recognition is favorable or unfavorable, the person experiences pride or humiliation. James seems to argue that people are universally sensitive to their appearance in the eyes of others, although he offers two important qualifications.

First, according to James, the person is not sensitive to different audiences in the same way for his self presentations:

Properly speaking, a man has as many social selves as there are individuals who recognize him and carry an image of him in their mind. To wound any one of these his images is to wound him. But as the individuals who carry the images fall naturally into classes, we may practically say that he has as many different social selves as there are distinct *groups* of people about whose opinion he cares. He generally shows a different side of himself to each of these different groups. Many a youth who is demure enough before his parents and teachers, swears and swaggers like a pirate among his "tough" young friends. We do not show ourselves to our children as to our club-companions, to our customers as to the laborers we employ, to

---

[4] William James, *The Principles of Psychology*, Vol. 1 (New York: Holt, 1890), pp. 291, 292.

[5] Charles H. Cooley, *Human Nature and the Social Order* (New York: Scribner's, 1902), pp. 174–175.

[6] James, *Principles of Psychology*, p. 293.

our own masters and employers as to our intimate friends. From this there results what practically is a division of the man into several selves.[7]

In this statement we have a forerunner of contemporary interest in variations in self presentation with different *reference groups.*

Second, says James, the person tends to select only certain of all possible areas on which to base his reputation, and to confine his feelings of pride or mortification to that area. James uses this example:

I, who for the time have staked my all on being a psychologist, am mortified if others know much more psychology than I. But I am contented to wallow in the grossest ignorance of Greek. My deficiencies there give me no sense of personal humiliation at all. Had I "pretensions" to be a linguist, it would have been just the reverse. So we have the paradox of a man shamed to death because he is only the second pugilist or the second oarsman in the world. That he is able to beat the whole population of the globe minus one is nothing; he has "pitted" himself to beat that one, and as long as he doesn't do that nothing else counts.[8]

Cooley similarly emphasized the sensitivity of people to the "imaginations" of themselves in the minds of others, but he believes that there is a great deal of temperamental variation in this tendency. The personal traits of *vanity* and *pride,* sometimes treated as synonyms, are considered by Cooley to be opposites in this respect.[9] The vain person is overly sensitive to the opinions of others about him, and he may develop a flighty disposition which allows him to be influenced by the opinions of those who happen to be around him at the moment. The proud person, by contrast, is relatively insensitive to others' views of him; his motto is frequently "the public be damned." Cooley sees both pride and vanity as "unhealthy" tendencies of the human self: pride because it closes the person to social influence, vanity because it leads to a kind of "self-dreading cowardice."[10]

Although James and Cooley document well the human tendency to be sensitive to the impressions that their behavior generates in the minds of others, they give little attention to the question of *how*

---

7 Ibid., p. 294.

8 Ibid., p. 310.

9 Cooley, *Human Nature and the Social Order,* Ch. 6.

10 Ibid., p. 226.

people present themselves in order to appear well to others. Contemporary work has focused more closely on this problem, as the next section will indicate.

PRESENTATION OF SELF IN EVERYDAY LIFE

A more recent study has attempted to show how even some of the most mundane interactions of people are influenced by their sensitivity to the impressions that their actions make in the minds of others, and how these impressions are manipulated in a process of "impression management."[11] Contrary—or complementary—to the Mead thesis that "the self arises in a social process," this kind of analysis *begins* with selves that have already "arisen," and looks at the social process in terms of the vicissitudes it presents for people attempting to *maintain* the respectability of that self.

To borrow the language of James, I have, let us say, pretensions to being a professor of sociology and am mortified if I learn that someone else (or that a great many others) know more sociology and can teach it and write about it better than I can. But I do not simply wait for my reputation as a sociologist to "wax and prosper" or to be "cast down." I prepare lectures and textbooks that I hope will impress students with my wisdom; I write scholarly papers to try to impress my colleagues with my professional caliber. Although I may show somewhat different sides of myself to these two audiences, in either case I am constrained to keep my best foot forward, avoiding courses and research topics in which I am the least competent to give impressive performances and concentrating on those few areas in which a "brilliant" performance is within my capacity.

Goffman's book is a description of some of the *techniques* that people employ to enhance their social selves and some of the *contingencies* that may arise in the course of social interaction which may threaten the integrity of these self presentations. Several features of his discussion of these techniques and contingencies will now be reviewed.

Idealization

The basic technique of impression management is the selective presentation to audiences of only the more creditable aspects of oneself and the concealment of more discreditable aspects. This

---

[11] Goffman, *Presentation of Self.*

process Goffman calls *idealization,* the fostering of the impression that one's performance completely conforms to normative standards. If there is "dirty work" associated with a performance, idealization will tend to conceal it. The polished lecture of the professor or the exquisitely tailored clothing of the playboy should give no hint of the professor's minor plagiarism of ideas or the playboy's frantic clothes-shopping. The saying that a man is not a hero to his valet (perhaps it could be also added, to his wife) expresses the view that it is difficult to be impressive to those people who "see him in his underwear."

There is an interesting reverse side of the idealization process, what Goffman calls the process of *dramatic realization.* For many people, the problem is one of bringing out favorable information about themselves rather than of concealing unfavorable information. The world is full of unsung heroes whose exploits are accomplished behind the scenes and who must use subtle ways of dramatizing their accomplishments. A housewife may, for example, suffer from the chronic sense that nobody appreciates the drudgery and complexity of the housework she does. Dramatic realization may occasionally be achieved by the housewife whenever her husband, for whatever reason, must take over the wife's chores for the day and, overwhelmed by crying babies and burned food, he comes to appreciate the value of his wife's performance which he previously had taken for granted.

Teamwork

Many kinds of self presentation involve impression management, not by individuals but by *teams* of individuals. A family may be concerned about its collective image or social self, and each family member is expected to support a consistent "line" of self presentation to outsiders. Frequently the expectation is that the family will give a show of solidarity to persons outside the family. It is only when the family members refuse to admit to themselves serious conflicts within the family that the pathological sort of *pseudomutuality* that we discussed in chapter 7 tends to emerge.

Teamwork in self presentation presents some special organizational problems. If impression management involves idealization or concealment, each team member is a potential danger to the team's presentation in that he might give away the team's secrets. A member of a president's cabinet may disrupt the show of solidarity of the administration by "leaking" to the public an account of a serious conflict of views within the cabinet. A young child may naively give away the polite line of a family by, for example, repeating to "Mrs. Jones," who is visiting, something disparaging about her that he has heard from his parents. Team members may have to be indoctrinated in the necessity of loyalty to the "party line"; otherwise, unreliable persons may be kept off the team or, if they are retained, given a minimum of information that they might betray to outsiders. Parents may watch what they say in the presence of children, and some bands of conspirators have a structure in which no one is given complete information about the organization or its membership lest some apprehended member betray the others to the police.

In addition to these loyalty problems, a team has the problem of finding ways to fill in each member of the team on the self presentational line currently being maintained. A husband and wife may be embarrassed to learn that they have told the same person somewhat different stories about some family affair. At work, a man is sometimes bawled out by his superior for the delinquent actions of one of his own subordinates. Not having been filled in by the subordinate, he suffers the flustering experience of having to admit to his superior that he does not know what's going on in his own shop.

A smooth and unified team performance requires that all members be kept currently informed of the team line. In democratically organized teams, this is accomplished by strategy sessions in which the members get together and decide on a unified position. In oligarchic teams, the line is determined by an elite and transmitted to the membership, often through the medium of a house organ, such as a union or political party newspaper.

Regions
Some of the impression-management problems of individuals or teams are alleviated by the *spatial* organization of self presentations. Goffman distinguishes three "regions" with reference to self presentation: back regions, front regions, and outside regions, with "barriers to perception" typically maintained between front and back regions and between front and outside regions.

Front and back. A front region is an area where actors and audiences come together for audiences to observe the performances of actors: a classroom with professors and students, a sports arena with players and spectators, the parlor or front room in which guests are entertained. Actors are on their best behavior in front regions, presenting themselves respectably and depending on their teamwork to help them sustain impressions to audiences. A back region is an area behind the scenes to which only actors are admitted (Authorized Personnel Only): the locker room in a sports arena, the cluttered and disorderly back room in a house that is off limits to guests.

In back regions two kinds of discreditable events are likely to occur. First, it is here that people do any dirty work that is required to present a clean performance in the front region. The restaurant kitchen is where the gristle and fat are removed before the meat is served to the customers up front. The back sides of stage props are nakedly utilitarian in appearance, often showing the frantic patchwork that has gone into putting together the set that the audience sees only in its finished or idealized form. Goffman points out that any area can be a back region if the audience is excluded from it. A theatrical company does its dirty work of rehearsing on stage without an audience. During rehearsals cast members can concentrate on the technical part of their work, wearing casual street clothing rather than costumes and not worrying for the moment about appearances. Their director may lose his temper and read out the cast for its poor performance, the kind of thing that only an excessively temperamental performer will do in the presence of an audience.

The other unseemly event that typically occurs in back regions is the relaxation of discipline that the actors are required to maintain in order to sustain the team line before an audience. A waitress can go into the kitchen, snarl at the cook, or otherwise drop the pose of geniality that she is required to maintain in the presence of her customers. Frequently this back region relaxation involves a team of actors poking fun at audiences who must be treated respectfully in their presence. Prostitutes refer to their clients as "Johns" or "creeps," teachers laugh at the naiveté of their students, students use derogatory nicknames in referring to their teachers, etc. One can easily give a functional interpretation to these behaviors. The maintaining of a consistent line creates tension that must be dealt with, and back regions are typically places where performers can let off steam out of the sight of their audiences and be able to go back to the front region with enough psychological stability to carry on the performance.

Outside and front. Just as audiences are excluded from back regions, "outsiders" are excluded from entering front regions where actors are performing for their audiences. The uninvited guest and the eavesdropper are examples of outsiders who intrude into front regions in which there are performances not intended for them. Such intrusions involve problems in self presentation if an individual or team is presenting different sides of himself to different audiences. A husband who presents himself to his wife as "perfectly loyal" would have one of his social selves threatened should his wife intrude upon a scene in which he is having a flirtation with another woman. Audience segregation is a persistent need of many actors: a school child cannot so easily act tough and rowdy with his peers and respectful with his elders if.members from each of these audiences observe him presenting himself to the other.

The problem of *how* to maintain audience segregation is an important issue in social life. Sometimes people protect their privacy by confining their acts to areas that are protected from unwanted intrusion: repairing to a secluded hideaway or locking oneself and his audience into a room with opaque and soundproof walls (with precautions, in some cases, that these walls are not electronically "bugged"). The usual rule is that one knocks at a closed door, breaks gently into an on-going conversation, or otherwise asks permission to join the party.[12]

Although some protection from the intrusion of outsiders is achieved by the use of such "barriers to perception," frequently the protection is based simply on the *tact* of outsiders in refusing to pay attention to performances that are "none of their business." One can observe much of this "civil inattention" in public places in which people carry on private conversations that can easily be overheard by bystanders.[13] If these bystanders pay any attention to such conversations, the rules of polite public behavior forbid their giving any indication of this attention. Some strain on this understanding may occur if the conversationalists say highly pro-

---

[12] In the typical bedroom farce, the knock at the door provides the cue to push the lover in the closet in anticipation of an intruder. The practice in some apartment buildings of requiring visitors to ring an apartment from the downstairs foyer provides additional resources for apartment dwellers to insure themselves that the "scene" is properly set for the arrival of a visitor in one's front region.

[13] Erving Goffman, *Behavior in Public Places* (New York: Free Press of Glencoe, 1963).

vocative things in a closely confined space, an elevator for example. A very funny story may be laughed at by all the occupants of an elevator but this is "in spite of themselves" since they literally "couldn't help overhearing."

Another rule, then, is one which forbids overly provocative actor-audience scenes in public places. People typically mute their discussion of politics or religion or their telling of risqué stories when they enter an elevator and, should they try to make love at noon on a park bench, they would probably overtax the "civil inattention" of police officials and perhaps lead others to observe that they should get a motel room for such performances.

SELF PRESENTATION IN UNUSUAL SITUATIONS

One frequent justification for "clinical" studies in social science is that an understanding of unusual or abnormal forms of behavior can provide a key to the understanding of more typical behavior. The sociology of self presentation may be advanced by an examination of the social interaction problems of those who are severely "questionable." The ex-convict, the physically handicapped, and the divorcee are a few examples of persons susceptible of being considered as having less than fully respectable selves. What is the nature of the "stigma" experienced by these persons and how do they attempt to cope with the self presentational problems arising from their stigmatizing condition?

Self Concealments

With some stigmas, there is the possibility of concealing from audiences that the actor is a member of a stigmatized category. Families, one of whose members suffers some affliction such as mental illness or pregnancy outside marriage, are likely to protect the family reputation by hushing up the matter, maintaining secrecy with the neighbors and discretion in discussing the affair before small children who might leak the family secrets.[14]

The basic problem of such "discreditable" persons is "information control,"[15] the necessity of trying to insure that audiences

---

[14] Marian R. Yarrow, John A. Clausen, and P. R. Robbins, "The Social Meaning of Mental Illness," *Journal of Social Issues,* 11(1955):32–48.

[15] Erving Goffman, *Stigma: Notes on the Management of Spoiled Identity* (Englewood Cliffs, N.J.: Prentice-Hall, 1963).

cannot get discrediting information about one's current involvements or historical background. Information control is likely to be very weak in small, traditional communities where "everybody knows everybody" and where any delinquencies or misfortunes are likely to be the topics of local gossip. Some other more artificial communities are designed to duplicate this interpersonal atmosphere of the small town. Goffman writes of "total institutions" such as prisons, mental hospitals, and training camps that are total, in one sense, because the institution aims at total information about the person's background and present activities.[16]

When a person enters such an institution as an inmate, the institution typically begins to generate a *dossier* on him, and this "service record" tends to follow him throughout his stay in the institution and may even go out with him. The small town and the total institution are the kinds of places in which the concealment of a stigmatizing condition tends to be very difficult. We can perhaps understand, then, the motivation of some people to remove themselves from these tight situations and to merge themselves into the masses of people in "civilian life" or in the big city.

Visible Handicaps
With some other kinds of stigma, concealment or information control is virtually out of the question. A person with a highly visible handicap, such as a paraplegic or a member of a stigmatized race,[17] informs people by his very physical appearance that he has the stigmatized condition. Although he may salvage some of his respectable self presentation by organizing interactions that do not involve physical appearances—if a black salesman, he might try to conduct as much of his business as possible over the telephone, or if a legless professor, he might specialize in writing rather than lecturing—most people have to meet the public on occasion, and these meetings are fraught with many dangers to a visibly handicapped person. A study by Fred Davis, which we shall now review, deals with some of the problems faced by the visibly handicapped

---

[16] Erving Goffman, *Asylums: Essays on the Social Situation of Patients and Other Inmates* (Garden City, N.Y.: Doubleday, 1961).

[17] The treatment of black racial features as "visible handicaps" in the following discussion does not, of course, imply any judgment of black inferiority. It is simply a fact that, in a country which has been characterized as a "white racist society," a black person *does* experience many deprivations, however exhilarating it may be in some respects to be "young, gifted and black."

and some of the devices they use to maintain respectable self presentations.[18]

One of the key consequences of a visible handicap for the social relationships of the victim is the "inundating potential" of his handicap. A person with a missing ear or of a distinctly alien nationality is likely to find that the people with whom he converses focus their attention—often in spite of themselves—on his external appearance rather than on the content of his verbal communication. This may lead to the kind of flustering that Goffman calls "alienation from interaction,"[19] the common experience of being too self-conscious about the sound of one's voice or about one's physical appearance to be able to concentrate on what one is trying to say.

A related difficulty is the character of visible handicaps as "ambiguous predicators" of social interaction. A person who must interact with a handicapped person is never *sure* exactly what he can reasonably expect of the handicapped. Should or should not a blind person be invited to a theatre party? Should or should not a one-legged person be invited to join a local bowling league? Would the black professor be flattered to join an otherwise all-white college faculty, or would he suspect that the offer was a token effort by the college to secure a "house nigger" as window dressing? Should an acquaintance offer condolences to a recently widowed woman or should he discuss "something light" with her? Although books of etiquette will provide many rules for dealing with persons in such situations, it seems that, on the whole, popular etiquette is inadequate to allow people to take behavioral stances toward the handicapped that will guarantee that the handicapped will not feel misused by others.

Given these and similar kinds of interaction problems of the handicapped, we can well understand why victims develop devices to manage the strained interaction to which they are subject. Davis discusses several such devices.

An early stage in this management process is called "fictional acceptance." Normals come to treat the handicapped as if he were "no different from anybody else." This level of acceptance can be achieved if the handicapped can show his audiences that, in every other respect, he *is* about like everyone else. A blind man

---

[18] Fred Davis, "Deviance Disavowal: the Management of Strained Interaction by the Visibly Handicapped," *Social Problems,* 9(1961):120–132.

[19] Erving Goffman, "Alienation from Interaction," *Human Relations,* 10(1957):47–60.

who succeeds in playing a game of golf may excite the wonder (sometimes a patronizing one that is hard to take) of normals, the performance showing them that any assumption of his *general* incapacity is mistaken. Most polite people can be counted on to grant this fictional acceptance to the handicapped, since one of the first rules of polite treatment of others is the requirement that one not embarrass the "face" of the other by bringing up discreditable matters.[20]

Some people, of course, are not polite in this sense. One of the basic techniques of the handicapped is to avoid interaction with such notorious "communication deviants"[21] as the mentally disturbed and small children (it was a child, recall, who was tactless enough to say, "But the Emperor isn't wearing any clothes," and perhaps it takes a child or a childlike person to ask pointedly, "How did you get that awful burn on your face?"). If avoidance is impossible, there still may be devices for dealing with the tactless: a staring person may be stared at in return, a tactlessly patronizing person may be abruptly put down (a normal to a cripple: "My poor girl, I see you've lost your leg." Cripple: "How careless of me!").[22]

Fictional acceptance is not a fully satisfactory adjustment between normals and the handicapped because there is a tinge of self-consciousness about the whole affair. The interacting parties have agreed to ignore handicaps of which the parties are perfectly aware, and the effort to be tactful may, on occasion, only accentuate the handicap, as when a person corrects himself in making such "innocent" blunders as saying, "Don't you see my point?" to a blind person or, "Would you like to take a walk down the hall with me?" to a person in a wheelchair. The quick corrections sometimes only make matters worse, revealing the tenuousness of the agreement to ignore the handicap.

Handicapped people, therefore, talk about a stage of "breaking through" in their relationships with normals. At this stage, normals forget the handicap or put it in a more normalized perspective. Whites and blacks become sincerely color-blind in their dealings

---

[20] Erving Goffman, "On Face-Work: An Analysis of Ritual Elements in Social Interaction," *Psychiatry,* 18(1955):213–231.

[21] Erving Goffman, "The Nature of Deference and Demeanor," *American Anthropologist,* 58(1956):473–502.

[22] Goffman, *Stigma,* p. 136.

with one another; a person literally never thinks about the facial blemishes of his friend. When normals and the handicapped *are* aware of the handicap, they talk about it without any evasion or sugarcoating of the topic: whites and blacks talk easily of racial matters, the sighted and the blind of the experience of blindness. The handicap becomes emotionally a matter of fact with little of the "inundating potential" of handicaps before the breakthrough.

Although a real advance toward satisfactory adjustment, the breakthrough stage has its own limitations. A handicapped person *is* handicapped, after all, and he must frequently remind his normal friend of this fact. A crippled person *cannot* go along as a full-fledged member of a skating party and, in some places, a black *cannot* accompany his white friend to certain places. The handicapped may need to carefully coach his normal companion in all the small "amendments and qualifications"[23] to the fact of the handicap that are necessary if the relationship is to survive.

SUMMARY

"The imaginations that people have of one another are the solid facts of society."[24] In this chapter we have examined the "solid facts" of society from a certain perspective: the view that people tend to experience pride or mortification, depending on how they imagine themselves to appear to others, and that they actively seek to foster favorable impressions of themselves. The adoption of such a perspective commits the social psychologist to a concern with those variables associated with variations in the ways in which people present themselves to others. The work of Erving Goffman suggests a number of these variables relative to such matters as teamwork, the availability of "back regions" to prepare impressive performances and to relax from the strain of presenting them, and the possibility of segregating audiences to insure that the right impressions are given to the right audiences. Investigation into the self presentation of people in discreditable or potentially stigmatizing situations can bring home more forcefully the nature of the taken-for-granted self presentational conditions of everyday life.

The idea of "impression management" strikes some critics as a too cynical view of human interaction, suggesting that people are always "putting on the style," that they never simply relax and "be

---

[23] Davis, "Deviance Disavowal," p. 130.
[24] Cooley, *Human Nature and the Social Order*, p. 121.

themselves."[25] But it may be that much of our easy self-confidence in performing to audiences is based on a set of social arrangements that make this kind of relaxation possible. When these arrangements break down, as when the rules of polite interaction are not quite adequate to cover the interaction of normals with the handicapped, we can see clearly enough the "management" devices used by people in such situations. Cooley suggests that, while we "normals" might not understand the painful self-consciousness of the "unfortunate," any of "us" would similarly experience a breakdown in the arrangements that guarantee our self-respect and our respectability in the eyes of others:

Many people of balanced mind and congenial activity scarcely know that they care what others think of them, and will deny, perhaps with indignation, that such care is an important factor in what they are and do. But this is illusion. If failure or disgrace arrives, if one suddenly finds that the faces of men show coldness or contempt instead of the kindliness and deference that he is used to, he will perceive from the shock, the fear, the sense of being outcast and helpless, that he was living in the minds of others without knowing it, just as we daily walk the solid ground without thinking how it bears us up.[26]

---

[25] Sheldon Messinger, Harold Sampson, and Robert D. Towne, "Life as Theatre: Some Notes on the Dramaturgic Approach to Social Reality," *Sociometry*, 25(1962): 98–110.

[26] Cooley, *Human Nature and the Social Order*, p. 208.

COLLECTIVE BEHAVIOR

PART SEVEN

Most of conventional sociology makes assumptions about the tendency of human beings, living together, to evolve certain social organizational arrangements that will make possible an orderly and predictable pattern for living together. The terms *society* and *culture*, two basic concepts for sociological analysis, suggest in different ways this tendency toward an established social order.

The field of collective behavior, by contrast, concerns itself with those relatively unorganized or unstructured forms of human social behavior. The term *relatively* should be emphasized since, as we shall see, any form of collective behavior that we discuss will have important elements of organization or structure about it. For example, leadership and rank-and-file roles may exist in a lynching mob as well as in a family or a bureaucratic organization, but this leadership tends to be less established or legitimated as authority; the mood of the mob perhaps determines the character of its leadership more than do any established rights of individuals to provide this leadership.

In studying collective behavior we are, then, concerned with human behavior at an underorganized level. The comments at the beginning of chapter 14 on the attitude of the sociologist toward deviant behavior should perhaps be repeated for collective behavior. Just as the sociologist does not *condemn* deviant behavior because it violates social expectations, he does not condemn collective behavior for its lack of organization. Only the most crusty conservative, perhaps, could wish for a society with complete orderliness and predictability. Not everyone would agree with Thomas Jefferson's view that there should be a political revolution every twenty years. But most people today perceive the various civil disorders and protests that prevail in contemporary life as containing within them at least the germ of "something better" than the presently established order.

Crowds and Publics

CROWDS

Modern social scientific study of crowds begins with LeBon's early treatise on *The Crowd*.[1] LeBon notes the popular conception of a crowd as any "gathering of individuals" but asserts that a psychological crowd is determined by a peculiar sort of "collective mind" and not by the mere fact of physical aggregation of people. The understanding of this collective mind was a major concern of early students of crowd behavior.

Nature of Crowd Behavior

LeBon observed that men, acting in crowds, differ from the way they would act as individuals. One of these behavioral features is the collective irresponsibility of crowd behavior:

The individual forming part of a crowd acquires, solely from numerical considerations, a sentiment of invincible power which allows him to yield to instincts which, had he been alone, he would perforce have kept under restraint.[2]

LeBon also emphasized the emotional contagion of crowd behavior, the tendency for the behavior of one person in a crowd to stimulate similar behavior in others; people become carried away or swept up in the spirit of the occasion.

A number of writers, including LeBon, emphasize the notion of the intellectual inferiority of crowd behavior; the collective mind

---

[1] Gustave LeBon, *The Crowd* (New York: Viking, 1960). First published in 1895.
[2] Ibid., p. 30.

"feels" but it does not "think" very effectively. Simmel, who wrote of the intellectual inferiority of the mass to the individual, asserts that:

Whoever wants to affect the masses always succeeds by an appeal to their feelings, very rarely by theoretical discussion, however concise it may be. This is particularly true of masses that are together in physical proximity. They exhibit something one might call collective nervousness—a sensitivity, a passion, an eccentricity that will hardly ever be found in anyone of their members in isolation.[3]

Simmel was interested in the effects of the numbers of members on group interaction, and the intellectual impoverishment of crowds is one aspect of the necessity for reducing interaction in large groups to the lowest common denominator intellectually. At the extreme, a mass of people may find that they can share only the experience of eating together: the tribal feast or the political banquet. An early American sociologist, E. A. Ross, argues that the crowd is inferior to its individual members not only intellectually but also morally:

The crowd may generate moral fervor, but it never sheds light. If at times it has furthered progress, it is because the mob serves as a battering-ram to raze some mouldering, bat-infested institution and clear the ground for something better. The better will be the creation of gifted individuals or of deliberative bodies, never of anonymous crowds. It is easier for masses to agree on a Nay than a Yea. Hence crowds destroy despotisms, but never build free states; abolish evils, but never found works of beneficence. Essentially atavistic and sterile, the crowd ranks as the lowest of the forms of human association.[4]

A more recent discussion of crowds which embodies many of these notions about crowd behavior is a major essay by Blumer on collective behavior.[5] Blumer identifies social unrest as the basic cause of collective behavior. "When people have impulses, desires or dispositions which cannot be satisfied by the existing forms of living they are in a state of unrest."[6] This unrest becomes social, however, only if people are subjected to the contagious influence of

---

[3] Kurt Wolff (ed.), *The Sociology of Georg Simmel* (Glencoe, Ill.: Free Press, 1950), p. 35.

[4] Edward A. Ross, *Social Psychology* (New York: Macmillan, 1908), pp. 56–57.

[5] Herbert Blumer, "Collective Behavior," in Alfred McClung Lee (ed.), *Principles of Sociology*, 3rd ed. (New York: Barnes & Noble, 1955).

[6] Ibid., p. 172.

other people in similar states of individual unrest. "It is only when restlessness is involved in circular reaction, or becomes contagious, that social unrest exists. One may view social unrest as the socialization of restlessness."[7] Blumer saw as a key mechanism in the development of crowd action the process of "milling" or the aimless wandering of restless people among themselves.

The approach to crowd behavior embodied in these notions has been challenged frequently by contemporary students of collective behavior who are less disposed to see irrationality and emotionality in the behavior of people in crowds.[8] A typical critical reaction is Skolnick's view that violent crowd behaviors such as race riots may be rational instruments of political action by minority groups rather than, as they are typically viewed, outbursts or explosions of pent-up emotions.[9] In the following pages we shall examine several varieties of crowd behavior and see that, in each case, there is controversy centered around the question of the rationality or irrationality of crowd behavior.

Rumor

The starting point for most social scientific discussions of rumor is the series of psychological experiments of Allport and Postman.[10] These authors emphasize the emotional context of the situation in which people inform and misinform one another about the events in their world. Rumors tend to form around topics in which people are emotionally involved; they are attempts to explain what happened or what is happening or will happen in areas that concern people. Persons involved in a war or a riot or who have heard of a political assassination are highly motivated to try to understand or predict events.

A second feature of rumor-generating situations is the *ambiguity* of more formal and established means of communication (newspapers and "official statements," for example). This ambiguity may arise from the weaknesses inherent in these formal channels (e.g., TV and newspaper spot-news coverage of inflammatory situations

[7] Ibid., p. 173.

[8] Carl J. Couch, "Collective Behavior: an Examination of Some Stereotypes," *Social Problems,* 15(1968):310–322.

[9] Jerome K. Skolnick, *The Politics of Protest* (New York: Simon & Schuster, 1969).

[10] Gordon W. Allport and Leo Postman, *The Psychology of Rumor* (New York: Holt, 1947).

such as riots or shootings tend, at least initially, to be contradictory or incomplete because of the time pressures of deadlines). However, it may also be that people distrust the objectivity of these "authoritative" sources.

A combination of emotional involvement and ambiguity can be seen in many rumor-generating situations. A war's end is usually rumored many times before it actually occurs; the wish for its end and the diplomatic secrecy typically surrounding the truce negotiations probably account for this. The assassination of President Kennedy was the occasion for many rumored versions of the assassination. Americans were highly involved emotionally in this event,[11] and a majority of them have come to doubt the authenticity of the official version of what happened as embodied in the report of the Warren Commission.[12]

The experimental studies in rumor reported by Allport and Postman are concerned with the distortion of information as it passes from one individual to another. Subjects who participate in a "rumor clinic" are asked to repeat, as accurately as possible, the details of a picture which is originally shown only to the first subject in the series of rumor transmissions. As many readers will know who have played similar kinds of party games, some severe distortions of information can occur by the time a story has gone through a number of retellings. Allport and Postman describe three kinds of distortion: (1) *leveling,* the elimination of details as the story is shortened: many rumors are reduced to a vague, "I heard something happened somewhere around here sometime recently"; (2) *sharpening,* the tendency of certain details to be retained and elaborated upon: a minor detail may become a center of focus; (3) *assimilation,* the tendency of people to reinterpret the story in terms of their own interests and stereotypes; we typically hear selectively in terms of what we expect or hope to hear.

Such studies have been criticized as being inadequate simulations of real-life rumor situations. For one thing, distortion may be reduced in these experimental situations by the lack of emotional involvement of the subjects. They are asked to repeat the story as accurately as possible and they know that observers will immedi-

---

[11] Paul B. Sheatsley and Jacob J. Feldman, "The Assassination of President Kennedy: a Preliminary Report on Public Reactions and Behavior," *Public Opinion Quarterly,* 28(1964):189–215.

[12] *New York Times,* January 12, 1967, p. 23.

ately detect any distortions or falsifications. In everyday life, a person may tell a fantastic tale at a social gathering and be "halfway to Phoenix" before his listeners realize that the story is a put-on.

Shibutani's study of rumor as "improvised news" takes to task the "serial-transmission" view of rumor on more fundamental theoretical grounds.[13] In everyday life, rumor formation is not typically a process of a single story about a topic's being passed along serially. Rather, ambiguous situations (those in which established news sources are inadequate) are likely to stimulate a variety of alternative and competing versions of the facts in the situation. Soldiers awaiting combat orders will usually hear a number of rumors about what their orders will be.

Following a Meadian view that social life involves a group definition of the situation, Shibutani argues that the rumor process or grapevine tends to evolve cooperatively developed definitions that frequently are surprisingly accurate versions of the real facts. Shibutani emphasizes the *deliberative* process found in many rumor situations. A storyteller tends to be subjected to cross-examination in the same way that a witness is interrogated in a court case and, just as witnesses may be disbelieved if shown to be unreliable, a notoriously inaccurate rumormonger tends to have his rumors rejected. By critical examination of the quality of evidence for one rumor or another,[14] people may arrive at definitions that are at least as accurate as the embellishments on the truth that are frequently made by officials, whose statements must take into account such factors as national security, or by the news media, whose circulation may depend on overemphasizing the sensational side of events.

Shibutani admits that sometimes this critical tendency is suspended under conditions of high "collective excitement." In such situations, the most dramatic rather than the most plausible rumors tend to be accepted. In any case, rumor formation is seen as a process of *interaction* among people who simultaneously face an ambiguous situation, and not as a matter of "serial transmission" from one person to the next.

---

[13] Tamotsu Shibutani, *Improvised News* (Indianapolis: Bobbs-Merrill, 1966).

[14] On the effect of a "critical set" in increasing the accuracy of a rumor as it is transmitted, see H. Taylor Buckner, "A Theory of Rumor Transmission," *Public Opinion Quarterly*, 29(1965):54–70.

Riots and Mob Actions

The terms *riot* and *mob* are frequently used to designate some of the more violent forms of crowd behavior, those involving destruction or the threat of destruction of lives or property. Mobs are violent crowd actions with a specific purpose: to lynch a murderer, to break up an ROTC dress parade, to heckle a speaker. Riots involve a more diffuse or less focused kind of crowd violence, with a rash of similar kinds of violent acts occurring in one time and place.

Perspectives on crowd violence. One viewpoint about riots and mob behaviors is that they represent *hostile outbursts* or "mobilization for action under hostile impulse."[15] A riot or a mob action is seen as a collective expression of anger by some group of people. Riots and mob actions are motivated by an angry sense that "something is wrong" and a righteous indignation that leads people to "do something about it." Since different people have different conceptions of what is wrong and what should be done about it, many riots become, in effect, clashes between crowds of righteously indignant persons.

In support of this view, consider the recurrent riots of college students and other young people in resort areas or at pop music festivals (Ft. Lauderdale, Newport, Woodstock). These events typically involve an "invasion" of a local community by outsiders. The indignation of the natives is likely to be reflected in an expressed desire that those "punks" should "get the hell out of town" while, from their side, the outsiders resent the inability or failure of the natives to provide services for them and may forcibly open bars or squat on private property.[16] Clashes also may occur when counterdemonstrators take it upon themselves to try to suppress the activity of a people engaged in nonriotous demonstrations or protests, as when veterans organizations attempt to break up Communist meetings[17] or when patriotic groups, indignant at the "trea-

---

[15] Neil J. Smelser, *Theory of Collective Behavior* (New York: Free Press of Glencoe, 1963), p. 226.

[16] The terrorizing of a town by an itinerant motorcyclists' gang was described in the motion picture, *The Wild Ones*. For a sociological account of a similar occurrence that "almost happened," see Robert Shellow and Derek V. Roemer, "The Riot that Didn't Happen," *Social Problems,* 14(1966):221–223.

[17] Robert C. Myers, "Anti-Communist Mob Action," *Public Opinion Quarterly,* 12 (1948):57–67.

sonous" behavior of peace demonstrators, attempt to disrupt such demonstrations.

A second perspective on riots is to see them as demonstrations or appeals to some audience with whom the rioters want to communicate. A prison riot, for example, may be a desperate attempt to call the attention of the outside world to the plight of the inmates.[18] A riot by members of a minority group may be an attempt to impress upon dominant groups the desperation of the rioters and the necessity of yielding to their demands if violence is to be avoided. From this viewpoint, a riot or a mob action is a weapon employed in a struggle to attain some political end: a threat of violence used to stimulate, for example, civil rights legislation, action to end the war in Vietnam, or acceptance of student-power demands by school administrators.[19] We shall discuss further the political uses of violence in the following chapter under the heading of "social movements."

A third perspective would emphasize that riot or mob participants may be motivated by the search for fun or excitement, rioting "for the hell of it." The college panty raids of the 1950s had much of this spirit. Often a "grievance" serves as a pretext to initiate a riot or mob action, but the ranks are swollen by participants who find it amusing to involve themselves. A student's arrest for jaywalking becomes the basis for a mass jaywalking demonstration by students which stops town traffic for several hours; the participants seem not to be especially hostile or angry but more motivated by the spirit of fun.[20] Even when there is a very serious protest involved in a riot or mob action—an antiwar student strike on a university campus, for example—there may be attracted many followers who see the crowd action as being, if not exactly fun, at least as providing the benefit of closing schools or getting a "moratorium" on class attendance.

Whichever kind of motivation for violent action is emphasized, it need not be assumed that people assemble with the preconceived notion of using their assembly for one of these purposes. Often enough, a riot begins with a relatively amiable crowd of people

---

[18] Don C. Gibbons, *Society, Crime and Criminal Careers* (Englewood Cliffs, N.J.: Prentice-Hall, 1968), p. 475.

[19] Skolnick, *Politics of Protest.*

[20] E. L. Quarantelli and James R. Hundley, Jr., "A Test of Some Propositions About Crowd Formation and Behavior," in Robert R. Evans (ed.), *Readings in Collective Behavior* (Chicago: Rand McNally, 1969), pp. 538–554.

assembled for some peaceable purpose, or loitering with no collective purpose at all. An especially provocative or amusing act may stimulate the "emotional contagion" that leads to an explosive crowd action.

Causes of riots and mob actions. In asking *why* these violent crowd actions occur, we shall follow the suggestion of Lieberson and Silverman and distinguish between the "precipitants" and the "underlying conditions" of riots.[21] The precipitating events are relatively easy to determine although, as these authors note, it is sometimes difficult to know which of several events is *the* precipitant. Lieberson and Silverman show that, in the United States between 1913 and 1963, race riots were most commonly sparked by some public and provocative act of physical aggression by members of one race against members of another: an interracial fight, the killing of blacks by white policemen, assaults by black men on white women. The National Advisory Commission on Civil Disorders (in its "Kerner Report") noted the tendency for most urban riots in the summer of 1967 to be touched off by confrontations between white policemen and black civilians.[22] In other cultures, riots may be more likely to be precipitated by some act of defamation of a sacred symbol: the burning of a flag or the theft of a religious relic.[23]

The underlying conditions of riots in American cities have been the subject of study by numerous government commissions, including the Kerner Report on the urban riots of 1967. These studies have emphasized such factors as the effects of urban migration in bringing together people from diverse social backgrounds (various ethnic groups, for example) and throwing them into contact in situations in which some of the traditional controls of the cohesive community or neighborhood are absent.[24] In the competition to get

---

[21] Stanley Lieberson and Arnold R. Silverman, "The Precipitants and Underlying Conditions of Race Riots," *American Sociological Review,* 30(1965):887–898.

[22] National Advisory Commission on Civil Disorders, *Report* (New York: Bantam, 1968).

[23] Lieberson and Silverman, "Precipitants and Underlying Conditions of Race Riots."

[24] Those areas of Detroit with the most cohesive neighborhood organizations were least likely to have many participants in the riot of 1967. Donald I. Warren, "Neighborhood Structure and Riot Behavior in Detroit: Some Exploratory Findings," *Social Problems,* 16(1969):464–484.

ahead in a competitive society, those who feel left behind may protest violently against their condition, while those who have a slight competitive advantage may employ violence to keep the subordinate groups "in their place." The interracial clashes in American cities that followed World War I, and also those during and after World War II, have been explained as results of this situation of chronic hostility between whites and blacks in economic competition with one another.[25]

A problem with many analyses of this kind is that most of them are post-factum explanations; moreover, they frequently ignore the fact that similar conditions have prevailed in other communities in which riots have *not* occurred. Lieberson and Silverman try to overcome this problem by comparing social conditions in pairs of American cities that are similar in most respects except that one had a race riot and the other did not. Their findings, although not definitive because of the low number of comparisons that could be made, suggest the following: Riots occur in those cities in which there is an accumulation of grievances by one or both races (a white grievance may be that blacks have advanced too rapidly compared with whites) and in which there is not a regularized machinery for the legitimate expression of these grievances (e.g., a political structure that elects all councilmen at large, thus denying council representation to minority groups). Similar conditions of chronic alienation of students from "establishment" institutions and lack of institutionalized mechanisms for dealing with their grievances may describe some of the underlying conditions of recent violent manifestations of student unrest.[26]

An additional factor of a *cultural* nature might be mentioned. Many mob actions, especially, involve outraged citizens taking the law into their own hands to enforce moral conceptions that law enforcement officials are not trusted to enforce. This kind of action may be more easily instigated in a culture in which there is a vigilante tradition of private justice. The recent mob violence in the United States—for example, the mobilization of "white militants" like the Ku Klux Klan—has been described as consistent with a frontier tradition of swift and informal justice to the cattle thief and

---

[25] For a description of commission findings on race riots, especially that following the Chicago riot of 1919, see Arthur I. Waskow, *From Race Riot to Sit-In: 1919 and the 1960's* (Garden City, N.Y.: Doubleday, 1966).

[26] Seymour M. Lipset and Sheldon S. Wolin (eds.), *The Berkeley Student Revolt* (Garden City, N.Y.: Doubleday, 1965).

other violators of community mores.[27] Although this vigilante orientation was a cultural adaptation to anomic frontier conditions, the tradition may persist as a "cultural lag" in a period in which the technological capacity of officials to enforce the law is greatly improved.

Mobilization of crowd action. Like other emotions, hostility is only intermittently expressed in overt action. Angry individuals or groups of them may repress their hostility, and they also may select carefully the targets of their aggression, directing it from frustrating agents to some safe target. Major sociological questions deal with why hostility bursts out at one particular time and place and why it is directed against specific targets. Two approaches to dealing with these problems will illustrate sociological viewpoints.

Role of publicity. A common notion is that the anticipation of publicity attending some violent crowd demonstration is a factor in promoting that violence. Demonstrations are aimed at impressing some audience, and demonstrators may select as occasions for violent action those situations in which widespread publicity can be expected. The visit of a sovereign or other head of state to a community is likely to stimulate crowd actions, since it is well known, for example, that the press follows VIPs closely and gives publicity to the events that occur around them.

Although news media are frequently accused of slanting the news to suggest more violence than actually occurs, it may also be suspected that violence *does* occur with disproportionate frequency in places in which crowds know that a television camera or a newspaper reporter is on the scene. The anticipation of wide publicity may, on the other hand, inhibit violent action if the crowd fears adverse publicity. Organizers of the various peace demonstrations and civil rights marches on Washington, D.C., have insisted on nonviolence by their participants under the stimulus of a perception that "the world is watching."

The effect of publicity seems to depend, then, on *what* a crowd is trying to demonstrate. If they want to show how much they care about some issue or how desperate they are, publicity will encourage violence by providing a wider public audience for the demonstrators' "heroic" acts. Publicity may well have encouraged the

---

[27] Skolnick, *Politics of Protest*, pp. 210–218.

heroics of Czech youth fighting Russian tanks in Prague with rocks and bare hands and of the idealistic young Americans in Chicago in the summer of 1968 or at Kent State in 1970, standing their ground against the police and the military. If, on the other hand, a crowd wants to demonstrate its respectability as a way of widening its appeal to the "respectable" world, publicity will encourage, for example, Eugene McCarthy's presidential campaign supporters to be orderly and "clean for Gene."

Publicity has another discernible effect on the timing of riots and mob actions in that publicity about one episode of crowd behavior tends to stimulate other episodes of the same kind shortly thereafter. The example of a riot in one urban slum may "suggest" the likelihood of a similar riot in other slums.[28] Publicity for one kind of riot may produce an atmosphere during an era or decade in which it is almost fashionable to participate in the given kind of riot: in the United States, the prison riots of the 1950s, the urban slum riots of the 1960s, and (perhaps) student riots in the 1970s.[29]

In such situations, publicity tends to replace the *milling* process described by Blumer as a means of interstimulation of persons similarly disposed toward some line of action. When sociologist (turned presidential assistant) Daniel P. Moynihan advises "benign neglect" of racial relations in the United States, he seems to have partly in mind the self-fulfilling effects that predictions of a "long hot summer" have on interracial conflict. A remedy sometimes proposed is for the news media to report more of the "good news" to keep the "bad news" in the proper perspective. In this way, proponents believe, a hostile outburst is not publicized as something that is happening everywhere, thereby giving it the prestige of apparent popularity.

These remedies overlook the nature of public expectation of what is newsworthy, however. Professional newsmen realize that

---

[28] These "suggestions" may travel across national boundaries, as in the speculation that violent race relations in the United States might set off similar events in Britain, a country in which interracial violence has so far been relatively rare. Daniel C. Kramer, "White Versus Colored in Britain: An Explosive Confrontation?" *Social Research*, 36(1969):585–604. In this context it is interesting to note that when Bernadette Devlin, leader of the Catholic civil rights movement in Northern Ireland, came to the United States in 1969 to raise funds for her cause, she made a point of visiting U.S. civil rights leaders to exchange views and observe tactics.

[29] The tendency of race riots to "bunch" into certain years in the United States between 1913 and 1963 was shown in Lieberson and Silverman, "Precipitants and Underlying Conditions of Race Riots."

the public expects to hear about the unusual; in many respects, "good news is no news." A story may not be "fit to print" in the *New York Times*, but it will be given space in the more popular press if the "news" is sufficiently interesting. Another problem of "benign neglect" is that it may deny protesting minorities an avenue of expression of their legitimate grievances. Certain newspapers, fearful of fomenting further violence if they "play up" grievances during a community crisis, may refuse to give any coverage to the demands of protesting groups.[30]

Selection of targets. The activation of a mob or of a riot typically requires that the crowd focus on a target for their hostility so that the action can be centered on a single event: the storming of a bastille, the overturning of food trays in a prison dining room, an attack on a Negro home in a "white" neighborhood. A specific target of hostile crowd action tends to be symbolic of a whole class of such potential targets. This is sometimes made quite explicit by members of a mob, who choose one victim to make an example of in order to intimidate potential victims.

One problem, then, is determining how a *category* of persons becomes defined as an appropriate target of crowd violence. In a society which emphasizes values of nonviolence and the due process of law in the punishment of offenders, it may require considerable rationalization or "neutralization" of any deviant use of violence against a group of people.[31] Just as individual deviance may be neutralized by the view that the victim of the crime "deserves it," so collective violence may be legitimated by a view of victims as subnormal or less than human and therefore not entitled to humane treatment.

Much of the process by which a target for crowd action is selected is thus a process of redefinition of victims as members of a highly undesirable category of persons. Negroes come to be perceived as "animals," student protesters as "hippies," peace demonstrators as "traitors," and the association of such people with derogated categories legitimates the violent mob actions against them. Turner and Surace have described a process by which

---

[30] David L. Paletz and Robert Dunn, "Press Coverage of Civil Disorders: A Case Study of Winston-Salem 1967," *Public Opinion Quarterly*, 33(1969):328–345.

[31] See the discussion of neutralization of deviance in chapter 14, esp. pp. 301–302.

Mexican-Americans in a California city became a target for mob action through their redefinition as "zoot-suiters," a category of people considered so despicable that any kind of violent action was justifiable.[32] With such rationalizations, crowd violence can occur without destroying the sense of crowd members that they are essentially law-abiding citizens of their community.

Another problem involves the selectivity of violent crowds in terms of the specific individuals singled out as victims: Why does the lynching mob kill one accused murderer and allow others to go free? Why is "burn, baby, burn" applied selectively in an urban conflagration? Contrary to the notions of LeBon and Ross about the amorality and the collective irresponsibility of crowds, mobs and rioters do seem to apply some moral principles in the selection of specific victims for their violence. Persons known to be friendly with members of a minority group may be spared damage during a riot. On the other hand, those individuals who develop a reputation for hostility to the demands of a group may be the first and principal victims of a violent episode. Beyond such "moral" considerations, violent crowds may select victims partly for the dramatic impact of their victimization. During a typical campus disorder in the spring of 1970 (that is known about by the author), the president of a college was "routed out of bed," according to the local press, and forced to participate in a demonstration march. A mob would undoubtedly not have concerned itself so deeply in victimizing another individual with less symbolic value attached to his person.

Behavior in Emergencies

Another variety of crowd behavior is displayed by people in emergency or stress situations. Some of these situations are in the nature of disasters: frightening "acts of God" like earthquakes, floods, and tornadoes. Others represent extreme situations created by man himself: concentration camps, where prisoners are kept under conditions of physical and psychological privation, or bombing attacks that destroy civilian lives and property. Still other emergencies may arise from misapprehension about some traumatic event that is believed to have occurred or to be about to occur: a bomb scare,

---

[32] Ralph H. Turner and Samuel J. Surace, "Zoot-Suiters and Mexicans: Symbols in Crowd Behavior," *American Journal of Sociology*, 62(1956):14–20.

for example, or the mistaken belief that there is an epidemic of debilitating insect bites,[33] or that a "mad anesthetist" is on the loose,[34] or that a mysterious substance is causing car windshields to pit.[35]

In all these real or fancied emergencies, the tendency is to suspect that people will react with *panic,* especially if they are influenced by the "emotional contagion" of observing other people in a state of fright. Panic may take either of two extreme forms: agitated and exaggerated movement—the rush to a doorway during a fire in a building—or passive resignation—e.g., the refusal of people to protect themselves when air raid sirens sound.[36] In either case, panic produces behavior that is dysfunctional in terms of coping with the crisis situation.

Panic does not always occur, however, and the conditions of its occurrence are a major concern for sociological study. We shall use one famous case study of panic, Cantril's *Invasion From Mars,*[37] as a point of departure for discussing several kinds of sociological variables associated with variations in degree of panic under conditions of threat or stress. Although the event itself was a relatively minor incident of mass panic, the problems in its study are identical to those involved in a great diversity of emergency social situations.

The Cantril study was based on public reactions to a radio broadcast on October 30, 1938 of a dramatization of H. G. Wells's *War of the Worlds,* a fictional account of a Martian invasion of earth. The Martians were depicted as landing their space vehicle in a field in New Jersey and, in spite of all control efforts by the local militia, moving relentlessly with their deadly poisonous gasses right into Times Square in New York. The narrator and principal character in the drama was Orson Welles, who assured listeners that the broadcast was a description of a fictitious event. Surveys indicated that

[33] Alan C. Kerckhoff, Kurt W. Back, and Norman Miller, "Sociometric Patterns in Hysterical Contagion," *Sociometry,* 28(1965):2–15.

[34] Donald M. Johnson, "The 'Phantom Anesthetist' of Mattoon: a Field Study of Mass Hysteria," *Journal of Abnormal and Social Psychology,* 40(1945):175–186.

[35] Nahum Z. Medalia and Otto N. Larsen, "Diffusion and Belief in a Collective Delusion: the Seattle Windshield Pitting Epidemic," *American Sociological Review,* 23(1958):180–186.

[36] Robert E. Forman, "Resignation as a Collective Behavior Protest," *American Journal of Sociology,* 69(1963):285–290.

[37] Hadley Cantril, *The Invasion from Mars* (Princeton: Princeton University Press, 1940).

some 12 million Americans listened to the broadcast; of these, some 30 percent believed that they were actually hearing a news broadcast and most of these were more or less frightened by the event. Cantril's analysis raised a number of research problems that are typical of sociological interests in panic reactions.

Context of general social conditions. Although some commentators remarked on the incredible gullibility of people who were frightened by the broadcast, Cantril suggests that the fright was understandable, given the situation in which people were exposed to the frightening stimulus. People were ready to believe that "anything can happen" in view of the incredible events—the beginning of World War II in Europe, for example—that were becoming the realities of the day. In troubled times, people are prepared to expect the unexpected. A television viewer who heard John Kennedy in 1962 announce a blockade of Cuba or who heard Walter Cronkite in 1963 say, "It is now official—the President is dead," is perhaps well prepared to accept as possible anything that he hears in an authoritative format.

The misinterpretation of the "War of the Worlds" broadcast as authoritative news was related to the realism of the broadcast, its high dramatic quality, and the peculiar radio listening habits of Americans. Many listeners tuned in late, missing the announcement at the beginning that a play was to be presented.[38] Other listeners, who followed the practice of having the radio on only for background noise or for company, were listening with one ear or not at all until their attention was caught by the increased tempo of the noise.

These points about listening habits could probably be generalized to other situations. Under restless social conditions in which people talk a great deal but often do not concentrate on what they are hearing, a person may catch an exciting or startling piece of news but miss the background information that puts a frightening situation in a more tolerable context. When this happens, individuals become susceptible to the "collective nervousness" of which Simmel has written.

---

[38] Much of this late tuning was related to the fact that the show competed with the Charlie McCarthy show, which was broadcast at the same time on another network. Listeners to this, the most popular radio broadcast of that day, sometimes listened until the end of Charlie's first act and then tuned at the commercial to another station, coming in late on the "news" broadcast of the invasion.

Personal and social devices for coping with panic. Very frequently people are momentarily startled by some unexpected event but quickly recover their composure when they realize that it is not a burglar downstairs but only the family cat in pursuit of a mouse. Prolonged panic—either of the flight or the passive resignation variety—will occur only if attempts to normalize the situation fail. Cantril describes some of the varieties of individual response to fright as people attempted to verify the existence of the feared emergency. These responses will emphasize certain features of the general problem of coping with stress.

Internal checks. Many of the "War of the Worlds" listeners thought about the plausibility of the events being reported and decided they logically could not be true. It would be impossible, for example, for news reporters to be on the scene reporting mass "gassing" without being gassed themselves; it would be impossible for military units to be dispatched to the scene as rapidly as they were reported being dispatched. One key to controlling panic is to find some device for getting people to "think about it for a minute" rather than "going off half-cocked." We might in this way understand the latent functions of a political practice such as requiring extended debate and successive readings of a bill when new legislation is being considered. These time-consuming practices give legislators time to think about the legislation and provide time for the contradictions in a proposed piece of legislation to be brought out. Constitutional checks on enactment of current popular will into law are devices to avert the half (or less) thought-out actions taken under the impulse, say, of a current war hysteria or witch-hunting mood in public opinion.

External checks. People subjected to false alarms frequently seek and receive disconfirming information from authoritative sources. Many people frightened by the "War of the Worlds" broadcast called newspapers or radio stations to ask, "Is it real?" Some consulted the radio log in the newspapers and discovered that "War of the Worlds" was scheduled for this hour. Others turned the dial to other stations on the theory that, if the report were authentic, other stations would be carrying it.

Again, we find that most societies institutionalize such sources of control of panic. During a crisis situation such as a campus riot or a disastrous flood, public officials are likely to remain on duty day and night to reassure people who hear frightening rumors about what is happening. As the earlier discussion of rumor will indicate, the degree of control of "improvised news" that can be achieved in this manner depends on the degree to which people trust officials and professional newsmen to give them the truth about disturbing situations.

Ineffective checks. One "War of the Worlds" listener looked out the window, saw the street "black with traffic" and interpreted this as independent substantiation of the report, since everyone was apparently "escaping." Another looked out the window, saw no cars, and concluded that all the people outside had been gassed. These examples illustrate a major limitation of the use of evidence to control panic reactions. Under stress conditions, people may selectively perceive those aspects of reality that tend to confirm their fears. A person who fears that he has heart disease will pay new attention to fleeting pains that he may once have dismissed as indigestion. Similarly, if the idea gets abroad that there is an epidemic of "windshield pitting" in a community, many people will examine their windshields closely for the first time (looking "at" them rather than "through" them) and conclude that the windshield is newly pitted as the result of the present epidemic.[39] Once a certain threshold of panic is exceeded, it is extremely difficult to calm people by assuring them of the incredibility of the situation they fear, or the existence of evidence against the reality of the feared situation.

Failure to check. Although most of the people who were frightened by the "War of the Worlds" broadcast attempted, successfully or unsuccessfully, to determine whether this fright was justified by the facts, about a third of them attempted no check at all. These people either quietly resigned themselves to their "fate" or they went into some sort of panic. There were panic flights, such as the college student who drove at a reckless speed from New York City to Poughkeepsie to be with his girl friend, and other instances of people who tried to protect themselves, such as the woman who "hermetically" sealed her room so that the "gas" could not penetrate it.

These subjects are especially interesting sociologically. Cantril's

---

[39] Medalia and Larsen, "Diffusion and Belief in a Collective Delusion."

interview materials suggest that some people are motivated to *want* to believe in the reality of a disaster, some because it gives them a sense of being a participant in an event of great historic significance (notice the pride with which people will tell of having been on the Eastern seaboard during the two-day electrical blackout, or in Alaska during the earthquake). People in the midst of traumatic events sometimes anticipate the pleasure in "telling their grandchildren."

Other of Cantril's subjects found pleasant fringe benefits in the scare, such as the thought of one person that, if the Martians came to his town, "I would not have to pay the butcher's bill," or of another that "knew it would at least scare ten years' life out of my mother-in-law." The author, who will tell his grandchildren that he was in New York City during the 1965 blackout, observed there a sense of great relief among many residents who could use the blackout as an excuse to miss a day of work or school. (The finding of an upsurge in the New York City birth rate exactly nine months after the blackout might be interpreted as a reflection of another enjoyable fringe benefit of the "disaster.")

The author also remembers with what fervor he wished for any disaster, natural or man-made, that would relieve him of an unwanted appointment, like a visit to the dentist or participation in a military exercise. Considering these sorts of motivation to believe in the reality of a frightening situation, we can understand that it is not necessary to condemn as simply "hopelessly gullible" those people who experience panic without actually trying to check out the authenticity of the source of their fear.

Differential susceptibility to panic. A major problem of sociological concern in the study of mass panic is the question of which people in a population exposed to a frightening stimulus will panic and which ones will make effective checks and otherwise keep their cool. There are two ways of distinguishing those persons who are more and who are less susceptible to panic: first, in terms of *personal* qualities and, second, in terms of the panic-inducing aspects of the *situations* which different persons are exposed to.

Personal characteristics. Some persons are clearly more suggestible or "gullible" than others, and these personality traits may be unequally distributed among the people in different social categories: age, race, sex, social class, etc. Studies of panic reaction in disasters like tornadoes and explosions have found that women somewhat more often than men experience panic,[40] a finding that corresponds to many popular notions about the special suggestibility of women. The most important personality variable studied by Cantril is the trait of "critical ability," the tendency to suspend judgment while new facts bearing on a situation are examined. The preponderance of lesser educated persons among the frightened listeners is explained largely by the effects of education in stimulating this ability.

Situational characteristics. Apart from such personality variables, the degree of panic seems to depend on the situations of different persons at the time of exposure to the frightening stimulus.

Persons were less likely to panic if they heard the broadcast alone than if they heard it in the presence of other people. Those who heard it in a crowd were more subject to emotional contagion incident to their exposure to other frightened persons. This generalization needs at least two major qualifications, however.

First, the presence of other people may have a calming effect on frightened persons, providing that these others include persons with a special capacity or obligation to keep a cool head in crisis situations. Many adults feel this special responsibility to provide an example of levelheadedness to the more suggestible children around them, and men may be expected to be more emotionally level than women. One subject in Cantril's study said she heard the broadcast with some other women and that they were very frightened until "the men came back and told us it wasn't real."

Second, panic may be induced not so much by the reactions of those in one's physical presence as by those "significant others" with whom one is personally associated. In the study of an "epidemic" of imaginary bug bites among women factory workers, it was found that, at least at the height of the epidemic, those who were more likely to be "bitten" had friends elsewhere in the plant who had been "bitten," suggesting that the women's social relationships were more influential in determining behavior than the example of those immediately around them.[41]

Another situational factor is indicated by Cantril's finding that

---

[40] Charles E. Fritz and Eli S. Marks, "The NORC Studies of Human Behavior in Disaster," *Journal of Social Issues,* 10(1954):26–41.

[41] Kerckhoff, Back, and Miller, "Sociometric Patterns in Hysterical Contagion."

panic reactions were most common among those who, for some reason, were unable to make effective checks on the authenticity of the "War of the Worlds" broadcast. Some people who were at parties felt constrained from checking other stations by the rule that you do not tune a radio at another person's house. A bartender was too busy tending bar to check, and other people with jobs requiring continuous attention (such as a nurse or night watchman) were unable by virtue of their situational involvements to take the time to get the facts.

This observation runs somewhat counter to a notion that, in a disaster, the involvement of people with caring for others is a major deterrent to their own panic tendencies.[42] Perhaps the difference can be reconciled by noting that interpersonal involvement encourages panic only when there is much ambiguity about "what happened" and much need to get facts as a preparation for rational action. In a situation such as an airplane crash or a burning building in which the deadly serious nature of the situation is apparent to all concerned, the inability to "check" the situation will not be a factor in differential panic.

Finally, people who are relatively close to the scene of a real or imagined disaster are more likely to panic than those further removed. The subjects whom Cantril interviewed were in New York City and in northern New Jersey, where the Martians were reported to have landed and, understandably, there was more evidence of fright among these subjects than in a national sample poll. Although we tend to think of fear of improbable happenings as irrational, a rational calculation may lead one to give at least a shred of credence to a danger that, though improbable, is also eminent. On this basis people buy life insurance on the mere improbable possibility that they *may* die tomorrow, in which case it would be most unfortunate not to be covered. Even the most sophisticated person may similarly "cover" himself by being prepared to take flight in some unlikely but immediately threatening situation.

PUBLICS AND PUBLIC OPINION

Publics are composed of a number of people who share an interest in some aspect of social life. Some popular names for publics will illustrate the sociological concept of public: the *market* for a

---

[42] Lewis M. Killian, "The Significance of Multiple Group Membership in Disaster," *American Journal of Sociology,* 57(1952):309–314.

commercial product, the *clientele* of a professional person, the *fans* of a baseball team, the *constituency* of an elected official.

While *common* interest unites the members of a given public, *differentiated* interests produce differences of attitude and behavior within the public. There are *issues* that arise within any public: disagreements within a medical public about effective ways to treat a disease, disagreements within an electorate about the relative qualifications of different candidates for public office. *Public opinion* is formed as different members of the public take different sides of these issues. The processes involved in the formation of public opinion are the principal focus of sociological interest in publics.

Three general sociological questions about public opinion will be discussed in this section. First, in what way is the structure of public opinion related to the more general structure of a society; what kinds of people (e.g., men versus women, young versus old) tend to hold which kinds of opinion on a given public issue? Second, what are the processes involved in the formation of public opinion; how do people "make up their minds" whether to support one candidate or another in a political election, whether to buy one product or another? Third, what kinds of devices are used with what effects by people with "vested interests" in influencing public opinion in one way or another; what constitutes an effective or ineffective political or sales campaign?

Structure of Public Opinion

In part five of this book, we discussed the idea that one of the major consequences of a given kind of social differentiation (e.g., sex, age, race, class) is the development of "life styles" peculiar to the different categories of people. One aspect of life that was not emphasized in this earlier discussion is the frequent expectation that a person will hold, or at least will express, opinions on social issues that are thought to be appropriate opinions within the individual's social circle. A businessman with prolabor attitudes may incur the disapproval of his colleagues, and a workingman who took management's side of a labor-management issue would likely be castigated as a "fink" or some other equivalent of the black's derogation of the "white" Negro as "Uncle Tom."[43] Although it is

---

[43] On the quality of reaction to racial "traitors," see Gary T. Marx, "The White Negro and the Negro White," *Phylon,* 28(1967):168–177.

popularly thought that a man is entitled to his own opinion, we do find very frequently that pressures are put upon a person to think as well as to act in ways that are appropriate to his social status.

Sociologists have been interested for various reasons in developing generalizations about which categories of people tend to hold what kinds of opinions on public issues. Suppose the problem is one of determining tendencies toward liberalism or conservatism on social issues. Sociological hypotheses are generated almost automatically by a survey of some of the major categories of social differentiation: Are men or women generally more liberal? the young or the old? blacks or whites? higher-class or lower-class persons?

Examination of such a question for any one set of categories tends to run into complications. Consider, for example, the relative liberalism of the different social classes. We may think that conservatism is more typical of higher-class persons, who have the most at stake in maintaining the social status quo, while lower-class persons would seem to have an equally strong interest in "progressive" programs that will change the existing social order in their favor.

To some extent this expectation is borne out: the advantaged tend to accept *ideologies* that justify the existing order (in capitalism, a belief by entrepreneurs in the sanctity of free enterprise) while the disadvantaged tend toward *utopian* or revolutionary opinions.[44] But, from another perspective, the relative liberalism of the social classes seems to be reversed. On issues involving the civil rights of persons accused of criminal, unpatriotic, or other deviant acts, as well as of those trying to remedy the discrimination inherent in their minority-group status, there appears to be a pattern of "working class authoritarianism" in which the lower classes hold less liberal attitudes than members of the higher classes.[45] "White backlash" against the extremism of the black civil rights movement seems especially concentrated in the white lower and lower-middle classes. The most vehement opposition to student protest movements has tended to come from "hard hats": laboring men from the construction, trucking, and other industries. The supposed

---

[44] Karl Mannheim, *Ideology and Utopia,* trans. by Louis Wirth and Edward Shils (New York: Harcourt, Brace, 1946).

[45] Seymour Martin Lipset, *Political Man: the Social Bases of Politics* (Garden City, N.Y.: Doubleday, 1960).

greater liberalism of the lower classes turns out to be confined mostly to the area of *economic* liberalism (e.g., sympathy for socialistic views) and to exclude civil rights liberalism.

Some sociological studies of public opinion introduce new complications by attempting to relate some kind of variation in public opinion to several different aspects of social structure and to make causal inferences about reasons for these variations. Typical is Stouffer's study of American attitudes toward communism and several kinds of nonconformity in the wake of Senator Joseph McCarthy's attempt to arouse the public concern about "Communists in government."[46]

Stouffer used sample survey data to determine which kinds of persons scored high or low on a scale of "tolerance for nonconformity" measured by responses to such questions as whether a man should be fired from his job if he were a Communist. Stouffer found that, in the following comparisons, people in the first listed category were more tolerant of nonconformity than those in the second listed category: (1) young versus old; (2) better educated versus lesser educated; (3) men versus women; (4) Westerners versus Southerners (Easterners and Midwesterners intermediate); (5) non-churchgoers versus churchgoers; (6) wealthy versus poor; (7) urban versus rural; (8) community leaders versus rank-and-file citizens.

Interpreting such findings involves some difficulties. First, it is possible that any one of these differences is accounted for by one or more of the other differences. The relative intolerance of older people may be entirely attributable to the lesser educational level of an earlier generation or to the fact that older people are more likely to be churchgoers or to live in rural regions. To establish any one of these differences as a genuine factor in accounting for variations in this kind of opinion, it is necessary to control for the effects of one of these variables when examining the influence of another on the dependent variable. (See chapter 2 for a general discussion of this problem.) Each of the differences listed above held up when what appeared to be the relevant intervening variables had been controlled for.

A second problem of interpretation involves the attempt to give some general theoretical meaning to a set of facts about variations in public opinion. Just as Durkheim studied a long list of facts about

---

[46] Samuel A. Stouffer, *Communism, Conformity and Civil Liberties* (Garden City, N.Y.: Doubleday, 1955).

variations in suicide rates among different kinds of people and abstracted a few generalizations about social conditions which contribute to suicide, so one might examine Stouffer's findings and arrive at some common denominators among these group differences in rates of tolerance.

Two such general explanations emerge from Stouffer's discussion. One is the suggestion that persons in positions of *responsibility* in a society are encouraged by their positions to take a "sober second thought" before taking an extremist political position. Dogmatic opinions may be one of the luxuries of social irresponsibility. This explanation seems to fit fairly well most of the group differences in tolerance listed above. The other explanation is that persons who are more involved in social contacts with a variety of people are more likely to develop a tolerance for deviance. From the viewpoint of this explanation, intolerance is a product of social isolation, of the provincialism or ethnocentrism of people lacking exposure to alien ways. Again, the fit of the interpretation to the data is not perfect, but the two explanations in combination provide a fairly coherent view of why different categories of people take different sides of issues involving the treatment of nonconformists.

Dynamics of Public Opinion Formation

A political campaign in the United States is a good illustration of the dynamism of public opinion. Pollsters predicting election results at different points in the campaign must qualify their predictions by saying, "If the election were held today, such-and-so would be the result." But successive reexaminations of public opinion may show violent fluctuations in the relative favorableness of reaction to the candidates, and an election held "tomorrow" may yield quite different results. Similar kinds of fluctuations of opinion may be found in any public: the rise and fall of popularity of public entertainers, the alternation between "bearish" and "bullish" moods among investors on a stock market. Explaining these fluctuations is a major sociological problem.

One sociological handle on this problem is the notion that in publics, as in crowds, the ideas of one person are influenced by his exposure to the ideas of others. Much of the analysis of change in public opinion deals with the nature of social influence on opinions about public issues.

With most public issues, people are exposed to two kinds of social influence. First, they see or hear persuasive appeals through the mass media: a televised appeal by a president for support for his foreign policy, advertisements for a brand of cigarettes, an editorial on the hazards of smoking. Second, people carry on two-way communications among themselves in which they exchange views on public issues. Boxing fans have heated arguments over whether Joe Louis could whip Cassius Clay, housewives compare notes on the effectiveness of different brands of detergents.

One noted study of how people make up their minds in a presidential election examined the relative influence of mass and interpersonal levels of communication about the election.[47] In 1940, as in every presidential election, the voters of Erie County, Ohio, were bombarded with mass media suggestions on how they should vote. Most local newspapers supported the Republican candidate editorially. But many people who read Republican newspapers voted for Roosevelt and, in general, the authors found relatively little influence of these mass appeals on people's decisions. One reason for this lack of influence is the fact that people who hold an opinion typically read only those editorials that support their opinions or listen only to the campaign speeches of candidates toward whom they are favorably disposed.[48]

Most decisions in Erie County were based on more direct interpersonal communication. There are a number of advantages of personal approaches to campaigning which led the authors to conclude that political parties should budget more of their money for the personal canvass or door-to-door type of campaigning. Three of these advantages of personal influence will be reviewed.

First, personal influence catches people with their defenses down. When a television announcer says, "First, this message," the viewer is cued to the fact that someone is about to try to sell him something, and his sales resistance may be reflected in his taking this opportunity to go to the refrigerator for a beer. A "casual" conversation, following Simmel's definition of sociable talk,[49] is devoid of any ulterior motive of gain for any of the parties other than the shared gain of pleasure in sociability. But this very lack of content in conversation may lead to a lessening of the normal

---

[47] Paul F. Lazarsfeld, Bernard Berelson, and Hazel Gaudet, *The People's Choice*, 3rd ed. (New York: Columbia University Press, 1968).

[48] Herbert Hyman and Paul Sheatsley, "Some Reasons Why Information Campaigns Fail," *Public Opinion Quarterly*, 11(1947):413–423.

[49] Georg Simmel, "The Sociology of Sociability," trans. by Everett C. Hughes, *American Journal of Sociology*, 55(1949):254–261.

resistances to persuasion. An extreme case is that of an Erie County waitress who decided to vote for Willkie because she had *overheard* so many of her customers saying good things about him. An overheard conversation is not usually one aimed at influencing the eavesdropper (although it is occasionally planned that a conversation be overheard), and his defenses tend to be drastically reduced.

Second, personal influence allows the persuasive message to be tailored to the idiosyncracies of opinion of the person being influenced. An advertiser or a political speech writer must operate with some notion of what will appeal to a "typical" member of the public but, in pitching the appeal to a middle range, will slight or offend many persons outside this range. An automobile salesman or a door-to-door campaigner, by contrast, can size up the person with whom he is dealing and adjust his sales or campaign message to the tendencies of that particular person. This variation in appeal with the situation is possible to some extent in mass media forms of persuasion, for example, regional advertising or "one speech for the North, another for the South," but these adjustments are limited by the more public nature of mass media appeals and the tendency of one's opponents to point out such inconsistencies.

Third, personal influence carries a more immediate reward or punishment for yielding to or resisting the persuasion. Probably not even the best copywriter could create an advertisement that would make a reader feel guilty if he did not buy a particular brand of automobile, but a good salesman in an automobile showroom can do just this, can make the person doubt his own sanity or moral probity if he fails to buy the car. The authorship of a mass media appeal remains essentially faceless, while one may react all too intensely to the clean-cut face of that "nice young man" in the salesroom who subtly dropped the hint that this sale would win him a company bonus or a trip abroad, which is a lifetime dream.

Propaganda

A different approach to public opinion study begins with the fact that certain persons or groups have "vested interests" in influencing public opinion in one way or another. The continued employment of a television star depends on his popularity with the television public; a president's reelection chances vary with fluctuations in public opinion about how well he is handling the job. Given such vested interests, we can understand the preoccupation of many people with influencing public opinion in a given direction. Such activities as the advertising campaign and the public relations activities of an organization become the focus of sociological studies that are concerned primarily with the "persuaders" rather than the "persuadees."

Following from the classic view that "masses" can be influenced more through the feelings than through the intellect, we can note that efforts to influence public opinion often take the form of *propaganda*, i.e., the presentation of one side of a public issue in a manner calculated to arouse mass feelings for that side and against the opposing side. Perhaps the basic technique of propaganda is to associate the favored cause with a range of "good" things and, through "guilt by association," to identify opposing views with a range of "evil" things.[50]

On the negative side there is a *scapegoating* process of attempting to blame one's opponents for all kinds of unfortunate events that have happened or may happen if the opponents should prevail. Women are urged to use a brand of dishwashing detergent on the ground that the alternative "Brand X" will produce dishpan hands, with all the dire effects on one's interpersonal relations that rough hands will inevitably produce. During an election campaign, one political party reminds voters of the recession or the war that occurred when the opposition party was in power, and raises the specter of a repeat performance if that party wins again.

Scapegoating tactics can be seen in operation during the recent struggle in the United States to influence American public opinion for or against American involvement in Vietnam. Presidential administrations that support the war have, with more or less subtlety, suggested that dissenters are in effect "encouraging the enemy" by making them believe that they can win a political victory where a military one is impossible. From their side, the dissenters have used slogans and arguments which associate the prosecution of the war with excessive profits by the defense industry, the extermination of non-Caucasian peoples, and other very negatively valued motivations.

The reverse side of the scapegoating process in propaganda is a kind of "halo" that people with a vested interest may attempt to construct around whatever viewpoint they are promoting. The

---

[50] Alfred M. Lee and Elizabeth B. Lee, *The Fine Art of Propaganda* (New York: Harcourt, Brace, 1939).

political party in power, in order to combat the opposition's attempt to scapegoat them by "viewing with alarm" the present deterioration of conditions, will "point with pride" at favorable aspects of contemporary existence, including those which are actually little influenced by the government of the day.

An instance of such tactics outside the political realm is the effort of some occupational groups to justify their incomes or other privileges by an emphasis on the value of the "services" provided by this group. American undertakers, caught in a situation of potential ruinous competition among themselves because of the large number of undertakers relative to the number of available clients, have needed to augment their incomes by providing a huge range of "services" for a funeral.[51] Typically, many hours are spent over a body, embalming and reconditioning it so that it will make a "Beautiful Memory Picture" when displayed at the funeral. Heavy caskets and above-the-ground vaults are sold with the implicit promise that these will preserve the body against the "elements" although, in fact, there is typically only enough embalming fluid used to prevent decomposition of the body for a few days. To justify the bill that will be presented to his client, these "services" must be glorified as essential to showing proper respect for the departed. The printed messages and the individual sales pitches "halo" the undertaker's services by associating them with these sentiments that are understandably strong among the people who pay for funerals.

A major study of propaganda that analyzed the haloing process was Merton's study of a Kate Smith war bond drive during World War II.[52] Treasury bonds can and have been sold with a variety of appeals, including the idea that it is a good investment (a safe place to put your money) or that saving excess income in wartime will reduce the inflationary pressure created by high incomes and shortages of consumer goods. In fact, however, these were *not* effective appeals to the American buying public at that time, and Kate Smith avoided them in her highly successful selling campaign on a radio marathon.

Americans at that time saw bond-buying as essentially a *sacred* rather than a *secular* act: people bought bonds to support their

---

[51] Jessica Mitford, *The American Way of Death* (New York: Simon & Schuster, 1963).

[52] Robert K. Merton, *Mass Persuasion* (New York: Harper, 1946).

country or to "bring the boys home" sooner. Miss Smith haloed the act of bond buying by emphasizing these associations with patriotic motives. However, this appeal required some subtlety of approach. Americans had frequently been exhorted to buy bonds as a patriotic duty, but most sales appeals were less effective than the Smith one. She apparently succeeded in eliciting an acute sense of guilt in many listeners by contrasting the insignificance of the "sacrifice" she was asking them to make by buying a bond with the much greater wartime sacrifices of others. Some of these sacrifices were the obvious ones: the boys "over there" who were risking their lives for their country and the families of these men back home who were sacrificing their loved ones.

A more subtle but highly effective appeal was the suggestion that Kate Smith *herself* was making a great sacrifice by going on the air "continuously" (actually, for a minute or two every fifteen minutes) for a sixteen-hour stretch. This example of Miss Smith's devotion to the cause, together with her already acquired patriotic reputation, gave her the *right,* as many of Merton's respondents saw it, to ask them to make a sacrifice by buying a bond.

This theme of the Smith sacrifice has an interesting implication for the nature of effective propaganda in general. Merton suggests that the American radio-listening public had become, by this time, rather immune to the flood of verbal appeals to form some opinion: "Buy Brand Y," "Vote for Senator Claghorn," etc.—they had become highly resistant to "propaganda-of-the-word." They were, however, susceptible to influence by "propaganda-of-the-deed," persuasion based on the personal example of the opinion-makers.

Contemporary examples of propaganda-of-the-deed seem to be plentiful. A congressman, bidding for public support, can give to his constituency the view that he is always hard at work for them in Washington and he typically reports the number of bills he has introduced or the number of miles he has traveled in their behalf. In a presidential campaign, the candidates may put in between sixteen and twenty hours a day, thereby creating the impression that they really believe in their own candidacy. An incumbent president can perform a different kind of "sacrificial" deed; he can, as did President Roosevelt in 1944, resist the temptation to campaign actively and instead remain "on the job." If he does go out to campaign, he may take personal risks that frighten his bodyguard or his physician but that demonstrate his desire to get to the people. (Merton cited an early example of political propaganda-of-the-deed: President Roosevelt's decision to ride hatless in an open-top car in the rain in New York City during the campaign of 1944, a highly impressive display, by all accounts, of his commitment to the people.)[53]

Recent political assassinations have led some critics of political campaigns to urge a greater use of television or other less risky campaign devices.[54] Since the public sees relatively little "sacrifice" in a candidate's sitting in a television studio for a few hours compared with the sacrifice involved in the traditional barnstorming campaign tactics, it may be doubted that political leaders will be very responsive to such suggestions.

SUMMARY

Crowds and publics represent collective behavior in some of its most loosely organized forms. Crowds involve emotionalized responses to unusual situations and, frequently, responses in which normal social controls against excessive behavior have broken down. The degree of this disorganization is a matter of controversy with each type of crowd behavior discussed.

Rumors involve the passage of information outside the formal channels of news dissemination. Most studies of rumor have emphasized the distortions that occur, but there may be other processes encouraging accuracy in unofficial news passage. Mob behavior and riots (crowd behavior involving expressions of anger) are stimulated by long-standing grievances and precipitated by provocative acts. The mobilization of this anger into violent action depends on a number of factors, including the role of publicity in focusing attention on some possible line of riotous behavior. Panic (behavior involving extreme fear) may be an outcome of reactions to emergency situations, although there are typically many social controls to encourage people to act more calmly and to get information about the situation before they act violently.

Public opinion is formed as the people who are interested in some area of social life take positions on the issues that arise among themselves. Problems in public opinion which have interested sociologists are: (1) What kinds of people tend to hold

---

53 Ibid., p. 92.

54 See the recommendation of the National Committee on Causes and Prevention of Violence that American presidents limit their public appearances to indoor rallies and use television more fully. *New York Times,* November 3, 1969, pp. 1, 2.

what kinds of opinions? (2) What influences people to develop one kind of opinion or another? (3) What devices are used by propagandists to influence opinion favorably in support of some vested interest?

Social Movements

NATURE OF SOCIAL MOVEMENTS

Sometimes the social unrest that produces emotionalized crowd behavior or rapid fluctuations of public opinion results in more organized and permanent kinds of collective behavior. In these situations, dissatisfied people mobilize their action as a more or less well-planned *protest* against prevailing social arrangements. These more organized social protests are called *social movements.*

Being protests, social movements always involve targets for the opposition of the movement. At least three kinds of targets are commonly found: (1) the prevailing cultural values of a society, e.g., spiritualistic protests against the materialism of the value system of the society or bohemian reactions to "philistine" value systems; (2) the prevailing forms of the basic social institutions, e.g., collective protest against the monogamous form of the family, the capitalist form of economy, the classical form of education; (3) the prevailing system of social stratification, e.g., protests against the unequal distribution of life chances. Such minority groups as women, students, and blacks may feel persecution against themselves and attempt to eliminate this discrimination.

Whatever the target of opposition of a social movement, there are two fundamentally different ways in which people can register their disillusionment with prevailing social arrangements. They may *withdraw* from participation in the society which contains the values, the social institutions, or the forms of discrimination to which they object. This withdrawal tends to be accompanied by an attempt to reconstitute a purified form of association limited to other protesters of their own kind. On the other hand, the protest may take the form of an active effort to eliminate the conditions to which the protesters object. The things of this world, evil though they may appear, are not something to be withdrawn from but something to be changed through the efforts of a social movement. These reforming types of social movements will first be discussed, then the movements of withdrawal.

MOVEMENTS TO ALTER SOCIAL CONDITIONS

Of those social movements aimed at changes in established social conditions, some protest a very specific condition for which remedy is sought. The movement is focused on a specific *demand*: stop the bombing in Vietnam, release political prisoners, reinstate a fired employee, increase pensions for the aged, repeal prohibition. In these situations there is no necessary challenge to the established order, only to specific decisions of established decision-makers. Other movements aim at more fundamental reforms in basic social arrangements: democratize the university, overthrow capitalism, eliminate all forms of discrimination against women, establish the Kingdom of Christ on earth.

Movements with Specific Demands

We consider first those social movements which are organized as pressure groups to accomplish some specific change in public policy. The initial problem of such a social movement is to get together enough "concerned citizens" to make some serious impact on people who have the power to institute the desired change. While many citizens are simultaneously concerned about a number of specific unsatisfactory social conditions (for example, high taxes, air pollution, highway safety, medical abuses), it may be a real accomplishment to organize sustained and effective action focused on any one specific reform.

Some traumatic experience may be required to mobilize people to a specific cause: a series of airplane crashes may activate citizens concerned about conditions of air traffic safety, a crippling flood may be the occasion for gathering backing for a much needed flood-control program. Also, a particularly charismatic person or simply a particularly persistent "fanatic" on a subject may finally attract a wide following: a Ralph Nader on auto safety, a Rachel Carson on pollution, a Margaret Sanger on birth control. Sometimes the traumatic event will focus attention on the fanatic who has been "telling us so" all along, predicting that just this population explosion or just this water contamination crisis would occur unless we mended our errant ways.

A major focus of sociological interest in social movements that make specific demands has been the question of the fate of such movements in relation to the fate of the goals they are pursuing. It might seem obvious that, if the aims of a movement were accomplished, the movement would cease to exist. Actually, this seems frequently not to be the case. People who have fought together for a "glorious cause" may develop affective attachments to one another and may be reluctant to break up their association when the original cause of the movement ceases to be an active motivation. After an election, volunteer campaign workers, who were usually attracted initially by a particular candidate, frequently are loathe to disband and seek ways to establish a more permanent organization, perhaps a political club of the "reform" variety.

When an almost totally effective vaccination for poliomyelitis was developed, the National Institute for Infantile Paralysis did not abandon its March of Dimes campaigns but shifted the focus to fund-raising for other medical purposes, especially to combat birth defects.[1] When the New Deal in the United States established a system of social security to provide income for the aged, a movement originally aimed at pensions for the elderly, the Townsend Movement, shifted its goals from pension agitation to the provision of a variety of social activities tailored to the interests of older people.[2]

A trend toward a more diffuse interest in wider social reforms can be observed in many movements originated around specific aims. Often the demands of some movement—for example, the demands of student protesters on some campuses—are rather vague or uncertain, suggesting that sometimes the specific demands are less important to the movement than the experience of "togetherness." It is sometimes said that the Berkeley disturbance of 1964 marked a turning point in the character of student protest movements.[3] The Berkeley affair started as a Free Speech Move-

---

[1] David A. Sills, *The Volunteers* (Glencoe, Ill.: Free Press, 1958).

[2] Sheldon L. Messinger, "Organizational Transformation: a Case Study of a Declining Social Movement," *American Sociological Review,* 20(1955):3–10.

[3] Jerome K. Skolnick, *The Politics of Protest* (New York: Simon & Schuster, 1969); for more detail on the Berkeley situation, see Seymour M. Lipset and Sheldon S. Wolin (eds.), *The Berkeley Student Revolt* (Garden City, N.Y.: Doubleday, 1965).

ment, a specific demand for the right of students to use university facilities to hear controversial speakers and to organize partisan political activity. The resulting confrontation of the campus protesters with the state's political administration gave students their first taste of victory and prepared the way for the more diffusely aimed "student power" features of recent student protests.

Reform or Revolutionary Movements

Most of the social movements that have attracted sociological attention have been those whose aims were of a more diffuse variety. Members of such movements demand more than specific policy changes by established decision-makers; they aim at a more complete replacement of existing forms of social institutions. A permanently organized "Reform Democratic Club" is clearly a different phenomenon sociologically than the ad hoc committee of volunteers who worked for Eugene McCarthy in the 1968 presidential election.[4]

The following discussion of reform movements will focus on one of several possible sociological approaches to the study of social movements. While Newton's second law of motion (for every action, there is an equal and opposite reaction) cannot apply literally to social movements (actions), the analogy will suggest a major sociological problem. Social movements, attacking as they do some established social arrangements, invariably step on the toes of someone, thus setting in motion a more or less vigorous reaction; any power for change that they exert is likely to stimulate a *countervailing* power to protect the status quo. Communist rallies have stimulated the counteraction of local "patriotic" groups to try to break them up.[5] Antiwar demonstrators and counterdemonstrators

---

[4] In many social movements promoting a cause, one finds a combination of participants, including groups with long-standing and permanent attachments to the cause—the Quakers with pacifism, for example—and groups newly created under the impetus of a specific situation—the National Mobilization to End the War in Vietnam. Often there is more than a tinge of jealously and hostility between these two types. Old established political organizations, for example, may view election-year volunteers as Johnny-come-latelies who missed the grinding discipline needed to sustain the party during less exciting times, and the newcomers may see the "pols" as mossbacks who are not fully in touch with the new spirit of things.

[5] For a description of a specific episode, see Robert C. Myers, "Anti-Communist Mob Action," *Public Opinion Quarterly*, 12(1948):57–67.

have frequently clashed. These clashes do not always occur, however, and the variation of counterreaction as related to variations in social conditions is a fit subject for sociological analysis.

To approach this problem, notice some of the variation in the aims and the tactics of social movements. The aims of a movement may vary from minor to complete alterations in the established social order, from a more complete integration of protesters into the general society to a more complete removal from it. The tactics of a movement may range from *moderate* to *radical,* as we shall define those terms. The wider social reaction to a social movement seems to be determined largely by the nature of the aims and tactics of the movement. The intensity and direction of "societal response" may, in turn, influence the subsequent aims and tactics adopted by the movement.

Aims. Generally, there is more tolerance for those social movements which accept important elements of the established order and aim at *reform,* not *revolution.* A policy of *gradualism* or tokenism in racial integration is more likely to be accepted by the dominant race than is an immediate and wholesale integration of the races. Of course, this statement has to be qualified as applied to the more fanatic opponents of a social movement. Here, the philosophy is likely to be, "Give 'em an inch and they'll take a mile." To some avid anti-Communists, any political reform providing social-welfare benefits is an instance of "creeping socialism"; to extreme racists, a single case of racial integration is the first step toward racial mongrelization. Objectively, there does seem to be a grain of truth in the extremist's fear of the effects of even the slightest compromise with the demands of a social movement. Once a "token" yielding to demands has been granted, the way is more easily opened to the view that, having given this much, one may as well yield to all of the demands.

The nature of the aims of a movement may also be an important determinant of societal response. Social movements, especially those that represent attempts to overcome discrimination against some group, may aim at the complete integration of their members into all of the privileges enjoyed by other members of the society. Other movements may attempt to "liberate" minority members from influence by members of the wider society. A program for the economic improvement of blacks might aim at more employment of black workers in "white" businesses, but it might also aim at an autonomous "black capitalism" in which black entrepreneurs would hire only black employees and reap the profits of providing services for black customers.[6]

The nature of opposition to the social movement may depend largely on which of these two forms the movement takes. Considering the social movement of blacks in the United States to improve their status, white lower social classes, as we noted in the last chapter, have provided the major source of opposition to the civil rights aims of blacks. Such persons are, after all, those who have the most to lose if civil rights legislation were fully implemented. It is they who send their children to the integrated public schools, they who might lose jobs if equal employment laws were enforced, they who would lose the prestige gain of being able to "look down on someone."

Recent changes in black militancy suggest, however, a shift from what Skolnick calls a "civil rights" to a "liberation" emphasis.[7] Recently many black leaders have derogated the goal of integration of the black man into "white society." They have urged instead black activities that emphasize the view that "black is beautiful" and have declared that the black American seeks not integration into but liberation from white society. Symptomatic, perhaps, of this shift has been the change of focus of racial conflict centered on American college campuses. Where once the drive was for black youth simply to get into segregated colleges, more recently the demand has been for Black Studies programs that will encourage the separate racial pride of the Negro.

Although our sociological studies do not yet prove this, it might be predicted that, as the aims of the movement shift from civil rights to cultural autonomy emphases, the major source of white opposition to the movement may shift also. We usually think of the middle classes as holding most dearly the values of Americanism and the free enterprise economic system. A black movement that looks to any extent to African rather than to American models will probably stimulate especially the ethnocentric reaction of these middle classes. As a de-emphasis on integration lessens somewhat the pressure of blacks on the privileges of the white lower classes,

---

[6] On the various dimensions of "black power" and of white reaction to it, see Raymond S. Franklin, "The Political Economy of Black Power," *Social Problems,* 16(1969):286–301.

[7] Skolnick, *Politics of Protest,* Ch. 4.

we might expect an increasing tolerance of blacks by these classes who, after all, are not so "respectable" themselves in the eyes of the middle class. It will be interesting to see where the white backlash occurs in future American elections: primarily in the middle-class suburbs or primarily, as previously, among the lower-class "ethnics" of the inner cities.

Tactics. The tactics of a social movement may be characterized as *moderate* or *radical,* and this distinction designates at least two kinds of variation. From one viewpoint, a moderate movement is one which employs only *legitimate* methods of accomplishing its aims; from another viewpoint, a moderate movement shuns violent methods in favor of *nonviolent* ones. Obviously these are not the same distinction in two guises, since a movement may be nonviolent but also illegitimate in its approach. The passive resistance and civil disobedience developed by Gandhi's anticolonial movement and borrowed by Martin Luther King for his sit-ins and freedom marches are examples. As a movement shifts from one tactic to another we may expect the reactions of people outside the movement to shift accordingly.

In the United States, a country in which, as we noted in chapter 10, there is a strong strain of legalism, the tactics of social movements are tolerated only so long as they remain within the realm of the legitimate and the nonviolent. We find frequently that, while most of the public are more or less favorably inclined to the aims of a reform movement, they reject strongly any radical tactics in support of these aims. Although most Americans say they are favorable to the civil rights aims of blacks, most white Americans reject any movement tactics other than the strictly legitimate ones, such as appeals to established authority; even nonviolent sit-ins and demonstrations are rejected by substantial majorities of whites.[8] The people of California were overwhelmingly disapproving of the nonviolent but illegal demonstration tactics used by students at Berkeley,[9] and Americans generally were even more rejecting of the violent forms of student unrest that developed in the spring of 1970. Even the majority of students and faculties at universities where protest movements have occurred—although certainly more favorable to radical tactics than is the general public—have re-

---

[8] Ibid., p. 186.
[9] Lipset and Wolin, *Berkeley Student Revolt.*

jected the tactics, for example, of the militant students who seized control of university buildings at Columbia University in 1968,[10] or of the young radicals who bombed the Mathematics Research Center at the University of Wisconsin in 1970.

This combination of public attitudes toward a movement—acceptance of its aims, rejection of its radical tactics—may be a severely anomie-generating situation for the adherents of the movement.[11] Given the tendency of established authorities to hear politely and to forget promptly the grievances of dissenters when expressed through legitimate channels, we can well understand why many social-movement adherents feel that only the more radical tactics will allow their aims to be accomplished. Perhaps it was really public fear of the long hot summers of the 1960s that produced the civil rights legislation of that period; perhaps it was the fear of further disruption of campus academic life that led to the increasing inclusion of students in the decision-making mechanisms of the university.

Many social movements face a severe tactical dilemma. They can remain within the bounds of legitimacy and nonviolence and risk having their aims ignored by a public which will, perhaps, be preoccupied with the demands of other and more radically oriented movements. Or, they can adopt radical tactics but hazard (1) alienating potential followers from among those who share their disillusionment with the established order but who also share the general cultural condemnation of violent and illegitimate tactics; and (2) creating a backlash among powerful persons who, while sympathetic to their aims when pursued with moderate tactics, turn against them when the movement switches to more radical methods. There seems to be no ultimately satisfactory resting place between these two horns of the dilemma.

WITHDRAWAL MOVEMENTS

In some social movements there is a minimal interest in making demands on established authority or in remaking society to correct some of its "defects." Rather, protest is expressed by the collective withdrawal of a group of people from this defective society and the establishment among themselves of a purified way of life. If *values*

---

[10] Allen H. Barton, "The Columbia Crisis: Campus, Vietnam and the Ghetto," *Public Opinion Quarterly*, 32(1968):333–351.

[11] See the discussion of *anomie* in chapter 14, esp. pp. 307–310.

are the target of protest—for example, if the protest is against the hypocrisy or intellectual mediocrity of "philistine" society—there may be established communities of bohemians whose way of life is dedicated to interpersonal honesty (e.g., openly acknowledged sexual relationships) or to the cultivation of art, music, and philosophy. If *social institutions* are the target—for example, a capitalist economic institution—there may be set up communes in which the Communist principle of providing the individual in accord with his needs is established. If some system of *discrimination* is the target—for example, the exclusion of the poor from social respectability—a group may establish its own system for the distribution of rewards in which the "first shall be the last," one in which, for example, it is the rich man rather than the poor whose entry into Heaven will encounter more difficulty than a camel passing through the eye of a needle.

Although withdrawal and the establishment of alternative social structures for their members are the defining characteristics of such movements, their interest for sociological study tends to revolve around persisting problems in the relationship of these movements (we shall here call them *cults*) to the world which the cult members have presumably left. There are two major facts of life for cults which make problems of this sort inevitable. First, members of a cult are typically recruited from the "outside world" (although some cults will try to increase their numbers by procreation among their own membership) and the cult must, at some point, be concerned about its appeal to this world. Second, the activities of a cult, while theoretically of concern only to the membership, are not a matter of indifference to people outside the cult. No matter how intent the cultists are about minding their own business, social movements of this kind are often seen as threatening because, if for no other reason, it is feared that the exposure of one's children to these strange ways may somehow corrupt their morals.

Recruitment

A basic problem of every cult is recruitment. Having a more or less esoteric set of beliefs and practices, the cult will attract only a relatively small part of a total population. A question of practical significance to the cult and of scientific interest to the sociologist is, What kinds of people are most likely to be converted to the peculiar way of life of a cult?

One set of sociological variables for explaining differential tendencies toward "conversion to a deviant perspective" has been proposed in a study by Lofland and Stark.[12] These sociologists investigated the membership of a tiny cult (never more than thirty members) of so-called World Savers who formed a community on the West Coast of the United States. The cult was a religiously oriented group of believers in the special prophecy of their leader, a "Mr. Chang" of Korea, where the movement originated. Given the fact that the aim of the group was literally to save *the world,* how is it that so few members of the world rushed to be saved in this manner?

Lofland and Stark suggested a "value-added" model of the sociological variables involved in recruitment to a cult. By this they mean that, before a specific kind of behavior will emanate from a person, he must be favorably positioned on two or more variables (e.g., if only young men join a particular cult, age and sex are two "value-added" variables). The total effect of the seven such variables discussed by these authors is to narrow severely the effective recruiting field from which a cult must find its members. In common with many sociological explanations of some phenomenon, attention is given both to *predispositional* and to *situational* variables, to the differential personal characteristics of people and to some of the contingencies that determine the situation in which people happen to be at the time of their potential exposure to some behavioral stimulus.

Predispositional factors. First, cult members appear to be recruited from among the more frustrated or dissatisfied members of a society. Few people who are "making out nicely, thank you" in the conventional social world are motivated to abandon this favorable position to take up membership in a cult in which they will be "despised and rejected." The World Savers described by Lofland and Stark are by and large people who have already experienced social rejection and have, relatively speaking, nothing to lose emotionally or socially by their participation in this cult.[13]

---

[12] John Lofland and Rodney Stark, "Becoming a World-Saver: A Theory of Conversion to a Deviant Perspective," *American Sociological Review,* 30(1965):862–875.

[13] For a description of the misfits of various sorts who participated in a far-fetched colonizing scheme, see Robert E. L. Faris, William R. Catton, Jr., and Otto N. Larsen, "The Galapagos Expedition: Failure in the Pursuit of a Contemporary Secular Utopia," *Pacific Sociological Review,* 7(1964):48–54.

Second, among chronically frustrated individuals, there are several alternative problem-solving tendencies by which different people typically deal with their frustrations. Lofland and Stark mention *political* and *psychiatric* perspectives on problem solution, in addition to the *religious* perspective adopted by the World Savers.

Some people faced with a frustrating personal situation will locate their trouble in the actions and decision of people in positions of political power and will attempt to solve their problems by writing congressmen or joining an ideologically oriented political party. Others will define their problems as resulting from the defects of their own personalities and will consult a psychiatrist, marriage counselor, advice columnist, or some other specialist in helping people solve problems by self-evaluation and personality development. There are psychiatrically and politically oriented cults, and they presumably recruit from among different kinds of people than do the religiously oriented cults such as the one described by Lofland and Stark.[14] Such cults encourage the employment of faith in the supernatural as an antidote to a range of personal and social problems. The recruiting field for the World Savers has thus been narrowed to the chronically frustrated and to the religiously inclined problem-solvers among the frustrated.

Third, many people are not disposed toward a cult like the World Savers because they are able to accept the beliefs and rituals of established religious bodies as devices to deal with the alleviation of their problems. (The same could be said about political or psychiatric cults. Many people can fulfill their needs through membership in one of the established parties in a two-party system rather than through joining a radical third party. Many people can use established personality counseling agents such as pastors and licensed psychotherapists without resorting to personality development cults like Yoga or Alcoholics Anonymous.) Those who *cannot* accept established religious orders have the kind of religious orientation characterized by a *seeker* tendency. There is a feeling that the supernatural world impinges more directly and profoundly on mundane human affairs than the established religious bodies will admit. The world is full of mystery (many religiously oriented cultists believe, for example, in the reality of flying saucers) and the

----

[14] Another viewpoint is that, through the process of "alternation" of intellectual perspectives, people may become disillusioned with one of these perspectives and take up another: from "dedicated Christian" to "dedicated Communist." Peter Berger, *An Invitation to Sociology* (Garden City, N.Y.: Doubleday, 1963), Ch. 3.

established churches are seen as derogating this mystery by reducing religious life to a set of ritualistic formulae.

Situational factors. The consideration of these predispositional factors has severely narrowed the recruiting field for a specific cult. Further narrowing is introduced by situational factors. While people may be predisposed to favorable response toward some proposed line of behavior, they frequently are prevented from so acting by certain features of their social situations. The "fair-weather liberals" and "fair-weather illiberals" that we discussed in chapter 12 are predisposed toward a line of action that they do not carry out because the "weather" or climate of opinion among others makes it dangerous or inconvenient for them to act. Similarly, only some people who are favorably inclined toward a given social movement will be in a position to "do anything about it."

The fourth factor, continued from the predispositional variables, is the existence of a *turning point* in the life of the potential recruit. Most people most of the time are too involved with conventional jobs, marriage, etc. to cut themselves loose and join an esoteric cult. Most adult American men may have the predispositions favorable to becoming a beachcomber or a member of a wife-swapping cult, but most of the time they are simply too busy with their conventional careers to pursue such will-o'-the-wisps. However, if someone with an unusual and interesting appeal (an offer to crew on a yacht bound for the South Seas, for example, or an invitation to a sex orgy) happens along when the man is at loose ends socially (having just lost a job or a wife, say), he may allow himself to be precipitated into a new and more esoteric set of involvements.

Most World Savers were people who had just flunked out of college, been fired from jobs, or were otherwise freed from usual social restraints. The disproportionate number of *adolescents* among the membership of many cults might be explained in this manner, although the usual explanation is the intensified frustration or storm and stress of this period. An adolescent typically has a minimum of settled social involvements, not yet being fully committed to a specific occupation or spouse, and he is in a better position to play around with esoteric cults.

A fifth factor, closely related to the previously discussed variable, has to do with the existence of social controls of an interpersonal nature that typically operate against the person's assumption of membership in an esoteric cult. Many a predisposed and situationally uninvolved person flirts with some cult activity, only to find that his "significant others" severely condemn the flirtation. Many a college student has received a letter from home asking him to cease and desist from wearing long hair or involving himself in radical politics or an unusual religious activity. The more favorable situations for cult recruitment are those in which either the person is exceptionally *isolated* from interpersonal relations with people in the conventional world or else these significant others are exceptionally tolerant of his deviance. In the weakness of what Lofland and Stark call *extracult bonds* lies a main chance for cult recruitment.

A sixth factor refers to what Lofland and Stark call the influence of *within-cult bonds*. If a close friend or relative of a person becomes an adherent of a cult, this fact becomes a situational contingency that is favorable to the person himself becoming involved, provided he is otherwise disposed and situated. Cult involvement, like other kinds of social behavior (adoption of an innovation, alcoholic addiction, hysterical medical symptoms), tends to spread in sociometric patterns of personal relations between people. In breaking into a sociometric chain, one finds that the first link is the hardest to force. An individual without such an interpersonal link to a particular cult is relatively unlikely to join it. One who has a close friend or relative who disaffects from the cult is also likely himself to experience disaffection.

These first six variables are seen by Lofland and Stark as both necessary and sufficient to account for a person's recruitment into a cult, but only to the point of his *verbal commitment* to that cult. Groups always distinguish between their devoted members and those who pay lip service, however, and one more situational contingency tends to determine the more radical involvement. Being typically esoteric and socially rejected groups, cults are sustained largely by the mutual reinforcement that cult members give to one another, a continual reassurance that the cult commitment is a "right" one.[15] This level of commitment requires what Lofland and Stark call a kind of "intensive interaction" of cult members with one another.

Given all the forces in the everyday world which tend to ridicule cult beliefs and commitments, it is understandable that the more

---

[15] J. L. Simmons, "On Maintaining Deviant Belief Systems: A Case Study," *Social Problems,* 11(1964):250–256.

devoted cult members tend to be those whose lives are more totally engrossed in interaction with their fellow cultists. A recognition of this fact is found in the typical requirement that cult members give up their separate residences and come to live permanently with other members of the cult. This requirement represents a situational contingency because only *some* cult members will be in a position to do this; some may be geographically separated, or have family obligations and job commitments that prevent their being present for many of the ritual occasions of the cult. The availability of people for intensive interaction is a major situational variable.

Cult Relations to the Wider World

Once people become committed to the separate way of life of a cult member, they typically still must sustain some kind of relationship with persons in the conventional world. The interaction of the "normal" with the "cultist" is likely to be tinged with the normal's perception of the cultist as "queer" and the cultist's perception of the normal as part of that "evil" world from which he has withdrawn. These orientations will suggest two major sociological questions in the study of the relationship of cults to the wider world: First, under what conditions are people willing to *tolerate* cultist social movements? Second, under what conditions do cultists shun association with the normals or, alternatively, attempt to convert them or bring them into the fold of the "true believer"?

Tolerance. One observation that ought to be made about general public tolerance of cults is that this tolerance tends to be rather *situational* in character; that is, the degree of the tolerance for a cult depends on varying circumstances. Because cultists hold beliefs and act in ways that no "sane adult" would imitate, there is often a considerable degree of tolerance of cultic behavior if practiced only by adults in the presence of other adults. Children, on the other hand, are more impressionable, and their elders may make vigorous efforts to insulate their children from the "bad influence" of cultists.

Another aspect of the situational character of public tolerance is the fact that special areas come to be set aside as territories within which a wide variety of cultic behavior is tolerated. Greenwich Village in New York and sections of southern California have acquired reputations as places where "kooks" and "fanatics" congregate. These places even have a kind of tourist attraction for the visitor, who amuses himself, for example, by going to the Village and clucking rather complacently about the variety of "specimens" of humanity that he observes there.

Proselytizing. The degree of interest of cult members in recruiting new members from the outside world is a major variable in determining the character of cult activity. Many cults are noted for their secrecy and the exclusiveness of their membership, priding themselves on the very smallness of their numbers and thinking of themselves as an elite who have been initiated into the mysteries of the universe. Others advertise in the mass media and otherwise actively seek to gain converts.

A social psychological case study of a group of cultists focuses on the question of why a cult frequently passes from an exclusive orientation to one of active proselytizing to gain new members.[16] Festinger and his associates studied a small group of believers in the prophecies about the end of the world provided by ethereal voices speaking through the agency of an American housewife. The group believed that the world would be doomed on a given date. At first they were very possessive about their secret and wholly disinterested in active recruitment of new believers. It was only when the prophecy was disconfirmed—when events predicted by the voices failed to happen—that the group began actively to seek new members.

The explanation offered is that, when a person or group is faced with events that discredit the beliefs on which action is being taken, there is strong "cognitive dissonance" which might be reduced either by abandoning the disconfirmed beliefs or by seeking group support for the belief by converting new members to it. The first direction of dissonance reduction—abandoning the cult—is difficult for devoted cultists who, according to the Lofland and Stark description, have strongly committed themselves by leaving home or otherwise "burning their bridges" to the conventional world. They cannot so easily "go home again."[17] In this situation, it is often

---

[16] Leon Festinger, Henry W. Riecken, and Stanley Schachter, *When Prophecy Fails* (Minneapolis: University of Minnesota Press, 1956).

[17] On the role of a public act of identification with a deviant life-style (in this case, talking in tongues) in fixing an individual's commitment to that life-style, see Virginia H. Hine, "Bridge Burners: Commitment and Participation in a Religious Movement," *Sociological Analysis,* 31(1970):61–66.

more feasible to hold to the esoteric belief and seek more group support for it.

Some of this crisis of self-confidence for a prophetic cult may be averted by the common practice of being nonspecific in the prophecy. By leaving vague the details of, say, an apocalyptic end of the world, the cult cannot be ridiculed for having made a prophecy that failed to be fulfilled. The Book of Revelation gives no precise date for the world's end, and although the "second coming" is frequently more specifically prophesied, the original account is not discredited by any disconfirming events. However, the question of whether "to specify or not to specify" a precise future event is not so easy for the prophetic cult to answer in many cases. A vague prophecy is relatively safe but it is also relatively unattractive to potential followers. If doomsday is projected to an indefinite future, persons worried about the world's end may put off indefinitely any tendency to take action on the belief.

The temptation of a prophet to attract a following by making a striking specific prediction is illustrated by the story of the old farmer who was preparing an "Old Farmer's Almanac" and predicting the weather for each day of the year. When he came to July 27, he wrote "snow." His wife, looking over his shoulder, said, "You old fool, you *know* it won't snow on July 27." He replied, "I know, but suppose it *did;* look what a prophet I'd be!" The public may be able to forgive a Jeane Dixon or other public prophet some of his errors if he has been bold enough to predict as unlikely an event as snow in July, the election of Harry S Truman in 1948, or the assassination of John F. Kennedy.

SUMMARY

Social movements represent the more organized and persistent forms of protest against social conditions. Social movements may demand specific reforms or more general reconstructions of basic social values, institutions, and distributions of privilege. Whether specific or general in demands, they aim at changing frustrating social conditions. Such movements may adopt relatively moderate aims and tactics or relatively radical ones, and the responses of different segments of the power structure tend to be determined by the character of these aims and tactics.

Sometimes a social movement takes the form of withdrawal from a world seen as "evil" because it incorporates negatively valued social arrangements. Such movements or cults recruit their members from the conventional social world, and a wide array of factors helps to determine which people join a given cult. Once having joined, they share with fellow cultists the likelihood of being treated with scorn by the conventional world, and much of their activity, including their attempts to gain new adherents from among outsiders, may be seen as efforts to convince themselves and others that they are "not so queer as all that."

HUMAN POPULATION

So far in this book we have treated the human beings who make up a society in a rather abstracted way: as role-players, as members of groups, as participants in collective or deviant forms of behavior. In this part we shall view the human material of society more concretely, focusing on the obvious fact that people have bodies that are located somewhere in physical space and that the numbers and locations of these human bodies, as well as the manner in which they are adjusted to their physical environments, have many fundamental sociological causes and consequences. This subject matter is usually considered under the headings of *demography* and *ecology,* studies that deal in one way or another with human populations in their physical aspects.

Population Size and Composition

18

Demography is the scientific study of human population. As we noted briefly in chapter 6, the sheer number of people in a group will influence the nature of the interaction and the organization of the group. As groups grow or diminish in size—as a "wide place in the road" becomes a city, for example—the character of the relations of people inhabiting an area may be transformed. The sociologist has every reason, then, to interest himself in the factors that determine the size or the change in size of a population. He also is interested in the *composition* of populations: the relative number of people of different types in the population—for example, men and women, young and old people, higher and lower social classes.

DEMOGRAPHIC VARIABLES

Whether size or composition is his major problem of interest, the demographer has only a few variables that he must consider, although the determinants of variability in each variable may be complex and perplexing. The number of people in a population is determined by two basic factors: natural increase and net migration.

Natural Increase

A population grows or declines in size as there is an excess of births or of deaths among its members. The number of births and deaths in a population are typically reported as ratios, with the number of births or deaths as numerator and some aspect of the total population as denominator. *Crude* birth rates and death rates indicate the number of births or deaths in a given year per 1000 of total population. In a United States population of around 200 million, there are some 3.6 million births and 2 million deaths annually, meaning a crude birth rate of around 18 and a crude death rate of around 10. The crude rate of natural increase is the difference between these numbers: 8 in the example cited.

The "crudeness" of these rates is based on the fact that the total population is used as the denominator. Since populations vary widely in their age and sex compositions, these crude rates tell us very little about such important matters as whether or not the birth rate is high enough to sustain population growth or how well people in a population are doing in keeping their members alive to older ages. A death rate of 10 per 1000 would be a remarkably low rate in, say, St. Petersburg, Florida, where there are many retired persons and the total population is a relatively old one. The same rate in a metropolitan commuter community with its many young couples would suggest some serious health hazard in that community. By the same token, a crude birth rate of 18 per 1000 would be remarkable in St. Petersburg but quite languid in the suburb.

To "refine" these rates, the denominator of the ratio may be not the total population but only some relevant part of it. A *fertility rate* would compare the number of births with the number of women in the childbearing ages, usually defined as women between the ages of fifteen and forty-nine.[1] An *age-adjusted* death rate would show the number of deaths of people of a given age compared to the total number of people in that age category.[2] These devices will control for the effects of unusual age and sex distributions on the birth and death rates of a population. However, crude birth and death rates are highly useful summary data because they show most directly the rate of growth or decline of a population.

Net Migration
In-migration and out-migration (immigration and emigration) are the only other demographic variables. Although these might also be expressed as ratios of migrants to total population, in fact they are usually expressed simply as absolute numbers.

DEMOGRAPHIC THEORIES
Demographers, like ordinary citizens, observe the frequent changes

---

[1] Donald J. Bogue, *Principles of Demography* (New York: Wiley, 1969), p. 659.
[2] Ibid., p. 550.

in size of populations, especially those rapid growths that are sometimes called "population explosions." The fact of population growth at an accelerating rate is one of the most obvious and, to some people, one of the most frightening facts of human history. World population in 1650 is estimated to have been about a half billion; it required nearly two hundred years for the population to be doubled but less than one hundred years for the population to double again, and population projections suggest another doubling within about forty years' time.[3]

How is population growth to be explained in terms of the demographic variables outlined above? Where world population is concerned, clearly only natural increase is involved, since there has apparently been no immigration to the earth from other planets. The population growth of any smaller territory—a nation, a city, or a county, for example—must consider both natural increase and net migration factors. Although some populations (rapidly growing cities, for example) are growing primarily through immigration, most larger regions have grown and are growing primarily through the influence of natural increase.

Even the United States, a country which is essentially a European colony demographically, has grown more by the internal reproduction of the resident population than by the infusion of new people through immigration. Bogue shows that, even during the decade of maximum immigration (1901–1910), net migration accounted for only about 40 percent of the country's population growth.[4] Recent natural increase rates have produced a population growth of about 1.5 million per year and net migration rates of somewhat under half a million; therefore, about 75 percent of recent population growth has been by natural increase.[5]

Migration Theory

Since migration is a relatively minor factor in the recent population growth of most countries, it is understandable that theory to account for migration is relatively sparse. The major approach to explaining migration is in terms of the expulsive forces that *push*

---

[3] Ralph Thomlinson, *Population Dynamics* (New York: Random, 1965), p. 13.

[4] Donald J. Bogue, *The Population of the United States* (Glencoe, Ill.: Free Press, 1959), p. 14.

[5] U.S. Bureau of the Census, *Statistical Abstract of the United States: 1969,* 90th ed. (Washington, D.C.: Government Printing Office, 1969), p. 6.

people into emigration and the attractive forces that lead them to immigrate to a given region.[6] People are pushed into emigration by such factors as economic depression, political persecution, objection to the established religious order, and lack of economic opportunity because of high birth rates which produce a surplus of people to the employment needs of the area. All these conditions were prevalent throughout much of the European continent during the nineteenth and early twentieth centuries, and such countries lost much population through a negative balance of net migration.[7]

Migrants are *pulled* into areas that provide antidotes to the conditions that precipitate emigration. To the oppressed and depressed European of the nineteenth century, the New World beckoned as a land of hope, offering those very opportunities that the Old World denied him. *Attractiveness* of an area is not the only reason for immigration, however; population gain through immigration is partly a function of closeness to a population being pushed by expulsive factors. Newly developed suburban areas close to large cities may be no more attractive intrinsically than some areas further removed, but their proximity to an outward-looking urban population seeking escapes from the city may lead to heavy immigration into them. This seems to be the crux of the "intervening opportunities" theory of migration: i.e., "the number of people going a given distance is directly proportional to the number of opportunities at that distance and inversely proportional to the number of intervening opportunities."[8]

If there are serious *obstacles* to immigrant entry into an area, such as geographic isolation or the exclusion of immigrants as a matter of policy, an area may not be selected as an immigration target even though it is otherwise attractive.[9] Likewise, immigration tends to follow the most easily traveled transportation routes.[10] Americans, for example, more frequently immigrate to European than to non-European countries partly because of the established airline flights between America and Europe and the much higher

[6] Bogue, *Principles of Demography,* pp. 753, 754.

[7] Oscar Handlin, *The Uprooted* (Boston: Little, Brown, 1951), Ch. 1.

[8] Samuel A. Stouffer, "Intervening Opportunities: A Theory Relating Mobility and Distance," *American Sociological Review,* 5(1940):845–867.

[9] Everett S. Lee, "A Theory of Migration," *Demography,* 3(1966):47–57.

[10] William F. Ogburn and Meyer F. Nimkoff, *Sociology,* 4th ed. (Boston: Houghton Mifflin, 1964).

rates charged for travel to other, perhaps equally attractive, parts of the world.

Natural Increase Theories

Malthus. Most contemporary theories of natural increase stem from the writings of Thomas Malthus, an English clergyman writing at the beginning of the nineteenth century.[11] Malthus noted the tendency for population to increase in a *geometric ratio,* doubling every generation (about twenty-five years). This tendency is based on a constant human sex impulse which insures that births will be kept at a level that is more than sufficient to reproduce the population. However, this growth rate is only a tendency that cannot be realized for any length of time, since actual population growth is limited by the expansion of resources to provide for people's material needs, and these cannot increase in anything like a geometric ratio.

In this situation, the inevitable balancing factor is a high death rate. Malthus wrote of "positive checks" on human population; the term is ironic since the positive checks that Malthus mentions are famine, disease, and war—calamitous events that carry off the surplus of population which cannot be provided for. Malthus also wrote about "preventive checks" or some form of contraception to limit births but, perhaps because he was a clergyman, he saw most forms of contraception as "vices" designed to encourage a morally degraded sexual promiscuity. The only morally acceptable preventive measures that occurred to Malthus were late marriage and sexual abstinence, rather unlikely checks in view of the constancy of the human sexual impulse. Altogether, Malthus gives a most gloomy prognosis for human population: the necessity for people to endure an excessively high death rate as the only effective balance for the pressures on resources created by high birth rates.

Critics of Malthus, favored with the advantage of being able to look back on demographic events that Malthus attempted to foresee, have pointed out two major flaws in his analysis: (1) Malthus failed to foresee—or perhaps refused to consider the legitimacy of —the great decline in European birth rates during the nineteenth

---

[11] Thomas R. Malthus, "A Summary View of the Principle of Population," in Frank W. Notestein (ed.), *Three Essays on Population* (New York: New American Library, 1960).

century because of the use of "preventive checks";[12] (2) he underestimated the capacity of an industrialized economy to support populations increasing at geometric ratios. The population of a number of countries, including the United States, did increase at such rates throughout much of the nineteenth century, and this population increase was matched with an expansion of economic productivity. Even today, the gross national product of the country increases at a rate far in excess of the rate of population growth.[13]

Demographic transition. Perhaps the most serious shortcoming of the Malthus approach to population analysis was its failure to anticipate the explosive rate of growth of population in the world. More recently, a theory of *demographic transition* has developed in the attempt to account for the recent accelerated rate of growth of world population.[14] According to this theory, most of the populations of the world have gone through or may be expected to go through a series of demographic stages.

Stage of high-growth potential. This is a population of the type described by Malthus as typical of all populations. High birth rates are balanced by almost equally high death rates, and natural increase is slight. This is taken to be a kind of primitive or preindustrial stage of population.

Stage of transitional growth. This stage is entered during an early phase of a country's industrial revolution. The first effect of modernization on population is a drastic reduction in death rates brought about by increased food supplies and improved medical care. Birth rates, being more responsive to a set of traditional social usages with reference to sexual relations and the desirability of large families, remain relatively high. The result is rapid natural increase without, usually, any rise in birth rates.[15] Most of the devel-

---

[12] Dennis H. Wrong, *Population and Society,* 3rd ed. (New York: Random, 1967), pp. 47–58.

[13] *Population Bulletin,* 26(February, 1970):10.

[14] Robert W. Notestein, "Population—the Long View," in Theodore W. Schulz (ed.), *Food for the World* (Chicago: University of Chicago Press, 1945), pp. 36–57; Irene Taeuber, "Demographic Modernization: Continuities and Transitions," *Demography,* 3(1966):90–108.

[15] In some countries, Bogue points out, there is a short-run rise in birth rates primarily because the lowered mortality is reflected in improved health of people at the childbearing ages. *Principles of Demography,* p. 56.

oping countries of the world have entered this stage. Mexico, for example, has maintained a steady birth rate of around 45 per 1000 for the last forty years or so; during the same time, the crude death rate has dropped from about 25 to about 10.[16] A similar pattern of increasing rates of natural increase with a stable or declining birth rate is shown in a recent study of the population of Brazil.[17] It is, in short, the *decline of mortality* rather than the increase of fertility in these countries that produces the explosive rates of population growth.

Stage of incipient decline. The population explosion of the preceding stage has been seen as only a temporary phenomenon. The countries of Western Europe—for example, Sweden[18]—went through the transitional growth stage in the nineteenth and early twentieth centuries and are now well established in the final stage. As industrialization proceeds, people acquire more of both the motivation and the know-how to voluntarily restrict the number of their children. In a fully industrialized and urbanized society, children are something of a hindrance, or at least a problem, since an urban apartment or house must be provided for them, and they must otherwise be "maintained" without contributing anything to family resources. Couples increasingly calculate how many children they can afford and adjust their reproduction accordingly. Population growth again becomes minimal, as birth rates finally "catch down" with death rates.

Postwar Population Growth

The theory of demographic transition has been challenged somewhat by demographic events since World War II in a number of countries. The birth rates in the United States, Canada, Australia, New Zealand and, probably, the Soviet Union *rose* considerably after 1945, an event which the demographic transition theorists did not foresee.[19] In the United States, the large crop of "war babies" (actually, postwar babies) arrived in 1946 and 1947. This rise in birth rates held up through the 1950s, a trend especially surprising since

[16] Ibid., pp. 76, 83.

[17] Rubens Vaz da Costa, "Population and Development: the Brazilian Case," *Population Bulletin*, 25(September, 1969):91–97.

[18] Bogue, *Principles of Demography*, p. 59.

[19] Ibid., p. 680.

the childbearers of this decade were born in the late 1920s and the 1930s, a time of depressed birth rates in the United States.

There were apparently two new factors at work here. One was the increased prosperity of the people of the United States and the apparent willingness of couples to have larger families as they could afford them. Another was the general reorganization of residential patterns in this period, a trend toward relocation of people from central cities toward outlying suburbs where, it appears, people feel that the environment is more favorable for child-rearing. Since about 1962, however, it has begun to appear that the rise in fertility during the 1950s may have been, after, all, a temporary disturbance of a long-term trend as described in the demographic transition theory. Crude birth rates declined in the 1960s and, more important, *fertility rates,* which indicate the ratio of children to women of childrearing ages, have declined: from around 120 live births per 1000 women aged fifteen to forty-four in 1959 to around 85 per 1000 in 1968.[20]

Perhaps the suburban flurry has spent itself, and perhaps the shift in values toward a child-oriented family was a passing postwar fashion. At any rate, the events of the 1950s indicated that birth rates can rise as well as fall as social conditions change, and much more caution will probably be exercised when trends are projected by demographic theorists of the future.

POPULATION COMPOSITION

For certain purposes it may be less important to understand trends in size of total population than to understand trends in the relative proportions of different population elements: men and women, old and young, rural and urban dwellers, etc. Trends in population composition involve the same combination of factors involved in explanations of total population size. The relative rates of natural increase and of net migration determine changes in population composition. We can illustrate this point by discussing two kinds of population composition: the relative numbers of men and women and the relative numbers of members of different social classes.

Sex Composition

One basic piece of information on any population is its *sex ratio,*

---

[20] Paul R. Ehrlich and Anne H. Ehrlich, *Population Resources Environment* (San Francisco: W. H. Freeman, 1970), p. 33.

defined as the number of men per 100 women in the population. The differential rates of migration is the main factor in producing imbalances of the sexes in many populations. In the United States, the western states have higher sex ratios than the eastern ones (more men than women, relatively) because more males have engaged in westward migration.[21] Urban areas have more females, rural areas more males, primarily because young women are more likely than young men to migrate from farms and small towns to the cities.[22] However, in many parts of the underdeveloped world—Africa, for example—there are more males in the cities, which have drawn mostly males from the rural areas to provide labor in the cities.[23]

The kinds of social problems implicit in unbalanced sex ratios are fairly obvious. Many American farmers have a difficult time finding wives in their local communities, and many single girls in the city have to go without male companionship. In African cities, there are the age-old problems of "vice" wherever unmarried men (or men away from their wives) congregate and, in the rural villages, there are the domestic hardships of families deprived of their able-bodied men for long periods of time.

In addition to these variations in sex ratio from place to place at a given time, there are fluctuations of the sex ratio for a given place over a period of time. For the United States as a whole, the sex ratio in 1910 was 106.2 males per 100 females; in 1968 it was 95.4.[24] The explanation of this shift to an excess of females involves both migration and natural increase factors. The sex ratio at the beginning of this century reflected the large foreign immigration to the United States during this period, an immigration very predominantly male; one estimate put the sex ratio of immigrants to the United States in the first decade of this century at 229.1.[25] The other factor favoring males at this time and place, as at all others, is the higher rate of births of male babies. The sex ratio at birth is between 105 and 106, an excess of male births that shows remarkable con-

[21] Thomlinson, *Population Dynamics,* p. 430.

[22] Bogue, *Principles of Demography,* p. 170.

[23] John C. Caldwell, *African Rural-Urban Migration: the Movement to Ghana's Towns* (New York: Columbia University Press, 1969); S. H. Ominde, *Land and Population Movements in Kenya* (Evanston, Ill.: Northwestern University Press, 1968).

[24] U.S. Bureau of the Census, *Statistical Abstract: 1969,* p. 24.

[25] Ernest Rubin, "The Demography of Immigration to the United States," *Annals of the American Academy of Political and Social Science,* 367(1966):17.

sistency over time and in different parts of the world, being apparently biologically determined.[26]

The more recent shift toward an excess of females in the United States must be attributed to a combination of migration and mortality factors (the fertility factor having remained constant). Although there is still a substantial rate of immigration to this country—around a half million per year—there has been a radical change in the sex ratio of this immigration. In recent years, more females than males have immigrated to the United States; the sex ratio of immigrants for the period 1960–1965 is estimated to be 80.0 males per 100 females.[27]

There has also been a rather dramatic shift in sex differentials in mortality to the advantage of females. In 1900, the average life expectancy (number of years lived) in the United States was 48 years for white males, 51 years for white females, 32½ years for nonwhite males, 35 years for nonwhite females.[28] This slight advantage in longevity for females was much extended by 1967, when the corresponding life expectancy figures were 67.8 for white males, 75.1 for white females, 61.1 for nonwhite males, 68.2 for nonwhite females.[29] The higher rates of male mortality *at all ages* requires explanation by some combination of biological and sociocultural factors. There are more miscarried or stillborn male than female fetuses, higher infant mortality rates among boys than among girls, higher male accident rates at the middle ages, and greater male susceptibility to fatal diseases of most kinds. Some of these facts are not attributable to differential medical care given to males and to females, but support a prominent notion about the "natural superiority" of the female in terms of her capacity for health and longevity.[30]

There are social and cultural factors involved in these mortality differentials, however, as demonstrated by the fact that the life expectancy differentials favoring females are less pronounced in some countries and in some times than in others. In a few cases, of which India is one, male life expectancy has even been higher than the female's, reflecting the possibility that medical care dis-

---

[26] Bogue, *Principles of Demography,* p. 166.

[27] Rubin, "Demography of Immigration," p. 17.

[28] U.S. Bureau of the Census, *Statistical Abstract: 1969,* p. 53.

[29] Ibid.

[30] Ashley Montagu, *The Natural Superiority of Women* (New York: Macmillan, 1953).

crimination in favor of men can overcome the "natural superiority" of women. The discrimination may, however, work in the other direction, as it seems to do in the United States and elsewhere. The male cultural ideal of "toughness" and the reluctance of males to admit they are sick (or, perhaps, of their families to allow them exemption from work obligations on grounds of sickness) are conditions not favorable to the attaining of effective medical care by men.[31]

Social-Class Composition

The relative numbers of people in different social classes are obviously influenced by the fact of social mobility: the changing of class position (up or down) by resident members of a population. We discussed social mobility, some of its causes and consequences, in chapter 11, and will not be concerned here with this major source of change in relative numbers of people in the different classes. Rather, we shall examine social-class composition from a *demographic* perspective, raising questions about the rates of fertility, mortality, and migration among members of the different classes. The point of reference for this discussion will be the population of the United States.

Considering first the matter of migration, the question can be raised whether immigration to the United States has served primarily to increase the ranks of the higher or the lower social classes. The popular stereotype of the social-class characteristic of the immigrant, given ritual statement in the poem inscribed on a tablet in the Statue of Liberty, is that America has welcomed primarily the "poor," the "homeless," the "masses yearning to breathe free." We reviewed in chapter 12 some evidence that immigrants have, indeed, tended to enter the lower social classes in the United States, whatever may have been their social statuses before immigrating. There has, however, been a significant recent shift in the status characteristics of immigrants to the United States, a change given official sanction and encouragement in the Immigration Act of 1965, which gives preference to applicants with high levels of talent. As Bogue summarizes the characteristics of recent immigrants:

---

[31] Women, for example, are more likely than men to complain of symptoms of mental disturbance. Derek L. Phillips and Bernard E. Segal, "Sexual Status and Psychiatric Symptoms," *American Sociological Review*, 34(1969):58–72.

Immigrants tend to be professional people, other white-collar workers, or craftsmen. Instead of being an in-movement of proletarians, modern United States immigration has more of the characteristics of a "brain drain," robbing Europe and many developing countries of their elite intelligentsia and talented leaders.[32]

It is quite clear that, if historically the size of the lower classes was increased by immigration to the United States, this is no longer the case.

In the area of natural increase, fertility and mortality differentials between the classes have tended to have offsetting effects. Mortality rates are negatively correlated with social-class position; it may be one of the major advantages in "life chances" of the higher classes that they have a better chance of attaining a long life.[33] On the other hand, fertility is higher among the lower classes in the United States, whether "class" is measured by education, income, or occupation.[34] Since there are both higher birth rates and higher death rates among the lower classes, it is difficult to reach any conclusion about the net effect of natural increase on the relative sizes of the social classes.

The explanation of these class differences in fertility and mortality is worth considering. The most obvious explanation of the mortality differential is that higher-class persons can better afford effective medical care. This is part of the explanation; if it were the whole story, we might expect these differences to disappear as medical care is extended more completely to the poor, through programs such as Medicare, for example.

One may well be skeptical that putting medical care within the financial grasp of the lower classes will necessarily eliminate the mortality differential. Perhaps it is part of the middle- and upper-class life style to tend to think in terms of preventive medicine (e.g., regular medical checkups) and of established daily routines in the areas of nutrition and cleanliness that are oriented toward considerations of healthiness. The hamburger-and-coke lunch that a lower-class parent might permit his child might well be denied a middle-class child being reared in a kind of vitamin-culture. The "present-oriented" style of lower-class life to which we referred in chapter 11 may be related in many ways to the failure of lower-class

---

[32] Bogue, *Principles of Demography*, p. 806.

[33] Ibid., pp. 603, 604.

[34] Ibid., pp. 693–708.

people to bother themselves to take health precautions or, for example, to subject themselves and their children to the immediate pain of an inoculation against a disease they may never contract or to undergo a medical test for a disorder they may not have.

Similar considerations may be involved in the differential fertility rates of the social classes. There may well be some fundamental differences of value-orientation between the classes where sex and reproductive behavior are concerned. Contrary to some opinions, the larger families of lower-class couples in the United States do not seem to reflect a greater desire for more children by the lower classes.[35] Family planning is largely a middle-class phenomenon in the United States, while for the lower classes, children are often the unwelcome but fatalistically accepted by-product of sexual intercourse. Lower-class people tend to be reasonably well acquainted with effective contraceptive techniques, but they may define their use as detracting from spontaneous enjoyment in the sex act. In one study it was found that this attitude was especially prevalent among lower-class *men,* many of whom refused to employ contraception in spite of the expectations of their wives.[36] The value pattern of "life for the moment—hope for the best—but be prepared for the worst" may explain a great deal about the existence of large families in the lower classes.

SUMMARY

The total number of people in a population and the relative number of different kinds of people are the outcome of a combination of an excess of births over deaths (natural increase) and of in-migration over out-migration (net migration). Demographic theory has focused especially on explanations of population growth through natural increase, starting from the ideas of Malthus, which postulate a stable population size based on high mortality rates inevitably offset by high fertility rates, given the limited power of the earth to support populations at the usual levels of procreation.

A theory of demographic transition has tried to show how, contrary to Malthus, populations may grow rapidly for a limited interval of time under the impact of social changes which lower mortality

---

[35] Ronald Freedman, "American Studies in Family Planning and Fertility: a Review of Major Trends and Issues," in Clyde V. Kiser (ed.), *Research in Family Planning* (Princeton: Princeton University Press, 1962).

[36] Lee Rainwater, *And the Poor Get Children* (Chicago: Quadrangle, 1960).

rates before they produce lower birth rates. The rises in birth rates that occurred in the 1950s in the United States and elsewhere do not fit the demographic transition model, but it may be that some very special circumstances of that decade produced these unanticipated events.

In explaining any changes in the composition or the relative numbers of different kinds of people in a population, it is necessary to keep in mind the influence of both migration and natural increase differentials between different elements of a population. To illustrate the demographic concern with explaining population composition, we considered the population of the United States in terms of changes in the relative numbers of men and women in the population and in terms of the effects of differential natural increase and migration on the relative sizes of the higher and the lower social classes.

Population Distribution: Communities

Human ecology is the branch of sociological study dealing with the spatial distribution of persons. The places in which persons live have a great deal to do with the kinds of social organization and culture they experience. A *community* is a special kind of human group. It has some of the same characteristics as *society,* as we defined that concept in chapter 5. The community provides a relatively self-sufficient base for the total life of its members. The various institutions tend to be organized on a community level. The distinctive thing about the concept *community* is that it has a definite territorial aspect as part of its definition. People live *in* communities, and communities can always be mapped or otherwise located in physical space.

TYPES OF COMMUNITIES

Places of residence vary in the degree of concentration of people within those places. Densely populated places are called cities and their populations are called *urban.* Places in which people are more widely scattered are called *rural.* Some further distinctions can be made. A *metropolitan area* is a community containing one very large central city together with the surrounding countryside and the *suburbs* or outlying cities which are economically and socially dependent on the central city. The Census Bureau of the United States distinguishes between those members of the rural population living on *farms* and what it calls the *rural nonfarm* population, composed mostly of people in towns of less than 2,500 population (the lower population limit for the Census Bureau's definition of an urban place).

The density of its population is not an entirely satisfactory criterion for classifying a community as urban or as rural. There is also a *cultural* dimension to these classifications; a community is defined as urban or rural in terms of the typical way of life in that community. Sociologists have attempted to define *urbanism* in such terms,[1] and one could presumably view *ruralism* from the same cultural perspective. The urban way of life emphasizes cultural heterogeneity: cities are the most congenial locale for a great variety of subcultures. Urbanism also features a relatively impersonal kind of interaction between persons. Simmel explained this "cool" or "hostile" character of social relations in the city as a necessity for the urban dweller, who could not withstand psychologically the stimulation of the constant presence of people around him unless he developed a blasé attitude of ignoring them or a hostile attitude to those who encroach on his privacy.[2]

The rural way of life represents the opposite in both of these respects. A city dweller is likely to be struck with the remarkable sameness of people in a rural community: a sameness which may extend to many details of appearance, manners, and social attitudes. Rural dwellers are often known as well for the warmth of their relations with one another and for their hospitality to strangers. Having few social relations, perhaps the rural man can afford to react more intimately with each of those few persons whom he does know.

The introduction of the cultural dimension to the distinction between rural and urban communities provides an additional tool for the sociologist in analyzing communities. Communities of a given size or density may vary widely in their degree of urbanism. Thus, the way of life in New York City may be more urban than that in Tokyo, although the latter city is the more populous of the two. The residents of Park Forest, Illinois, or some of the towns in Westchester County, New York, are highly urban persons, despite the fact that, technically, they live in small cities. Sociologists who hypothesize that certain kinds of behavior—for example, juvenile delinquency—are related to conditions of urbanism have been able to test their hypotheses by measuring the degree of cultural urban-

---

[1] Louis Wirth, "Urbanism as a Way of Life," *American Journal of Sociology*, 44 (1938):1–24.

[2] Kurt Wolff (ed.), *The Sociology of Georg Simmel* (Glencoe, Ill.: Free Press, 1950), pp. 409–424.

ism of different cities and examining the correlation between these differences and the kind of behavior in question.[3]

CHANGES IN COMMUNITIES: ECOLOGICAL PROCESSES

An examination of any society over a length of time will show that the population is changing in terms of the types of communities in which people live. An analysis of these changes would indicate two types of changes: (1) changes in the distribution of people and activities in physical space, which we shall call *ecological processes;* and (2) changes in the degree to which people are engaged in a rural or an urban way of life. The sociologist is interested in the social origins and the social consequences of both of these kinds of changes in communities.

Ecological processes may refer to: (1) the redistribution of people and activities between types of communities, or (2) changes in the distribution of people and activities within a given community.

Redistribution Between Communities

Urbanization. A major ecological trend in the history of the world has been a long-range tendency toward *urbanization,* the movement of people from rural communities. In the United States, for example, the percentage of the population living in cities has increased from about 5 percent in 1800 to about 73 percent in 1968.[4] Several countries of Western Europe are even more highly urbanized than the United States, while the populations of most countries in Asia, Africa, and South America are still predominantly rural but are undergoing rapid urbanization.[5]

Causes of urbanization. There are two different dimensions to sociological explanation of urbanization. One is the explanation of the shift of population generally from rural to urban communities. A second is the explanation of the location of cities at particular geographic locations.

The general tendency toward population concentration may be

---

[3] For example, Marshall B. Clinard, *The Sociology of Deviant Behavior,* 3rd ed. (New York: Holt, Rinehart & Winston, 1968), Ch. 3.

[4] *Population Bulletin,* 26(February, 1970):6.

[5] Kingsley Davis, "The Urbanization of the Human Population," in Editors of Scientific American, *Cities* (New York: Knopf, 1965).

seen as the result of changes which have negated the necessity for population to be widely dispersed. Perhaps there are inherent motivations for population concentration: the desire to associate with others, the advantages of specialization of activity which requires concentrated population,[6] the need for the protection of massed numbers. But there are also forces making for deconcentration: the need for men to live close to the land that supports them; the dangers of disease and violence associated with concentrated living. Cities existed in the Middle Ages, and they gratified the needs for concentration listed above. But they were necessarily small because of the dangers of fire and pestilence and the economic impossibility of many persons being separated from agricultural occupations.[7]

Technological changes in agriculture associated with the industrial revolution made possible an agricultural surplus to support city populations. (In the United States today only about 5 percent of the population lives on farms, and still agricultural production is more than adequate to support the nation's population.) A related factor was the development of forms of social organization that made it possible for city dwellers to appropriate this agricultural surplus for their own use.[8] The development of efficient mechanisms of taxation, land rent, and religious tithes made it possible for urban dwellers to support their specialized occupations. An additional factor of recent importance has been the development of public health and law enforcement practices to a level sufficient to enable people to live in dense aggregations in relative safety.

In urbanized populations, the specific location of cities involves other problems of explanation. The factor of *transportation* is one of obvious importance. Cities live by the movement of people and materials into and out of them, and they have tended to locate at places favorable for transportation. Most of the world's largest cities are located near natural harbors because water has been the cheapest form of transportation. Inland cities have grown up along existing railways or highways. Cooley argues that cities tend to develop at a "break in transportation"—a point at which goods

[6] Fenton Keyes, "The Correlation of Social Phenomena with Community Size," *Social Forces,* 36(1958):311–315.

[7] Gideon Sjoberg, *The Preindustrial City* (New York: Free Press of Glencoe, 1960).

[8] Kingsley Davis, "The Origin and Growth of Urbanization in the World," *American Journal of Sociology,* 60(1955):429–437.

are removed from one form of transportation and reshipped by another means.[9] Port cities are the most obvious examples; here goods are transferred from oceangoing freighters or transoceanic airlines to trucks, trains, and cargoliners for domestic distribution.

Beyond this generalization, the location of cities seems to depend somewhat on the type of city involved. *Industrial* (manufacturing) cities, such as Pittsburgh, Manchester, and Cologne, are located for access to raw materials, a labor supply, and a market. *Commercial* cities, such as Chicago, Kansas City, and Boston, that specialize in servicing a large trade area, tend to be located at points accessible to all parts of that trade area or "hinterland." *Political* cities, i.e., the seats of governmental activity such as Washington, D.C., Bonn, and The Hague, are also often located at points near the geographic or population centers of an area at the time they were established.

Consequences of urbanization. Some of the more negative consequences of the movement of people from rural to urban communities have been recorded in sociological studies. The *disorganization* of both rural and urban life has been especially noted.

The effects of rapid urbanization of life in cities might be treated as an instance of *cultural lag,* a concept discussed in chapter 4. Masses of people have moved into the cities before institutions could be evolved to regulate the relations of these people. Although few large cities in the United States have grown rapidly in the past forty years, these cities are still concerned with problems of inadequate housing and with conditions of demoralization that have produced such characteristic phenomena as high rates of crime and continuing racial violence. Attempts to solve these problems through political action have been retarded by another consequence of urbanization. State legislatures, which control the taxing powers of city governments and the allocations of state funds, are often dominated largely by rural interests, reflecting the more rural composition of the country when legislative seats were first apportioned.[10] Under the pressure of Supreme Court decisions requiring legislative reapportionment, some of this difficulty of rural domination of urban people has begun to be eliminated.

---

[9] Charles H. Cooley, "The Theory of Transportation," in Robert C. Angell (ed.), *Sociological Theory and Social Research* (New York: Holt, 1930).

[10] Gordon E. Baker, *Rural v. Urban Political Power* (New York: Random, 1963).

Rural communities also experience the disorganizing effect of urbanization. As rural population emigrates, those remaining on farms and in small towns find a dearth of people to operate such local agencies as schools, churches, and medical facilities. (Some of the small towns in western New York State have recently advertised in newspapers and on billboards for a town physician.) The continuity of rural families is broken as the sons and daughters of rural people find little economic opportunity in their home communities compared to that available in the cities.[11]

Not all of the disorganizing consequences of urbanization are the result of the rapidity or the massiveness of the movement; some result from the fact that different parts of the rural population tend to emigrate at different rates. In the United States, young adults migrate to cities in larger proportion than either the young or the old, and more young women than young men participate in this movement.[12] The result is, for cities, a surplus of young unmarried women and, for rural areas, a deficit of economically productive persons, which means a high *ratio of dependency:* a large number of old and young to be cared for by a relatively small number of working people.[13]

Suburbanization. Probably the most important recent ecological process in the United States has been the movement of persons from the centers of large cities to the outlying areas of these cities. Between the federal census of 1950 and that of 1960, all except two of the country's ten largest cities (Houston and Los Angeles) declined in population, while there was a very high rate of growth of the suburbs around all these cities.[14] The 1970 census will probably reveal a continued although much slowed process of suburbanization of American cities.

Causes of suburbanization. In numerous sociological studies sub-

---

[11] Calvin L. Beale, "Rural Depopulation in the United States: Some Demographic Consequences of Agricultural Adjustments," *Demography,* 1(1964):264–272.

[12] On the general problem of the selectivity of persons in rural-to-urban migrations, see the articles in T. Lynn Smith and C. A. McMahan (eds.), *The Sociology of Urban Life* (New York: Dryden, 1951), Ch. 9.

[13] Warren S. Thompson and David L. Lewis, *Population Problems,* 5th ed. (New York: McGraw-Hill, 1965), p. 97.

[14] *Population Bulletin,* 19(March, 1963):25–50.

urban residents have been questioned about their motives for abandoning the city for the suburb.[15] Most answers seem to reflect the desire of urban dwellers to gain some of the advantages of the rural way of life for themselves. The suburb, like the small town or farm, is thought to be a more desirable place for raising children because of its "open space" and fresh air and freedom from the presumed violence and unhealthiness of city streets. There is also apparent among many respondents a reaction against the impersonality of city living and a desire to settle in a place with a stronger sense of community and more of the joys of neighborliness. Finally, apart from its supposed inadequacies for family life, city living can be costly. With its high premium on space, the large city is an extremely expensive place in which to acquire the living space necessary for raising large families. This economic factor, operating in reverse, may be a partial explanation of a recent ecological phenomenon: a return of older couples to the city (and to apartment living) after their children have left home.

Consequences of suburbanization. One easily demonstrable consequence of the suburban movement is that it has introduced an increased amount of residential segregation of several types. The composition of suburban migrants shows a high proportion of whites, married persons, children, and members of the upper and middle classes, leaving an increasing concentration of blacks, single persons, and lower-class persons in the central cities.[16] The Negro population of every major city of the United States increased substantially between 1950 and 1960, a period when white population was declining in most of these cities.[17] Suburbs typically have few apartments or other facilities for unmarried adults. The movement from city to suburb has been one element in the process of

---

[15] Sylvia F. Fava, "Suburbanism as a Way of Life," *American Sociological Review,* 21(1956):34–38; Wendell Bell, "Social Choice, Life Styles and Suburban Residence," in William M. Dobriner (ed.), *The Suburban Community* (New York: Putnam, 1958).

[16] Reynolds Farley, "Suburban Persistence," *American Sociological Review,* 29 (1964):37–47; Leo F. Schnore, "Urban Structure and Suburban Selectivity," *Demography,* 1(1964):164–176.

[17] Only very recently have blacks begun to join whites in the "flight" to the suburbs. Reynolds Farley, "The Changing Distribution of Negroes Within Metropolitan Areas: the Emergence of Black Suburbs," *American Journal of Sociology,* 75(1970): 512–529.

social-status mobility, and few lower-class persons have succeeded in making this move.[18]

The movement has also introduced problems of institutional functioning for both the large cities and their suburbs. Central cities are faced with the problem of constructing and paying for facilities for *commuting,* a phenomenon closely related to the suburban movement. Traffic problems in the city ensue,[19] and suburban residents typically pay no taxes to support the transportation facilities that they require (New York City has, however, instituted a personal income tax on nonresidents of the city who earn incomes there). Suburbs have the problem of providing educational facilities for the numerous children in their communities and, being almost entirely residential, many suburbs have few industrial or commercial establishments to tax for school and community needs.

Ecological Patterns Within Communities

A city, a town, or a rural countryside is not a static entity but is continually undergoing change of some kind. Museums will often display photographs or drawings of an area of a city showing how it looked some years ago that surprise us by the discrepancy they reveal between that area then and now. The student of communities is interested in more than physical change, however; he is interested in understanding the patterns of community structure and the processes of change in that structure. There have been several models advanced for the explanation of these patterns.

Concentric zone model. Within a city, one finds that different kinds of activity tend to be concentrated at different places. These "natural areas"[20] include residential areas, wholesale and retail commercial areas, and manufacturing areas, as well as many finer specializations within each of these categories. The most prominent generalization about the patterning of urban activities is that it can be summarized as involving a distribution of people and

---

[18] Recent studies have found more frequency of working-class suburban residence than had previously been thought to be the case. See Herbert Gans, *The Levittowners* (New York: Pantheon, 1967).

[19] Francis Bello, "The City and the Car," in Editors of Fortune, *The Exploding Metropolis* (Garden City, N.Y.: Doubleday, 1958), pp. 97, 98.

[20] Robert E. Park, "The Urban Community as a Spatial Pattern and a Moral Order," in Ernest W. Burgess (ed.), *The Urban Community* (Chicago: University of Chicago Press, 1927).

activities in *concentric zones.*[21] One finds, in many cities, a central business district for retail, wholesale, and light manufacturing activities surrounded by an area of relatively poor housing, which is surrounded in turn by rings of housing of successively improved quality as one moves from the center of the city.

One question of interest to sociologists has been whether this patterning of cities in concentric zones is primarily or exclusively a phenomenon peculiar to the United States. An older study of a small French city—Aix-en-Provence—raises a critical question of the universality of this typically American pattern of social status as negatively correlated with closeness to the center of the city.[22] However, a specific comparison of Paris with Chicago, the city whose ecological pattern forms the basis for the concentric zones theory, finds a high degree of similarity of patterning in the two cities.[23] In many cities of Latin America and India, by contrast, there is quite a different pattern, the slums of the city tending to be located in the hillside regions outside large cities.[24] The question of the applicability of this model of ecological patterning outside the United States is still rather controversial.

Sector model. Even in large American cities there are significant departures from the concentric zones model which sociologists have attempted to explain. Certain kinds of activities, rather than clustering in zones, tend to follow major transportation lines out of the city. Instead of a section of automobile showrooms or a section of slums, we find an automobile row or a slum row strung along a major city street. The *sector theory* of urban patterning attempts to account for these departures from the concentric zone model.[25]

[21] Ernest W. Burgess, "The Growth of a City: an Introduction to a Research Project," in Robert E. Park, Ernest W. Burgess, and Roderick D. McKenzie, *The City* (Chicago: University of Chicago Press, 1925), pp. 47–62.

[22] Theodore Caplow, "Urban Structure in France," *American Sociological Review,* 17(1952):544–549.

[23] A. Lewis Rhodes, "Residential Distribution and Occupational Stratification in Paris and Chicago," *Sociological Quarterly,* 10(1969):106–112.

[24] Surinder K. Mehta, "Patterns of Residence in Poona (India) by Income, Education and Occupation," *American Journal of Sociology,* 73(1968):496–508; Leo F. Schnore, "On the Spatial Structure of Cities in the Two Americas," in Philip M. Hauser and Leo F. Schnore (eds.), *The Study of Urbanization* (New York: Wiley, 1965), pp. 347–398.

[25] Homer Hoyt, *The Structure and Growth of Residential Neighborhoods in American Cities* (Washington, D.C.: Federal Housing Administration, 1939).

Multiple nuclei model. Another model emphasizes the effects of recent changes in the pattern of transportation lines around cities. As bypass expressways have been built around certain cities—St. Louis, Indianapolis, and Boston, for example—commercial establishments have been relocated toward the periphery of metropolitan areas. The suburban factory and the sprawling shopping center are reflections of this decentralizing tendency in cities today. Some urban sociologists have suggested that we need a *multiple nuclei* model of urban ecology to account for some of these tendencies of certain types of traditionally "downtown" activities to move toward urban fringes.[26]

Process of Ecological Succession

The process by which a given area changes in the character of the activities carried on therein is called *ecological succession.* There have been various theories about this succession process. One of the more interesting is that there are predictable consequences for an area that is a "zone of transition" between one of these kinds of land use and another.[27]

Slums are formed near the point at which the central business section of a city terminates and the residential section begins. As the central business district expands, large homes that were once on the periphery of the city become threatened by this central expansion, and the original owners of these homes "flee" to a new periphery. The homes remain, however, and they are typically divided into apartments to be occupied by lower-class persons. Rentals on such subdivided buildings are highly remunerative, but the slum landlord knows that the central business district will soon expand into the area and that the buildings will be removed, bringing him a premium price for the land. Therefore, he has no motivation to spend money maintaining this property. Thus, according to one theory, does the deterioration of housing conditions near the centers of cities occur.

Not all slums are found in "zones of transition," but the idea is probably a useful one, especially if we notice that there are other relevant kinds of transition, such as when the businesses along a certain street deteriorate in anticipation of a new superthroughway

---

[26] Chauncey D. Harris and Edward L. Ullman, "The Nature of Cities," *Annals of the American Academy of Political and Social Science,* 242(1945):7–17.

[27] Burgess, "The Growth of a City."

to be built in that area. Also, we can apply the idea to explain certain kinds of agricultural slums, farms near the periphery of cities that are not adequately maintained as farms because their owners anticipate selling the land for a new housing development.

CHANGES IN COMMUNITIES: CULTURAL URBANIZATION

Our earlier discussion of urbanism and ruralism will suggest that it is possible for a population to be undergoing change in the rural-urban dimension even if people are not moving physically between urban and rural communities. Urbanization may mean the growth of cities or suburbs, but it may also mean the process by which the people in a society are becoming more urban in their ways of life. Rural as well as urban residents may be undergoing a process of urbanization in their ways of living.

It may be useful to compare the degree of cultural urbanization of urban and rural residents. In some societies there is a striking difference in the ways of life of urban and rural people. Rural life represents "the bush" with all its traditional ways, while urban life represents modernity and sophistication. Many countries in South America, Asia, and Africa display this pattern, their cities being "very urban" while their countrysides are "very rural," and there is much hostile feeling between people in the two types of communities.[28] Rural-to-urban migration is likely to be a traumatic personal experience in these countries.

In the case of the United States, it appears that the nineteenth century was a period during which the gap in the degree of urbanization of urban and rural dwellers was considerably widened. Social change proceeded rapidly in the cities and very slowly in rural areas. Violent labor strife and heavy foreign immigration into American cities in the late nineteenth century encouraged many rural people to see the cities as especially "wicked" places.[29] By the beginning of this century, country folk could view the life of the city with a mixture of fascination ("Everything's up-to-date in Kansas City," sang the farm boys of *Oklahoma*) and moral outrage, as exemplified by William Jennings Bryan's fundamentalist championing of the Bible against the newfangled theory of evolution at

---

[28] Nathan Keyfitz, "Political-Economic Aspects of Urbanization in South and Southeast Asia," in Hauser and Schnore, *Study of Urbanization*, pp. 265–309.

[29] Constance M. Green, *The Rise of Urban America* (New York: Harper & Row, 1965), pp. 104, 105.

the "Scopes Monkey Trial" in Dayton, Tennessee. From their side, urban dwellers could look at their country cousins as "hicks," somewhat in the disdainful manner of H. L. Mencken at the same Scopes trial.

Since about 1930, this situation appears to have changed drastically. Rural life has been transformed by such "urban" comforts as electricity, radio, television, and supermarkets. At the same time, the suburbanization trend suggests that urban residents have attempted to move somewhat in the direction of rural ways. The net result is a situation in which the degree of cultural urbanization of the rural and urban populations is not so very different. City and country dwellers have a common base of information and outlook, even if this common denominator is as superficial as a common concern for last week's moon landing or next week's World Series.

SUMMARY

People live in some variation of urban or rural communities and this residence tends to affect their style of life in a number of ways. The overall world trend toward urbanization (the movement from rural to urban communities) tends to produce problems of social organization, both for the communities into which people move and for those which they leave. These problems involve a combination of factors: the necessity to rearrange institutional facilities to accommodate more or fewer people; the need to reorganize ordinary social relations disrupted by the selective migration into the cities of different types of people (e.g., in the United States, productive adults, particularly young women). Similar problems can be raised about the most recent population redistribution in countries like the United States, namely, the movement of people from large cities to outlying suburbs. Although these movements are motivated by the search for a more congenial living environment, the results are not always entirely satisfactory for the persons involved.

The distribution of people and activities within a city tends to follow some sort of pattern; the sociological problem has been to find some general model to explain the nature of this patterning. The *concentric zones* model has been the most influential, but it must be modified by the observation of recent changes in urban life and by variations in pattern from one country to another. These patterns change over time, and the redistribution of land uses within a city tends to produce such phenomena as residential and agricultural slums.

Urbanization is not always a matter of physical redistribution of people; it may involve changes to a more urban way of living *(urbanism)* by people living in both rural and urban communities. Differential rates of urbanization of rural and urban populations produces fluctuations in the character of the feelings of rural and urban people toward one another and in the nature of their social relations.

People and Resources:
The Human Environment

As this book is being written, it is being widely predicted (and with some signs of fulfillment of the prediction) that the concern of the American public with environmental problems will replace earlier preoccupations with such matters as race relations and war. There is a feeling among many people that man has been unduly careless with the employment of the resources of his natural environment and that a better use must be made of these resources.

Recalling our discussion in chapter 1 of the controversy among sociologists about the necessity for sociology to be relevant to contemporary concerns, the reader can anticipate that the more academically oriented might take a less lively interest in environmental matters. Even from the more academic viewpoint, however, the fact that people become concerned enough about certain situations to define them as problems and to seek solutions for them *is* an elementary fact about human behavior that no sociologist can rightly ignore.

ADAPTATION OF MAN AND ENVIRONMENT
The relationship of a plant or animal species to its external environment is a major problem of interest in the study of the ecology of any species. The adaptation of a species to its environment is strikingly shown in many cases: for example, in the protective coloration of an insect species that allows its members to blend into the physical environment as a protection against its enemies. The most prominent theory of the origin of biological species, that of

Darwin, emphasizes the process by which species change in the direction of closer adaptation to their environments.[1]

As we suggested in chapter 4, the relation of the human species to its physical environment is more complicated than this. Although there have been biological adaptations of man to climatic conditions in the history of Homo sapiens, the technological development of *culture* has come to dominate the relation of man to his environment.[2] Man has learned to manipulate his environment in accord with his own needs; he has learned, for example, to build fires for warmth and to kill animals for food with efficient hunting weapons. The mastery of the environment has been a major theme of human history.

There is another side of this story, however. The very technology that has made it possible for man to master the physical environment for his own purposes has also produced the instruments for creating serious environmental problems for himself. His mastery of the air has resulted in environmental conditions of air pollution and, in some places, bothersome or even physically destructive noise levels. His use of pesticides to control crop-destroying insects has created major problems of contamination of his water supplies. Indeed, it seems that every technical solution to an environmental problem tends to bring in its wake new problems, anticipated or unanticipated. The recent rise in public consciousness of environmental problems probably reflects the fact that many of the problematic consequences of the application of technology are just now beginning to be felt acutely.

Once a human problem rises to the level of human consciousness and is perceived as a problem, it becomes a major focus of interest of the sociologist. Worried about some situation, an individual may attempt to convince others of its gravity and, perhaps, of the need for some proposed remedy. Others may share his concern and support this remedy, or they may minimize the gravity of the situation, or support other solutions. Social problems, environmental or otherwise, thus involve the social relations of men with one another.

Our discussion of environmental problems in this chapter will

---

[1] Charles Darwin, *On the Origin of Species* (Cambridge: Harvard University Press, 1964).

[2] Alfred L. Kroeber, *The Nature of Culture* (Chicago: University of Chicago Press, 1952), pp. 23–30.

emphasize the efforts of people to organize action with reference to these problems. It should provide the reader with some introduction to an important area of sociological analysis: the study of social problems.

OVERPOPULATION
One possible source of maladjustment of man to his environment is the situation of there being too many of his kind for the comfort of the individual member.

Nature of the Problem
Overpopulation is usually seen as a matter of too many people for the available supplies of the material necessities of life. The rapidly growing populations of many of the world's underdeveloped countries are problems because these countries apparently cannot expand their economic productivity as rapidly as the population expands. The result is inevitable: the per capita income in such countries is kept at very low levels since many more people must be provided for from limited resources.[3]

Not all overpopulation involves this kind of material deprivation, however. In countries like the United States, recent population growth has not threatened the material standard of living of the population. The country's economic productivity has grown much more rapidly than has the population.[4] But if competition for material necessities is not a grave problem, competition for living space and for certain kinds of social services has been severe. A commuter, vacationer, or weekend tourist is likely to find the roadways and the other means of transportation jammed with other people competing with him for a seat on the train or a parking space for his automobile. A student who tries to enroll for a college course finds that the course is already oversubscribed when he gets there.[5]

Perhaps all these problems are ultimately resolvable by the expansion of facilities to meet expanded demands by more people. But these expansions require time and, sometimes, some other painful environmental adjustments (such as cutting down trees to

---

[3] Georg Borgstrom, *Too Many* (New York: Macmillan, 1969).

[4] *Population Bulletin,* 26(February, 1970):10.

[5] Lincoln H. Day and Alice Taylor Day, *Too Many Americans* (Boston: Houghton Mifflin, 1964); Edward Higbee, *The Squeeze: Cities Without Space* (New York: Morrow, 1960).

build new campus buildings or replacing public parks with parking lots). Somehow, the facilities never quite seem to catch up with the demands of human comfort.

Proposed Solutions

The possibilities for population control are indicated by the nature of the demographic variables discussed in chapter 18: fertility, mortality, migration.

Migration control. Occasionally, it is proposed that either the promotion of emigration or the discouragement of immigration would be a plausible solution to the overpopulation of a territory. Overpopulated countries have instigated invasions of adjacent territories with open spaces on the theory that settlement by residents of the invading country would improve the population situation of the invaders.[6] Restrictions on immigration have been motivated at least partly by the feeling of a people that their country is already full and that newcomers would only produce overpopulation.

These migration-policy solutions are seldom proposed today, however, perhaps because of an increasing awareness of the interdependence of national fates and the realization that one country's population solution may be another country's population problem.[7] It is also recognized that population growth results from natural increase (the excess of births over deaths) and that any solution to overpopulation must involve a reduction in this rate of increase.[8]

Fertility control. Our discussion in chapter 18 of the theory of demographic transition indicated that population explosions are frequently the result of rapidly declining mortality rates rather than

---

[6] Japanese invasion of the mainland of Asia at the beginning of World War II was motivated at least partly by a desire for possession of "open space" for resettlement of Japanese population.

[7] This is not always the case; sometimes two countries have a mutual interest in migration between them, one country needing additional population and another needing relief from overpopulation. For a discussion of this kind of relation between Canada (underpopulated) and Holland (overpopulated), see William Peterson, *The Politics of Population* (Garden City, N.Y.: Doubleday, 1964), pp. 307–322.

[8] "It is a significant fact that the great emigration from Europe between 1800 and 1910 did not prevent a long-sustained and slowly increasing rate of growth of the populations from which it came." Warren S. Thompson and David L. Lewis, *Population Problems,* 5th ed. (New York: McGraw-Hill, 1965), pp. 489, 490.

increasing fertility rates. Although population-control policy could conceivably aim at slowing the rate of decline of mortality, the cultural emphasis on the sanctity of human life guarantees that there will be almost no tendency to advocate higher death rates as an instrument of population control. To most people in the world, population control is synonymous with birth control. Zero population growth, it is felt, can be achieved if couples will employ contraception and "Stop at Two."

Like other technical solutions to social problems, contraception seems to introduce problems of its own. As is typical of many solutions to social problems, some proposed remedies will involve value conflicts with major social values. Two of these will be mentioned.

First, effective birth-control programs may require a certain amount of duress to prevent reproduction by some persons. One of the difficulties of most programs of voluntary fertility control is that they appeal to people who have already committed themselves to the idea of contraception. (Applicants for voluntary sterilization, for example, are usually people who have already had several children and do not want more and who have reached a stage in life when they might not have had more children even without sterilization.)[9] To be effective in reducing births, the use of a contraceptive technique would have to be increased among people who are less committed to the idea of birth control. It is sometimes proposed, seriously, that couples with large families be forced to stop procreating by requiring, for example, the sterilization of the husband or the wife. Such proposals usually run aground because, in the process of attempting to promote one value (population control), they violate another value (the right of people to make their own decisions about the number of children they want to have).

A second difficulty in contraception as a means of population control is illustrated by the public concern with some of the unwanted by-products of the application of contraceptive technology. Many women, alarmed by reports of negative medical effects of oral contraceptives (susceptibility to blood clotting, for example), discontinued the use of a highly effective device for the prevention of conception. Some leaders of the population control movement in

[9] Joseph M. Stycos, "Obstacles to Programs of Population Control: Facts and Fancies," *Marriage and Family Living,* 25(1963):5–13.

the United States—officials of the Planned Parenthood Federation of America, for instance—deplored this discontinuation on grounds of its supposed effect in increasing the number of unwanted pregnancies. This situation is typical of many in which the negative effects of some consumer product—e.g., cigarettes, cyclamates, diet pills, DDT—become a matter of social controversy and hence of disagreement about whether efforts to control the harmful by-products by controlling the use of the product are worthwhile.

RESOURCE DEPLETION

One problematic aspect of overpopulation is the possibility that, as more people draw on the fund of natural resources available to man, the depletion of this supply will be hastened. Even though resources may be sufficient to the needs of those presently alive, the resources of future generations might be threatened. Resource depletion does not necessarily depend upon increased population, however. Even in a stable population, people may become increasingly wasteful in their consumption of natural resources.

Nature of the Problem

There are several kinds of natural resources whose supply is rather severely limited. The topsoil on which agricultural production depends is limited to a layer of a few inches on an otherwise infertile earth. If this soil is washed away or rendered infertile by overactive cultivation, a major human resource has been lost. Water, in quantities sufficient for irrigation farming or in a quality satisfactory for drinking, is a limited resource in many places. Many plants and animals are natural resources for man's use (redwood trees, for example, or trout or deer). Depletion of these resources is likely to be treated as a problem. Whatever the nature of the resource in question, the problem is always the same: a limited supply in relation to human demand.

Proposed Solutions

As in any scarcity situation, there are two possible solutions to the problem of resource depletion. Their supply may be expanded, or the effective demand for them may be restricted. We shall consider each of these possibilities and some of their difficulties.

Supply expansion. Every situation of resource depletion seems to stimulate efforts to increase the supply of that resource. New topsoil can be created in limited quantities by composting operations. The supply of usable water can be improved by constructing lakes and ponds to collect rain water and by building facilities to desalt sea water. Property owners are encouraged to plant trees or to stock their property with fish or other wildlife.

The main limitations of most such efforts are the expense and the time required to accomplish them. The cost of building a pond or of terracing the land to prevent soil erosion can be very high. Few individuals can afford such programs, and financial support from governmental agencies, in recognition of the public interest involved, may be necessary. But even governmental support is limited, since most government agencies operate on limited budgets on which heavy demands are made. Some resource-expanding activities are prohibitively expensive for *any* agency: the desalination of salt water is a good example.[10]

Beyond such cost considerations, the expansion of many natural resources is an extremely time-consuming operation. Trees planted today may not reach maturity for thirty or more years; the revitalization of depleted soil may require many years of exemption from normal agricultural use. Understandably, the feeling of many people is that these resources will "last my time" and, while it would be "nice" to plant trees, etc. for the benefit of later generations, a person's main obligation is to use his time and money to provide for the immediate needs of his own family. This attitude was encouraged in the United States and elsewhere by the historical situation in which there appeared to be an inexhaustible supply of natural resources. If this piece of land were to become depleted, there would be plenty more "out West" for later generations. If mining operations were wasteful or poorly designed to maximize production in one spot, there would be plenty more spots to mine in the future. The supply of resources was not defined as any cause for concern until the depletion had already reached an advanced stage.

Use limitation. The other direction for dealing with the resource depletion problem is the limitation on use of natural resources. If a species of animal—e.g., the whooping crane—is in danger of extinction, it may become a protected species with laws forbidding

---

[10] Roy Popkin, *Desalination: Water for the World's Future* (New York: Praeger, 1968).

the killing of any of its members. Sections of woodland may be set aside as "forest reserves" with strict enforcement of laws against the damage of plant life within the reserves. Sometimes use limitation is by persuasion rather than by coercion: farmers may be persuaded to remove land from agricultural use by Soil Bank payments for their participation in land conservation programs.

Some limitations of use restriction as a solution may be noted. There may be a feeling among many people that they have a "right" to the use of natural resources, especially to resources located on privately owned property. Ownership of anything generally implies the right to determine the use of that thing. Actually, in no social system apparently is the individual owner given complete freedom to determine the use of his property; there is a recognition of a public interest, for example, in forbidding property's being used as a junkyard or to harbor an illicit business. But any attempt to assert this public interest is likely to encounter the sense of the owner's right to the disposition of his property. As is true of so many social problems, solutions in the interest of one value (resource conservation) are limited by the fact that the solution conflicts with another value (the property rights of private owners).[11]

Another value conflict in this area concerns the problem of determining precisely what is the "public interest" in matters of resource use. Urban middle-class Americans may treat it as an incontestable truism that the public interest would encourage the reserving of Western lands from resource-depleting activities such as sheep grazing. Also, what morally sensitive person could doubt that the public interest forbids the extensive cutting of redwood trees that have required hundreds of years for their growth?

From the perspectives of local residents of certain Western states, these matters may look quite different, however. Mexican-Americans in New Mexico, who depend on sheep grazing for a livelihood, resent bitterly the efforts of the United States government to divert lands to forest reserves.[12] Residents of Pacific coastal communities in California and Oregon recognize the eco-

[11] For a typical statement of the view that values and value conflicts are data for the sociologist rather than an expression of his own preferences, see John F. Cuber and Robert A. Harper, *Problems of American Society* (New York: Holt, 1951). For critical questions about this approach to the study of social problems, see Howard E. Freeman and Wyatt C. Jones, *Social Problems: Causes and Controls* (Chicago: Rand McNally, 1970), p. 15.

[12] Stan Steiner, *La Raza: the Mexican Americans* (New York: Harper & Row, 1970).

nomic value of the timber industry to their communities and resist the efforts of Save the Redwoods and similar conservationist groups. The sociologist cannot, of course, arbitrate such value conflicts. He can only hope to clarify, for the benefit of the combatants or to satisfy his own curiosity, the nature of the values that are brought into conflict.

POLLUTION

To many people today, "environmental" problems are virtually synonymous with some of the ways in which parts of the environment become too contaminated for safe or comfortable human use. Beaches are closed for swimming because of water contamination. The "air pollution index" of a city reaches a level at which people become apprehensive, if not physically discomforted. In such situations, pollution comes to be defined as a condition requiring remedial action.

Nature of the Problem

Environmental pollution is a by-product of two kinds of human activities: (1) the disposal of waste products; and (2) the attempt to increase productivity.

Human waste has always been a problem wherever urine and fecal matter have not been put to use productively. With the domestication of animals, the disposal of animal waste also became a problem. When man began to manufacture goods, and to distribute and preserve them, he was faced with new problems: how to find ways to dispose of the waste materials produced by the manufacturing process, of the packages used in shipment and storage, of the contaminants formed by the combustion of fuels used in the vehicles which distributed the goods and, finally, of the manufactured goods themselves after their usefulness was exhausted. Whether buried, burned, or dumped in water, there is a strong possibility of environmental contamination resulting from these disposal practices. The industrial smokestack emitting fly ash over a city and the rural junkyard are among the more visible manifestations of the waste disposal problem.

Contamination is also a by-product of efforts to force a greater productive yield from the environment. Insecticides and fertilizers are essential to agricultural production in most areas. But they are also a contaminating factor, polluting water supplies and endangering wildlife species such as birds and other animals that feed from the land or the water.[13]

Pollution from either of these sources may be a major factor in the depletion of environmental resources. An illustration of the unanticipated adverse effects of technological processes on environmental conditions is the matter of "thermal pollution," the heat from industrial processes being a waste which, when disposed of in water, may kill marine life. Many industrial plants, located on lakes or rivers, use the water for their industrial operations and return it to the lake or river slightly warmed from its use. The resulting rise in the temperature of the river or lake has resulted in a multiplication of algae or other plant life to a level at which fish have not been able to survive.[14] Perhaps there could be no better indication of the delicacy of the balance of nature and the danger of human activity in upsetting this balance.

Proposed Solutions

There seem to be some obvious solutions to environmental pollution, as to other social problems. The person who dumps garbage in a lake or the power company which pollutes the air could be constrained by law and public censure to cease and desist from these practices. If a laundry detergent has contaminating chemicals, alternative detergents could be developed without these contaminants. If commercial fertilizers are contaminating, organic ones may be used instead. Communities which border lakes may be required to construct treatment plants to decontaminate sewage before it is put into the water.

Any of these obvious solutions will bring new problems in their wake. Consider the matter of the sewage treatment plant. Although all may agree on the undesirability of dumping raw sewage into a lake, the mechanism for the elimination of this practice may be cause for social controversy. A frequent issue, for example, is the manner in which sewage treatment plants will be financed. If local taxpayers must bear the burden of the cost, it may be necessary to institute property taxes that make property prohibitively expensive

---

[13] Rachel L. Carson, *Silent Spring* (Boston: Houghton Mifflin, 1962); Paul R. Ehrlich and Anne H. Ehrlich, *Population, Resources, Environment* (San Francisco: W. H. Freeman, 1970), pp. 129–134.

[14] Ehrlich and Ehrlich, *Population, Resources, Environment*, pp. 187, 188.

to own. Many towns bordering Lake Erie have traditionally used the lake for raw sewage disposal. Recently, residents have been faced with the prospect of, from their viewpoint, paying for a facility that is really a matter of general public concern. Such communities have been understandably resistant to the construction of sewage treatment plants.

There is also the problem that some of the proposed noncontaminating alternatives to aids to productivity are less effective than those containing contaminants. An insecticide, to be effective, may *have* to contain elements with polluting potentials.[15] Automobile gasolines freed of contaminants may, in the process, be freed of elements that contribute to the running efficiency of automobile engines.

A decision to combat pollution in any given way will tend to encounter the opposition of persons who feel most acutely the disadvantages that the solution would entail. The sociologist cannot tell the citizen whether the advantage to be gained from the solution is worth it when the problems created by the solution are taken into consideration. He can, perhaps, provide a reasonably comprehensive description of the vested interests opposing a solution, so that people are at least apprised of what to expect in the way of opposition if they try to adopt a proposed solution.

SUMMARY

The adjustment of man to his physical environment is a perennial but apparently an increasingly prominent problem of human concern. The technology which gives man control over some features of his environment may also be used, often inadvertently, to deplete or contaminate resources in that environment. We have discussed three types of environmental social problems: overpopulation, resource depletion, and pollution.

In the case of each of these problems, there are solutions that are more or less within the grasp of human technological capacity. The limitations of these solutions involve, in some way or another, cost considerations, either financial expenditures or inconveniences to some persons who have been accustomed to behaving in ways that produce negative environmental effects. The relative weight to be given to the advantages of the solution and the dis-

---

15 Ibid., pp. 181, 182, for a contrary insistence that there *are* effective alternatives to the more persistently contaminating chlorinated hydrocarbon insecticides.

advantages to those injured by the solution is a matter of human valuation. Different people will value the different elements of these problems and solutions in different ways. Environmental problems, like other social problems, are thus an arena of social controversy in a situation of values in conflict. The sociologist *as a sociologist* cannot impose his own values to settle these controversies; he can only hope to clarify for all concerned the dimensions of the problem by examining the values implicated both in the problems and in the solutions.

Name Index

Subject Index

Social interaction—*Con't.*
patterning of, in social
relationships, 123–27
Social mobility
and ethnic groups, 271
of groups, 240–41
of individuals, 242–45
Social movements, 372–88
definition of, 372
reform or revolutionary
types of, 375–79
for specific demands,
373–75
of withdrawal, 379–87
Social organization, 73–132
Social problems
relevance for sociology,
8–11
sociological study of,
418–29
Social relationships
personal, 124–25
status, 125–27
See also Social inter-
action
Social stratification, 215–46
Social system, 76–78
Socialization
of children, 141
definition of, 292
process of, 292–96
Society, 75–93
definitions of, 75–78
as social system, 76–78
Sociology, 3–16
European origins of, 5–7
methods of studying, 17–
39
motives for studying, 5–
11
and other social sci-
ences, 11–15
in United States, 7–11
Solidarity, as religious function, 168–70
Statistics, 31
State, the, 186, 190–92
Status, as basis of primitive
society, 65
Status ascription, 142, 240,
241
Status crystallization, 226–
28
Status relationships, 125–
27
Stereotypes, 126, 256

Stigma and self presenta-
tion, 333–37
Structural change, 89
Subcultures
and cultural integration,
47, 48
definition of, 42
and deviance, 299, 300,
310–13
ethnic groups as, 260–62
social classes as, 231–34
and social differentiation,
214
Suburbanization, 410–12
Suburbs
definition of, 405
growth of, in U.S., 410
Suicide
Durkheim's study of, 303,
307
and homicide, 303

Taste, cultural definition of,
46
Technological determinism,
68
Technology
changes in, 69, 70
definition of, 44
as modifying geographic
influence, 62
as source of social prob-
lems, 419
Telesis, 8
Tension management, 85
Total institutions, 194, 292,
334
Totalitarianism, 194
Traditional authority, 194,
195

Upper classes
economic and social
power of, 218
as past oriented, 232
Urban ecology, models of
concentric zone, 412–13
multiple nuclei, 414
sector, 413
Urbanism, 406, 415, 416
Urbanization
as growth of cities, 407–
10
as growth of urbanism,
415, 416

and social mobility, 242,
243

Validity of sociological
measures, 23–26
Values
as element of culture, 45
ethnic differences in, 261
social-class differences
in, 232–34
and social stratification,
216
in sociological study, 21
Variables, 30
dependent, 33
independent, 33
intervening, 34–36
Violence
and social control, 186–
88
in social movements, 378,
379
Voluntary associations, 113,
116, 374
Voting
influences on, 364–66
and party affiliation,
204–6
participation in, 207–9

War
effects of, on ethnic relations, 265, 266
and human instinct, 52,
53
and the modern state, 191
War bond sales and propa-
ganda, 368–70
Welfare, as political function, 189
Working classes
deviance and anomie
among, 308–10
discrimination against, in
law enforcement, 315,
316
life styles of, 227
as present oriented, 233,
403
relative liberalism of, 362,
363
and revolution, 234–40

Youth culture, 47, 48, 279